Materializing Ritual Practices

Materializing Ritual Practices

EDITED BY

Lisa M. Johnson and Rosemary A. Joyce

UNIVERSITY PRESS OF COLORADO
Louisville

© 2022 by University Press of Colorado

Published by University Press of Colorado
245 Century Circle, Suite 202
Louisville, Colorado 80027

 ASSOCIATION of UNIVERSITY PRESSES   The University Press of Colorado is a proud member of the Association of University Presses.

The University Press of Colorado is a cooperative publishing enterprise supported, in part, by Adams State University, Colorado State University, Fort Lewis College, Metropolitan State University of Denver, University of Alaska Fairbanks, University of Colorado, University of Denver, University of Northern Colorado, University of Wyoming, Utah State University, and Western Colorado University.

∞ This paper meets the requirements of the ANSI/NISO Z39.48-1992 (Permanence of Paper).

ISBN: 978-1-64642-238-8 (hardcover)
ISBN: 978-1-64642-239-5 (ebook)
https://doi.org/10.5876/9781646422395

Library of Congress Cataloging-in-Publication Data

Names: Johnson, Lisa M. (Lisa Marie), editor. | Joyce, Rosemary A., 1956– editor.
Title: Materializing ritual practices / edited by Lisa M. Johnson and Rosemary A. Joyce.
Description: Louisville, CO : University Press of Colorado, [2020] | Includes bibliographical references and index.
Identifiers: LCCN 2021049430 (print) | LCCN 2021049431 (ebook) | ISBN 9781646422388 (hardcover) | ISBN 9781646422395 (ebook)
Subjects: LCSH: Ritual—Mexico—Case studies. | Ritual—Central America—Case studies. | Indians of Mexico—Rites and ceremonies—Case studies. | Indians of Central America—Rites and ceremonies—Case studies. | Interdisciplinary research—Case studies. | Indians of Mexico—Antiquities. | Indians of Central America—Antiquities.
Classification: LCC F1219.3.R56 M38 2020 (print) | LCC F1219.3.R56 (ebook) | DDC 972/.01—dc23/eng/20211018
LC record available at https://lccn.loc.gov/2021049430
LC ebook record available at https://lccn.loc.gov/2021049431

Financial support for this publication was provided by the University of Nevada, Las Vegas.

Front-cover photograph of Francisca Tejero by Alessandro Lupo; back-cover photograph by Philippe Nondedeo.

Contents

This volume is a product of an International Scientific Coordination Network (GDRI) funded by the French Centre National de la Recherche Scientifique (CNRS), involving collaboration by the Université de Paris Ouest–Nanterre La Défense, Paris X; the Université de Paris–Panthéon-Sorbonn, Paris I; the Centro de Estudios Mayas, Instituto de Investigaciones Filológicas, Universidad Nacional Autónoma de México; the Centro de Investigaciones y Estudios Superiores en Antropología Social, Mexico; the University of Texas, Austin; the Rheinische Friedrich-Wilhelms Universität Bonn; the Università degli Studi di Napoli L'orientale; la Sapienza, Università di Roma; and the University of California, Berkeley. The editors and contributors gratefully acknowledge the support of CNRS for the conferences and workshops undertaken by the network.

The editors would like to acknowledge the funders of the conference held at Berkeley as part of campus participation in the broader RITMO project Ritual Actions and Time: Creation, Destruction, Transformation in Mesoamerica from 2015–2018, the Townsend Center for the Humanities, the Department of Anthropology's Alice S. Davis Endowment, and the University of California Institute for Mexico and the United States (UC MEXUS). The Department of Anthropology graciously provided event space for the conference's first evening.

The editors also wish to acknowledge permission from the Universidad Nacional Autónoma de México to include as chapter 11 of the present work a revision and translation into English of a paper that previously appeared in Spanish in 2018 in *Revista Península* 13 (2): 97–123, as "La importancia del tunk'ul en el ritual y canto ceremonial del carnaval de Pomuch, Campeche: Un estudio interdisciplinario" by Francisca Zalaquett Rock, Juan Carrillo González, Giovani Balam Caamal, and Olivier Le Guen.

Materializing Ritual Practices

1

This book examines a long history of ritual practice, illuminating the way the temporalities of ritual—duration, timing, and rhythm—are instantiated through materialities. It takes an interdisciplinary approach, engaging ethnographers, linguistic anthropologists, and archaeologists with a common focus: the long-term reproduction of social relations in Mexico and Central America accomplished through ritual practice.

Materiality pervades many aspects of ritual. Even actions such as singing, chanting, or praying, often treated as if they were ephemeral or immaterial, may be anchored in material objects and substances, produced through mobilization of the material—whether that material is conceived of as moving breath, sound waves, or vibrations perceived through bodily sensations. Materialities have tempos, durations, and rhythms. The contributors to this volume highlight just how deeply dependent ritual temporalities are on the rhythms of materiality, expanding the way ethnographers and linguistic anthropologists describe and recognize the production of ritual rhythms.

Both of the co-editors are archaeologists, specialists in understanding action through material residues. The contributions to the volume, taken as a whole, challenge the way materialities are sometimes understood when discussion takes place solely among such specialists. The result is more than simply mourning the absence of the kind of materialities of gesture, voice, and posture and of substances consumed or destroyed

Introducing Materialities and Temporalities of Ritual Practice

Rosemary A. Joyce and Lisa M. Johnson

https://doi.org/10.5876/9781646422395.c001

3

that ethnographers witness. Instead, as archaeologists, we are moved to recognize how the material traces we can document imply these other forms of materiality. This volume thus exemplifies the power of interdisciplinary exchanges. Ethnographers, linguists, and archaeologists have specialist procedures that practitioners of each discipline need to understand to fully assess the potential for cross-disciplinary work.

What emerges from the confrontation with detailed methodological discussions presented here are some convergences and some absolute differences. The scale of observation is one aspect of methodology that is worth attention. Multiple contributors use approaches that allow analysis of ritual temporalities and materialities at the micro-level. In archaeology, this includes documenting microscopic residues; in linguistic studies of the ethnographic present, attending to the smallest performative level of enunciation: the breath. As the contributors demonstrate, the microscale is always made more intelligible by linkage to macroscale phenomena, including the macroscale of long-term temporalities in which ritual action is reproduced over centuries through action at the fleeting scale of the moment, the event.

In the chapters that follow, the contributors explore temporalities of the event, ritualization of place, and the materiality of sound as three axes that unite practitioners from different research disciplines attempting to illuminate the historical trajectory of ritual in Mexico and Central America. These three axes grew out of a multi-year sequence of exchanges among participants in an international working group. Starting with temporality of ritual and with the critical junctures of repetition, transformation, and destruction as key sites of engagement, participants were free to explore multiple dimensions of the topic. In initial discussions in Paris in 2015, the emphasis was on temporalities at multiple scales, involving defining sequences, processes, and procedures through which ritual actions were coordinated. Repeated performance of rituals—some represented by new observations, some by older records, some by archaeological observations—formed the focus. At this point, the articulation of different research practices was bridged by the shared subject matter: rituals in Mesoamerica. Ethnographers and archaeologists found common ground in the ways ritual practices instantiated spatial settings, ritualizing place. In a second major conference held in Rome in 2016, discussion shifted to the question of the recomposition of time through ritual, directly engaging participants across methodological boundaries. The third major conference was held at the University of California, Berkeley, in September 2017, where all the contributors to this volume participated. Observing the salience of materialities in the previous events, the 2017 conference took the materiality of ritual as its central focus.

The specific focus of this volume, like the conference from which it was developed, is thus on materiality: the form through which temporal effects are produced. The sequences of creation, destruction, and transformation that are produced through ritual action always involve a variety of materialities. From a contemporary theoretical perspective, we argue, materialities must be understood as active and agential, as composing assemblages of humans and non-humans that come together to make things like transformation effective (Barad 2003, 2007; Bennett 2010; Chen 2012; Connolly 2013; DeLanda 2016; Dolphijn and van der Tuin 2012). Materialities may persist at temporal scales beyond the lives of humans or be as fleeting as spoken words, music, or scents. Yet they always contribute their own specific tenor to the practices we recognize as ritualized.

GEOGRAPHIC AND METHODOLOGICAL SCOPE

The authors in this volume connect the kinds of observed material discursive practices ethnographers witness to the sedimented practices from which archaeologists infer similar activity in the past. They address the way specific materialities encourage repetition in ritual actions and, in other circumstances, resist changes to ritual sequences. Contributors are attentive to the broader sensorium and the potentials to understand materiality in ritual performance through more than the study of representation of symbolic concepts in visual form, a well-established aspect of research by iconographers on ritual in Mexico and Central America. Contributors use the concept of materialities, understood to encompass visual, aural, olfactory, and tactile phenomena, as a focus to explore intersections that cross differences in methodological approaches to sounds (including words and music), actions (including historical sediments that are residues of action), and material context (including altars and buildings).

All contributors consider a wide range of agential, active, animate, and vital entities that extend beyond the human to include non-human and suprahuman actors and force in what Perig Pitrou (2012, 2016a), a participant in the project who was unable to contribute to this volume, describes as "coactivity." Together, the chapters illuminate a deep history of ritual practices in an area extending from Mexico to Costa Rica (figure 1.1), where such coactivity is indicated in both ethnographic and historical times. Expanding the scope of the working group from Mesoamerica to encompass adjacent Central American traditions in Honduras and Costa Rica acknowledges that the boundaries drawn by scholars delimiting "Mesoamerica" in the early

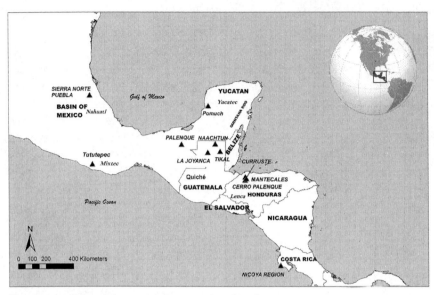

FIGURE 1.1. *Map of sites and regions mentioned in the text*

twentieth century did not describe a fixed cultural entity (Joyce 2004, 2021). It opens the way to consider how ritual practices reproduced at the level of the individual, household, and village proved resilient even as government structures changed, so we can delineate long histories of related ritual practice.

A central focus of the contributors to the volume is the long-term historical tradition that links contemporary speakers of Maya languages with the architects of archaeological sites of the Classic Maya culture, inhabited in the first millennium AD. Three chapters, on Palenque (Johnson, chapter 2), La Joyanca (Arnauld, chapter 5), and Naachtun (Nondédéo and his coauthors, chapter 6), examine ritual over long historical spans of time that resulted in deposits visible at monumental scale today. The products of actions directed and carried out by the ruling and non-ruling noble families of highly stratified city-states, these contributions introduce some of the most enduring and unusual materialities, from large-scale carved stone monuments to precious stone crafted into items deposited during rituals. The same settings, however, allow us to focus on the more ephemeral and less visible traces of ritualized events, from the structuring of sediments observed at microscale (Johnson) and macroscale (Arnauld) to the micro-residues of substances used in part for fleeting affects, such as scent.

These chapters on early Maya history are complemented by studies of contemporary Maya ritual performances in Yucatan involving detailed analysis of discourse (Vapnarsky, chapter 4) and of music (Zalaquett Rock and her coauthors, chapter 11). Here, the scale of observation and analysis using specialist methods mirrors the microscale achieved by the archaeologists, demonstrating the potential utility in both cases of a clearly articulated notion of the ritualized event (discussed by Johnson). The contemporary observations also reinforce the idea that materialities are not simply those things that are resistant to decay, such as stone and ceramics that preserve in archaeological sites. Instead, Valentina Vapnarsky shows us that in Yucatec ritual practice, breath, the animating force of speech, must be treated seriously as a materiality. Francisca Zalaquett Rock and her colleagues add a useful illustration of the way ritual implements, such as the wooden drum made and played in the case they study, are actively agential, reproducing specific performance effects.

Maya ritual practices, both ancient and contemporary, anchor the integrative study of a specific set of rituals carried out across the territory historically occupied by speakers of a range of Maya languages—stretching from Mexico to Honduras—by Johann Begel, Marie Chosson, and Cédric Becquey (chapter 7). For the archaeological examples, they draw on the kinds of stable, enduring objects that predominate as evidence of ritual in other archaeological studies. They emphasize certain kinds of assemblages that occur emplaced in particular ways, evident also in the archaeological studies by Johnson, Arnauld, and Nondédéo and colleagues. To navigate the methodological distinction between the materialist approach of archaeology and the performative observations possible for ethnographers, they examine sacralization of specific places—buildings—showing that while the observable contents of ritual deposits in the present are different, the temporality of these rituals is comparable. Repeated instances of ritualizing structures are, in the ethnographic present, repetitions of the terms of agreements with animating forces of the earth. While the same cannot be asserted based solely on the structural similarities of the archaeological examples, the cross-disciplinary discussion directs us to consider whether there were similar compacts with animate spirits involved in more ancient rituals.

Taking a similarly long-term, integrative view, Rosemary Joyce and Russell Sheptak (chapter 3) expand the cultural range of the volume beyond Mesoamerica. The Lenca-speaking peoples of western Honduras were closely tied to the prehispanic Maya world, and there are aspects of their ritual practices that align them with those studied by Begel, Chosson, and Becquey. Yet Lenca history offers an interesting contrast to the Maya tradition. In the prehispanic past, Lenca political organization never developed the extreme levels of inequality seen in Classic Maya city-states (Hendon, Joyce, and Lopiparo

2014; Joyce 2017a). As a result, there are no monumental architectural complexes like those at Palenque, La Joyanca, and Naachtun in Lenca territory. Yet similar practices ensuring reproduction of continuity are evident in ritualized deposits in Lenca sites (Joyce 2015a; Joyce and Pollard 2010).

Joyce and Sheptak emphasize the methodological challenge of linking evidence created through different practices to trace continuity and change in materialities of ritual over the long term. Drawing on ethnographic studies that document rituals of payment to animate forces of the earth, like those central to Maya ritual in the analyses of Begel, Chosson, and Becquey, Joyce and Sheptak explore how the precise vehicles and performances involved in relations with such forces are differently visible in historical documents and archaeological sites. Treating the long term as a product of active interventions by Lenca people engaged in colonial projects, their chapter frames the question of ritual temporality at the largest scale as one in need of explicit consideration in each area where a deep history of ritual practice can be traced. The structural equivalences they trace between ancient fired clay figures and modern saint's images are not simply products of reproduction of practices. Instead, they demonstrate the continuing requirement for material vehicles for the animating spirits, which can equally be manifested in plants collected from the countryside. What endures is not the iconic form but the relationship humans forge with non-human spirits that come to rest in specific materials.

The chapter by Valeria Bellomia (10) also deals with a long-term history in which colonization is a context in which ritual materialities are reinterpreted. Her analysis of bone rasps removed from Mexico and taken to Italy early in the colonial period brings us another example of how microscale methodologies specific to one discipline can inform our understanding of phenomena observed using other disciplinary approaches. The product of these instruments in their past use was ritualized sound, music that formed part of the performance of ritual. Their preparation and use in producing ritual music can be reconstructed from the traces of manufacture and wear that are presented in the material itself. In their contemporary setting as museum display objects, they signify through sheer physical form, as icons of cultural identity.

The study of musical instruments is represented by two additional chapters, the ethnographic and historical research of Zalaquett Rock and her coauthors on a specific wooden drum used in modern Yucatec performance and the discussion of a large collection of archaeologically recovered fired clay ocarinas by Katrina Kosyk (chapter 9). In both cases, the focus is on the way instrumentalists engage with the things through which they produce sonic materialities of ritual. Kosyk expands the geographic and cultural scope even further, to the Nicoya region of Costa Rica. Like the Lenca area discussed by Joyce and Sheptak, Nicoya did not see the kind of growth of inequality that resulted in monumental construction typical of the Mexican and Guatemalan Maya lowlands. Kosyk emphasizes the importance of ritual practice, including performances of music, in political structure in this area.

Kosyk brings to the volume an explicit emphasis on the way instruments imply both individual practices and the existence of communities of practice, groups of people who learn a way to carry out a practice (a ritual, a performance) and reproduce that way of acting in part through embodied gestures and in part due to internalized ideas of what the right way to act might be. Like Bellomia, Kosyk uses the material studies method of reconstructing the *chaîne opératoire*, the sequence of actions that results in the making of a specific object and in its repetitive, structured pattern of use. It is the repetition of actions that results from learning in a community of practice that makes it possible to link individual things to patterns of action such as those observed in the contemporary studies.

Zalaquett Rock's chapter demonstrates this kind of linkage well, even though it does not use the explicit vocabulary rooted in the material culture studies methodology employed by Bellomia and Kosyk. The wooden drum she and her coauthors discuss has agential capacity to enable the reproduction of a specific performance, in the hands of practitioners who have learned to play the drum in what Kosyk would recognize as a community of engaged performance. It is not just the drum that ensures the continued transfer of performative practices. The words of the song Zalaquett Rock and her colleagues analyze—rhythmically recapitulated in performance—also convey the sentiments, orientations, and meanings associated with the event they historically marked.

The capacity of words structured as song to assist in the repeated reproduction of ritual echoes the arguments made in the two chapters that examine ritual language in contemporary settings. Vapnarsky's case study, like that of Zalaquett Rock, takes place in Yucatan, although the kinds of ritual performances are quite different: highly personal, even intimate rituals for Vapnarsky contrasting with the community-wide celebrations of Carnaval studied by Zalaquett Rock. Vapnarsky's case is more closely paralleled by the contribution of Alessandro Lupo (chapter 8), who carefully analyzes the effective force of Roman Catholic prayers in rituals among the Nahua people of the Sierra of Puebla in the highlands of Mexico. Using a combination of Spanish and Nahuatl, the modern language descended from that spoken by the makers of the bone rasps studied by Bellomia, the ritual specialists Lupo discusses

produce intertwined ritual discourses. Roman Catholic prayers, Lupo emphasizes, are marked by their repetition, included in measured numbers, and treated
like material objects that can be "heaped" on the altar. Where Vapnarsky gives
us an account of ritual speech as a corporeal phenomenon, Lupo gives us an
account of the corporeality of a kind of speech act. The materiality of the
prayers Sierra Nahua ritualists produce is demonstrated in their potential to
over-stuff the bodies of the people for whom the rituals are performed.

The integration of different disciplinary approaches united by a common focus
on ritual practice as materialized at a variety of temporal scales that this volume
represents is a challenge to discipline-specific and even culture-area–specific
understanding. Bringing together researchers who work by observing living
people in action and those whose understandings of action are mediated by
residues, and thus shaped in the face of chronological disjunction, required a
degree of convergence in initial terms of engagement that was produced by the
series of conferences that preceded the one represented by this volume. Before
returning to the content of this volume, we briefly frame the main domains in
which practitioners using different methodologies sought ways to coordinate
their observations about ritual, temporality, and materiality.

TERMS OF ENGAGEMENT

Archaeologists who once used definitions of ritual that separated them
from ethnographers have increasingly drawn on theories of ritual practice that
were developed for understanding ritual in ethnographic situations (Bradley
2003; Joyce 2017b; Swenson 2015). As this transformation took place in the
last decades of the twentieth century, the work of religious studies scholar
Catherine Bell (1992, 74) proved especially influential, including her call for a
shift away from identifying ritual objects and places to understanding ritualization, defined as "a way of acting that is designed and orchestrated to distinguish and privilege that which is being done in comparison to other, usually
more quotidian, activities." Building on Bell's work, archaeologist Richard
Bradley (2003, 12) proposed that treating ritual as action made it possible "to
consider the contexts in which particular rituals are created and performed,
and the consequences of such actions, whether they have been intended or
not." He identified ritualization as both "a way of acting which reveals some
of the dominant concerns of society, and a process by which certain parts of
life are selected and provided with an added emphasis" (12).

Ritualization is a process, and as a process it takes place in time, directing
attention to changing relations among participants in action. Ritualization

is accomplished "through materialities that produce the effect of a ritualized body, ritualized spaces, and ritualized things" (Joyce 2017b, 143). Joyce (144) notes the way the editors of the journal *Material Religion* follow in this framing, linking religion (and thus ritual) to materiality: "Religion is about the sensual effects of walking, eating, meditating, making pilgrimage, and performing even the most mundane of ritual acts . . . what people do with material things and places, and how these structure and color experience and one's sense of oneself and others." For Joyce (144), this connection implies that "the materiality of religious practice is both a productive site for recommitting to existing beliefs, and also provides the only medium through which to transform beliefs."

Johnson (chapter 2, this volume) links ritualization explicitly to contemporary theoretical perspectives on the co-activity of humans and non-humans acting together, arguing that ritualization "occurs through a stylized way of acting that illuminates relationality between humans, places, things." A growing number of scholars working in Mesoamerica are addressing the idea of the animacy of such assemblages (Brown and Emery 2008; Harrison-Buck 2012; Hendon, Joyce, and Lopiparo 2014; Joyce 2018). The materiality that is the focus of contributors to this volume concerns how humans, places, and other beings are organized relationally during the events contributors recognize as ritualized performances.

The shift from thinking of rituals to considering ritualization paralleled a shift in anthropology and archaeology to thinking of materials as active, as materializing practices. Active things, vital materiality, and animist ontologies are now common elements of scholarship in these fields (Alberti and Marshall 2009; Brown and Walker 2008; Hill 2008; Hodder 2012; Ingold 2010, 2011, 2012; Jones and Boivin 2010; Joyce 2008, 2012a, 2012b, 2015b; Kohn 2013; Walker 2008; Watts 2013; Zedeño 2008). The differences among various theoretical approaches often lie in how agency is understood, either as an inherent quality, in which case objects can be alive and active in ways symmetrical with humans (Olsen 2003), or as a capacity to act, typically through relating to other materials, humans, plants, and animals (Barad 2003, 2007; Bennett 2010).

In all contemporary theoretical perspectives, materiality is understood as relational, shifting the human from the center of all things to a position in relation to a larger world of materials and recognizing that other forms of matter are agential, having the potential to cause effects alone or in concert with humans (Barad 2007). This is different from simply granting human-like intentionality to non-human things. A concept of agential materiality is especially useful in ritual studies, where it is understood that a wide range of entities can exercise agency. The ways materiality is perceived as active vary, but generally, we can say that materials—including nonliving things, animals, and plants—can have an effect on outcomes, outside of direct human intervention, and can alter the outcome of human action as well as human perception of those actions (Van Oyen 2018).

Materiality should not be confused with physical substance. When we discuss materialities, we are including everything with a presence that enables relational action, or what Karen Barad (2003, 2007) calls intra-action. Intra-action, Barad argues, is the way phenomena are configured in action, through the drawing of boundaries around regions of what in fact is a continuous plane of material in action. Intra-action implies the coming into existence of phenomena through the definition of topologies that demarcate them rather than labeling the instantiation of relations between preexisting things. Intra-action aggregates the potential for action with the definition of that which acts and is acted on: entities emerge as bounded agential materialities in action; they do not precede action.

We thus include in our understanding of materiality things that would be recognized conventionally as objects and substances, some ephemeral or invisible to the human eye, alongside living landscapes of plants and animals—not because any of these are given but because they have the potential to produce effects. What is material, understood as having agential possibility, may act through media that are not observable visually but can be sensed through its effects. Sound, produced as instrumental music, singing, or chanting, has a substance, a materiality, as contributors to this volume demonstrate.

What materiality implies, then, is a capacity to have an effect, an effect that is consequential enough to become observable. Ritual materialities have effects, among them maintaining, changing, and ending social worlds. The effectiveness of ritual materialities is seen in the way worlds proceed and change over time. In examining apparently common things that recur in ritual, we are exploring time and temporality as nonlinear and examining multiple kinds of time, exploring ritual as a stylized, materially potent phenomenon through its effects. In the process, contributors to this volume are interrogating the relationality of matter and subjectivity and the presence and distribution of agency within ritual, recognizing that subjectivity is fluid and agency is active.

Some of the contributions to this volume discuss non-human things and spaces as animated. We want to distinguish this from a proposal that these societies were or are "animist." This would undermine the goal of agential realist thinking, which is to assert the intra-activity of materialities as a condition of existence, not simply a belief some people hold (Barad 2003, 2007). There is a history of anthropological debate surrounding animism that has brought the idea that things, plants, and animals have souls, or are the same as human persons, under scrutiny (Wilkinson 2017). The recent revival of animism was an attempt to move away from a "Western ontology" in the consideration of non-Western ritual practices (Haber 2009). In a Western—or, better, Enlightenment—ontology, there were clear divisions between subjects and objects, nature and culture. Yet materials never ceased to be active, despite the temporary dominance of this philosophical framework. Ritual practices provide one of the clearest domains for exploring how materials, in relation with human and non-human persons, are agential. This volume presents one such exploration, with a particular history, that of ritual in a specific geographic area: Mexico and Central America. Here, it is clear that animating force inhered in other-than-human materialities and that ritual, among other things, engaged these animating forces in rhythms from the moment to the generation and beyond.

THEMES

The contributors to this volume provide case studies from locations across Mesoamerica and Central America. Throughout the volume, contributors discuss the materiality of ritual, considering such things as instruments, altars, mausoleums, and houses as active. Each section of the book is organized around a common theme that extends across different research approaches: events and temporalities, ritualizing place, and the materiality of sound.

In part 1, authors consider the temporality of ritual and the ways ritual temporality can be distinct from temporalities in other contexts. Johnson discusses how actions and experience inside ritual events can produce a special temporality. Using methods developed in recent microarchaeology, she presents microstratigraphic residues as archaeological evidence for sequences of ritual actions practiced over multiple generations in a non-ruling noble residential household at the Classic Period Maya city of Palenque. Johnson links the repetition of action she can detect at the fine scale of microstratigraphy to the concept of the event, described as an inflection point in the ongoing flow of activity. She shows how events, visible in microstratigraphy, contribute to longer cycles of historical reproduction. She describes the event as having "an impact that extends beyond the moment and place of its occurrence" (Gilmore and O'Donoughue 2015, 6). Johnson argues that "what constitutes the 'event' is its memorable, effecting qualities. It is set apart from other repetitive moments that blur together in memory." From this perspective, ritualization is a particularly important way moments become events with agential effects.

In their chapter, Joyce and Sheptak combine ethnographic, historical, and archaeological data to consider the historical depth of ritual practice in western Honduras. They consider two types of rituals carried out historically by Lenca people, speakers of a group of non-Maya indigenous languages who occupied most of western, central, and southern Honduras. These rituals are called *compostura*, or "payments to the earth," and *guancasco*, ceremonies in which the statue of a patron saint of one town moves to visit the patron saint of a partner town. Joyce and Sheptak examine historical documents to understand the link between prehispanic period and modern Lenca rituals, a process of relating temporalities observed at the scale of the event to temporalities of the long term. They argue that relating modern ritual practices to archaeological predecessors requires taking historical change into account. They thus relate the ritual event (in the present, the colonial past, and the prehispanic past) to a punctuated rhythm of long-term repetition, transformation, and disruption. They find that in the contemporary world, ritual events repeatedly relate Lenca people to spirits understood to animate places. The historical examples of ritual events in which Lenca people related to spirits animating places can then be seen as part of a sequence of repetition and transformation of ritual. The longer rhythm includes changes in the ways rituals engage with materialities and vary even at the same point in time for these rituals to have effects.

Johnson, Joyce, and Sheptak deal with ritual temporalities mediated by materialities over long periods of history. In the final chapter in this section, Vapnarsky turns our attention to a temporality and rhythm of the shortest possible duration: the "breath group," defined as "a stretch of speech between two pauses of sufficient length for an intake of breath." Vapnarsky considers the sensorial perception of voice in ritual among the Maya of Yucatan. To understand variations in tempo and rhythms, she argues, one must also consider the relationship between voice and other gestural actions. An important argument she makes is that voice has physical, material effects. When expended through strong force, the breath of the voice can be felt. Sound, she demonstrates, is material, producing the temporality of ritual as its effect.

Where Johnson examines the materiality of sediments and Joyce and Sheptak look to three-dimensional images and two-dimensional documents as the material ground of ritual temporalities, Vapnarsky demonstrates that breath and articulated speech itself are materialities. She considers ritual speech as a timing mechanism, setting the pace for the temporality of ritual. She argues that the materiality and temporality of voice creates the rhythm of the contemporary Yucatec Maya rituals she observed and analyzes. Chants or prayers, she demonstrates, are considered as substance in these rituals and can serve as offerings much like candles and incense, substances whose materiality has never been in question even though they, like breaths, are ephemeral and are consumed and disappear with time.

These chapters serve as an introduction to the nesting of multiple temporalities in action and their relationships to materialities from the most ephemeral to the most enduring. In part 2, we turn to case studies of ritual materializing place. Again, the theme crosses boundaries among ethnographic, linguistic, and archaeological analysis and involves temporalities of different durations that overlap in the same context. What binds these chapters together is a concern with how places—from the short-term place represented by the altar constructed for a contemporary ritual to the long-enduring ritual places, built thousands of years ago, that remain as parts of archaeological sites—are produced through the transformation of materialities in ritualized events.

Arnauld provides an introduction to "ritual stratigraphy" as an investment in place and place making. Ritual stratigraphy recalls Bradley's (2003) discussion of ritualization through "structured deposition" (Richards and Thomas 1984). We argue that a concept like this is critical to linking archaeological scales of analysis to ethnographic ones (Joyce 2015a; Joyce and Pollard 2010). Structured deposition produces ritual stratigraphy, recognizable traces of stylized actions repeated over time as part of sequences of ritual action.

Like Johnson, Arnauld explores the layering of materials stratigraphically on a temporal scale equal to human lives and generations, a scale that her work again shows can span centuries. Arnauld avoids interpreting offerings buried in house platforms and monumental structures in functionalist terms, as intended to animate the structure, departing from a long-established approach in Mesoamerican studies. Instead, she argues that the burial of materials, forming ritual stratigraphy, constitutes acts of place making—the same conclusion reached in studies of structured deposition through which the Neolithic landscape of Britain was shaped. Approaching the Maya lowland example, she analyzes ritual stratigraphy with an eye to ethnography; she likens the insertion of caches and offerings in a stuccoed surface or temple as similar to farmers preparing a field and planting seeds, invoking ideas of futurity at different scales, in distinct cycles. "Place making," she writes, creates "a 'common ground.'"

The building of structures takes on greater significance when it is understood to be place making. Archaeological analysis allows for observations of ritualized place making over time, across the space of a settlement, that might not have been recognized without a self-conscious orientation to observe the creative, repeated acts that produced the ritualized stratigraphy. Arnauld suggests that inhabitants of one influential household at La Joyanca may have intentionally excavated occupational debris and soils from their original homesite, to be transported and used as fill material inside a newly constructed public structure. This practice, she argues, not only kept exterior spaces clean, but the discarded occupational debris may have served as "ritual rubbish," carrying personal knowledge and history with it into this new space.

The relationships Arnauld demonstrates between the apparently inert medium of sediments and the active constitution of place, at scales ranging from the house to the city, are complemented by the discussion by Nondédéo and his colleagues of place making in engagement with stone sculptures identified as altars, material agents in ritual action. The altars they discuss from the site of Naachtun are constructed of stone, but they arguably served the same purpose as altars of more perishable material constructed in contemporary rituals out of wood and other organic materials, examples of which are discussed in other ethnographic cases (see chapters by Vapnarsky [4], Joyce and Sheptak [3], and Lupo [8]).

As in the instances described by Arnauld, Nondédéo and his colleagues recognize both longer-term temporalities and fine-scale events in the ritualization of place associated with the placement of the two altars they document. The stone altars they describe were ritualized by the placement of ceramic vessels in a series of events that would have involved repeated emphasis on the sacrality of the place. Among the usually ephemeral materialities they are able to suggest were engaged in these events, organic traces suggest the burning of resin to produce scent. More durable inclusions in the deposits resulting from these ritual events, jade and marine shell and coral fragments, may be viewed from the perspective of agential realism as media for intra-action relating the newly created place to the places where these materials originate—the stony earth and marine waters. They conclude their detailed discussion of the stratigraphic history of events related to the two altars they document by pointing to the agential role of the altar stones themselves. Rather than serving simply as objects on which ritual actions took place, the altars forged "a link between a deposit and a building."

An integrative study of ethnographic rituals of house building and archaeological deposits viewed as likely residues from analogous practices in the Maya past serves as a bridge from the two archaeological chapters that open this section, to the final chapter in the section, by Alessandro Lupo, which examines contemporary ritual activity. In their comparative archaeological and ethnographic study, the penultimate chapter in this section, Begel, Chosson, and Becquey demonstrate that built structures in contemporary Maya towns require repeated rituals to bring the occupants into harmony with entities that own and control the earth. The reciprocity they demonstrate between humans and non-human entities recalls the description by Joyce and Sheptak of the effect of Lenca rituals. It appears that in both cases, humans must maintain relations with a landscape of living beings, structuring the reproduction of ritual practices, even as the kinds of buildings constructed and the available materialities for ritual practice change.

Begel and his colleagues describe ritual deposits interred in archaeological sites, like those associated with the altars at Naachtun discussed by Nondédéo and his coauthors, as agential, based on their equation of these deposits with those created in the practice of house building rituals today. In her work at Palenque, Johnson (2018b, chapter 2) discussed such combinations of active material agents as "assemblages," following Manuel DeLanda (2016). His assemblage concept accounts for the ways humans and materials emerge intra-actively, through relating, with their boundaries and properties defined only in relationship to each other. In considering an assemblage, no one component is given priority. The components and the agency that is enacted through their coming together must be described as potentially unique, even if similar to other instances.

DeLanda's assemblage theory reminds us that even when the elements assembled look similar, the historical moment is different, as is the effect of their agential possibilities. In the Classic Maya archaeological sites discussed by Johnson, Arnauld, and Nondédéo and his coauthors, the agential effects of buried deposits take place at very large social, temporal, and spatial scales. They create monumental histories of dynasties and noble families, appropriate to the durability of the stone materials used. Yet like the ethnographic rituals of more modest scale in the lives of individuals and their houses documented by Begel, Chosson and Becquey, the archaeological rituals create ritualized place through repetition at intervals timed by human life events.

In the final chapter in this section, Lupo provides an ethnographic examination of prayers as materialities that, like other things employed in rituals, can be heaped up on altars, ritualizing these critical active places. He shows that the way prayers are produced has a material impact on the participants in the ritual. As in Vapnarsky's Yucatec Maya example, Lupo's Nahua case study demonstrates that verbal forms need to be treated as weighty materialities, no more or less ephemeral than many of the other things assembled for ritual events—the flowers, incense, and food that will decay or be burned or consumed. As the capacity for archaeological detection of micro-residues of such fleeting substances increases, it is becoming ever more possible to harmonize descriptions of ancient ritual events with those observed today, in which flowers, burning resin, and foodstuffs play prominent roles on the altar (Morehart 2017). Lupo's account of the effects prayers have should remind scholars also to attempt to account for the materiality of the vocal (or better, aural) performances we can assume accompanied rituals in the past, even when we have no direct way to assert their existence.

The third section of the book turns deliberately to this question of the aural as material, using both archaeological and ethnographic studies to extend implications of the linguistic work by Vapnarsky and Lupo. Collapsing any possible distinction between studies of living performance and studies of things, the contributions to this section all involve consideration of the activity of musical instruments in a variety of historical contexts. They demonstrate that it is through relating that things act, from the interrelation of wooden drum and singing in a Carnaval celebration discussed by Zalaquett Rock and her coauthors, to the ancient, historical, and contemporary engagements of bone rasps examined by Bellomia, or the assemblage of fired clay, human breath, and moving fingers considered by Kosyk.

This section opens with work by Kosyk on ritual performance and its embodiment implied by the form of musical instruments, ocarinas recovered in excavations at a site in Costa Rica. The large number of instruments present makes this an especially good place for rethinking the materiality of sound. Similar instruments are present in archaeological sites throughout Mexico and Central America, usually in smaller numbers. In ethnographic rituals recorded in the recent past and the present, other instruments, including instruments introduced through colonization, may be employed; but the same kind of analytic efforts can be brought to bear on their particular implications, as the chapter by Zalaquett Rock and her colleagues demonstrates.

Musical instruments are exceptionally rich ritual materialities because they implicate three different subject positions contributing to ritual practices: those of the makers of instruments, those of the players, and those of the participants who listen to the music and respond to it in the ritual. Attentive to the creation of agential possibilities through the making of instruments, Kosyk explores the intertwined agencies and relationalities of makers of instruments and performers. The breath that flows through the fired clay of the aerophones in her case study animates the instrument intra-actively. It would have produced material effects similar to those seen in the studies of contemporary verbal performances described by Vapnarsky and Lupo. The bodily effort involved in producing sound from instruments underlines how verbal performances in ritual are more than merely uttering words. They have, as both Vapnarsky and Lupo emphasize, material force, felt in the body of the speaker (who must not be exhausted by the effort, Lupo's Nahua interlocutors tell him) as well as in the body of the subjects of the ritual.

The preservation of musical instruments made of fired clay is in one sense incidental, an outcome of the need to fix the material to produce specific tones. As Kosyk notes, the fired clay of the Costa Rican ocarinas actually absorbs moisture, creating a challenge for the musician. In another sense, when the instruments are viewed as ritual agents themselves, the choice to produce highly durable instruments allowed for inter-generational rhythms of ritual reproduction. This is one of the points made by Bellomia in her study of Mexican bone rasps preserved in a museum in Italy. It is also a central lesson of Zalaquett Rock's study, with her colleagues, of the performance in Yucatan of a specific song using a traditional wooden drum.

Bellomia demonstrates that archaeological instruments continue to exercise agential possibility today. Following Igor Kopytoff (1986), she considers the "cultural biographies" of two bone rasp instruments. She argues that "in a museum context, this means recognizing the ability of materiality to dynamically act as a cultural agent, able to convey meanings, stories, knowledge, and creativity." Kopytoff's highly cited work marks one of the first attempts to follow and account for the shifting values, meanings, and functions of objects as they moved from context to context. Kopytoff (1986, 66) explains:

> In doing the biography of a thing, one would ask questions similar to those one
> asks about people: where does the thing come from and who made it? What
> has been its career so far, and what do people consider to be an ideal career for
> such things? What are the recognized "ages" or periods in the thing's "life," and
> what are the cultural markers for them? How does the thing's use change with
> its age and what happens to it when it reaches its usefulness?

Recent reconsiderations of this approach have proposed alterations, describing the historical movement of things as "itineraries" rather than biographies (Joyce 2012a, 2012b; Joyce and Gillespie 2015). This involves two main changes: first, acknowledging that the itineraries of things "have no real beginning other than where we enter them and no end since things and their extensions continue to move" and second, not subsuming the experiences of things to the life course of humans with birth, death, and "afterlives" but allowing for different biographies with moments of renaissance and revision (Joyce and Gillespie 2015, 3–4).

Tracing the itineraries of things can be a means to follow an object's changing relationships, as in the instance when musical instruments are transformed from active agents of ritual performance to agents producing multiple temporalities in their new museum context, bringing to Europe a feeling of antiquity, of being outside of the modern, while simultaneously indexing their colonial acquisition. As does Kosyk, Bellomia employs technological and use-wear analyses to determine how things were made, used, and altered after being transported away from their use-context, to identify the rhythms they produced. She shows that the temporality of rhythms created by these instruments extends to their contemporary incorporation in museums.

In the final chapter in this section, Zalaquett Rock and her colleagues present a multi-layered study of the materiality of music that links the performance of a specific song to the activity of a specific wooden drum. In a wide-ranging exploration of the joined histories of the song and the drum, Zalaquett Rock and her coauthors explore materiality at scales ranging from the event of the Carnaval to its annual repetition and the generational reproduction of skill required to play the song using the drum. Bringing oral narratives into the assemblage, they add more temporalities, including those of the creation of the category of instrument and its socialization.

Like Kosyk and Bellomia, Zalaquett Rock and her colleagues are concerned with the specificities of the musicality of the instrument, a materiality itself that produces additional materialities in the form of sound. Like Vapnarsky and Lupo, she is also concerned with the performative weight of the sung narrative, with its powers to effect ritualization. The song she and her coauthors explore is agential on its own, reproduced both through performance and through documentary media—recalling the role of documentary media in bridging long stretches of time demonstrated by Joyce and Sheptak in their study of Lenca ritual practice and implicit in the archaeological studies of Classic Maya Palenque, La Joyanca, and Naachtun, where the documentary media involved were produced using Maya script.

A person acting as part of assemblages with any of the musical instruments described in the final section of this book would be immersed in the materiality of the grouping, evoking a multiplicity of the senses. Authors of many chapters address aspects of the sensorium, from acoustics (Kosyk, Bellomia, and Zalaquett Rock) to the smell of copal incense or burning food in a ritual feasting event (Johnson). These represent efforts to adopt a more embodied approach to materialities that can account for human perceptions as well as material relationships. The senses are both culturally and contextually constituted. In ritual, the senses are heightened through engagement with matter, which includes the material effects of sound generated through song or instrumental music.

CONCLUSION

What became apparent after the sequence of conferences that led to the present volume was that we were all witnessing the ways indigenous peoples of Mexico and Central America establish, maintain, and reinvent relationships with active beings, including ancestral and earthly spirits. Those relationships temporarily coalesce into material assemblages that were experienced directly by the ethnographers and linguists of this volume and indirectly by the archaeologists. The experience of those assemblages extends beyond visual display; they are heard, ingested, and felt in ways distinct to the time and place.

Following a consideration of the case studies presented in this volume, we can argue that the perception of things as agential only takes place through intra-action-producing effects (Barad 2007). We are essentially describing material transactions between humans and non-humans that are accessible across our diverse disciplines. Inside some events, those transactions take the form of song and instrumental music; in others, they are collections of materials inserted into the earth.

The ritualized event, its material components, and its temporality form an assemblage that takes on its material form through a process that is historical. As DeLanda (2000, 11) argues, "All structures that surround us and form our reality (mountains, animals and plants, human languages, social institutions) are the products of specific historical processes." From this perspective, we can see why interdisciplinary exchange such as the initiative we have formed here is not only beneficial but necessary. Archaeologically recovered material assemblages provide evidence of a deep history to ritualized transactions among the peoples of Mexico and Central America. Ethnography and linguistic anthropology reveal the ways those transactions have emerged as similar to or distinct from the history of transactions that took place before, highlighting the fluidity of materiality and temporality in intra-action.

This volume shares similarities with other works, particularly in our efforts to bring together a multidisciplinary consideration of ritual in the Mesoamerican region (Mock 1998b; Tiesler and Scherer 2018). We do not focus here on specific practices and religious themes but rather, bring discussion of ritual in the region in line with larger theoretical discussions surrounding ritual, materiality, and temporality—discussions we see happening in many other parts of the world among physicists, historians, and political scientists, as well as anthropologists and archaeologists. A widely held consensus across these various disciplines is that space, time, and material configurations occur as a series of possibilities afforded by a history of configuring in particular ways—emergent, but also shaped by the past. What we present in this volume is consequently a series of distinct configurations and re(con)figurations of making time. The rhythm of ritualization in this part of the world began centuries ago and continues to flow in a series of overlapping, nonlinear temporalities mediated by the intra-action of materialities that become ever more visible as practitioners of different disciplines compare their insights.

PART ONE

Events and Temporalities

2

Measuring time and examining the materials produced, used, and deposited over time is fundamental to the practice of archaeology. We interpret time through stratigraphy and often present a linear historical narrative, sometimes exceeding a thousand years in just a few meters of layered soils, artifacts, and built features. But archaeological time can feel abstract and removed from the present, a point that is increasingly problematic when we consider the larger anthropological and philosophical discourse surrounding the varied concepts of time and temporality. Anthropologists and social theorists have long recognized a diversity in perceptions of time and temporality, both cross-culturally and from context to context. Temporalities may follow a physical dimension with the movement of celestial bodies and changing seasonality. Lived time is another temporal dimension not as evenly measured but nonetheless ongoing. From a scientific point of view, time is a universal, can be measured and divided precisely, and can exist outside of human experience or organic growth and transformation. Archaeologists, in efforts to establish typologies and time lines, often present an interpretation of past actions and events as a chronological sequence of development, but some have argued for archaeologists to expand their reckoning of time to account for multiple temporalities (Bailey 2007; Murray 1999, 2).

Time, as perceived and as materialized, is multiple. And so, we are challenged to explore the ways these

From One Moment to the Next

Multiple Temporalities in Classic Maya Ritualized "Events"

Lisa M. Johnson

https://doi.org/10.5876/9781646422395.c002

multiple temporalities materialize into a single "archaeological record." As Joyce (2015b, 182) has argued, even the most straightforward archaeological excavation handles multiple scales, durations, and granularities of temporality at the same time. There are various archaeological strategies for dealing with these multiple durations, some accounting for seasonal time through pollen and phytolith studies (Morehart 2017) and others employing an ethno-archaeological approach to consider lived temporal scales (Boivin 2000).

In her contribution to this volume, Arnauld discusses the "social stratigraphic perspective" as put forth by McAnany and Hodder (2009), which understands the formation of layered sediments and materials as a result of the continual tempo of social action over time. To that I would add that the tempo of humans moving about occurred in a complex web of organic and inorganic growth, decay, and movement. Consider the time-elapsed video of a jungle floor: human feet may scuff and move about at one pace, burrowing microfauna, twisted vines, and roots at another, and all lend to the formation of "strata" as the archaeologist encounters them. From this perspective, the "social" and "natural" mechanisms for stratigraphic layering cannot be disentangled. On the contrary, they cease to be separate categories, and this is what one sees in micromorphological thin section.

Multiple temporalities in this case are twofold: they are the varied "granularities of temporality" (after Joyce 2015b) evident in archaeological excavations through the integration of microscopic methods and the detection of single episodes of deposition alongside macroscale sedimentation of strata spanning multiple generations. They are also the consideration of the multiple temporalities that are produced and experienced in those episodes of deposition or sedimentation of strata. The experience of time is no doubt varied and highly subjective. Many perceive time at different rates in different contexts. As I will discuss in this chapter, some contexts constitute what I call "eventful" moments, particularly ritualized contexts.

The temporality of ritual has been described as one in which the past and the present are brought together synchronously, or "ritual time" (Bloch 1989). In addition to the lived experience of "ritual time," there are other temporalities at work, which include seasonal and calendrical time. And no discussion of time or temporality can ignore materiality. The experience of time occurs through an intermingling of performativity and substance. Sights, smells, and tactile qualities of substance lend to the ways time is perceived. While asking questions of subjective experience, emotions, and memory in the past may be an experimental exercise, it is one worth considering rather than ignoring some of the most fundamental aspects of eventful moments in the past (Joyce

2001; Kus 1992). To do that, I revisit discussions of temporality and the concept of the "event" to understand discrete archaeological deposits as residues of materially rich, sensual, emotional, and memorable moments. The concept of an event has a history in anthropological discourse that often stresses temporality and structural change (Beck et al. 2007; Sahlins 1985; Sewell 2005). A more recent take on the event expands on the concept to include a consideration of its materiality as well as its temporality (Connolly 2013). I argue that the bounded moment that is the "event" as described in this recent theoretical work materializes as a depositional episode that is detectable archaeologically. The event and the structured deposition that forms within it are utilized in this study as methodological constructs through which the process of ritualization and the material relations that emerge in ritual can be studied. The ritualization of an event and the assembled materials within occurs through a stylized way of acting that illuminates relationality among humans, places, things, and, in some cases, the supernatural (Bradley 2003; Humphrey and Laidlaw 1994; Swenson 2015).

This chapter considers the materialization of ritualized events and multiple temporalities through micromorphological studies carried out in a residential plaza group at the Classic Maya city of Palenque known as "Group IV," occupied by non-ruling nobles, to consider some of the most intrinsic qualities of ritual: temporality and materiality.

TEMPORALITY, MATERIALITY, AND THE EVENT

In a recent review of archaeological approaches to ritual, Swenson (2015, 333) describes ritual as a distinct material process that occurs through a special quality of action, or a "material reframing of action that often sets apart recognized events (initiations, pilgrimages, festivals, etc.) from the stream of everyday practice, events that often afford alternate experiences of time, place, and being." Similarly, Walker (2008, 144) has argued for "an expanded understanding of practice that focuses on the material relations between people and nonhuman agents" as an alternative to older models that placed too much emphasis on symbolism and belief.

The growing consensus in what has been termed the "material turn" in social theory is that non-humans can be active and that humans act alongside other non-humans. This perspective is one that takes the relationships that emerge between the coming together of humans and the physical world in which they dwell as primary. The ways we investigate the human experience are shifting. Instead, we are asking, how does the human articulate alongside these other vibrant materials? How do material relations shift in a given situational context? For those of us pursuing these questions, we no longer deny subjectivity to non-humans but rather seek to understand how subjectivity varies from situation to situation and across matter (e.g., humans, plants, animals, objects). It can be argued that what is identified as ritual are those contexts in which non-human matter and the landscape in which it occurs are experienced as active. As Swenson (2015) notes, citing Fowles (2013, 103), ritualization is marked by a "heightened awareness of interconnectedness and the relations between things." Along these lines, we can explore the potential contributions of a new materialism (Barad 2007; Bennett 2010; Dolphijn and van der Tuin 2012) in an archaeology of ritual to examine shifting subjectivities, relationality, and materiality in the emergence of the ritualized event.

"New materialism" refers to a revitalization and expansion of older materialist philosophies, in which material relationships are reconsidered as emergent, transformative, and historically constituted (DeLanda 2000; Dolphijn and van der Tuin 2012). Among the host of scholars often associated with this theoretical movement, Manuel DeLanda's (2000, 2016) "assemblage" theory provides an interesting approach to map material relationships. As DeLanda explains, assemblages are heterogeneous collectives, a whole made up of parts. That whole not only includes persons but materials as well. Assemblages can become components of larger collectives, such that an intimate household mortuary ritual emerges within a larger assemblage that is the social house (Joyce and Gillespie 2000), which itself is part of an even larger collective, the Maya city. DeLanda (2016, 20) refers to this as "nested assemblages." They vary in scale and duration. Some assemblages, often larger assemblages such as communities or cities, can exist over longer terms, while other, shorter and smaller assemblages can form and dissipate within them.

As heterogeneous collectives, power is not typically equal across the individual components of an assemblage (Bennett 2010). Humans and non-human organisms, things, and substances make up assemblages; and across the collective, agency and subjectivity are unevenly exercised. The new materialist paradigm does not place the human at the center of all things, and it does not restrict subjectivity and agential capacity to humans alone. While assemblages, or events, are rooted in historical processes, "all assemblages should be considered unique historical entities" (DeLanda 2016, 6). Assemblages are historical constructions. They emerge from the coming together of components that existed prior, components that had been part of other previous assemblages and that may assemble again. Thus, the event-as-assemblage is temporal, has spatial boundaries and is material, and is experienced differently from non-eventful moments.

Traditionally, the event as concept has been considered a happening, often of historical scale, that can alter or cause a rupture in social structures (Beck et al. 2007; Gilmore and O'Donoughue 2015; Sahlins 1985). Just as there is a multiplicity of temporalities, there is multiplicity in the event. Events can vary in scale and effect. While some may indeed overturn or destabilize the equilibrium of social structures, others may be a momentary rupture, a moment that stands apart from other moments. These events, although not dramatic or large scale, are still experienced and remembered differently.

Archaeologists have previously stated that matter shapes the experience of space and time (Jones 2004, 331; Olsen 2003). But to reorient ourselves within the new materialist paradigm that stresses the emergent nature of things, we could consider another point of view, in which space and time are produced, and do not exist independent of, matter interacting. Ritualization, as a distinct quality of action, can produce a temporality that is experienced and remembered differently from the tempo of daily life. The temporality of ritual does not follow a presumed universal, often abstract concept but rather, follows—as a number of social theorists have argued—a multiplicity that is not always linear, is often subjective, and is produced differentially from moment to moment. The subjective experience of so-called nonlinear time can coincide simultaneously with other temporalities (Bergson 1999; Bloch 1989). Archaeologist Richard Bradley (1991, 209) describes multiple temporalities as including "substantial time" being marked by human experience and "abstract" time as measured and divided precisely. Within that "substantial," or lived, time, some moments stand apart. Similarly, anthropologist Alfred Gell (1992) describes multiple temporalities as A-series and B-series events. A-series are considered time-immanent in passage of events, while B-series are isolated happenings. Tim Ingold (1993, 157) describes this view as one "in which events are strung out in time like beads on a thread." In visualizing events as heightened relationality of matter, we could liken them to waves cresting and receding.

Perhaps we can conceive of certain moments as episodic for the impacts they have on individual and social memories. On the one hand, Gell's A-series events can produce what Tulving (1993) defines as "semantic" memories, a repetitive tempo of daily life that creates a blurring of memory. In contrast, Tulving's "episodic" memories arise from significant events, or Gell's B-series events. It is through memory of the event that future events can be structured and materialize in similar ways.

This can be the case with something like a mortuary event in a residential plaza group among a small group of Maya living in the city of Palenque during the Classic Period (AD 250–900). A funeral brings memories of past events, a previous time when the newly deceased was living. The present moment of the funeral itself is episodic, creating memories that will be carried forward. When discussing the event and what distinguishes eventful moments from non-eventful moments, Gilmore and O'Donoughue (2015, 6) suggest that at the very least, an event has an "impact that extends beyond the moment and place of its occurrence." Events inform the moments that follow, so that a history of practice emerges that is shared across space and over multiple generations. We can examine a history of practice and the creative, emergent nature of individual events archaeologically through a comprehensive approach that attempts to account for the range of materials present and their repetition across events. This can be difficult in warm tropical environments when most of the expected materials are organic and thus potentially perishable as macro-artifacts. This challenge calls for the use of microscopic approaches.

EXAMINING THE MATERIALITY OF THE EVENT IN MICROSTRATIGRAPHIC SEQUENCES

Distinguishing the single, individual event from the continual traces of material deposition, alteration, and disturbance can be difficult. These material traces, like past actions, and the work of memory making share similar features. The rhythms of daily life and the traces they produce through those actions can blend together, creating the archaeological palimpsest. In following ritualization as a stylized or emphasized action but also the assemblage as a set of material relations, the event presents a concept through which we can consider ritual not as an abstract idea but as a bounded phenomenon that produces material traces that can be identified. Micromorphology provides a microscopic view of some of those traces, often detecting multiple moments of deposition where only one is visible to the naked eye. For this kind of analysis, blocks of soil are retrieved to be impregnated with epoxy and cut into thin section for microscopic analysis of components in situ (Macphail, Courty, and Goldberg 1990). Because it is a bulk sample rather than a loose sample, we can see the mixing and layering of components over time. Our understanding of the microstratigraphic sequences in thin section is based on analysis of taphonomy and depositional relationships between sediments and artifacts and bioarchaeological remains (Matthews et al. 1997, 281). This includes post-depositional alterations to components, such as weathering.

Micromorphology interprets past actions and material processes through comparison. To understand the actions and processes that formed the soils and sediments seen in thin section, one needs to be familiar with a range of actions and processes that are different. Like ritual itself, to understand what is ritual (or, even better, to identify traces of ritualization) for a given cultural and historical context, one needs to be familiar with actions and performances that are not ritualized in the same time and place. It is through this process that materials, even materials recognized in any other context as utilitarian, can become ritualized as the result of a ritual event. Ritualization is a relationship of difference that leaves traces.

Originally developed to examine soil formation processes (Kubiëna 1938), archaeologists have increasingly turned to micromorphology to identify anthropogenic alterations of the soil as well as the distinct patterning of material components produced by different actions (Courty, Goldberg, and Macphail 1989; Nicosia and Stoops 2017). This has enabled archaeologists to identify discrete activity areas (Goldberg et al. 2009; Matthews et al. 1997; Shillito and Ryan 2013) as well as the temporality of repeated actions (Boivin 2000). Existing examples of archaeological analyses using micromorphology are largely from outside the Maya area. Micromorphological studies in the area in recent years are mainly concerned with soil formation, sustainability (Sedov et al. 2008), and environmental change (Solís-Castillo et al. 2015). My analyses of samples from the Classic Period city of Palenque demonstrate that micromorphology, as a method for studying microscopic traces of deposition and relationships between material components, when incorporated into a larger archaeological study, allows for the identification of eventful moments.

Human actions are often evident in micromorphological thin section, as they can alter the composition, arrangement, size, and shape of constituents in a soil fabric (Macphail and Goldberg 2018). For example, broken and angular components or coated aggregates can be suggestive of trampling (Matthews et al. 1997), while the layering of phytoliths or grassy plant remains may be evidence of a mat laid down (Goldberg et al. 2009). Or a stratum of burning may macroscopically appear to be one event but under the microscope multiple layers of burning may be visible, indicating repeated events over time. The integration of methods such as micromorphology allows for a reconsideration of a life history of place through lived, generational time. Rituals as distinct events may produce traces that are recognizable when considering the stratification produced by actions over time, as seen in archaeological excavations. The daily rhythms of everyday actions—such as trampling, depositing bits of charcoal, remnants of food, broken pottery, or lithic tools—can blend into the soils and are then further transformed by yearly rainy seasons, intrusive rodents, and microfauna such as worms and other living organisms. Over hundreds of years, those factors can create a visibly blurred mixing of material residues. At the microscopic level, however, the orientation of constituents, their form, and their spatial relationships can enable examination of discrete episodes of patterned deposition, burning, or the presence of distinct materials such as pigments and incense distinctive of ritual events.

Micromorphology is best interpreted within a well-integrated research design, one that includes complementary sampling of larger artefactual materials, flotation for macrobotanical remains, and sampling for phytoliths and starches. Micromorphological and other microscopic studies integrated alongside traditional macroscopic archaeological analyses provide an opportunity to recover and analyze the many residues of the human experience in the past, including both the anthropogenic sediments and, simultaneously, the climatic and geological landscape within which those events occurred. This is evident in my results from Palenque's Group IV.

Here, multiple temporalities affecting deposits begin with deep geological time in the shaping of the parent materials that make up much of the fabric seen in thin section and extend to the single depositional episode that occurs during the event, leaving a distinct material signature. The remains from events cover generations that would pass before later events were recorded in stone on a monument, Group IV's so-called Tablet of the Slaves.

Interpreting distinct events in thin section required a comparison between different samples of the same soil profile as well as across different profiles. In the Maya region, it can be difficult, sometimes impossible, to recover the necessary sequence of overlapping block soil samples from inside stone-built structures. Often, Maya structures are constructed primarily of large limestone cobble construction fill with few, if any, internal surface areas. Of two mausoleum structures excavated in Group IV, only one showed evidence of discrete contexts and surfaces that could be sampled for micromorphological analysis. The comparison of different contexts seen in micromorphological thin section in this structure provides a means by which we can investigate what constitutes ritualization among the Maya of Classic Period Palenque.

THE MAYA WORLD OF ACTIVE MATTER

Swenson (2015, 340) concludes his review of archaeology of ritual with an important point: "Ultimately, a focus on ritual as a materially marked process (often demarcating specific events and times) allows archaeologists to analyze ritual as a historically particular experience without abandoning the anthropological project of comparison." Ritualization and the material process of ritual are unique from culture to culture. This study is concerned with the

Maya who lived during the Classic Period (AD 250–900). Hieroglyphic text and iconographic scenes of ritual events among the Classic Maya suggest that Maya rituals materialized through the participation of a range of human and non-human actors. Offerings of plant and animal food, smoke, fire, and pigments were among the animating substances involved in Maya ritual events. This aligns the Classic Maya with what has been called relational ontologies.

A review of ethnographic accounts of contemporary Maya communities suggests that a relational ontology in which matter is active persisted throughout the long and painful experience of European invasion (Harrison-Buck 2012; see also Begel, Chosson, and Becquey, chapter 7, this volume). Changes to practice in contemporary Maya ritual events do not appear to reflect a shift in ontology or worldview but rather, the addition of participants such as Catholic saints and priests. Consulted with awareness of historical processes, ethnographies can be used along with Classic texts and artistic imagery to provide models for the experiential qualities of the materialization and temporality of ritual, to inform interpretation of archaeologically recovered traces of past ritual events.

The archaeologically recovered material traces of ritualized events in Classic Maya sites suggest specialized treatment of materials and spaces that was distinct as compared to other, non-eventful moments. To understand how non-human things can temporarily take on life during an event, we can consider recorded descriptions of contemporary Maya practices. Previous discussions of a Maya ontology have considered at length the perception of animate things, animal co-essences, and sacred plant stuffs as active (Harrison-Buck 2012; Stross 1998). The world of living things is in a perpetual cycle of birth, death, and regeneration. This does not mean, however, that things, animals, plants, temples, and caves are the same as humans but rather, that they participate in the same process of birth, death, and regeneration. Ethnographic accounts describe the Maya concept of soul and animating forces at length. In most cases, animating energy is not inherent in any human or non-human thing or organism but is exercised through action. Among some contemporary Maya, *ch'ulel*, considered a life force, exists outside of the body and is accumulated over the course of a lifetime (Scherer 2015, 12). In highland Maya communities in Guatemala, everything has the potential to carry *k' u'x* (a heart), but only humans have both *k' u'x* and *anima*, or soul (Fischer and Hendrickson 2003). Among the Yucatek Maya, *ik'* winds are a vital essence that can move into bodies, often bringing sickness or death (Love 2012). For the Maya who wrote inscriptions of the Classic Period, a force labeled *ik'* also brought life (Taube 2004). *Ch'ulel* and *ik'* are examples of free-flowing energies that move in and out of material bodies including humans, non-human substance, things, animals, and other living organisms.

For the Maya of the Classic Period, things such as stone monuments, pottery, temples, and houses were not inherently active. They were activated through dedication ceremonies, burned offerings, painting, or inscription (Stuart 1998). Stone carved into a stela or monument and "planted" during calendrical rituals was activated and "invested with *ch'ul*" (Stuart 1996, 157). A house or temple was activated once it was censed in a "fire-entering" ceremony (Stuart 1998).

The ritualized events that materialized in Palenque's Group IV include the setting of a stone monument, the activation of an ancestral house, and the burial and subsequent feeding of the ancestral dead. All of these evoke multiple temporalities, and the actions of each event informed the materialization of subsequent events. The grave is a space of liminality, a place in which ritual events transition the once living body to the realm of the dead and, later, elevate the dead to the role of ancestor (Scherer 2015). The timing of ritual events, their duration, and their scale most likely varied from context to context. In some cases, the calendar might have determined the duration or timing of an event; in others, a life event or unanticipated need might have initiated a ritual event.

Epigraphic information suggests that life-cycle events, including accessions, birthdays, and death, were celebrated events that included the participation of supernatural beings as well as the spirits of the ancestral dead (Fitzsimmons 1998). Some of those events may have occurred over an extended period, involving activities such as dancing, music, feasting, and burning of incense. While the death of a person was part of a life cycle and might have been unanticipated, the rituals that surrounded the death might have been timed by the Maya calendar. Such events, as described in inscriptions, could last multiple days (1998). Fitzsimmons (1998) discusses calendrical anniversaries, with actions including the opening of tombs, or "houses," for the dead to be censed. The timing of mortuary events among ancient Maya may have occurred around calendrical anniversaries, as the living returned to commemorate and honor the dead at a *k'atun* anniversary following the death of the individual (1998).

To demonstrate the integration of fine-grained stratigraphic analyses in the consideration of multiple temporalities, namely, daily rhythmic time and the heightened moments of events, I now turn to the Classic Period city of Palenque, located in the western limits of the Maya region, Chiapas Mexico (figure 2.1). The mausoleum structure in Palenque's Group IV acted as a house for the influential dead person and was an active participant in ritualized feasting events. For the Maya, the consumption of food was one way in which things, spaces, and humans could be transformed or enlivened. But

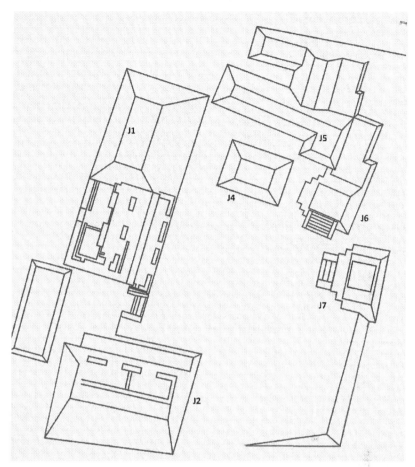

FIGURE 2.1. *Plan of Group IV, Palenque, indicating the location of Structure J7 on the east side of the plaza*

houses are not equivalent to persons; they consume substance through different means, such as burning. Micromorphological analyses, along with other analyses, allow the identification of these distinct forms of participation in ritualized events.

EXCAVATIONS IN GROUP IV, PALENQUE

Palenque was a densely occupied city situated along a Paleocene age limestone ridge midway up the heavily folded Chiapas-Tabasco foothills. The city—occupied by a population of roughly 6,000—encompassed a small area of 16 linear km, with just 2 km² forming the city center, bounded by the steep foothills to the south and vast alluvial plains to the north (Barnhart 2007). A number of springs, streams, and rivers run through the city. The sierras on which the city was built were composed of micaceous sandstones and limestone outcrops with ancient fossilized inclusions (Riquelme et al. 2012). These material features, sedimented over deep geological time, characterize the fabric seen in micromorphological thin section. The soils are rich in clay, yellow in color, typical of equatorial tropic climates, and soft enough to cut when in a fresh state (Kubiëna 1970, 124). The continual flow of water throughout the city in addition to the annual downpours during the rainy season lend to the qualities of the events that emerged in this hot, humid, tropical city in the forest. The onset of heavy rains each year typical of Palenque may have also influenced the times when events were carried out and the duration of those events.

The excavations in which I participated were carried out in the residential group of structures known as Group IV (figure 2.1). This is a large, elaborate plaza group located just 300 m northwest of the central palace district. Group IV was designed with multiple structures situated around a central patio area. The largest of the structures, J1, is a two-story structure on the west side of the plaza that was built with a series of small rooms and may have served as a primary sleeping and living area. Another structure in the southwestern corner of the plaza (Str. J2) appears to be a later addition, connected to Structure J1 by a stairway and platform area. There is a long L-shaped range structure on the north side of the plaza (Str. J3) and three small pyramidal structures clustered on the eastern and northern corners of the plaza (Strs. J4, J6, J7). These served as mausoleum structures, or houses for the remains of deceased influential members of the household (Johnson 2018b).

Group IV was the site where an elaborately carved limestone panel bearing an inscribed text was discovered while a road into the archaeological park was being built (Ruz Lhuillier 1952). From the text on the tablet, we can deduce that the social group living in Group IV was a wealthy, politically connected household. The panel, known as the Tablet of the Slaves, has been deciphered and is understood to be the recorded narrative of the life events of an influential *sahal*, or lower lord, Chak Sutz' (Izquierdo and Bernal Romero 2011; Schele 1991). The dates recorded on the Tablet of the Slaves span the late fifth and early sixth centuries. As is common for Classic Maya narration of life-cycle events, each event mentioned in the text is fixed in the calendar (Josserand 1991). One date precedes the description of the events, producing a distinct temporality of its own. Dates like this, inscribed in stone, appear more fixed and were likely experienced differently than dates in the flow of living activity.

The recorded events inscribed on the panel were not listed in order as a kind of chronicle; rather, as in most Classic Period Maya texts, later events are situated in relation to past figures and their actions while also situating the narrative within the political landscape contemporary with its creation. The text begins by listing the accession of three generations of Palenque rulers. The rest of the text is a narrative of key moments in the life of an important member of the house, Chak Sutz' (Josserand 1991). The latest of the rulers listed at the beginning of the text, Ahkal Mo' Knab, was in power during the time of the panel's creation in the early sixth century and may have been the one to confer titles on Chak Sutz' (Stuart and Stuart 2008). The moments in the life of Chak Sutz' selected for recording include his participation in multiple war events and his capture of three captives. Just two years before the first war event, he celebrated an event of succession, apparently as a lower lord (*sahal*) under the Palenque ruler. Following two successive war events and the capture of captives, Chak Sutz' celebrated the completion of three *k'atuns* since his birth, suggesting he was roughly sixty years of age in AD 730.

The recorded historical events on the Tablet of the Slaves evoked a specific kind of long-term temporality derived from the Maya calendar but also recalled lived time through the recording of Chak Sutz's life events. As Stuart (1996) noted, the setting of stone monuments was often a marker of significant period-ending events, with the word *tun* as "stone" often used in statements recording time. Temporal markers inscribed in stone provided a longer time depth than other forms of commemoration, with many recording thousands of years. Stuart (1996, 151) explains that "dedicated *tuns*, whatever form they took, served in some capacity as representations—one might even say 'embodiments' of time itself."

An estimated seven or eight generations of continuous occupation and expansion occurred in this house over the course of nearly 300 years, from roughly AD 500–750 (assuming the average life expectancy of thirty-five years). Chak Sutz's generation was one of the last to live in Group IV. Excavations have revealed a lengthy occupational history beginning hundreds of years prior to the installation of the Chak Sutz' monument. This history is primarily understood through the superposition of burials on the east side of the plaza. Multiple projects have encountered burials in this area, including the recent excavations during 2016 and 2017 (Liendo Stuardo 2016; Lopez Bravo 2004; Rands and Rands 1961). The living members of the house continually buried their dead on this side of the plaza, including men, women, and children.

Most burials were found clustered around the basal steps of Structures J6 on the northeast corner of the plaza and Structure J7 on the east side of the plaza, the two mausoleum structures from which I analyzed materials.

STRUCTURE J7

Structure J7 is a 3.5-m-tall square structure located on the east side of the plaza (figure 2.2). The unusual stairs, wide and shallow, were a result of continual modification and expansion. The series of external modifications were an early sign that this particular space was one of the oldest for the group. Excavations inside the structure reached a depth of nearly 5 m below the summit of the structure, ending at bedrock, enabling a full reconstruction of the sequence of events that took place in this area of the plaza (Johnson 2018b).

The earliest living surface, just above bedrock, was dated to the early to mid-500s AD. There were repeated episodes of burning intermixed with high concentrations of broken storage vessels and coarse wares in addition to a whistle in the shape of a woman's headless torso. In micromorphological thin section, these earliest moments of deposition showed the highest level of complex soil formation, with weathered limestone bedrock material, bioturbation, and weathered and crystallized fragments of plaster that appear to have descended and washed down from above. Evidence of trampling in these earliest layers can be seen by the presence of subrounded and clay-coated silt aggregates most likely transported from elsewhere (table 2.1). Micromorphological samples taken from the plaza area outside of the structure did not reveal the quantity of materials or any patterning indicating a primary depositional event. In contrast, the samples taken from the plaza were relatively devoid of artifacts, as if this area was intentionally kept clean. The area on the east side of the plaza appears to have been a marked ritual space from the beginning of occupation. Only after the initial marking of that space was the space considered sacred, and the nature of those ritual events shifted.

The marking of that space followed a larger Maya tradition. The eastern cardinal direction was ritually significant. As the direction from which the sun rises, it was associated with the planting of crops and, by extension, the cyclical reckoning of time. From the east, the sun god would rise each morning before making his way across the sky and descending into the western entrance to the dark underworld (Freidel, Schele, and Parker 1993; Taube 2004). The sacred cycle of life, death, and regeneration was intimately tied to the movement of the sun along this path, and so the ancient Maya often marked spaces on the east side of a bounded plaza group for ceremonial events, both in the home and in public spaces (Ashmore 1991). A tradition of funerary events and shrine building on the eastern side of a residential plaza group emerged in the eastern lowland Maya region (Becker 2003) but did not seem to be common in the western lowland region where Palenque is located. However, here in Group IV, we see from the initial occupation and first generations of Maya living in this home that the eastern area was of special significance. These earliest deposits are distinct from other areas in the plaza group, outside of Structure J7.

Soon after these earliest depositional events in the east, the occupants of Group IV dug into the bedrock to construct a stone crypt with double niches, making a cruciform-shape grave. This contained the body an older man. These events took place between AD 576 and 651 (with a 95.4% probability), if we were to place them back into a linear archaeological chronology.

Themes of foundation and the centering of sacred space proliferate in the earliest periods of Group IV's ritual events, in the actions performed and the materials active in ritual events. Digging into bedrock to place human burials was common across the Maya region. Classic Maya inscriptions likened the burial of the dead to "planting" or "sowing" (Fitzsimmons 2009, 68). To dig into bedrock was to anchor the ancestor into place so they might regenerate in their new form, much as corn is sowed, dies, and returns (Scherer 2015). The man buried in the crypt may have been one of the first influential members of the group to pass away, and his burial event transformed the east side of the plaza. His cruciform crypt was constructed in a form reminiscent of the world tree depicted later in the central ceremonial precinct of the city, the best-known example being on the Palenque ruler Pakal's sarcophagus lid constructed more than 100 years after the burial in Group IV (Freidel, Schele, and Parker 1993). Placing the body in the cruciform crypt positioned it along the center of the world tree. In Classic Maya cosmology, the world tree provides a conduit connecting the living world, the underworld, and the worlds of the supernatural above.

The event whose traces these deposits constitute emerged from the death of a man who presumably lived in this house and had some influence in this community. The dead body itself was an active participant in these events, a primary agent. Mortuary events that had happened among the community before informed the ways this event materialized, but as Connolly (2013) has said, events are creative and novel and through their emergence, something new materializes. This specific burial event produced ritual time, a folding of the past into the present (Bloch 1989). The placing of the dead body in the crypt may have been a moment in a prolonged series of moments. The body was most likely prepared and received visitors from the surrounding community while the crypt was being constructed. Traces of cinnabar inside the man's eye orbits suggest that one of the ways the body was prepared was through spreading red pigment over him. He was also dressed in jade and shell ornaments, including shell L-shaped ear ornaments with hanging jade beads and a jade bead necklace, before he was lowered into the crypt. A carved limestone spindle whorl was placed on his groin, and a small flat-bottom bowl was placed in the western niche of the crypt. The bowl most likely contained food or drink for the initial departure of the man's spirit.

Death is an emotional process. The events that occur around the death of a community member are memorable, as the death is out of the ordinary. Using Gell's definition, we can describe the temporality of this mortuary event as episodic. Inside that moment, time may have been experienced differently across the group of mourners. We can imagine this event as dramatic, as emotional, and as one that triggered the senses—as can be inferred by the series of actions that took place and the distinct material deposit left in the archaeological stratigraphy. In inferring the sensory impact of these events, I recall a point made by Susan Kus (1992, 172), who argued that "sensuality may not be directly recoverable in the archaeological record. This does not imply that we are free to ignore its place in our theoretical formulations." The death of this man in a tropical landscape most likely produced a distinct smell that would have fixed that moment into the memory of the community that experienced the event. As with many ritual events among the Maya, copal may have been burned, fires lit, and food prepared and served, creating an overwhelming agglomeration of matter. Smells, sounds, and substances—including the smell of the dead body, copal, food, the tropical forest, the sound of chatter, crying, possibly music or chanting, the substance of smoke from copal, from fire, of mineral pigment applied to the dead body—materialized an event, a punctuation of temporality.

The funeral event was a moment of rupture in the flow of activity of non-eventful moments. In that eventful moment, the community was made aware of the potency of death. The materialization of the moment cemented into memory and marked that space. One obvious rupture was the altered state of an influential member of the group from living to dead. From an archaeologist's perspective, we encounter traces of the event and can infer multiple actions that left these traces, which punctuate our experience of the deposits.

After the funeral event, a series of large flat limestone slabs were placed on top of the crypt, sealing the man's body below. A thick layer of bright, white, loose plaster was deposited between each layer of limestone slabs. Just above his crypt, the descendants and living members of the group gathered food typical of Palenque cuisine, including fish, turtle, jute snails, and beans. They burned copal in a small unslipped pedestal-based incensario. To transport the feast to the realm of the dead, everything was burned in situ (Johnson 2018b). The eating of food typical of everyday meals would have been experienced differently in that moment. It was ritualized by the inclusion of the dead and by the marked space in which the feast was located. The pottery vessel forms associated with this event shifted from storage vessels and cookware (as was seen in the earliest moments of deposition) to finely decorated serving ware, including polychrome plates and thin-walled bowls and vases. This episodic moment no doubt stood out in living memory as the ancestor was actively there, called upon to receive his food. This was not a typical everyday occurrence. Copal smoke intermingling with the smoke of the burning fish, turtle, jute, and plant foods most likely produced a distinctive smell that lent a distinctive quality to the event.

The feasting event was a depositional episode that was spread across the area directly above the crypt. In thin section, this event left a distinct material signature as compared to samples taken from the plaza at similar depths. The groundmass had a series of planar voids, creating a moderately separated crumb microstructure with large components including lithic, ceramic, charcoal, and plaster fragments—many of which were oriented parallel to the ground surface, typical for accumulated occupation deposits on floors (Matthews et al. 1997, 289). In contrast, middens and secondarily discarded materials are typically unoriented and randomly distributed throughout. In addition to durable materials, phytoliths were present in the sample. There were no identifiable boundaries in the thin section (sample 400-04), suggesting that this was a single depositional event. The residents of Group IV did not return and feast again in this spot.

The death and subsequent burial of the body was not the final moment in the transformation of a living member of the community to an ancestor. Elaborate meals and events of feeding and eating among the Maya were often structured by multiple socio-temporal frameworks, including those that followed the calendar, the harvest of crops, and the human life cycle (Hendon 2003). The mortuary feasting event that emerged following the sealing of the burial was a single moment among a series of protracted moments that Scherer (2015) argues were meant to placate the spirit of the dead and ensure a smooth transition in this liminal stage. Food and the act of feeding and eating was a common component in the ritual events that materialized on the east side of Group IV's plaza space.

The burned remains of the feasting event were left scattered above the grave, but carbon dates suggest that shortly after, the residents built a square stone altar to provide a space for continued reciprocal interaction with the ancestor buried below. The altar covered nearly half of the feasting area and was positioned perfectly over the burial, suggesting a memory of the grave's location below the surface. The construction of the altar coincided with a series of meaningful acts. Samples taken at the base of the altar for micromorphological analysis revealed another moment in between (table 2.1). In thin section, it appears that a thick layer of clay-rich material, "clean" of artifacts, was laid as a foundation to prepare a surface for the subsequent construction (sample 400-03).

During construction of the altar, three square stones were set into the center, layered one on top of the other. The square stones were distinct from rough cobble fill that made up the bulk of the altar. The central positioning of the stones and their layering formed a pattern evoking the Maya "three-stone-hearth" referred to in inscriptions about cosmological origins (Freidel, Schele, and Parker 1993; Taube 1998). The upper stone was scorched from burning, transforming the space into an active hearth. Burning activated the altar, opening the path of reciprocity between the world of the living and the supernatural realm. Afterward, the altar was completely plastered. A generation of living members of the house returned to that altar to burn offerings, particularly plant matter, on the plastered altar surface.

Micromorphology samples taken in this excavation reveal that all of the thin sections share similar characteristics in their fabric due to the geological and climate conditions of Palenque's local landscape (table 2.1). A sandy clay matrix with traces of single mica grains is evident in all samples both inside and outside of identified ritual contexts. Clay coatings and intercalations of clay are frequent throughout all samples, indicative of high amounts of water movement and weathering. But the weathered matrix and clay-rich fabrics are not the backdrop on which an event of deposition occurs; they form together. This sheds light on the feeling of the event. The wet tropical conditions and soft soils lend specific sensory effects to the material qualities of the events that materialized in that space.

The sample taken from the altar surface was characterized by massive microstructure with weakly separated peds, planar voids throughout, and mono-striated b-fabric of yellow-orange clay in a fabric of fine micaceous sand. The total fabric is carbonate-rich, with frequent abundance of fine sand– to gravel-size plaster fragments. The largest plaster components are oriented parallel to the surface. The rainy season caused wear on stucco, and the altar needed to be maintained—we see at least one episode of re-plastering in thin

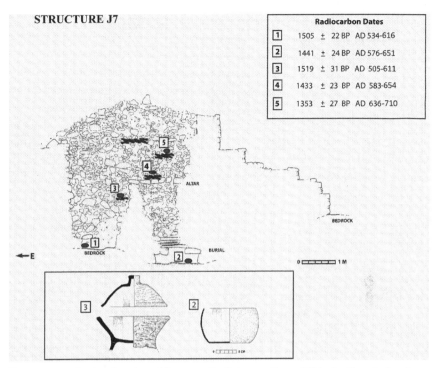

STRUCTURE J7

Radiocarbon Dates		
1	1505 ± 22 BP	AD 534-616
2	1441 ± 24 BP	AD 576-651
3	1519 ± 31 BP	AD 505-611
4	1433 ± 23 BP	AD 583-654
5	1353 ± 27 BP	AD 636-710

FIGURE 2.2. *Section drawing of Structure J7, Palenque Group IV, indicating the location of micromorphology samples, carbon samples, and burning events*

section, 400-01 (figure 2.2). One plaster component shows a laminated boundary indicative of a layering of plaster. There is a single small gravel-size component of burned plant tissue oriented parallel to large plaster components and the surface. This was most likely a remnant of the visible burned material on the surface of the altar, suggesting that whatever was burned in the offering event was plant-based.

The re-plastering may have coincided with a ritualized event meant to maintain the ancestral altar. Contemporary Mesoamerican people often visit the graves of the dead during calendrical events, most notably the Day of the Dead. During such repeated visits, the gravesite is cleaned, swept, and washed (Brandes 1997). The timing of altar or grave maintenance and the feeding of the dead is less clear for pre-conquest Maya. Whether altar use and maintenance occurred outside of the rainy season or on the anniversary of a death is not known. Classic Period inscriptions at Piedras Negras describe rulers revisiting the graves of their ancestors to cense them or clean them with smoke during anniversary events (Fitzsimmons 1998). This practice may have extended to non-royal Maya.

Other events materialized in this same space but had different effects. The events that occurred later were of a different sort, in both material and context. A generation after the construction of the altar, the living members of the group constructed a formal mausoleum structure, burying the altar and the remains of the founding ancestor within. The structure was to become a living house for the dead, the kind of building that needed to be "fed" to become alive (Fitzsimmons 2009, 134–135; Stuart 1998). Like the earlier feast for the dead, the meal offered for this purpose was burned. Burning the food offering transported the offering through smoke (Brown 2004, 37). The first feeding for this building was carried out after laying roughly 50 cm of loose cobble fill.

It is unclear how long the construction of the mausoleum would have taken or how many members of the group or extended community were needed to construct the house for the ancestor buried within, but before they finished, they fed the house once more by burning food and pine directly on the cobble fill. Inside those events, the stone construction itself was a primary material force. While the body and ancestral spirit buried deep below the buried altar initiated the sequence of events that would follow, subjectivity and power shifted from event to event. Rodrigo Liendo Stuardo suggests that later events materialized with the incorporation of newly deceased members of the group, when additional burials were placed inside the stairs of the structure (personal communication, 2018).

Each sequential event was related in historical process. They were each in some way initiated by that first funerary event and placement of the body that would become a founding ancestor. But the effect of the events that followed differed from moment to moment. The construction-related events, including the building of both an altar and the larger mausoleum structure, emerged as a result of the presence of the dead. However, inside those events, the structures themselves were primary agents. The burning of plant foods and pine had the effect of activating that space and was not directly for the dead person, who moved to the periphery of those events. The burning of plant foods and pine was a necessary action to take, just as important to the process as laying the stones and plaster.

The mausoleum structure was completed between AD 636 and 710 (with a 91.6% probability) and may have been witnessed or even commissioned by a young Chak Sutz', the man whose life events would be inscribed into stone and put on display in the main structure of Group IV (J1). The inhabitants

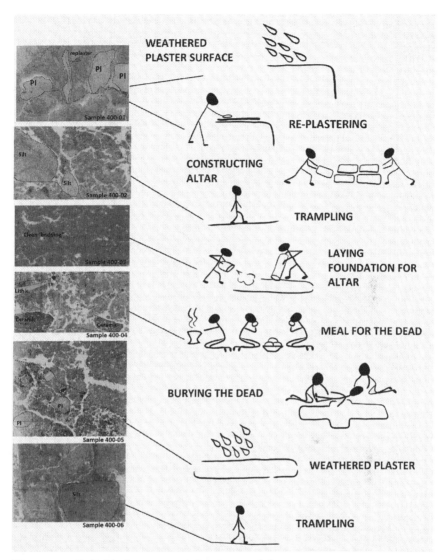

Figure 2.3. *Individual events as seen in micromorphology*

of Group IV and possibly extended members of the community continued to return to this space and inter their dead around the base of the structure, in the inset corners of the structure, and, finally, on the stairs—effectively closing the structure in the way Arnauld and colleagues (2013) have described in other Maya Classic settings.

Many years later, the panel installed in Structure J1 describes the celebration of Chak Sutz's completion of three *k'atuns*, or his sixtieth birthday. In hieroglyphic text found at Piedras Negras, ancestral dead are described as dancing at birthday events (Fitzsimmons 1998). Chak Sutz' may have celebrated his birthday with the spirits of his ancestors whose remains were buried deep inside Structure J7.

CONCLUSION

Archaeologists, epigraphers, and art historians have been fascinated with Classic Maya ritual for centuries. Ritual "deposits" are often some of the most materially rich archaeological contexts and include finely crafted objects and artworks that are seldom found in non-ritual contexts. Ritual and cosmology figured prominently in Maya art and text during the Classic Period. The ethnographic, archaeological, epigraphic, and iconographic studies of Maya ritual and cosmology are too numerous to mention. It is through those studies that most scholars are familiar with the Maya worldview and ritual practices in the past. It is well-known that rituals often centered around death and commemoration of the dead and that ancestors were influential in the lives of their descendants. The meanings generated by certain configurations of materials—such as the cruciform-shape crypt and the layering of stones inside the altar found inside Structure J7—interpreted as the foundation of sacred space and the connection between the earthly realm and the supernatural realms, are also concepts that have been discussed at length. In that respect, this study is not groundbreaking by any means. But this volume is concerned with two primary features of Mesoamerican ritual: temporality and materiality. For the Classic Maya, text, images, and excavated ritual offerings serve as evidence of events such as burials and "termination" rituals. However, surprisingly, we know very little surrounding the timing of those ritual events, their repetition, or even the range of materials present in those events.

In addition to ethnographic analogies as well as epigraphic and iconographic considerations, the increasing implementation of microscopic analyses such as micromorphology may provide crucial information surrounding the timing of Classic Maya rituals. A few other studies have demonstrated the utility of integrating other microscopic methods to understand the temporality of ritual events in Mesoamerica. For example, the recovery of archaeobotanical remains associated with an altar in the Basin of Mexico revealed a high degree of domesticated maize and beans; the varieties and their length of maturation led the investigators to conclude that they were most likely

Context	Accumulated Deposits in Thin Section	Post-Depositional Alterations	Absolute Date
Altar surface Sample 400-01	Single-space porphyric-related distribution weakly separated, carbonate-rich, dense microstructure, orange-yellow silty clay, mica and quartz randomly distributed throughout. 30% dislodged and weathered plaster components oriented parallel to the surface, single burned plant component oriented parallel to surface and plaster components	Crystal formation, clay intercalations, striated b-fabric	1433 ± 23 BP
Immediately below stone altar Sample 400-02	Close porphyric-related distribution weakly separated, massive microstructure, orange-yellow silty clay, fine sand–size mica and quartz randomly distributed throughout, silt aggregates single ceramic sherd fragment	Crystalline pedofeatures, bioturbation clay aggregates/ intercalations of clay, clay coating	
Below altar Sample 400-03	Double-space porphyric-related distribution massive microstructure, few zigzag planar voids orange-yellow silty clay, fine sand–size mica and quartz randomly distributed throughout, devoid of artifacts.	Interlaced intercalations of clay, clay nodules	
Below altar Living surface Sample 400-04	Single-space porphyric-related distribution, partially accommodated crumb microstructure, components of fine sand–size mica grains and quartz, coarse components of lithics, ceramic sherds, phytoliths, charcoal, plaster fragments of sand to gravel size. The largest components are oriented parallel to the surface.	Cross-striated b-fabric clay nodules, crystal formation	1519 ± 31 BP
Above bedrock Sample 400-05	Single-space porphyric-related distribution, partially accommodated blocky microstructure, components of fine sand–size mica grains and quartz. Lower boundary a crystallitic groundmass; coarse components include weathered plaster, charcoal, phytoliths.	Random striated b-fabric, crystal growth	

continued on next page

TABLE 2.1.—*continued*

Context	Accumulated Deposits in Thin Section	Post-Depositional Alterations	Absolute Date
Directly above bedrock Sample 400-06	Close porphyric-related distribution moderately sorted crumb microstructure very fine sand–size quartz and mica grains distributed randomly throughout groundmass, coarse components of small gravel-size bone, one ceramic sherd, plaster, and phytoliths largest components, oriented parallel to the surface	Speckled b-fabric crystallization	1505 ± 22 BP

deposited not long after harvest, between August and September (Morehart 2017). The integration of analytical methods not common in previous decades of ritual studies in the Maya region can potentially recover entirely new data sets. Paleoethnobotany, soil chemistry, and micromorphology are proving invaluable for detecting organic and perishable materials and substances. Those methods can also detect evidence of past actions that may not be visible macroscopically.

Archaeologists know very well that method and theory are intertwined. In this regard, the material sciences and a new materialist theoretical approach are highly complementary. Thinking through past ritual events as assemblages provides a mode by which we can explore the way relationships with materials, animals, plants, and the space around us can shift from one moment to the next. The analytical vocabulary we use has to change along with the techniques we employ. By emphasizing the concept of the event, in this chapter I have equated microstratigraphy to inflection points in the ongoing flow of activity. Events, visible in microstratigraphy, have memorable qualities that are effective beyond the moment they occur. The historical effects of each event in the sequence on the next event link the microscale with the macroscale of history. The agential capacity of these events is in part the product of their ritualized nature, seen in action and long-term effects.

Acknowledgments. This work was carried out as part of a collaborative project directed by Rodrigo Liendo Stuardo and would not have been possible without him and the members of the Proyecto Regional de Palenque. Support for this work was provided by dissertation grants from the Wenner-Gren Foundation (Grant 9543) and UC Mexus (Grant DI-15-7).

3

How can we think about the multiple temporalities involved in ritual action and meaningfully link ethnographic, historical, and archaeological accounts? This chapter uses our own research in Honduras, which spans the prehispanic, colonial, and Republican periods and involves analysis of a variety of material registers—including Spanish-language documents—to try to work through the challenges involved in tracing a historical tradition of ritual practice without collapsing into a normative and atemporal idealized account. Our research takes place in northern Honduras, in the drainage of the Ulua river. While today the local population does not identify with an indigenous past, based on a number of lines of evidence, we recognize the region as likely ancestral territory of Lenca-speaking people (Joyce 1991, 2017a; Sheptak 2007, 2013).

In the twentieth century, ethnographers observed the Lenca people of Honduras practicing rituals of the fields called *compostura*, identifying some elements as "syncretized" from the Roman Catholic religion and singling out others as "traditional" (Chapman 1986; Meluzin 1997). Ethnographic accounts of *compostura* have been used by some archaeologists as a basis to interpret deposits excavated in sites occupied during the centuries from AD 500 to 1000, corresponding to the Maya Classic and Terminal Classic periods. This use of twentieth-century ethnographic observations to interpret the deep past has been attempted despite the absence of recognizable colonial descriptions of

Over Time

From Compostura *in the Present to Lenca Rituals of the Prehispanic Period*

ROSEMARY A. JOYCE AND
RUSSELL N. SHEPTAK

https://doi.org/10.5876/9781646422395.c003

compostura that would allow security about the continuity of these practices from the prehispanic period.

In this chapter, we offer a new analysis of the evidence for practices in prehispanic Honduras that can be compared to *compostura*. We draw on colonial documents from and about indigenous communities, read "against the grain," that while not describing the practice of rituals (which, if they took place, would most likely have been kept from the eyes of Spanish officials), do provide a basis to understand the reproduction of Lenca philosophies of materiality and spirituality, or ontologies. We support the assertion that there was a continuing Lenca tradition of ritual practice throughout the colonial period engaging the present and the prehispanic past but question the precise way archaeologists, ourselves included, have previously approached linking the material registers produced through excavation with the observed behavior and oral tradition of the contemporary, living Lenca.

We conclude that there does exist a historic tradition connecting the people of the period AD 500–1000 to the Lenca of the present. We focus not on identifying specific modern rituals in archaeological sites but on the identification of the bodily gestures, significant materials, and evidence of underlying beliefs that formed a tradition of Lenca rituals for the earth that was maintained and reproduced throughout this long history. We include in our analysis a second type of Lenca ritual, today known as *guancasco*. We demonstrate that *guancasco* most likely emerged during the colonial period in new structures of governance of Lenca communities that, although part of the Spanish imperial apparatus, also were engaged by Lenca people to assist in their survivance. These structures created challenges that gave communities a particular reason to invest in *guancasco*. Rather than seeing *guancasco* as wholly a product of Spanish colonial power and economic relations, we emphasize the connections between *compostura* and *guancasco*, which are especially important to our goal of relating modern Lenca ritual practice to a long historical tradition.

ETHNOGRAPHIC ACCOUNTS OF LENCA RITUAL

The mesoamericanized zone of western Honduras was historically occupied by people who spoke either a Maya language (ancestors of the modern Chorti) or one of multiple variants of Lenca (with dialects or ethnic labels cited by different scholars under the terms Care, Cerquin, Colo, Guaqui, Popoluca, Poton, and Toquegua, in addition to Lenca). While once considered a language isolate or unconvincingly related to Xinca, Maya, or both, we follow Adolfo Costenla Umaña's (1981, 1991) arguments that Lenca languages are the northernmost Macro-Chibchan languages. Lenca people, from at least 2100 BC and arguably as early as 6000 BC, shared a suite of practices that are recognizably Mesoamerican. The archaeological evidence for mesoamerican-ized practices in the earliest periods of village life extends from as far south as the border with El Salvador to the Caribbean coast on the north, with a boundary evident between the extensive Ulua and Comayagua valleys and smaller drainages to the east, where it is likely that ancestors of the Torrupan, Pech, and Misumalpan speakers of eastern Honduras and Nicaragua were located.

While the Lenca region is extensive, ethnographic research with Lenca people has, unfortunately, been limited. Doris Z. Stone (1948) contributed a brief sketch to the *Handbook of South American Indians*. While always cited as a fundamental source on Lenca ethnography, this was a very generalized summary, with no details on sources of information or any account of research on which the claims might have been based. Some of the descriptions of what are in fact colonial practices present them through an extreme exoticizing lens. All of this urges caution in using this source. However, it has heavily influenced subsequent research, in particular by archaeologists, by presenting a normative picture of Lenca culture.

In this account, we are told that the Lenca marked "sacred mountains and hills" with wooden crosses; that they made "periodical offerings to the seasons or to the crops" in "planting and harvesting ceremonies" involving the drinking of chicha, burning of copal, and placement of "straw or corn shuck crosses" in fields, and at harvest, "masked men dance around the piles of grain to the music of drums, rattles, and whistles" (Stone 1948, 215). Complementing these agricultural rituals, which are all located in or near fields, we are told that on the patron saint's day, "often the saint is carried on a visit to the patron of a friendly neighboring town," accompanied by dancing, drinking, and feasting (216). These two relatively vague and generalized descriptions correspond to what later ethnographic accounts describe as *compostura*, or payments to the earth, and *guancasco*, or "paisanazgo" (sometimes called *convite* in Lenca communities in El Salvador). A third generalized ritual practice described by Stone (215), visits to a sacred cave, is not covered in this chapter due to specific problems with the reliability of the account. It is nonetheless worth noting that caves were used as sites of ritual deposit of objects and sometimes of already defleshed human remains in secondary mortuary rites throughout the prehispanic Lenca territory from at least 1400 BC to the time of Spanish invasion (Joyce 2011).

The two ritual complexes, *compostura* and *guancasco*, have been studied in sufficient detail in ethnographic situations for us to begin to think about how contemporary practices might relate to Lenca ritual life in earlier historical epochs. *Guancasco* fundamentally features inter-settlement movement of the statue of a patron saint or patron saints, characterized as a visit by one patron saint to the home place of the other. Reciprocity between communities is not always practiced or may be organized in a complicated cycle in which saints visit other places whose saints, in turn, visit the original participating town. The study of *guancasco* has been episodic. Stone (1954) provided one of the earliest significant descriptions, followed decades later by the Honduran folklorist Mario Ardón Mejía (1987) and historian Manuel Chávez Borjas (1992). Anne Chapman (1986, 132–145) included a brief section on *guancasco* in her major study of Lenca religion. Recent decades have seen a considerable increase in research on *guancasco* in specific communities, rooted in the study of folklore, oral tradition, and theatrical performance (Ardón Mejía 2015; Carias et al. 2004; Orellana Peña and Orellana 2015; Sagrario Torres and Lobo Morales 2015).

Archaeologists and ethnohistorians often characterize *guancasco* as the affirmation of a pact of peace between communities, subordinating religious aspects to a functionalist explanation rooted in an image of the prehispanic Lenca as in a state of habitual war (e.g., Joyce 1991, 20–21; Lara Pinto 2011). This is based on a report of a single informant who said "the *guancasco* is a pact of peace as previously those towns were always at war" (Chapman 1978, 30). There is no actual archaeological or historical evidence for extensive inter-community conflict among prehispanic Lenca. Many recent studies view *guancasco* as primarily a form of mass or popular culture, with little or no religious or ritual meaning. Oscar Rápalo Flores (2008) provides an exception, returning to *guancasco* from a perspective rooted in the anthropology of religion.

Compostura, in contrast to *guancasco*, has always been discussed exclusively from the perspectives of anthropology and archaeology of ritual and religion. Researchers routinely compare *compostura* to better-known rituals of the contemporary and ancient Maya, such as those discussed in this volume by Johann Begel, Marie Chosson, and Cédric Becquey (chapter 7). For example, summarizing scholarship on *compostura* and the related "payment to the earth" ritual, Claudio Sagrario Torres and Raquel Lobo Morales (2015, 75) write:

> They correspond to the ancient Maya offerings to the gods as a sign of gratitude for the goods received by humans . . . with these ceremonies, the Lencas offer goods to their gods in exchange for divine favors. The earth produces because the Lencas offer something in exchange. The "payment to the Earth" is

an offering in which the human sacrifices turkeys and chickens . . . The Earth requires nutrients to assure a good harvest . . . The *compostura* implies to arrange something, to repair, to cure, and it concerns ceremonies in which good health, community services, and good works are asked. (translation by Rosemary Joyce)

Jorge Orellana Peña and Leivi Orellana (2014) offer a more locally rooted assessment of the meanings of such ceremonies in an explicitly post-colonial study aimed to understand multiple epistemologies, viewing these practices not as primordial traits but as "strategies of survivance" (*estrategia de supervivencia*) and "collective imaginaries." This leads these authors to characterize Lenca ceremonies for the harvest and for the success of pottery making, both forms of *compostura*, as "veneration of nature" rather than payments to deities (104). We argue that this perspective is more consistent with historical and archaeological evidence in the Lenca area of Honduras, where identifying personified divinities such as those of Maya beliefs is not only difficult ethnographically but also in prehispanic media.

The main substantive resources for our comparison of the practice of Lenca ritual today to its historical predecessors are the two volumes based on extensive ethnographic research carried out between 1967 and 1986 by Chapman, published in Spanish as *Los Hijos del Copal y la Candela*. The first volume (Chapman 1985) details agrarian rituals and corresponding oral traditions collectively known as *compostura*. While the second volume (Chapman 1986) is intended to separate those rituals and narratives that are primarily rooted in Roman Catholic practice, in fact, the materials in the two volumes complement each other, and the language of *compostura* occurs in both.

This classic ethnography is placed in the context of two other major ethnographic works dealing with Lenca ceremonies and oral traditions. The first is an ethnographic account of research in the remote Lenca community of La Campa by Catherine M. Tucker (2008), whose dissertation research took place in the 1990s. The second is a volume of oral tradition from Yamaranguila in the Department of Intibuca, collected by a Honduran team composed of Claudia Marcela Carias, Hector Miguel Leyva, Róger Martinez Miralda, Emma Leticia Ordoñez, and Jorge F. Travieso (2004), a second edition of an original published in 1988. Yamaranguila is a well-known participant in *guancasco* and was the source of a large amount of the ethnographic information used by Chapman. La Campa, located in the Department of Lempira, is described as "the third major center of national pilgrimage in Honduras" for the traditional *baile del garrobo* held on the feast of San Matias el Marinero, to whom there is "regional devotion" shared with two other neighboring Lenca communities, San Manuel Colohete and Santa Cruz (Ardón Mejía 2015, 169). Tucker (2008) describes this performance as part of a fully developed practice of *guancasco*. By drawing on these three ethnographic resources, we are able to explore Lenca ritual practices in communities maintaining aspects of both community celebrations engaging neighboring towns (*guancasco*) and those carried out within the community, often by individual families (*compostura*).

GUANCASCO

Guancasco actually labels a relationship that exists between two towns that engage in reciprocal visitation of saints' images. Ardón Mejía (1987, 129) used a Spanish term, *paisanazgo*, for what he recognized as related traditions. He specifically mentions that people from paired communities using Spanish called each other *paisanos*, a term identifying people from the same territory. In the literature on *guancasco*, the word is normally described as a Lenca term of unknown derivation. The participating communities call each other *guanco*, understood to mean something like double or partner. Tucker (2008, 41) describes the relationship of *guancos* as defined by the sex of the corresponding patron saints: friendship between towns with male patron saints, marriage when the saints are of opposite sexes.

The *guancasco* between Ilama and Gualala, Santa Barbara, that we witnessed in 1998 is typical. The visiting patron saint was carried to a point on the outskirts of the visited community, where it was greeted by its counterpart and invited back to the town church. The crowd of people accompanying the traveling saint played music. Traditionally, this involves playing drums and flutes (Ardón Mejía 2015). Town dignitaries such as *alcaldes* lead the processions and give speeches of welcome and thanks (Tucker 2008, 41). A variety of celebratory dances are part of traditional *guancasco* visits. Ardón Mejía (1987, 2015, 179) identified a regular pattern of associated dances in Honduras, starting with a dance of *moros y cristianos*, followed by a *baile del caballito*, and ending with the *baile del zopilote*. Many towns have specific local aspects to these dance performances.

COMPOSTURA

Chapman (1985) provides the classic model for understanding Lenca *compostura*, synthesizing observations of multiple performances in communities in the Department of Intibuca. In first-person narratives that she recorded, participants referred to the rituals as directed to the earth (*tierra*) and spirits (*espiritus*) or earth owners (*dueños*). In her account, the performance of these ceremonies begins with the construction of an altar, a framework decorated with bromeliads of the genus *Tillandsia*, called *zomos*. Candles, chicha, copal, and cacao seeds are normally employed in the *composturas* she described, often along with chickens or turkeys. Intercession with the appropriate spirits was initiated by burning copal and lighting candles.

Chapman's descriptions of *compostura* focus on the altar. In contrast, Tucker (2008), based on her work in the 1990s at La Campa in the Department of Lempira, provides a view of these rituals that emphasizes spatio-temporal movement. On the scale of individual performance, human participants move from the prepared altar or table (*mesa*) to the location of the selected spirit and back, while the spirits come to the table from their own location and then return to it. The rituals for maize, called *pagos* (payments), traditionally took place on an annual basis, timed to planting and harvest, while those for most other resources reportedly took place during one period of the year—the rainy months between harvest and planting, from January to May.

A different temporal cycle was begun by the building of houses: "When a new house was constructed, a *pago* was conducted to reassure the resident spirit, and periodically thereafter a *pago* took place in gratitude for the use of the house lot" (Tucker 2008, 45). Tucker (42) describes the rituals the people of La Campa called "*pagos a la tierra*" as acts "to put things into balance." She quotes a woman from La Campa who said: "We should pay the earth, because if someone gives you a gift, shouldn't you repay that gift? Wouldn't you return it? Of course. It's the same with the earth: it gives us food. And it seems to me we should pay back the gift. The earth has owners, each place has spirits that live there, and the water has owners too" (42). Tucker (table 2.2) enumerates the focus, location, and timing of the main payments to the earth in La Campa. *Pagos* were practiced for maize, cane, or bean fields, for orchards, clay beds, and sand beds at the pottery-firing location, at water sources, in the house yard, and in the forest. At a minimum, when a full ritual could not be carried out, the people of La Campa might substitute a practice called *punto* (translatable as moment or spot), placing a single candle at the location where the full *pago* should be completed.

The majority of the ceremonies Tucker reported were preferentially carried out between January and May, the months of the rainy season preceding field preparation and planting. She reports that a single maize field *pago* had replaced what once were a series of four *pagos*, historically held at planting (April–June), first ripening of maize (August–September), harvest (October–January), and when the harvest was completely consumed. When they were carried out in the past, these four maize *pagos* would have created an annual cycle.

For our purposes, one of the more significant aspects of these rituals in La Campa is the role played by Catholic saints. *Pagos* in La Campa employ saints' images and crosses in place of the plants that provide vessels for spirits that are part of the *compostura* described by Chapman for Intibuca. In La Campa, a major *pago* is actually addressed to San Antonio, as patron of farm animals (ideally offered on June 13). In La Campa, disentangling Catholic and indigenous ritual temporalities and materialities is impossible, as, in fact, it is in Intibuca.

Pagos begin with a display of materials on a table decorated for the purpose, followed by movement out to the point on the landscape where the spirit in question resides to invite him or her back to the table (Tucker 2008, 47–48). After sharing a meal with the invited spirits, they are discharged back to their own places. The ritual leader prays at each of these stages: "The prayers speak to the spirit as the owner of the place, and request that it accept the sacrifice of the bird that is being offered. The prayers also thank the spirit specifically for the resource that has been consumed or used, especially water, clay, sand, vegetation, or a crop" (48). Catholic saints' images provide materialization of the spirits associated with places and materials when they come to be part of the *pago*.

DISCUSSION

While *guancasco* and *compostura* have often been discussed as separate religious practices, the first rooted in Catholic history and the second in a specifically Lenca past, the Lenca people of contemporary Honduras who practice both do not separate them in this way. Reciprocity is emphasized in both: reciprocity between settlements in the case of *guancasco* and between humans and non-human agents in the case of *compostura* or *pagos*. Spatiality is involved in both cases, with movement away from a fixed center of the celebrating human community into a periphery, where spirits (sometimes materialized as saints) reside, and then back to the center of the human community. Many *compostura* rituals mark points in a life course of an entity, such as pottery (where mining of clay, acquisition of sand, and firing are points in the making of pots), a house (where rituals mark the building and inhabitance of the building), or plants such as maize, with their seasonal cycles.

Guancasco and *compostura* have both been explored as models for interpretation of excavated assemblages from archaeological sites in Honduras dating between AD 500 and 1000 (Joyce 1991, 2017a; Lopiparo 2006; Wells 2007; Wells and Davis-Salazar 2008). Archaeologists have relied on modern Lenca ethnography from the southern states of Intibuca, La Paz, and Lempira to interpret excavated materials from sites far to the north, in the modern Honduran Departments of Santa Barbara and Cortés. This displacement in space is a consequence of, on the one hand, the lack of archaeological research in the southern Lenca area and, on the other, of the lack of ethnographic research from the northern zone. The likely occupation of ancient Santa Barbara and Cortés by speakers of Lenca languages has been supported by studies of the distribution of ceramic materials in consistent painted and modeled styles throughout these areas (Hendon, Joyce, and Lopiparo 2014; Joyce 2017a) and by analysis of colonial Spanish documents (Chapman 1978; Sheptak 2007, 2013). What has not been fully justified is how Lenca communities in northern Honduras between AD 500 and 1000 can be linked to those observed by modern ethnographers in southern Honduras without using assumptions of static and uniform normative culture. The linkage between the distant past and the present lies in the colonial period, for which very few studies of cultural practices related to ritual exist.

COLONIAL TRACES OF LENCA RITUAL

Conventional accounts of *guancasco* and *compostura*, and archaeological uses of them, do not fully address this issue. Chapman (1978), summarizing Spanish colonial chronicles spanning the sixteenth and seventeenth centuries, found little direct commentary on Lenca ritual and religion. She cites one early primary account, from a 1576 letter to the crown by Diego Garcia de Palacio, in which a group of Lenca carried out sacrifices to a stone image in a remote area, apparently a mountaintop (32), and tentatively equates this with contemporary *compostura* because of the location away from the settlement and the use in the ritual of materials overlapping modern *compostura*. One major difference, of course, is that the modern *compostura* rituals she described do not involve any identified equivalent of the carved stone iconic image central to Garcia de Palacio's account but rather use bromeliads or other plant materials as vessels for spirits.

Chapman identified no primary references to ritual practices she could equate to *compostura* postdating the sixteenth century. We use different kinds of colonial documents to attempt to trace ritual practice through the colonial period. Rather than return to the chronicles and reports of early religious and military campaigns, which provide very little direct or reliable information, our approach is to examine petitions from indigenous communities to Spanish authorities. While never overtly talking about indigenous ritual practices, when read "against the grain," petitions by *pueblos de indios* provide insight into how we might understand specific local practices in the past in terms of a widely distributed historical tradition of ritual belief and practice (Sheptak 2013). They attest to continuous attitudes of care for the fruitfulness of the earth as a social responsibility. They underline the conservation by indigenous Honduran people of materials such as cacao that were of importance for ritual practices, even when those ritual practices are virtually unattested otherwise. We also draw on rare comments from Catholic clergy about indigenous religiosity. Together, these more intimate colonial documents demonstrate an emphasis on ritual use of spaces away from and between settled places, in cycles linked to community churches that associate religious practice with the care of the earth. In these documents, one material agent, cacao, receives special attention.

CACAO AND CARE OF THE EARTH

In the seventeenth and eighteenth centuries, multiple *pueblos de indios* in the district of San Pedro Sula suffered from incursions on their cultivated land, initially from mercenaries and privateers and later from cattle ranchers (Sheptak 2013). A remarkably uniform discourse of the earth emerges in petitions these towns made for assistance in relocating and reestablishing themselves. The community leaders of one town, Jetegua, asked in 1679 for aid to protect their town from attacks by mercenaries and pirates who could come upriver to the settlement. In their petition, the community leaders repeatedly describe cacao as a gift from God (*frutos que dios nos da*) with which they give comfort (*se socorre*) to the earth (*tierra*), which will suffer (*padecer*) without them and be lost (*perdida*):

> With the fruits of cacao that god gives us we give comfort to all the earth . . .
> we are in fear that a second invasion at this time will lose the harvest of cacao
> that god gives us so that this time the earth will suffer . . . we ask aid in the
> name of Your Majesty . . . because otherwise all of those of the *partido* will have
> to go away to seek a place to resettle leaving uncared for our haciendas of cacao
> that we have, with which the earth would be left lost and lacking the fruits that
> god gives us, and the poor earth lost. (AGCA A1.60 legajo 5364 expediente
> 45339, page 4)

In our original translation we used "land" as the English translation of *tierra* where, through engagement with ethnographic sources, we later realized we should be reading "earth." This reading, consistent with ethnographically attested Lenca discourse on the purposes of rituals of the field, shows that this petition was drawing on the same concepts underlying modern rituals of *pago a la tierra*, "payment to the earth." Without the cacao produced by Jetegua, the poor earth, talked about as an animate being, would be deprived of care, suffer, and be lost.

The importance of preserving cacao groves was repeatedly cited in petitions from Jetegua and other neighboring towns throughout the seventeenth and eighteenth centuries. The use of this argument for administrative action suggests that cacao was grown for significant cultural and social purposes, but those were not the purposes of the Spanish colonial economy. Historian Linda Newson (1986, 147n144), commenting on the long persistence of cacao cultivation in northern Honduras, noted that Honduran cacao was no longer a commercial product at the time. The language of the Jetegua petition is Spanish, recorded at a time of transition toward monolingualism in the region. The concepts expressed, however, come from an indigenous frame of reference.

The use of cacao, a gift of God, for the benefit of the earth had a history in northern Honduras extending from before 1150 BC, with residue analysis confirming continued use to at least AD 400 and vessel forms suggesting no break in the presentation of cacao beverages in succeeding centuries, for which we do not have residue studies (Joyce and Henderson 2007). In the sixteenth century, the *provincia del río de Ulúa* entered the Spanish documentary record as one of the major cacao-producing areas in Central America (Sheptak 2004). The leader of local military campaigns against Spanish colonization was described by Diego Garcia de Celis as a great merchant in cacao whose main town was "of great enterprise for the abundant cacao which they collect" (1535 AGI Guatemala 49 N. 11). The seventeenth-century petitioners from Jetegua were town leaders who called themselves *tlatoques chicos y grandes*, "great and minor nobles," using a cosmopolitan language of trade: Nahuatl. Their Lenca family names, Toquegua, Sima, and Calao, had been attested as names of autonomous settlements in the region in the early sixteenth century (Sheptak 2007, 2013). While most of our historical attention has gone to the role cacao cultivation played in connecting Honduras to trade extending into Maya and Mexica territory, the later colonial history of cacao cultivation underlines that it was significant in local practices in these cosmopolitan, polyglot Honduran towns.

By 1588, tribute in cacao from Honduras only came from towns in the Ulua valley, and some towns in the region continued to render cacao as tribute payment to second- and third-generation *encomenderos* as late as the 1660s. The cacao produced in the northern Honduran zone occupied by the people of Jetegua and their ancestors must have provisioned other communities farther inland, where conditions for growing cacao were not propitious. In the twentieth century, Chapman (1986, 17–18) could record oral tradition from such an area, Yamaranguila, in which Adam and Eve performed the first *compostura*, prominently featuring cacao. God tells Adam:

> I am going to give you nine grains of dead maize, and nine cups and one large jar will appear; you're going to throw one grain into each cup . . . Look over there, there by the rocks there is a palm frond. You're going to throw a drop of palm juice in each cup and another in the jar . . . On your return from where you are going, you'll find some pods, cut them right there. In the pods you are going to see some seeds, those are cacao. And there a tree nearby there, you are going to pierce it and it will throw off a resin, that resin is copal. Over there will also appear to you a tablet of wax, produced by bees. From this you will make candles: nine little candles and a large one. This is what you are going to do. And when all that is done, you will bring me the zomos. [our translation]

Maize, palms, and tillandsia are all plants that grow in the highlands around Yamaranguila. While the copal tree, *Protium copal*, prefers lower elevations, it can be cultivated in these higher elevations. Cacao, in contrast, was provided for the first *compostura* by divine action in the form of pods, products of plants that required the lower elevation, heat, and humidity found in the river valleys of Caribbean coastal Honduras.

The continued production of cacao loomed so large for colonial *pueblos de indios* on the Ulua river that they cited establishing groves as a founding action for their towns (Sheptak 2013, 2019). It enabled continued relationship of Lenca people across western Honduras with the animate earth. It is the relationships of people with the earth that provide the framework of ritual over the long-term history of Lenca social life, linking the distant past and the present. Starting with this ontological perspective as our guide, we can re-read the colonial and ethnographic sources to understand the space, time, and materiality of Lenca ritual.

THE SPACE AND TIME OF RITUAL PRACTICE

Petitions from colonial indigenous communities that deal overtly with ritual life never allude to indigenous payments to the earth or anything like *compostura*. Instead, petitions from multiple communities cite the importance of the church building and the Catholic sacred images held within it, objects repeatedly robbed during coastal pirate raids (Sheptak 2013). It has been easy for scholars of Honduran history to treat these texts as evidence of purely Roman Catholic religion. Our search for a colonial history for contemporary Lenca ritual, however, leads directly to these same texts and the focal objects they fore-ground as traces of a history for *guancasco*, indigenous ritual entangled with modern *compostura*: saints' images carried in processions on visits between towns.

While it is common for archaeologists to cite *guancasco* as likely a prehispanic ritual preserved through syncretism, in its structure and the focus on images of saints, *guancasco* (and its equivalents) recalls the Spanish Catholic institution of the *cofradia* charged with caring for saints' images used in church rituals. Indeed, Ardón Mejía (2015, 163) explicitly says that the *guancasco* cycle tying together Ilama, Gualala, and Chinda in the Department of Santa Barbara "very probably . . . was initiated with the arrival of the images of patron saints of the three towns." Chávez Borjas (1992, 38) defines *guancasco* as "a ritual in which two religious images meet, dance, and talk, through the representatives of the top level of two *cofradias* (or their historical remnants)." Yet this is not to say that *guancasco* has nothing to tell us about the long tradition of Lenca ritual; it simply suggests that we need to consider *guancasco* alongside other colonial rituals in which images of saints played a significant role.

References to *guancasco* (or its equivalents) are not hard to find in nineteenth-century documents. Land titles created or reconfirmed in the Republican period include comments linking official milestones marking town limits with practices of inter-town visits of saints (Lara Pinto 2011, 190). These spots themselves could be marked by Catholic ritual images; Chapman (1986, 173) remarked that even in the late twentieth century, crosses were placed at the town boundary markers. This may be the basis for Stone's (1948, 215) claim that the Lenca marked "sacred mountains and hills" with wooden crosses.

Mention of *guancasco* earlier than the nineteenth century is less common. In an unpublished land title from 1893 that we have analyzed, for land that was formerly part of a *pueblo de indios* called Yamalá in Santa Barbara, we have a chance to compare two surveys offering a description of the same key points on the landscape in 1893 and 1766. It is only in the later description that we see comments on the location of the former meeting point between Yamalá (by then abandoned) and its *guancasco* partner, Posta, at *un acervo de piedras colo-cado a orillas de un barranco colorado* ("a collection of stones placed on the edge of a reddish gully"). While the surveyor in 1893 was concerned to reject the identification of this landmark with the boundary marker he was seeking, his concern reflects the fact that the local people included both kinds of markers in a single geography, using the same kinds of physical signs to indicate them: piles of stones, sometimes with a cross added.

The earliest explicit references to *guancasco* we have found come from slightly after the 1766 Yamalá survey and date to the last two decades of the eighteenth century. These are repeatedly cited statements included in religious documents condemning the expense indigenous Lenca communities invested in celebrations of the saints. Ardón Mejía (1987, 133) cites a commentary from 1788 on practices in El Salvador called *convites* and *guancascos*, described as "entire towns going out on the roads carrying the images of their patron saints up to thirty and forty leagues away." The same source describes "reforms" enacted to require celebrations of patron saints to take place "solely in the same towns on the days of their fiestas." Thus, while the form of the *guancasco* seen today may be rooted in the arrival of images of Catholic saints, it appears that the way those images were used was seen by authorities as out of conformity with sanctioned Catholic practice.

This is, in fact, characteristic of the materialities through which the new Catholic religion was enacted in persistent Lenca places. We have previously argued that colonial documents show that *pueblos de indios* controlled the sacralized spaces of the newly built churches required by Spanish policy, which were visited only a few days a year by missionary priests, making them centers of religious practices through which towns ritually identified their own community (Sheptak, Joyce, and Blaisdell-Sloan 2011, 159–163). *Cofradias* dedicated to specific saints were a significant part of such town-level indigenous religious practice in the colonial period. By the early eighteenth century, towns like Yamalá had multiple *cofradias*, each with its own responsibility for a specific saint, including a *cofradia* that cared for the patron saint of the town. Indigenous religious confraternities became a focus of concern for the colonial government as part of the Bourbon reforms, starting with orders to enforce provisions in existing law requiring both ecclesiastical and secular licenses for these groups. In 1742, in response to this mandate, the head of Honduras's provincial government circulated a questionnaire seeking information about all the known *cofradias* in the country (AGCA A1 legajo 222 expediente 2479).

In response, indigenous *cofradias* were identified as self-governing and described as having origins known only to their members. In the Lenca area of Santa Barbara, the priest of one *pueblo de indios*, Despoloncal, reported that he could say nothing of the origins of the *cofradia* there because it was something only the *indios* knew. In a second town in the same area, Petoa, the *cura*, reported there was a *cofradia* of *indios*, saying that due to its antiquity, there was no account of its founding or regulations. The independence of *cofradia* practices in *pueblos de indios* was part of a broader picture troubling to some of the clergy. The priest of Petoa went on to ask "that there be named an *indio* of Christian practices so that he might take care of and assist in the churches" where, he warned, "not a few times the *indios* on entering exercise their ancient idolatry" (AGCA A1 legajo 222 expediente 2479; transcribed and translated by the authors). He goes on to say that this person would need to be prepared to "walk out in the *montes* (wilderness areas)" to bring the people in to the church (AGCA A1 legajo 222 expediente 2479; transcribed and translated by the authors). While these two claims would seem to be contradictory, we can see them as reflections of the *cura* of Petoa's belief that the local Lenca people were carrying out non-Christian rituals both in the hinterland and in the church itself.

Cofradías were ultimately subject to stronger regulation, and beginning in the 1770s and 1780s, the property they held in common came under scrutiny. This, perhaps not coincidentally, is the same period when colonial sources from Honduras and El Salvador began to reflect (negatively) on the excesses of patron saint visitation between communities, characterized as the *guancasco* or *convite*. Even as community ownership of property used for the support of saints' festivals was under official pressure, Lenca people elaborated festivals in which saints' images were carried between towns on a regular schedule as part of a range of indigenous rituals in which saints' images and crosses figured.

DISCUSSION

Guancasco instantiates an annual tempo of spatializing community links to neighbors, in some places through to the present day, in a framework of Spanish Catholic materialities. Payments to the earth, made in rituals called *compostura* today, occupy the same spatial-temporal framework, operating at a punctuated tempo within communities at the scale of smaller groups engaged in the creation and maintenance of fields, houses, and productive spaces. Although normally treated as contrasting syncretized (*guancasco*) and traditional (*compostura*) religious practices, detailed studies usually end up talking about them together because they are interwoven in life.

Images of Catholic saints are central to *guancasco* and are present in some places in payments to the earth, taking the place of other items (bromeliads and reportedly corn husks) used in some communities. Saints' images often are spirits of place for the modern Lenca. They may be found in trees or in rocky faces along streams; often, they did not wish to stay in places to which they were brought, so the saints' images returned to where they were found until persuaded to stay in the churches or until a church was built where they were stationed (Chapman 1986, 30–57). Some saints' images are described as alive, their skin color changing in response to external events, responding to bells or music, and even leaving their church to bathe—tracking back sand as a material sign of their movement.

If we understand churches not solely as spaces for Roman Catholic ritual but, in the case of those with saints with recognized animacy, as the proper places of those spirits, a final distinction between *compostura* and *guancasco* dissolves. Both now involve spirits localized in the landscape, whose intercession is important to the well-being of people, families, and towns. As animate beings, they move back and forth from their proper places to others where they participate with human agents in events marked by consumption of offered foodstuffs and, in the case of the larger-scale events involving whole communities, singing and dancing. With this framework in mind, we can revisit the archaeological materials that provide the deeper history of modern Lenca practice, not looking for *compostura* or *guancasco* as distinct practices like their modern forms but for material traces of compacts between spirits of place and humans.

ANCESTRAL LENCA RITUALS

Archaeologists working in Honduras have long endeavored to use Lenca ethnography to help interpret archaeological data. In our research, we suggested that political relations between the apparently independent towns that developed in northern Honduras between AD 500 and 1000 would have required something like the periodic ritually sanctioned festivals marking positive relations between neighboring towns (Joyce 1991, 20–21). Jeanne Lopiparo (2006), emphasizing the common orientation of performative architecture (ball courts and large platforms) and burials to shared points on the horizon, used *guancasco* as a structural model for ritual processions and movement between communities in archaeological sites in the lower Ulua valley, evident in distributions of non-local figurines discarded in different communities.

The most sustained argument for identifying archaeological ritual practices of this period with modern Lenca rituals has been offered by Christian Wells (2007) and Wells and Karla Davis-Salazar (2008). Drawing on survey and excavation data from the Naco and Palmarejo valleys, small upland basins in the Department of Santa Barbara, they singled out the distribution of incense-burning vessels as possible evidence of the practice of *compostura* (2008). They noted that small field houses had especially elevated proportions of these vessels, suggesting a concentration in these locations of incense-offering activities.

Such studies have, for the most part, proposed generalizations about behavior on a regional scale without identifying counterparts to the kinds of highly structured events that are represented ethnographically. Our argument is that in understanding *guancasco* and *compostura* to be transformations within a historical tradition based on a common philosophy of relations in space and

time, we can link contemporary rituals to evidence of a broader range of rituals practiced in a deeper past. In this final section, we discuss three instances
in which we can describe specific structured deposits produced by ritualized
practices that exhibit central features of modern Lenca ritual: reciprocity,
returning gifts to the earth, and bringing spirits into the cultivated spaces of
town and house compound.

MANTECALES: RITUALS FOR THE EARTH

Excavations at the Mantecales site in 1995 were aimed at documenting features that were slated to be destroyed for construction of a gasoline station. The
site was typical of the central Ulua valley: four large, low earthen terraces created
by repeated remodeling of domestic structures on river levees in an otherwise
easily inundated landscape (Joyce and Pollard 2010). Two of these platforms,
tested by local archaeologists of the Honduran Institute of Anthropology and
History, produced remains of two to three small structures with stone features
and trash, including pottery, grinding stones, and chipped stone tools.

Excavations by a Cornell-Berkeley project focused on a third platform.
Measuring 40 m by 60 m, this platform produced evidence in multiple locations of burned material, but nothing like the small house features in the other
two platforms. Here, in an area approximately 14 m by 6 m near the center
of the platform, the original archaeologists had "encountered remains of clay
surfaces, circular patches of carbon and ash, and great quantities of broken
ceramics, including complete figural whistles and figurines . . . Throughout
these excavations, the team encountered ashy deposits, figural artefacts, and
broken pottery, along with occasional unusual objects, such as small quartz
stones contained in a jar, polished celts, and chipped obsidian bifaces . . . the
deposits were composed of surfaces with circles of ash, in some places thicker
lenses of ash, alternating with clay, with several dense piles of broken pottery"
(Joyce and Pollard 2010, 300).

Excavations by the Cornell-Berkeley project explored a single part of this extensive set of features, reaching depths of 1.65 m below the modern ground surface where a rectangular stone chamber, open to the north, had previously been
identified. The first 90 cm of the deposits we excavated consisted of lenses of
burned materials layered around broken ceramic vessels. A feature on the west
edge of the cist was made up of seven jar necks (28–42 cm in diameter), stacked
one on top of another. Analysis of associated painted pottery and detailed depositional history showed that the jar necks had been placed in three episodes,
extending over at least 100 years, during which the area was repeatedly used as

a focus for burning incense. A large number of incense-burning vessels were represented: half a dozen large lids with modeled decoration to be placed over vessels containing burning resin, including two with effigies of felines and one supporting a standing human figure; ten ladle censers with handles; and portions of at least ten other bowls used for burning resin. Pieces of polychrome painted serving vessels, red-painted and incised jars, and unslipped jars with handles, used to serve drinks, and a series of unusual items (jade beads, obsidian blades, and portions of at least one and no more than two mold-made figurines) were carefully placed in the area bordered on three sides by stone walls.

The repeated burning of incense at a focal point away from residential buildings, and the suggestion that some beverage was imbibed in conjunction, relate this deposit to modern descriptions of *compostura*. The inclusion of figural artifacts, however, is strikingly different from the classic descriptions of *compostura* in Intibuca, where spirits occupy non-iconic plant materials: bromeliads. However, it is consistent with the payments to the earth in La Campa, where the vessels for visiting spirits are Roman Catholic icons.

The deposits at Mantecales, while the most elaborate known to date, are not entirely unique. Other archaeological sites in the Ulua valley produced examples of effigies from incense burner lids and figurines, in complex deposits likely stemming from discard of materials from related ritual practices. They allow us to examine the spatiality implied by these ancient ceramic images and support the argument that these were, like the saints' images used at La Campa, containers for spirits otherwise normally located in the landscape, brought into human spaces for the purposes of communication and participation in ritual.

CURRUSTÉ: BRINGING SPIRITS AND NEIGHBORS TOGETHER IN THE CENTER OF THE TOWN

Currusté is located within easy walking distance of Mantecales, but where the latter site was made up of a series of simple low earthen platforms, Currusté was composed of almost 200 stone terraces, including a large number defining a plaza area (Hendon, Joyce, and Lopiparo 2014). Excavations at Currusté by Lopiparo documented the remains of an installation along one side of this plaza area in which multiple incense burner lids were left in place. The figures crowning most of these were gone, except for a large collection of fragments of the body of a near life-size statue of a pregnant woman carrying a box on her back. A series of three jar necks were encountered stacked in another location at the site. Fragments of mold-made figurines were more common here than in the Mantecales deposits.

Lopiparo (2006; Hendon, Joyce, and Lopiparo 2014) sees the deposits at Currusté as evidence of rituals involving burning incense and consumption of brewed drinks by a group including visitors from outside Currusté. Her argument for visitation between settlements was developed by analyzing the distribution of figurines with different headdresses at sites throughout the valley, showing that those found at Currusté came from multiple external places. The mold-made figurines at Mantecales, although rarer, might be thought of as connections to their places of origin as well. Where in modern Lenca rituals, spirits are invited to occupy bodies provided by *zomos*, or small images of Roman Catholic saints, in the prehispanic Ulua valley, we see figural artifacts at two scales that provide potential vehicles for such spirits.

If we take location as a distinction between modern rituals of payment of the earth and reciprocal visitation by patron saints, then we might see the Mantecales deposit as likely a location of payment to earth spirits and the Currusté deposit as a product of a reciprocal visit to the community center by spirits normally living elsewhere. Both kinds of deposits use the same repertoire of ritual gestures: burning incense to animate vessels for spirits, creating a mouth into the earth through stacking of jar necks (perhaps to receive poured liquids such as cacao beverages, indetectable without chemical residue analyses not completed at either site), and bringing figural images from one place to another. We cannot separate the two kinds of practices. They took place in a landscape unified by orientation toward specific mountain peaks and seasonal solar markers. In each case, the temporality of what Lisa Johnson calls the ritual-as-event is potentially identifiable, but only if we take each deposit apart as a unique residue of human actions of the moment. At Mantecales, in contrast to Currusté, we can see the repetition of such rituals-as-events over and over and measure the time elapsed between first and last incidents. Yet each ritual of burning recapitulates the same temporality, whether we see these as a sequence over time (as at Mantecales) or an event in its historical moment (as at Currusté).

CERRO PALENQUE: BRINGING THE SPIRITS HOME

A final example will serve to underline that this kind of ritual place making was widely distributed, using similar materials. It also demonstrates that ritual actions most comparable to modern *compostura* are potentially evident within archaeological sites, not only in spaces away from settlements where archaeologists would rarely be likely to excavate them.

Cerro Palenque was the single largest settlement known from the prehispanic Ulua valley (Joyce 1991). It began as a small hilltop place and, in the ninth and tenth centuries, grew dramatically as other settlements in the valley lost population. Excavations at a series of house compounds here produced two examples of ritual deposits in small, low platforms in the center of house compound yards. One of these dated to the period before AD 800. Although the buildings in the house compound where it was located were stucco-coated and ornamented with stone sculpture, this ritual deposit began as a hole dug into the loosely consolidated marl. In the marl placed back in the pit, a set of pebbles and one single obsidian blade were recovered. The location remained a site of ritual practice after this initial event and ultimately was closed with a plaster floor capped with a *Spondylus* (thorny oyster) shell containing a jade bead. While not located on the periphery of the settlement, the excavation of a pit here whose contents were apparently largely perishable is similar to the key moment in modern payment to the earth. Coming at the beginning of the construction history of this household compound, it may be the one material trace we have of something like *compostura* for the building of a house. Between the first detectable episode and the closure of the place, a second deposit was made, of a single obsidian artifact, this time a biface. This recalls Tucker's (2008) statement that payments to the earth for house construction in La Campa required renewal at intervals.

After AD 800, residents of a second excavated house compound at Cerro Palenque also built a low platform in the center of their house yard as part of an initial stage of construction of a building that in this case was never renewed. Excavation here recovered an assemblage of broken pottery with high proportions of brewing vessels and incense burner fragments. In the heart of this small platform, inside a pit dug into the underlying clay, two artifacts were placed: a pair of figurines, standing upright; on the west, a woman carrying a water jar on her head and on the east, a man wearing a bird costume and carrying a *Strombus* whistle in his hand. While the image reproduced by the female figurine is rare, multiple fragments of figurines similar to the male figurine exist in museum collections, the majority attributed to Cerro Palenque. We might consider these as possible bodies of spirits invited to share in payments to the earth in this house compound, with the vessels for palm wine, chicha, or cacao and for burning copal resin—the ingredients of the first *compostura* as described in Yamaranguila—the residues of the *pago* itself.

The actions memorialized in the imagery of this pair of figurines, serving drink and masked dancing, are central today to the reciprocal visits between towns of patron saints' images, known as *guancasco*. Contemporary with this household ritual offering, at the far edge of Cerro Palenque, an isolated platform served as the base for the installation of at least one nearly life-size effigy figure from the lid of an incense-burning vessel. While looters destroyed most of this context, its position makes it like the boundary markers where the people of Posta brought their saint to the edge of Yamalá, which in 1893 was still remembered and marked with a pile of stones.

CONCLUSION

Our proposal, then, is that we can talk about relations between rituals observed using archaeological and ethnographic methods, but we need to account for historical change and emphasize the values embodied in rituals and the materials used over the expectation that formal actions will look the same. Although ethnographers certainly can differentiate between rituals that involve the whole community and movement from one town to another of images of saints and rituals that involve smaller groups of residents in fields and house yards, the line between them is actually a good deal less solid than has been argued. Because *guancasco* has been seen as a more syncretized ritual, it has not often been seen as a basis for interpreting archaeological data. Our consideration of a series of well-documented ritual deposits, however, suggests that the archaeological sites in this area show evidence of a mixture of elements today taken as specific to distinct ritual complexes. By using the contemporary ethnographic accounts as a source for definition of a set of gestures that form Lenca ritual practice today, we were better able to see the archaeological evidence as potentially related to the modern rituals.

A long-term perspective shows that the contemporary Lenca have developed a number of more distinct ritual practices from grounding in a common philosophy of relations to the earth to spirits associated with the use of various materials from the landscape. In the prehispanic period, we can define repeated ritual sequences, but they cannot be simply mapped onto modern *compostura* or modern *guancasco*. They are the ancestors of the modern practices, which were and continue to be shaped by histories of conquest and reinvention. The temporality within each ritual event constructs cycles, while the temporality of continued engagement with spirits of place creates a specifically Lenca ongoing history through ritual practice. This is not stasis, homogeneity, a mentality, or a deep-seated structure. It is a philosophy of substance, an ontology, that was developed in a long-enduring historical tradition as people engaged with an ever-changing world. If we understand that ongoing tradition as one of identity in change rather than sameness, we can see temporalities and relations that unfolded over generations.

4

Voice Matters

Vocal Creation and Manipulation of Ritual Temporalities

VALENTINA VAPNARSKY

Studies of rituals in Mesoamerica have been concerned with rhythms of occurrence of ritual performances, either in their cyclicity or their sequentiality or both, most often linked to external cycles and specific calendars—for example, the periodic recurrence of a given ritual, the position of a ceremony in a sequence of rituals, or the coupling of ritual periodicity with seasonal natural elements, cycles of life, and calendars. But rhythmic patterns also give shape to and characterize the ritual performance internally, contributing in an essential way to its dynamic and efficacy. To our knowledge, this has been the focus of much less attention (except to some extent in ethnomusicology). Rhythms inside the performance are generated from various modalities: gestures, complex actions (e.g., disposal of offerings, displacements), music, dances, words (e.g., the parallelistic and repetitive components of Mesoamerican ritual speech), and elocutionary patterns of the words said. I will concentrate in this chapter on the rhythms set by the voice. Rhythmic patterns will be considered based on different units (syllabic, breath group, pause, relation between vocal and textual units) within a ritual and between rituals of two different kinds, agricultural and therapeutic, as practiced today by the Yucatec Maya of Quintana Roo (Mexico).[1]

The main idea explored in the following pages is that voice is physical matter that can be easily manipulated rhythmically with different effects, in particular on how the temporal flow is acted and perceived, and that this

https://doi.org/10.5876/9781646422395.c004

plays a significant role in the pragmatics of ritual performances. In other words, the use of voice appears as a crucial aspect of the multimodality of rituals, with special effects on ritual temporalizations and on the interactions and actions that are performed in the ritual and define it. I conceive temporalization as "the phenomenon of assigning time to and managing the time of something" and use it as a heuristic concept to acknowledge the fact that time (in particular, ritual time) is not given a priori but rather is the result of dynamic, procedural, creative, and selective processes of configuration of temporality.

THE FLOW OF TIME, THE FLOW OF SPEECH, THE FLOW OF RITUAL

In "The Notion of Rhythm in Its Linguistic Expression," Benveniste (1951) showed that before Plato, *rhuthmós* (ῥυθμός or ῥυσμός in Ionian) contrasted with *skhèma, morphè,* or *eídos,* which referred to fixed forms and immobile realities. *Rhuthmós,* from the verb *rhéin* "to flow," was used in contrast to refer to the ephemeral form of unsteady things: a cloth, someone's character, water flowing in a river. Because the word is suffixed with *–(th)mós,* meaning "a way, a manner," *rhuthmós* referred not only to a dynamic reality observed at one precise moment but also to the form of this dynamism itself. It is *"une manière de fluer"* "a way of flowing," said Benveniste (1951).

The present study aims at illuminating the special rhythm, in the sense of "way of flowing," the manipulation of the voice by the ritual specialist imposes on ritual. It also seeks to understand what this way of flowing generates per-formatively. Based on the analysis of two types of contemporary Yucatec Maya rituals, I will argue that voice is a matter the ritual specialist transforms for two interdependent reasons: on the one hand, to create a flow of time proper to the ritual that allows for the interaction with spiritual entities (guardian spirits, harmful airs) and, on the other hand, to act physically on them (fight them, move them) as well as on other participants (i.e., to calm the patient).

The pragmatic force of the vocal rhythm seems to be based on two main basic properties. First, the elocution rhythm is a powerful tool (together with gestural rhythm) for transforming the sensorial experience of the flow of time. Speaking very fast makes it feel as though time is running quickly, whereas decelerating the pace of speech triggers the feeling that time slows down. I argue that this vocal quality of "shaping" time is used to create a ritual tempo-rality distinct from that of the mundane world.[2] This distinctive temporal flow, generally heterogeneous within the same ritual (with sometimes several ways of flowing running in parallel), combines with other forms of temporalization.

It corresponds to what one could consider the most intimate temporality of the ritual: its breath.

A second meaningful and powerful quality of voice is that, contrary to the ritual words that are largely opaque for non-specialists, it can be heard and felt without specific esoteric knowledge. It constitutes a sensorium that any participant who is able to hear or overhear the words can feel, affecting her or him and his or her perception of time as well as of the ritual actions that are taking place. The specific vocal rhythm induces the sensation for the different participants in the ritual that time moves at a different pace. As part of the ritual soundscape, it also acts as an index of the interaction with the spirits. For the rituals analyzed below, I would suggest that it is one of the most basic ways by which human participants in the ritual, even those who overhear, become aware of the spirit's presence, even if spirits can also be present in silent moments of the performance—but as we will see, these are delimited by a specific vocal flow as well.

VOCALITY IN RITUALS

Half a century after ethno-poetics first drew attention to the rhetorical, aesthetic, and semantic importance of voice transformations in certain oral genres (Hymes 1977; Tedlock 1971), vocal anthropology is still an emerging field (Feld et al. 2004; Harkness 2014; Revel and Rey-Hulman 1993). Yet it has proven its relevance in many sociocultural domains. Voice can no longer be taken as a mere "paralinguistic" extra component of the performance or as a mostly idiosyncratic creative means but should rather be considered a key cultural parameter of speech multimodality and interaction, with significant pragmatic properties and a diversity of effects on social life. As for rituals, ethnographic data show that manipulations of the voice have complex pragmatic functions, which are linked to constitutive transmitted rules and are intimately related with the agentive modalities of the ritual. For instance, it has been argued that the alternation between a falsetto voice and a throaty voice in the *anent* incantations of the Amazonian Achuar is the index of an inter-subjective and intra-subjective interlocution within the chant (Taylor 2017, 56), that voice breaks in related Amazonian genres are icons of emotional attitudes (Briggs 1993; Sherzer and Urban 1986), and that the regular, pulsed, and sometimes staccato-like rhythm of these chants is related to breath and breathing, in a cultural context where all performative enunciations are accompanied by ostensive breathing (Brabec de Morí, Lewy, and García 2014; Hill and Chaumeil 2011; Taylor 2017). Except for a few ethnographic contexts, it is surprising, notwithstanding, how little these vocal aspects—especially the rhythmic ones—have been taken into account in the analyses of rituals. Such is the case in Mesoamerica, but it even holds true for traditions where there has been a flourishing literature on ritual chants, as in Amazonia. More generally, attention has been given to pitch, timbre, and intonation rather than to rhythm and to those aspects when the ritual words are chanted rather than merely "said" or spoken.

The spoken nature of ritual enunciation is what precisely defines many Mesoamerican rituals. Even in this context, however, the way of speaking is the object of much elaboration. In Maya studies and restricting our attention to rhythm, Monod Becquelin (2000, 519) notices that among the Bachajon Tseltal, the prayers in church, the ritual speech of therapeutic ritual, and the *pat'o'tan* ritual dialogues of cargo transmission during the carnival all imply precipitated and accelerated rhythm. Monod Becquelin and Breton (2002, 299, 306) interpret the acceleration of the talk found in the *pat'o'tan* as forming part of the set of devices used in the verbal battle that takes place between the two orators, alongside other means such as speaking with the fewest possible pauses to prevent the addressee from taking the floor. For Yucatec rituals, in his study of a curing ritual of the same kind that I will analyze here, Hanks (1984, 151) explains that the speed of both the verbal articulation and the shaman's bodily rhythm is varied according to the age and strength of the patient. The ritual specialist he has worked with also insists on the correlation between breath groups and the invocation of meaningful groups of spirits as essential to the performance (Hanks 2000, 233). Such comments on voice's use found in the periphery of previous work give precious insight for the development of more thorough analysis on this topic.

As a last introductory remark, in linguistics, rhythmic properties of speech have been the object of increasing research over the last few decades (Auer, Couper-Kuhlen, and Müller 1999; Couper-Kuhlen 1993). Speech timings have been shown to be an essential aspect of the production of meaning and speech acts, syntactic organization, and the deployment of communicative interaction. Rhythmic norms of speech appear therefore to be context-sensitive and pragmatically governed (Barth-Weingarten, Reber, and Selting 2010; Couper-Kuhlen 2009; Wichmann, Dehé, and Barth-Weingarten 2009). However, most works have dealt with speech turns in conversational data, in a few well-described languages. Ritual discourse represents an interesting contrasting case, where the rhythmic rules and their pragmatic effects seem to be of a different nature than those identified by conversational analysts. Their analysis should bring new evidence to nourish the long-debated question of the relation between ritual discourse and ordinary talk.

RHYTHMIC COMPONENTS OF RITUAL SPEECH

Before going into the details of the rituals that will be analyzed below, the main rhythmic components distinguishing their speech should be outlined. They apply at three levels:

1. Text with its rhythm and rhythmic variations (syntactic structure of the lines, rhymes)
2. Voice with its rhythm and rhythmic variations (flow and tempo of elocution, length of breath groups and pauses)
3. Asynchronies between the rhythm of the text and the rhythm of the voice.

The first concerns the textual level (textual refers to the spoken words themselves; the ritual genres under study do not involve any written text as a base for learning or performing). As is common in Mesoamerica, these discourses are characterized by a very dense parallelistic structure and by the cyclical form of certain central sections. In the present cases, these sections concern the invocation-ex-vocation of spiritual entities (in the agricultural ritual) or their expelling (in the cure). Both parallelisms and cycles are subject to varied variations, in such a way that the repetition associated with the variation creates a constant but variable beat; this irregular pattern is what gives the words life, individuality, and effectiveness (Vapnarsky 2008). However, this structure of complex textual variations is superimposed with the rhythmic vocal structure of the elocution. The latter is also organized on the basis of certain regularities with relevant variations. Here, the unit of the breath group, a stretch of speech between two pauses of sufficient length for an intake of breath to be made at each (two inbreaths), is of clear importance, as has been argued for discourse genres in other Amerindian oral traditions from north to south (Hanks 1984; Hymes 1981; Tedlock 1971). Furthermore, the vocal structure is not correlated in a simple way to the textual structure, thus creating a third rhythmic level, generated by the relationship between textual rhythm and vocal rhythm.

The speech genres analyzed here are very little melodized, and no pitch or timbre changes were observed. As voice is concerned, it is the rhythmic pattern that is most distinctive compared to non-ritual speech. This feature also contrasts the two major corpora of Yucatec ritual speeches among the Maya group under study: the ritual genre analyzed here, where rhythm is the main vocal operator, versus the *k'aybil reesa* "sung prayers," a corpus of prayers of the *reesa* genre (from Spanish *rezar* "pray"), which are a Maya appropriation of the Catholic liturgy and include marked melodizations, as their name signals.

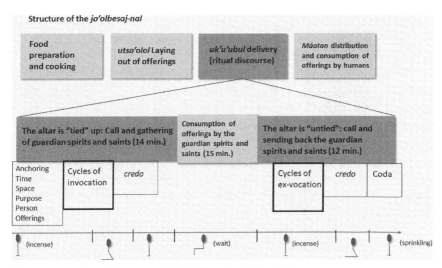

Structure of the *jo'olbesaj-nal*

| Food preparation and cooking | *utso'olol* Laying out of offerings | *uk'u'ubul* delivery (ritual discourse) | *Máatan* distribution and consumption of offerings by humans |

| The altar is "tied" up: Call and gathering of guardian spirits and saints (14 min.) | Consumption of offerings by the guardian spirits and saints (15 min.) | The altar is "untied": call and sending back the guardian spirits and saints (12 min.) |

| Anchoring Time Space Purpose Person Offerings | Cycles of invocation | *credo* | | Cycles of ex-vocation | *credo* | Coda |

(incense) (wait) (incense) (sprinkling)

FIGURE 4.1. *General structure of the* jo'olbesaj-nal *first-fruit ceremony*

SPEECH RHYTHMS IN THE *JO'OLBESAJ-NAL* "EAR OF CORN BENEDICTION"

The *jo'olbesaj-nal* is a first-fruit ceremony that is carried out for the first fruits of maize, before the harvest. The first cobs are offered to the guardian spirits (often referred to as *yuuntsilo'ob* "fathers/masters" in non-ritual contexts) who helped throughout the cultivation process in various ways and to the superior deities of the celestial or terrestrial world. This ritual is integrated into a larger series of rituals that mark out the agricultural cycle in which the guardian spirits themselves are rewarded for their *meyaj* "work" (Hanks 1990, 361; Vapnarsky and Le Guen 2011; Villa Rojas 1945). In the *jo'olbesaj-nal,* offerings are made of corn on the cob baked in the *píib* (earth oven) or a special drink made from fresh corn (*x iis-uul*), as well as incense, candles, and prayers of the creed (a section of *credo* prayers in Maya translation that do not represent performative words of dedication and delivery but rather form part of the offerings). The structure of the first-fruit ceremony follows the fairly regular form of agricultural rituals that extends, contracts, or unfolds according to the specific sub-genre, apart from the burning ritual (figure 4.1).

Whereas the family responsible for the ritual prepares the offerings and sets up the table that will become the altar, the ritual specialist, called the *jmeen* (literally, "the doer"), is in charge of laying out the offerings. It is only once the offerings are displayed and the candle lit that, standing in front of the altar and incensing the offerings, he starts to pray. It is common knowledge that the *jmeen*'s speech serves as a dedication and a handing over of the offerings and, most important, that it will be responsible for the invitation of the spirits and beyond, their moving to and away from the altar. For specialists and non-specialists, *ut'aan*, which can be translated by "his speech," "his word," "his voice," "his language," is the key modality of the performance. To know how to perform the ritual is expressed as *uyoojel ut'aan* "he knows its speech" (in this case, the third person marker *u* in *ut'aan* refers to the ritual itself). In this type of ritual, the discursive performance appears therefore to be predominant over the gestural action, although it is highly connected with some postures and significant gestures. The *jmeen* stands or kneels according to the speech sections; he crosses himself at certain distinctive speech internal turns. He also blesses the offerings with incense while praying and, by the end, pours a small amount of the drink from each gourd toward the cosmos's cardinal points.

The *jmeen*'s discursive performance is divided in two main phases. In a first phase, the ritual specialist sends his words/voice to gather the spiritual entities to come and consume the offerings. In a second phase, he returns them to their proper places, always with his words/voice; it is said that the altar is "tied" in the first phase and then "untied." (In other agricultural rituals, in particular the major *jaanli kool* "the milpa's food," the food offering is preceded by an offering of fresh corn drink.) In our field data, each phase lasts between twelve and fifteen minutes. The two phases are separated by a more static moment, without ritual words, lasting approximately the same as each phase. This moment is the time allocated for the spiritual entities to consume the offerings. It is a moment of calm waiting for the other participants but with the tension induced by being aware of the co-presence of the spiritual entities. The central section of each speech phase is when the *jmeen* sends his voice toward different places in the surrounding geography to summon and gather and pile up the guardian spirits on the altar (invocation) or to send the spiritual entities back to these places (ex-vocation). This is done by way of textual cycles (Monod Becquelin et al. 2010, 126–132). Each cycle consists of an introductory formula, the mention of the trajectory of the words and of the movements of the guardian spirits, the naming of the guardian spirits, and lastly, the place they are attached to (table 4.1). These discursive cycles implement the main actions of each phase, which are enunciated with special and repeated words, such as for the invocation, "for me to gather and pile up they say my true lord, for me to gather and pile up they say your true beauties," and for the ex-vocation, "for me to make rise my true lord, for me to make rise your true beauties, for one of your beautiful pure holy altars to get untied."

TABLE 4.1. Excerpt from the *jo'olbesaj-nal*

Yucatec Text	English Equivalent
[25] Jats'aknaak topoknaak	Hats'aknaaak topoknaak
kubin int'aan	my words/voice go
tunoj uk'a' biin	to the right hand they say
u'aj kanan káakbilóo'	of the guardians of the dark soils
ti' bin u'aj kanan montanya'ilóo'	to they the guardians of the high forest
beej San Bartolo'e'	toward San Bartolo
yumeeeen (. . .)	my lord (. . .)
[26] (. . .)	(. . .)
je'ix ka' oorapaj men injajal yet injajal koolel	as when time made itself by my true [lord] with my true lady
uti'il injunts'ankunsik bin ajajal ki'ichkemile'ex	for me to gather and pile up they say your true beauties
way tuxuul meesa	here at the edge of the altar
way tuni'yooke	here at its feet
kayuum senyor santisima kruus	# my father lord Santisima cruz
uti'il ink'ub bin	for me to offer they say
tunoj uk'a' jajal ki'ichkemile'ex	to the right hand of your true beauties
treese asujuy laake'ex	thirteen pure plates
treese asujuy luuche'ex	thirteen pure gourds
oorapaja men uti'il injajal ko'lel	time made itself by for [*sic*] my true lady
uti'il ink'ubik (. . .)	for me to offer (. . .)
[28] Jats'aknaaak topoknaak	Hats'aknaaak topoknaak
kubin int'aan	my words go
tunoj uk'a bin	to the right hand
u 'aj kanan-káakbilóo' xan	of the guardians of the earth
beej Sajka-ch'éene'	toward Sahkach'éen
yumeen	my lord
[29] Jats'aknaak topoknak	Hats'aknaaak topoknaak
kubin int'aan	my words go
tunoj uk'a	to the right hand

continued on next page

TABLE 4.1.—*continued*

Yucatec Text	English Equivalent
u 'aj kanan-káakbilóo'	of the guardians of the earth
beej Yo'ts'ono'ote'	toward Yo'ts'ono'ot
yumeeen	my lord
[30] Jats'aknaaak topoknaak	Hats'aknaaak topoknaak
kubin int'àan bin	my words go
tu noj uk'a bin	to the right hand
u 'aj kanan-káakbilóo'	of the guardians of the earth
aj kanan-montaanya'ilóo'	guardians of the high forest
ti' bin u 'aj balam-k'áaxilóo'	to the jaguars/guardians of the forest
ti' bin u 'aj tepalilóo'	to the rulers
beej Ts'uts'enbaake'	toward Ts'uts'enbàake'
yumeeen.	my lord.
[31] Jats'aknaaak topoknaak (. . .)	Hats'aknaaak topoknaak (. . .)

As mentioned above, the discourse is characterized by a very dense parallelistic and cyclic structure that is subject to varied variations. On a temporal level, the variation applied to a rhetorical organization based on different types of repetitions creates perceptible changes in rhythm that are an integral part of the specific temporal flow generated during the ritual.

This structure of variations is made more complex by the rhythmic vocal structure of the elocution. To elucidate this rhythmic pattern, the vocal rhythm—the rhythm of the enunciation—was considered in light of two aspects of the speech flow that appeared to be manipulated by the ritual speaker during the performance: first, the speed of syllabic pronunciation and second, the length and distribution of the breath groups and pauses. These were analyzed with automatized segmentation programs adapted to Yucatec Maya (for a precise description of the methodology, see Vapnarsky, Barras, and Becquey 2018; Vapnarsky et al. 2015).

The speed of syllabic pronunciation was calculated taking into consideration the number of syllables per second in each unit of breath. It is illustrated in figure 4.2, which is a representation of the evolution of syllabic rhythm during

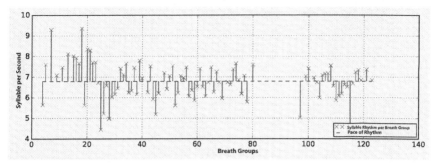

FIGURE 4.2. *Syllabic rhythm during the course of phase 1 of the* jo'olbesaj-nal *agricultural ritual*

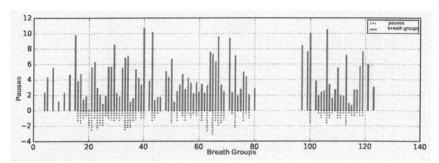

FIGURE 4.3. *Length of breath groups and pauses during phase 1 of the* jo'olbesaj-nal *agricultural ritual (above). The length of each breath unit appears on the upper part of the time line (in plain lines), and the length of the pauses appears below the time line (in dotted line).*

the first phase of one prayer of *jo'olbesaj-nal* recorded in 1994. We observe an initial very rapid rhythm, then a deceleration and continuous variations in the central part.

Figure 4.3 indicates the length of the breath groups and of the pauses during the same stretch of ritual speech. The very marked differences in length of the vertical lines on the upper and lower parts of the central line show the variety in the duration of breath groups and pauses during the prayer. The breath groups are generally much longer than the pauses, revealing a very dense and sustained speech flow. In a corollary way, we note exceptionally long breath groups. In the example shown in figure 4.3, several breath groups exceed eleven seconds duration. They can be followed by even longer ones, as in the second phase where the *jmeen* utters two nearly successive breath

TABLE 4.2. Example of enunciation cut in the text
(the separation between lines corresponds to a pause)

//Jats'aknak topoknaak; kubin int'aan; tunoj uk'a' bin
u'aj kanan káakbilo'; bej Yo'ts'ono'te'; yumeen;
//jats'aknaaak topoknaak; kubin int'aan; tunoj uk'a' bin
u'aj kanan káakbilo'; ti' bin u'aj kanan móontanya'ilóo';
ti' bin ubalam k'áaxilóo'; ti' bin u'aj tepalilóo';
bee x Ts'uts'enbaake'; yumeen; //Jats'aknaaak topoknaak; (. . .)
//Jats'aknaak topoknaak; my words go; to the right hand they say of the guardians of dark soils; my lord;
//Jats'aknaak topoknaak; my words go; to the right hand they say
of the guardians of the dark soils, to they say the guardians of the high forest; to the, they say, jaguars/spirits of the forest; to the, they say, sovereigns,
on the way to Tsutsenbak; my lord;// Jats'aknaak topoknaak; (. . .)

groups of eleven and fifteen seconds. All these lengths are significantly longer than what occurs in ordinary speech.

Finally, no clear correlation exists between the length of the breath groups and the length of the pauses, a fact that confirms the very elaborate character of the sound rhythm and of the use of the voice by the ritual specialist. The crosses indicate the number of syllables (calculated on the basis of the vowels) per second in each unit of breath. The horizontal line in the middle indicates the rhythmic average, the superior vertical lines show an acceleration of the tempo, and those in the lower part indicate a deceleration.

The analysis of the vocal rhythm in this ritual shows that on the whole, the speech tempo tends to be faster and breath groups notably longer than in non-ritual genres. Some ritual specialists have, in fact, an impressive and acknowledged dexterity in uttering long breath groups at an incredibly fast tempo (see, for instance, the recording of don Victor Hau, *jets' lu'um*, in Gubler 2017). For the non-specialist, this is a sonorous signature of the genre. But the speech vocal rhythm also shows significant variations in both speed and length of breath groups and pauses. As a general pattern, this echoes the irregular regularity found in the textual rhythm, although as we will now see, this similarity of principle only accounts for part of the picture.

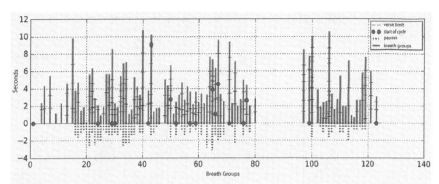

FIGURE 4.4. *Relationship between textual units and vocal units in the prayer (the dots signal the beginnings of textual cyclical units)*

At this stage, it is fitting to compare the vocal rhythm to the textual rhythm. Most, if not all, published transcriptions of Maya ritual discourses represent speech in chunks corresponding to complete textual cycles or groups of lines. However, in our data, correlating the textual and the vocal units shows that their limits are not always aligned. This can be seen, for instance, in table 4.2, which corresponds to cycles [29] and [30] that were represented in table 4.1, based then on the textual structure. The separation by a blank line corresponds to a pause in enunciation, while the semicolon (;) indicates separations between lines and the two slashes (//) signal borders between textual cycles.

We observe that the first cycle mentioned starts at the beginning of a breath group, but the next cycle follows immediately within the same breath group, without a pause. Then a pause is made before the last two lines of the cycle and the next breath group starts with the last lines of the previous textual cycle. Taking into account the articulation between the textual and the vocal rhythms reveals, therefore, a non-synchronous rhythmic organization.

Based on such analysis, figure 4.4 shows the precise relation between textual and vocal units throughout the first phase of the prayer. The beginning of the cycles is signaled with dots. Two major aspects can be observed. On one hand, the beginning of the textual cycle units often corresponds to beginnings of vocal groups (that is, when the dot is on the median line separating the pauses from the breath groups), but not always. On the other hand, the discrepancy between both types of units is concentrated mostly in one section of the prayer phase (between lines 40 and 80).

In sum, the analysis shows that each rhythmic level presents internal variations throughout the verbal performance. The *jmeen* starts with a very fast flow, which he sustains during the performance as a whole but with significant pace variations within it. Breath groups can be notably long, but, as do the lengths of pauses, they also vary in duration. Finally, the rhythm of the text and the rhythm of the voice can be synchronous, but they are marked by clear asynchronies in some parts, especially in one main section.

Collating the different rhythmic levels together and in relation to other features of the performance helps us further our understanding of the pragmatics of these rhythmic patterns. First, the moment when the disparity between textual rhythm and vocal rhythm is at its highest, between lines 40 and 80, also corresponds to a phase of higher variation of the syllabic rhythm or tempo. This period of higher rhythmic variation is also correlated to other speech features. In particular, it is a period when the mention of an expression *kuyoorapaja* "to make time," which operates like a leitmotiv referring to the *hic et nunc* generation of ritual time in the prayer, is repeated most iteratively, giving special intensity to this process. This period also corresponds precisely with the sections when the voice travels to gather and pile up the guardian spirits or to send them back. Therefore, the moment of major rhythmic vibration and tension equates with a central phase in which the orator invokes and properly moves the spirits toward (or, in the second phase, from) the space of the altar. In other words, greater variations and asynchronies are correlated with moving the guardian spirits.

To better understand the use and function of voice and rhythmic patterns in the ritual performance, I shall now analyze another type of Yucatec Maya ritual, a therapeutic ritual to expel malign airs. This ritual, like the agricultural rituals, forms part of the *jmeen's* repertoire, though internal specialization does exist. In the cases analyzed here, the *jmeen* conducting the agricultural ritual and the one conducting the therapeutic ritual were different people, each a specialist in his own ritual field. However, the details of their lives, practices, and "client list" reveal transmission lines, relations, and specializations that constitute an important background when it comes to comparing practices and styles. We shall see that in spite of corresponding to two different ritual practices carried out by specialists dedicated respectively to just one of them, both rituals show notable similarities in the treatment of time through speech and voice but also some critical differences arguably related to the ritual actions involved.

SPEECH AND BODY RHYTHMS IN THE
SÁANTIGWAAR THERAPEUTIC RITUAL

The *sáantigwaar* therapeutic ritual corresponds to what is known in the American continent as a cleansing ceremony. It is carried out when the

TABLE 4.3. General structure of the ritual discourse for *sáantigwaar*

Sequence of Actions and Phases in Ritual	Time for a Sick Baby*	Time for an Adult Woman
(drinks and spits on the branches to wet them; crosses himself)		
First phase—expulsion of the airs	3:15	3:43
Silence/pause—(drinks and spits on the branches)	0:16	0:18
Second phase—expulsion of the airs	3:01	3:40
Silence/pause—(drinks and spits on the branches)	0:15	0:10
Dedication—supplication *k'áatmatik*	1:10	1:50
(drinks and spits on the branches; crosses himself; sweeps the body with branches)		

* Times given are minutes and seconds, representative of common durations.

supposed cause of illness in a person is that she or he has been "caught" (*chuk*), "seized" (*mach*), or "aerated" (*sáalt*) by one or several potentially harmful airs or winds (*iik'*), of the great variety that exists for the Maya. The purpose of the ritual specialist's performance is to identify the air(s) that caught the body, *pa'iik'* "to break air," and to send them away.[3]

The *sáantigwaar* can occur as a single session or be integrated into a series of sessions, depending on the condition of the sick person. It is associated with a drink offering, sometimes food, dedicated to the deities, the bad winds, or the guardian spirits; but this is not obligatory and depends on the etiology of each case. For the cure, the sick person is invited to sit on a chair close to the ritual specialist's altar. If the sick person is a baby—a very common situation since they are the most vulnerable to certain winds—the mother sits holding her or him in her arms. The *jmeen* then lights a candle, seizes a *sip'che'* branch and his small bottle of alcohol, takes a long sip, and spits the liquid on the branches. Then he starts to "sweep" (*míistik*) the patient's body, beating it lightly with the *sip'che'* leaves as he shakes them with a regular movement of his hand. With the exception of a brief moment at start and finish, as well as two pauses between discursive sections when the *jmeen* takes a sip and spits on the branches, his voice and words accompany the entire sweep and its regular beating gesture in an incessant flow and a fast rhythm.

For the present study, I analyzed three performances filmed between 2006 and 2008 in the house of one *jmeen*, where he treats his patients. The general structure of the ritual discourse is illustrated in table 4.3. It is divided into two main phases of expelling airs, which are almost identical, and a final phase of supplication to God and other deities.

In previous work, based on the analysis of the different temporalizations created by the words in this therapeutic performance, I have argued that the curing is realized in part by a calibration of cosmic time with the performance's time in terms of the airs' movements, as well as by a kind of resetting of time, which links the moment of the seizure of the body by the airs with the curing time (Vapnarsky 2017). But there is more to it. As in the agricultural ritual, here, too, rhythmic components play a crucial role in what is going on and in the prayer's performativity. They result in a polyrhythmic texture composed of at least three modalities: textual, vocal, and gestural.

At a textual level, the fabric of the speech is constituted of prolific parallelistic series, with short parallel lines used to invoke a considerable number of airs in extensive—and ideally exhaustive—enumerations. The invoked airs are organized in sub-series according to the qualities that define them (e.g., airs qualified by the disease they cause, linked to poisonous animals, linked to specific places). The relative exhaustiveness of their mention aims at identifying the ones responsible for the disease. Cyclicity is also operative, especially for the mention of the airs and the actions and movements that affect them. Table 4.4 shows part of one cycle of invocation, formed by the enumeration of a series of winds and ending with a group of lines referring to the *jmeen*'s action of passing the branches over the patient's body ("we are sweeping its layers, we are sweeping its pain") and expelling the airs toward their place of origin.

One salient distinctive element by which any Maya person can recognize a *sáantigwaar* is the rhythm of its elocution, particularly fast and regular. After a few introductory slow *dyos yúumbi dyos mejembi dyos el espiiritu saantos*s "God the father, God the son, God the holy spirit," with which the *jmeen* blesses any person present, he initiates his naming of the long series of winds at a very fast pace and without further preamble, over about fifty lines. This rhythm is maintained over about seven minutes and only slows down at the end, with the imploration to God and other deities that closes the speech. Beyond this general fast tempo and although the vocal rhythmic parameters made explicit for the agricultural ritual remain relevant, the *sáantigwaar* elocution shows some sharp distinctions with regard to the previous ritual. First, the *sáantigwaar* involves a much more regular rapid tempo than the agricultural performance (except for a strong structural variation in the *sáantigwaar* final dedication). The speaker uses a tempo of about 100 beats/minute, which he often subdivides into 4s, with his syllabic articulation following the same rhythmic measure as his hand shaking the leaves while "sweeping" the body. Second, whereas the *sáantigwaar* is composed by some very long but also lengthwise

TABLE 4.4. Excerpt from a *sáantigwaar* made for a sick baby

Yucatec Text	English Equivalent
uyiik'al xan kruseero i kaayes	the air of streets' crossroads
uyiik'al kruseero i beejo'	the air of paths' crossroads
uyiik'al la'la' soolare'	the air of the old patios
uyiik'al la'la' ch'e'en	the air of the old wells
uyiik'al la'lajkajtali	the air of the old villages
uyiik'al x jala'ap	the air of the ravines
uyiik'al xmulu'uch	the air of the mounds
uyiik'al muulu' **	the air of the ruins
uyiik'al aj kanul	the air of the guardians
uyiik'al xan kulpach iik'	the air also of the backward wind
yiik'al xkuulpach taankaso' **	the air of the backward tankas
uyiik'al xan k'asap iik'al	the air of the k'asap wind
k'asap tankaso'	the k'asap tankas
uyiik'al xan **	its air as well
k'ak'al mosoon iik'o'	the air of the closing whirlwind
k'ak'al moson taankaso'	the tankas of the closing whirlwind
(…)	(…)
táan kmíistik uts'aapa'	**we are sweeping its layers**
táan kmíistik uk'iinam	**we are sweeping its pains**
te' kuka'bina'	there it goes again
tu'ux kutaalba	to where it came from
ti' yóol iik' kutaal	on the wind it comes
ti' yóol kuka'bin xan tuka'atene'	on the wind it goes again
x kok iik'	air of the asthma
x kok oojo' iik'o'	air of the asthma evil eye
(…)	(…)

varied breath groups as in the agricultural ritual, in contrast with the latter, its pauses are always very short and regular in duration (figure 4.5).

If we consider the relation between the textual and the vocal rhythms, we do find asynchronies as in the agricultural performance. But the asynchronies are now more predictable, regular, and subtle. The shift only concerns a few morphemes rather than groups of lines: instead of marking the pause at the end of the line, as is done in most cases, the *jmeen* sometimes marks a pause

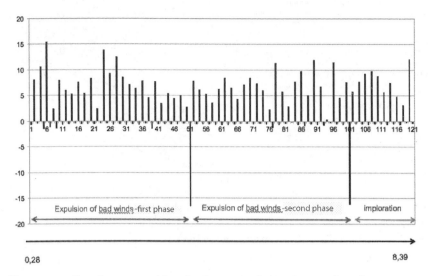

Figure 4.5. *Breath groups and lengths of pauses in the* sáantigwaar. *Breath groups are represented by the vertical lines above the medial horizontal line and pauses by the vertical lines below; the number of the ordinate represents seconds, and the abcissa gives the number of the line of verses.*

after two line-starting morphemes, the determiners *le* and *x* (table 4.5). This creates a brief suspended time, which carries with it the projection of the next phrase. The projection results from the syntactic incompletion, the prosody, as well as the subjacent model of parallelistic structure, which implies a subsequent equivalent line. This regular asynchrony has several effects: to lessen the feeling of interruptions in the speech flow and to create a projective tension as well as a distinctive small rhythmic mismatch or vibration.

The rapid tempo, the long breath groups, the brief pauses, and the type of recurrent rhythmic asynchrony between textual and vocal units used by the ritual specialist all generate at the sensorial level a very fast speech flow, with a relatively regular pulsed rhythm, sustained without interruption. Now, the phase where the intent of constant speech flow is most manifest is the one that corresponds to the section where the *jmeen* sends the bad airs back to the cardinal directions. Remember that the phase with the most rhythmic tension in the agricultural ritual was also the one in which the spirits were moved. Although the vocal techniques are not exactly the same in both rituals (variations in length of breath groups and pauses in the agricultural ritual versus variations in rhythmic mismatch creating the feeling of a nonstop flow in the therapeutic

TABLE 4.5. Asynchronies between textual rhythm and vocal rhythm in the *sáantigwaar*

Yucatec Text	English Equivalent
ti'(a)l ubinba te' lak'in	for them to go to the west
wáa te' j lak'ina'	or to the west
wáa xan te' j xamano' utaal xan	or also from the north it also comes
le x => # (2 :21,1-21,7) INTERNAL VERSE PAUSE	**the #**
k'íinam pool oojo' iik'o'	evil eye air of the headache
x chokoj pool oojo' iik'o'	evil eye air of the hot head
x weenel oojo' iik'o'	evil eye air of the sleeping
x jaaya' oojo' iik'o'	evil eye air of the yawning
x jak' oojo' iik'o'	evil eye air of the fright
x # ja'as óol oojo' iik'o'	evil eye air of the frightening
x k'íinam pool oojo' iik'o'	evil eye air of the headache
x chokoj pool oojo' iik'o'	evil eye air of the hot head
pribaasyon oojo' iik'o'	evil eye air of the swooning
x xikin oojo' iik'o'	evil eye air of the ear
x xikin oojo' t'ankaso'	evil eye tankas of the ear
ti'(a)l ubinba' (xa)no' te' j xamano'	for them also to go to the north
# (2 :34,3-34,9) FINAL VERSE PAUSE	
ti' yóol iik' kutaal	on the wind it comes
ti' yóol iik' kuka'abin	on the wind it leaves again
(. . .)	(. . .)
(. . .)	(. . .)
x chokoj pool oojo' iik'o'	evil eye air of the headache
x wéenel oojo' iik'o'	evil eye air of the sleeping
x jaaya' oojo' iik'o'	evil eye air of the yawning
x => # (3 :0,8 :07,3) INTERNAL VERSE PAUSE	**the #**
ja'k'óol oojo' iik'o'	evil eye air of the being frightened
x ja'as óol oojo' iik'o'	evil eye air of the frightening
x k'íinam pool oojo' iik'o'	evil eye air of the headache . . .

one), in both cases the means used to set the spiritual entities in motion rely on the principle of text/voice asynchrony and imply a projective tension.

The tense flow and the beat that shape *sáantigwaar* ritual speech drop abruptly with the mention "in the name of the father, of the son, of the holy spirit" in Spanish, then in Maya, for which the *jmeen* moves quickly to a much slower non-measured rhythm. Then, the *jmeen* resumes a faster rhythm for the imploration, with very long breath groups but of different rhythmicity from those in the phase of the expulsion of the airs. Last, the *jmeen* concludes his speech by declaiming three *dyoos yuumbi dyoos mejembi dyoos el espiiritu saanto*s "God the father, God the son, God the holy spirit" and the coda *Amen*, again extremely slowly. This rhythm, in sharp contrast with the fast and regular pace that animated most of the ritual, structurally distinguishes the section of the expulsion of the airs from the section of the summoning of the deities, each one dedicated to very distinct groups of beings. It also creates a sudden lowering of the tension that marks the end of the ritual, arguably playing a role equivalent to the formula that opened the *sáantigwaar* speech—that of a rhythmic border between the mundane and the ritual temporalities.

SPEECH RHYTHMS, RITUAL ACTIONS, AND SPIRITUAL CONFIGURATIONS

What motivates and generates the complex imbrication of rhythmic manipulations, vocal but also textual and gestural, observed in the ritual performances? Based on the previous analyses and some new ethnographic data, I suggest a few hypotheses in this regard. They concern the use of fast tempo in both rituals as well as the distinctive rhythmic manipulations found in each ritual.

We have seen that both rituals require rapid elocutionary rhythms, despite the differences that define them. In the therapeutic *sáantigwaar* the rapid pace is continuous; in the *jo'olbesaj-nal* (first-fruit ceremony) the rhythm is much less regular, but it is still faster than ordinary talk and, noticeably, the prayer also starts with an initial fast tempo. As noticed in the introduction, rapidity of elocution is shared with other Maya ritual contexts. Although the fast tempo seems to be endowed with different forces depending on its specific elaborations and ritual contexts, I suggest that it has the two main basic functions of, first, generating a specific sensorial temporality for the ritual and, second, creating and indexing an agentive interaction, engaged in by the ritual specialist toward the spiritual or more generally non-human entities.

At a sensorial level, the sustained fast tempo, often associated with especially long breath groups, contrasts neatly with the flow of speech in ordinary discourse and other formal genres (such as petitions between humans or narratives). It generates a specific temporal flow that defines the now of the ritual. This flow is for all participants a palpable experience of temporal otherness, functioning as an icon of the non-mundane composition of temporalities that occurs in ritual events. Opening and closing formulas of markedly slower non-measured rhythm may actually operate as a sort of rhythmic border that helps the transition between mundane and ritual times. In addition, the fast flow works as an index of the intense and direct interactions of the *jmeen* with the spiritual entities and hence of the presence of the latter. This leads us to the second main function of fast speech in the rituals under study, that of creating, I argue, the agentive interaction of the ritual specialist toward the spiritual entities.

This may be understood by considering speaking fast as one facet of the regimes of communication and action that for the Yucatec Maya hold between ontologically distinct participants. According to this view, speaking fast integrates a complex frame of asymmetrical modes and channels of oral interaction among human beings, the ritual specialist, and spiritual entities. Among the latter, the *yuuntsilo'ob* guardian spirits incite most Maya metadiscursive comments. The *yuuntsilo'ob* have two main means of oral communication with humans. First, they can signal their presence or a danger through a specific type of whistle (hissing, *xuuxub*). This is a warning that most people have heard and requires that they leave the place or take some precautionary measure.

Second, the *yuuntsilo'ob* can enter into dialogue with a ritual specialist or a person who might become one in verbal exchanges whereby they teach their interlocutor esoteric knowledge. Such exchanges usually occur in dreams or during some ecstatic experience in the forest, typically when the person "gets lost" (Hanks 1993b). They are held in ordinary speech, except when the guardian spirits guide the *jmeen* in his learning of ritual speech. In none of these oral interactions (I use oral because only the second one is properly verbal, using articulated speech) is rapidity ever involved, by which I mean it is never mentioned by the experiencers or others as a special feature of the exchange or the lived situation. On the contrary, as is common throughout Mesoamerica, there is a typical extra slowness of the lived time in the underworld or in the spiritual world. This slowness is encapsulated in the frequently heard comment that one day there is equivalent to one year in the mundane world.

The *yuuntsilo'ob* are also supposed to talk among themselves. People comment that most probably, they use the same ordinary Maya language as people do. As with the visual mode, humans cannot hear them except when the spirits want them to.

The ritual involves yet another interactional frame. Whereas the guardian spirits are the interlocution leaders in the type of interactions previously mentioned, in the ritual, the human specialist is at least ideally the leading performer. He must drive the performance and keep control over the interaction. Moreover, in this case, the interaction is not, strictly speaking, a verbal exchange, since the *jmeen*'s words as directed to their spiritual targets do not aim at transmitting communicative content or at receiving a verbal answer. (In case of addressees' discontentment, non-verbal answers are expected in the forms of signs, uncooked offerings, the fall of a candle, an unknown animal in the surroundings, and the like). The purpose of the *jmeen*'s words is rather to act on the spirits in a very physical manner (e.g., move them). We suggest that the fast tempo functions as a condition for triggering this type of highly performative and asymmetrical interaction.

This hypothesis should be further elaborated to take into account the more diverse ritual contexts where rapid tempo is used. In particular, it is also used when addressing divinities and saints with explicit speech acts (e.g., imploring, asking). Although the "airs" invoked in the therapeutic ritual share properties with the guardian spirits, starting with the basic fact that all are invisible *iik'* "air" or "wind" and that a body of them (in particular, those linked with ancient living places) seem to overlap, they are not ascribed the same intentional and communicative properties.

To further our understanding of the rhythmic use of the voice by the *jmeen* beyond the speed parameter, some considerations of the "spiritual" configurations that characterize each ritual we analyzed now seem necessary. The *jo'olbesaj* and the *sáantigwaar* rituals differ not only in terms of the kind of spirits involved but also, and more critically for our point, in terms of their co-presence settings and the nature of the actions at play. The agricultural ritual is dedicated to a set of guardian spirits who are not present at the beginning of the performance. A crucial and delicate aim of the performance and of its illocutionary force is to make them come to the table—which is part of the process of the table becoming an altar—and, after they consume the offerings, to take them back to their abode. This is tense action because the presence of these entities is full of potential danger, but it is not an agonistic one: the *yuuntsilo'ob* "masters" are addressed with reverential formulas such as *ajajal ki'ichkemiléex* "your beauties" and invited with all due verbal forms. By contrast, the *sáantigwaar* presupposes that some dangerous airs are (or at least might be) present from the start. The cure takes place when the patient goes to see the *jmeen* because the patient feels or conjectures that she or he is carrying harmful airs with her or him. The purpose of the performance is to expel them and send them back to "where they came." The airs' presence from the beginning can explain why there are no verbal premises to the interaction with them (recall that the prayer starts by naming their long list without innuendo) except from the blessing of the attendee, which aims at protecting the latter from getting caught by the airs being moved during the session. Also, in contrast with the polite and dialogic form of address used for the guardian spirits in the agricultural rituals, in the *sáantigwaar* performance, the airs are only referred to as third persons with no sweet formulas. The second person and the verbs for asking in a sweet-polite way for help and blessing are restricted to divinities and saints in the final section of imploration.

Moreover, even if the motion of the spiritual entities involves a similar cyclical textual structure in both cases, the words used for it differ greatly. Whereas in the agricultural ritual the voice goes to gather and pile up the guardian spirits and then raise and lead them back to their abode, in the *sáantigwaar* the actions evoked (and performed) are those of "sweeping" airs and pains but also more forcefully of "breaking-airs" (*pa'iik*). In contrast with other traditions (see, for example, Figuerola Pujol 2010 on Tzeltal Maya prayers), here the expelling is not based on any negotiation, convincing, or seducing of the target entities but rather on very physical acts of disconnection, separation, and relocation. All this reveals that in the *sáantigwaar*, the action of moving away the airs comes under much more strain (it is a proper expelling) within an agonistic interactional frame.

I argue that specific rhythmic manipulations are used to perform the two actions of setting in motion and expelling essential to these two rituals. Both these actions are multimodal, and the voice plays a crucial part. In addition to the textual words, the expelling in the *sáantigwaar* is performed jointly by the gestural and vocal modalities: on the one hand, the sweeping of the body with the branches, imbued with a special force by blowing alcohol on them, and on the other hand, the regular flow of uninterrupted fast speech. Recall that in addition to fast speech, this flow is created in the *sáantigwaar* by using the most minimal pauses and by rhythmic projective mismatches. All these gestural and vocal manipulations are outward and centrifugal: sweeping away, blowing, but also talking fast with a minimal inbreath and long outbreaths. They act physically and iconically like a proper expulsion.

By being based on a very physical action and at the same time carrying the words, the voice operates as a nodal articulation between the gestures and the textual components. The gesture sustains a continuous regular beat, which gives support to the pace of the talk (even when the talk stops for inbreath, the beating of the hand holding the leaves continues), while in parallel, the textual semantic components shape other temporalizations, at a different level from the rhythmic properties of the voice but thanks to this enunciation.

In the *sáantigwaar*, the tempo may also be determined by a third central participant: the patient. Hanks (1984) reported that the *jmeen* is careful to adapt the pace of his voice to the state and frailness of the patient: more *cháambel* "slow, low (tone)"[4] for the weaker ones, more *péeka'an* "fast" for the stronger ones. The patient appears therefore, metaphorically or not, as the battle ground of the tense interaction that takes place between the *jmeen* and the airs. We can imagine the action and the sensitivity of the patient as the delivering of a battle either on crystal glass, softening the movements to avoid breaking the floor (vocally: speaking not slow but less fast), or on a hard and resistant *floor*, pushing and beating with less fear (vocally: speaking faster and in a tenser way). These rhythmic adaptations more fundamentally highlight the effect of the elocutionary pace on the patient: the fast-uninterrupted regular tempo works on the expulsion of the harmful air while at the same time clearly acting as a calming balm for the sick person, helping bring balance back to the body. Although this topic cannot be developed in the context of this chapter, it is worth noticing that the vocal rhythm used in the curing ritual is not unrelated to that of Maya mothers patting their babies' backs to calm them (or other corporal movements used to the same effect, e.g., rhythmically moving the baby sideways or up and down).

The term used to refer to the fast pace of the talk is *péeka'an*, literally "moved" (from the root *péek* "move" + participial *–a'an*). Thus "going fast" is "being moved." And indeed, fast talk *makes for movement*, but the rapid tempo of the ritual discourse does not seem to suffice to generate the air's or spirits' movements. The data under study show that the displacement of the spiritual entities is in fact more effectively performed when an asynchrony (or a desynchronization) is produced between the vocal rhythm and the textual rhythm. The desynchronization occurs in both ritual genres. I propose, by way of hypothesis, that the shift between the vocal rhythm and textual rhythm is the temporal expression of the spatial movement. Following a principle of iconicity, it is by a rhythmical displacement that the *jmeen* generates the spatial displacement of the spiritual entities.

The temporal desynchronization is more marked in the *jo'olbesaj-nal* than in the *sáantigwaar*. This is also seen in the greater variations of the duration of breath groups and of the pauses' lengths that occurs in the phase of the agricultural ritual when the *yuuntsilo'ob* are moved. The rhythm becomes more irregular, additive, and no more divisive. Although firmly proving this would require more comparative analysis, I suggest that the major desynchronization observed in the first-fruit ceremony is linked to a major emphasis drawn in this ritual to the displacement of the guardian spirits between precise locations and the altar. By contrast, in the *sáantigwaar*, the strained agonistic outward force needed for the expelling appears as the main factor governing the specific vocal alterations (uninterrupted regular fast flow) used by the specialist.

CONCLUSION

In conclusion, the detailed and multimodal analysis of ritual discourses in two distinct Maya rituals shows that voice matters—greatly—in the transformative processes aimed for, even in the Maya genres under study where ritual words are not chanted but spoken. In this tradition, voice's manipulations are mostly rhythmical. They play with enunciation rhythms of various sorts as well as with the textual and the gestural rhythms, introducing meaningful asynchronies. Voice plays with rhythms to generate a specific flow of time, which sensorially and pragmatically distinguishes the ritual from other mundane temporalities. The specific vocal tempo is also a way for the ritual specialist to trigger a highly agentive and performative verbal interaction toward the spiritual entities involved and, beyond, to produce specific actions. The two kinds of rituals analyzed share common vocal devices but also show differences in the rhythmic patterns and alterations by the ritual speaker, which are linked to the praxic, interactional, and co-presence configuration of each ritual. Consequently, vocal rhythms operate as an index of spiritual presence and the interaction and actions going on and hence also act on the human participants in their awareness or quasi-awareness of what is happening and who is there and, consequently, in their behaviors, feelings, and states of being. Voice is the breath of ritual time. Much further research is needed to deepen our understanding of this intimate yet potent temporal matter as a transformative and agentive process.

Acknowledgments. This research was developed within the RITMO international network (funded as GDRI-CNRS, France). A first version of the comparison of the temporalization means in the rituals under study was presented at the conference "El tiempo en recomposiciones: Enfoques interdisciplinarios sobre los rituales mesoamericanos" at the Sapienza Università di Roma, November 3–5, 2016 (org. Alessandro Lupo and Perig Pitrou). A more thorough comparison of the voice patterns was developed for the meeting "Materializing Temporalities" at the University of California at Berkeley, September 21–23, 2017 (org. Rosemary Joyce). I thank the organizers and all the participants for their insightful comments.

NOTES

1. The data used in this chapter were collected and recorded in southern villages of Felipe Carrillo Puerto, during extensive fieldwork realized by the author since 1994.

2. The passage of time in the spiritual world is different from that experienced by humans, something we are reminded of in every account about them. However, in the

rituals that will be studied, ritual time does not seek to reproduce an external tempo-rality but rather create its own, with agentive properties.

3. Hanks (1996, 175) reports that the *jmeen* he worked with in Yucatan distinguishes the *sáantigwaar* from the *pa'iik'* ceremony, the latter rarer and closer to an exorcism. In my data, the action of *pa'iik'* "breaking air/wind" is central to the *sáantigwaar*, it is mentioned as such in the ritual speech and also used as a metadiscursive comment about the ritual

4. *Cháambel* literally means "little going," and it also refers to a sound (including voice) being low. *Cháambel t'aan* means either "speak slowly" or "speak softly."

PART TWO

Ritualizing Place

5

The study of place making in the political sphere of the ancient Maya has recently attracted much interest, not only in relation to urbanism (Fash and López Lujan 2009) but also directly in relation to sedentism (Inomata et al. 2015). Place making relates to the creation of a "common ground" in agglomerating communities and to the stability of dwellings for their inhabitants. In agrarian societies evolving in a tropical forest environment, residential stability seriously challenged subsistence systems. Based on swidden agriculture, these systems involve slash-and-burn practices with long fallow periods to naturally restore the fertility of cultivated land, a cycle that requires the frequent displacement of residence to minimize distance to cultivated fields. In contrast, stable agglomerations were basically required for political institutions to form and function. This profound contradiction, which Maya societies faced (Pohl and Pohl 1994), leads us to consider place making as an important issue.

This chapter gives attention to the hypothesis of Ian Hodder, that religion had a primary role in the origin of settled life because it allowed the production of the two main supports of settled life: historical depth and attachment to place (Çatalhöyük Project, Templeton Foundation, https://www.templeton.org; see Hodder 2007). One possible application to the Maya lowlands would be that Maya sedentary people may have resorted to religious practices through ritually materializing central places located in the heart of their

House, Floor, and Soil

Fixing Residence

M. Charlotte Arnauld

https://doi.org/10.5876/9781646422395.c005

spatial mobility system (for a more specific model, see Inomata et al. 2015). In other words, carrying out particular rituals would have allowed them to create historical depth and attachment to a place even though they eventually maintained relatively high mobility patterns necessary for their very subsistence. Fixing one's house at a specific spot represented a risk and a source of internal tension for families, and rituals would have been among the various strategies used to mitigate both risk and tension.

The present chapter focuses on patterns of rituals interpreted in relation to the creation of fixed, settled places in urban contexts by ancient Maya people. I briefly explore the meaning of the notions of "historical depth" and "attachment to place" (Hodder 2007) in relation to the archaeological record of place making in the Maya lowlands. As this chapter is part of long-term research on the beginnings and transformations of Classic Maya kingship (Arnauld 2016a, 2016b), I emphasize the pivotal relevance of place making for royal Maya dynasties. Finally, I briefly present and discuss an example of complex "ritual stratigraphy" (after McAnany and Hodder 2009) in La Joyanca Structure 6E12sub, which was excavated from 2000 to 2003.

MATERIALIZATION OF HISTORICAL DEPTH AND ATTACHMENT TO PLACE IN THE MAYA REGION

Archaeologically expressed, historical depth corresponds to the stratification of earth layers and deposits containing artifacts and vestiges studied through stratigraphy, that is, the study of change through time as reflected by stratified layers (by analogy with geology). This is the basic archaeological materialization of time, which implies not only culture-historical phasing (based on stylistic change in artifacts through stratigraphic sequence) but also an understanding of the tempo of strata formation and taphonomy. For the most part, this tempo was socially determined, and within this "social stratigraphic" perspective (McAnany and Hodder 2009) it was, in some cases, ritually determined. Joyce and Pollard (2010, 297) have made salient the very peculiar character of what they call "structured deposition": "These shifts from the geological model of stratigraphic accumulation representing an uninterpretable coincidence of materials removed from cultural systems over vast periods of time, to the assumption that deposits can be understood in terms of the temporalities of human lives, are irreversible changes in archaeological perspectives."

We are far from culture-historical phasing—although this basic task can (and must) still be conducted through ritual stratigraphy, even though its premises are distinct from those of routine accumulations resulting from non-ritual building and living activities. Structured deposition implies temporalities of centuries through which the same depositional rites were repeated but also generation and other human life temporalities that situated their enactment. Moreover, if, as in this chapter, structured deposition is focused on religious practices referring to place making, we must envision still new temporalities that became available to sedentary farmers in forested environments like the Maya lowlands. Once settled in agglomerations and installed in masonry houses, farmers were to experience times less constrained by the cycles of their milpas (maize fields) and perishable-material field houses, domestic time shared with neighbors, generational and ancestral time, time of socioeconomic enterprises, and more complex religious and political temporalities—calendrical and others. As I hope to argue in this chapter, some of those desired temporalities were included in ritual stratigraphy materialized by horizontally expanded layers and vertically buried deposits at the place being built.

Attachment to place is also related to a stratigraphy that is not strictly ritual, that of permanently elevated structures (e.g., masonry walls and roof) built, occupied, dismantled, then rebuilt on the same spot as many Maya examples show, until the entire stratified structure forms a high platform or substructure—an equivalent to the tells studied in the Middle East: "dans un contexte marqué par l'augmentation supposée de la sédentarité, ces pratiques jouent un rôle moteur dans la fixation et la création de centralités en contribuant à ancrer les groupes dans le paysage, à un lieu et à une mémoire. [In a context marked by the supposed increase in sedentary lifestyles, these practices play a leading role in the fixation and creation of centralities by helping to anchor groups in the landscape, place, and memory]" (Hadad 2017). The layering of recycled dismantled houses and middens raised the earth's surface on which to build the house. The domestic platform was then a visible cue of past and future occupation of the spot, even when its inhabitants were periodically away living closer to their milpas in field houses. Today, the platform is still the best type of evidence to indicate an ancient presence in rural contexts, a basic tenet for present-day Maya farmers (Vapnarsky and Le Guen 2011) and archaeologists alike, but it is also the main type of evidence for demographic evaluations of the ancient Maya. Platform-building practices were common in Preclassic and Classic Maya villages, towns, and large cities to raise simple domestic houses and monumental, politico-religious buildings as well.

Along with the burials it covered, the platform was the primeval marker for the adoption of sedentary life, even when mobility was still required and largely practiced. Here, burials are thought of as "deposited objects" that resulted from "a history of practices that did not originate specifically for the purpose of commemorating a human person by incorporating his or her body in the dwelling site" (Joyce 2011, 41). They instead fixed the dwelling site through their deposition within a raised platform that incorporated repeatedly built houses on the same spot, creating longevity and thus sedentism or the appearance of sedentism (see also Joyce 2008).

Structured deposition appears in the caching practices that had punctuated the various fill layers of platforms or pyramids produced by dismantling previous constructions. In these caches or ritual deposits, artifacts were purposefully diverted from current life and buried in a way archaeologists easily distinguish from artifacts dispersed through stratified layers by the effect of routine formation processes. Caches are found in all kinds of Maya buildings (although less frequently in perishable houses; Arnauld et al. 2013), yet archaeologists tend to give them more consideration when associated with monumental architecture (Walker and Lucero 2000). Caches are also found in locations away from elevated structures, in ball court alleys or plazas (Aoyama et al. 2017; Inomata 2017; Inomata and Triadan 2015) and other public, collective places. The relevance of caches lies first, in their ubiquity and second, in their vertically buried, circumscribed (for example, within a covered ceramic recipient), often intrusive situation. Together, these features may be referred to as "bundling" (Guernsey and Reilly 2006) or, even better, as "bundling-burying" due to the double ritual action of assembling valuable offerings and inserting them into the earth at a specified locale. Considering their ubiquity in relation to building uses, the place-making aspects of both gestures may be plausibly said to "anchor social groups in the landscape to a place and a memory" (citing Hadad again, see above; on the "intentionality" of caches, see Harrison-Buck 2004; Joyce and Pollard 2010; Mock 1998b). Instead of the place-making concept, animation or nourishment of houses has often been cited as an explanation of caches, following the ethnography of ritual house building (Vogt 1965), yet Begel has assembled evidence and arguments that question such notions (Begel, Chosson, and Becquet, chapter 7, this volume).

In the most ancient caching practices known in the Maya and Olmec lowlands, when people were settling in large villages (Early–Middle Preclassic, 1200–400 BC or even earlier; Henderson and Joyce 2001; Inomata and Triadan 2015; Inomata et al. 2015), bundled-buried valuable artifacts were often jade celts. Those specific artifacts were unused tools evoking forest-clearing activities for milpa cultivation, made of precious stone symbolizing fertility (Aoyama et al. 2017; Ortiz and Rodriguez 1999, among others). Celts were also the symbol of thunder, lightning, and rain as aspects of the *k'awiil* divinity, a figure of kingly power (Stuart 2010, 292). The cruciform shape of a number of those early caches confirms the importance of the specific place-making ritual as it created one sacred locus in the world's "horizontal configuration" (Matthews and Garber 2004), where people assembled, settled, and initiated their collective experience. Admittedly, as Trigger noted (1996, commenting on the discussion of materialization by DeMarrais, Castillo, and Earle 1996), such "caches" were invisible in the urban landscape. But the repeated ritual performance of caching jade celts would have stimulated political interactions between acknowledged leaders who probably shared the memory of created ritual stratigraphy. The latter would have been part of the political processes that gave shape to the early sedentary communities through the creation of specific political landscapes. What should be emphasized here is that the materialization involved in those place-making rituals (within sedentary contexts) was tightly related to agriculture (bundling-burying as planting, jade celts, *k'awiil* symbols), implying the creation of a deforested place as a shared, inhabited locale endowed with plant fertility and human fecundity through the implementation of collective but exclusive rites with controlled knowledge addressing non-human entities. It is from this agrarian complex that the role of early Maya rulers would have emerged.

PLACE MAKING AND SACRED MAYA KINGSHIP

Following a suggestion by James Porter, David Stuart (2010, 291) has presented epigraphic arguments in favor of stelae being understood by the Maya "not just as vaguely precious stones, but as large, monumental celts and axes" and as "massive axe[s] or celt[s] piercing the ground" (295). Those erected stones helped create political landscapes and also embodied time units (289). At Middle to Late Preclassic Ceibal (around 400 BC), Inomata (2017) observes that cached jade celts were replaced by cached clusters of small stones or pebbles deposited in ceramics, and he hypothesizes that they referred to the early shaping of the calendar (as a count of days). Buried (invisible) and erected (visible) stones, both sunken into the earth at specific locales, may have come to materialize the divine power Maya kings exerted on space and time according to culturally specific forms and practices in particular period-ending rituals.

The political landscape of those sedentary communities was not only made of buried and erected stones; in fact, a few Classic cities never erected any stela. Yet all of them had pyramids, ball courts, and palaces gradually built around public plazas; and among those edifices was the residence of living and dead rulers with their families. It is well-known that Preclassic and Classic Maya cities show a wide diversity of planning with regard to their monumental epicenters, reflecting complex local histories. An analysis of a sample of site layouts indicates that to be installed with a degree of legitimacy and stability, royal dynasties needed to spatially transform the locus of their domestic cults into the collective focus of the community (Bazy 2010). Whereas most Mayanists admit that many different architectural layouts effectively articulated funerary pyramids with semi-public palaces and public plazas, only a few of them have worked out the constructive sequence of monumental groups of a city interpreted as a dynastic sequence (examples include Bazy and Inomata 2017; Houston et al. 1998). On their spatio-temporal scale, political displacements within the city involved place-making rituals, just as place-making rituals had been required when settling communities created their houses and initial common spaces. In the place-making perspective, the general distribution of ritual cached deposits suggests there was a symbolic equivalence between rituals anchoring the place of the house and those creating the built landscape of public plazas with monumental politico-religious edifices, both reflecting long-term house histories central to house societies (Joyce and Gillespie 2000). Their materialization may have differed in their degree of richness or elaboration, and certainly the implied temporalities also differed from simple farmers to divine rulers, but all place-making rituals shared specific material projections of past/present/future times by settling farmers and rulers seeking legitimacy.

This is the perspective I take to present my specific case study. Of critical importance for Classic Maya dynasties were the practices of anchoring the residence of their dead and living members in one place. As indicated by the symmetrical abandonment rituals carried out during the subsequent period of collapse, the stakes were high in the Maya lowlands with regard to the stability and continuity in residence and collective action at one place. Thus, this required an elaborate set of ritual actions to ensure correct placement in the world and a prosperous future, in much the same way as sowing maize.

RITUAL STRATIGRAPHY OF A MASONRY TEMPLE-HOUSE AT LA JOYANCA, STRUCTURE 6E12SUB

La Joyanca was a medium-size city with 632 structures situated across 1.6 km², with a population of roughly 1,300 to 1,600 inhabitants by AD 800 (Lemonnier 2009). It is located in northwest Petén, Guatemala, 20 km west of El Perú-Waka and 15 km north of Zapote Bobal, both first-rank cities in terms of their numerous inscribed stelae (Arnauld, Breuil-Martinez, and Ponciano Alvarado 2004; Arnauld et al. 2012). Although La Joyanca was arguably a larger settlement than Zapote Bobal, the site had only one inscribed stela,

TABLE 5.1. Radiocarbon assessments of charcoal fragments from Structure 6E12sub (in stratigraphic order, top to bottom)

Carbon Sample ID	Provenience	Interpretation	Years BP	Calendar Date Range and Central Intercept (2 sigma)
VERA-2491	6E-12sub on floor, strata 574-575, charcoal fragment 575	Termination ritual	1210 ± 40	**680–900 cal AD** (AD 740)
GifA 100622	6E-12sub in stucco covering roof comb, charcoal fragment 556	Construction date	1330 ± 70 BP	**603–875 cal AD** (AD 620)
GifA 100620	6E-12sub sub-floor stratum 512, charcoal fragment 512	Construction date	1230 ± 60 BP	**671–950 cal AD** (AD 720)

erected in AD 485. Its population boomed by AD 500–600, largely through immigration (Arnauld et al. 2017).

Its only public locale, the Main Plaza (figures 5.1 and 5.2), was entirely rebuilt after AD 600, with the earliest vaulted building at the site, Structure 6E12sub, located on its west side. Three radiocarbon dates are directly associated with the structure (table 5.1), while ceramics suggest that the construction took place by 600–650, and glyphic elements of the inscription engraved in an inner wall indicate that it was still occupied after 680 (A. Lacadena, personal communication, 2003). In any case, the building was structurally unstable and was likely occupied only briefly. The shortest possible interval for its construction and occupation, based on radiocarbon and other dates, is AD 650–720. By 720 it was carefully infilled with stones and covered by a pyramid supporting a temple, Structure 6E12. As will be shown, 6E12sub "anchored" the new public space, together with superimposed Temple 6E12 to which a collective building, Structure 6E13, was also attached (figure 5.3; Arnauld, Breuil-Martinez, and Ponciano Alvarado 2004).

Commenting on McAnany and Hodder (2009), Barbara Mills (2009, 39) noted that to interpret archaeological deposits in social terms, "one needs to have a strong contextual understanding of the specific historical trajectories of each case study." By the time 6E12sub was being built, the local community was going through the simultaneous processes of urbanizing and installing a new rulership. Of the four inscribed texts so far discovered at La Joyanca, one was within Structure 6E12sub on an inner wall (as mentioned above), one was within superimposed Structure 6E12 on a portable stone altar, and the other

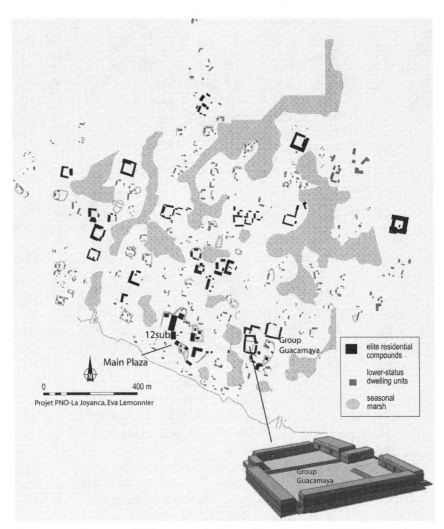

FIGURE 5.1. *Site map of La Joyanca with elite residential compounds (ERC) in black (mostly vaulted structures) and their associated neighborhoods, including clusters of lower-status dwelling units; seasonal marshes or bajos separate neighborhoods. Modified from Arnauld, Breuil-Martinez, and Ponciano Alvarado (2004, 77).*

two are spatially associated with the largest residential compound at La Joyanca, the Guacamaya Group, located 400 m to the east of the Main Plaza (figure 5.2). This compound is where the only stela of the site was found, spatially associated with monolithic altars and a royal burial (Arnauld, Breuil-Martinez,

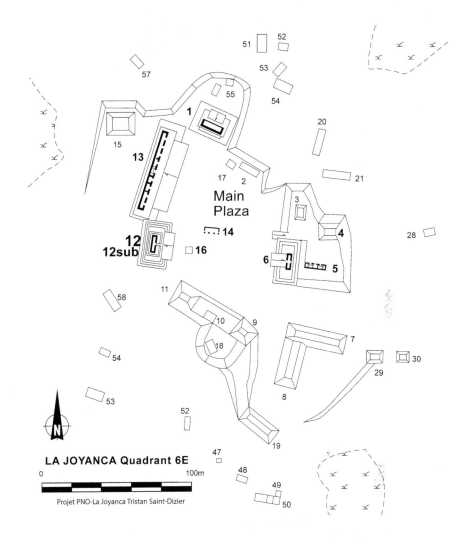

FIGURE 5.2. *Main Plaza of La Joyanca during the Late Classic, AD 600–850.* Courtesy, *Project PNO–La Joyanca.*

and Ponciano Alvarado 2004). On the basis of the distribution of written texts, it can be argued that the social group inhabiting the Guacamaya Group commanded the construction of Structure 6E12sub, of subsequent 6E12, and possibly of the entire new plaza by AD 600–700. Exclusionary knowledge and memory were firm bases for power in ancient Maya cities, as confirmed

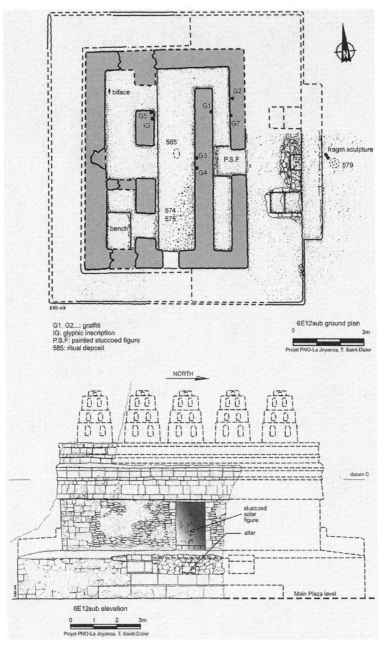

G1, G2...: graffiti
IG: glyphic inscription
P.S.F: painted stuccoed figure
585: ritual deposit

biface

G2

G1

G7

G5
IG

585

G3

P.S.F

G4

574
575

bench

fragm. sculpture

579

6E12sub ground plan

0   3m

Projet PNO-La Joyanca, T. Saint-Dizier

NORTH

datum C

stuccoed
solar
figure

altar

Main Plaza level

6E12sub elevation

0   1   2   3m

Projet PNO-La Joyanca, T. Saint-Dizier

FIGURE 5.3. *La Joyanca Structure 6E12sub, ground plan and elevation. Drawing by Tristan Saint-Dizier, Projet PNO-La Joyanca.*

FIGURE 5.4. *East facade of La Joyanca Structure 6E12sub taken from the Main Plaza.*
Author photo.

by the ritual practice of depositing into the earth visible stelae and invisible caches, some of them with written texts. Another argument for the association of Structure 6E12sub with the Guacamaya Group is its location in the line of sight with the Guacamaya stela-altar-burial complex (Early Classic in date; Arnauld 2004; Bazy 2010). Some sort of a road might have existed between this complex and Structure 6E12sub, as indicated by the absence of structures in the line of sight and the purposeful infilling of a swampy area west of the Guacamaya compound. Structure 6E12sub would have materialized the presence of the Guacamaya social group on the west side of the Main Plaza, while the physical residential compound could not have been displaced. We surmise that it represented the political ambitions of the Guacamaya social house holding sway over the Main Plaza.

Structure 6E12sub (figure 5.3) presents a labyrinthic inner organization with four narrow, dark rooms, religious graffiti, and an engraved inscription on its walls—along with one polychrome-painted, stuccoed, anthropomorphic solar figure modeled on the wall in front of the entrance door (coded PSF on figure 5.3). It displayed an eastern facade (plaza side, figure 5.4) with an anthropomorphic sculpture, modeled-stuccoed decoration (fragments of which were found on the exterior floor), and an altar inserted in its access stairway, still preserving charcoal. Rather than a residence, it might have been a "sacred house" (Valdés 2001, 142) inaugurating the hold of the Guacamaya social

TABLE 5.2. Elements of the ritual stratigraphy of Structure 6E12sub, in stratigraphic order (top to bottom). Strata 579 and 512 were excavated only partially; 512 possibly exists under all parts of the structure; all other features were entirely excavated.

Stratigraphic Position and Timing in Sequence	Layer/Pit Location	Recording Code	Associations	Ritual Gestures (interpreted)
Within inner stucco floor Terminal infilling	Pit in central room, center	Cache 585	33 individuals: small and/or juvenile animals, all aquatic and bird species (analysis by Emery and Thornton 2008); one small piece of jade	Piercing stuccoed floor; depositing animals directly within hole; sealing with three stones, floor left unrepaired
Above inner stucco floor Terminal infilling	Layer in central room, south half	Strata 574-575	Sherds, charcoal, ashes, a few human bones	Carrying domestic midden-hearth, and burial materials; layering directly on stuccoed floor
Below inner floor Initial construction	Pit? in 6E12sub center, −5 cm under floor	(looted cache?)	Large spherical jade bead, blackened with soot from Stratum 512	?? Depositing in unknown context (disturbed; edge of central looter trench)
Below inner floor Initial construction	Layer under most parts of 6E12sub	Stratum 512 (ceramic lots 512, 565, 567)	Black earth (2–14 cm thick), charcoal and soot, many sherds, polychrome sherds, one flint blade	Carrying domestic midden-hearth materials; layering just below the stuccoed floor
Below exterior floor, within layer 579 Initial construction	Pit in central axis, plaza side	Cache 579	In one Aguila Red large bowl covered by a similar inverted bowl, no content (except for one small invertebrate individual, doubtful)	Piercing Stratum 577; depositing a bowl with unknown organic material; covering with an inverted bowl
Below exterior floor Initial construction	Layer below platform, plaza side	Stratum 577	Black earth, small bits of charcoal, many sherds, flint flakes, 1 fragmented mano, no bones	Scouring-carrying domestic midden materials and cultivated soil? layering just below the stuccoed floor

house over the Main Plaza located 400 m distant from its residential compound (figure 5.1). This hypothesis is valid at least during the seventh century, whereas the later construction of residences on the plaza may have canceled the initial pattern.

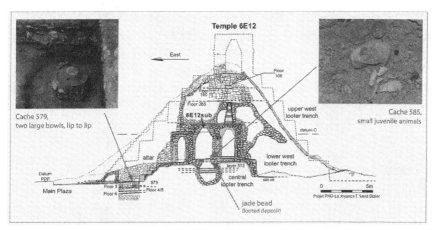

FIGURE 5.5. *East-west section of La Joyanca Structure 6E12. Drawing by Tristan Saint-Dizier, Projet PNO-La Joyanca.*

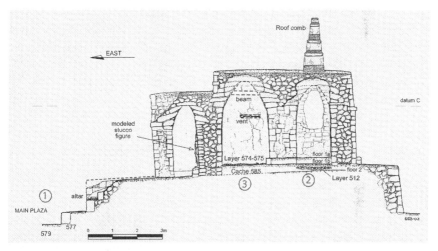

FIGURE 5.6. *East-west section of La Joyanca Structure 6E12sub. Drawing by Tristan Saint-Dizier, Projet PNO-La Joyanca.*

This small building presents a complex ritual stratigraphy (table 5.2). Although the excavation of the deeply looted 6E12sub buried beneath Temple-Pyramid 6E12 was risky and difficult, we were able to determine that at least five ritual deposits were made during its construction and just before its terminal infilling (figures 5.5 and 5.6). Two deposits consist of horizontal layers expanded beneath the exterior and interior stuccoed floors; they date back to the initial construction. A third layer, which partly covered the interior floor, must thus be associated with the terminal infilling. The remaining two deposits were made in pits—that is, they were purposefully buried in the earth: one is associated (contemporaneous) with the aforementioned exterior construction layer, the other with the inner terminal layer. A sixth, hypothetical buried deposit would have been associated with the inner construction layer.

RITUAL STRATIGRAPHY OF STRUCTURE 6E12SUB: TIME AND PLACE MAKING

The first feature to be noted in this stratigraphy is the general structured deposition of repeated pairs associating vertically buried deposits (or caches) with horizontally extended layers (Arnauld et al. 2013; see Joyce and Pollard 2010, 303 on the same duality involving "caches/production of sediments" in research carried out by Pauketat and Alt at the Cahokia site). In other words, specifically produced layers were added on fill layers to directly support the floors, and these specific layers contain intrusive exterior and interior caches (the latter apparently looted); in addition, one specific layer covered the inner floor before infilling the structure with stones, again with an intrusive cache. All caches were cut into layers and floors in the central east-west axis of the structure. This duality of layers and caches is what should help us interpret the entire ritual stratigraphy: "What the concept of depositional practices allows us to do is consider these unusual structured deposits not simply as the residues of rituals, the ceremonial trash of the updated behavioral archaeological framework . . . but as the evidence of a historical sequence of human actions" (Joyce and Pollard 2010, 301).

In the 6E12sub historical sequence, two heuristic levels must be distinguished: first, the level of the usual *chaîne opératoire* articulating domestic construction practices with agrarian practices and second, the more circumstantial creation of a sacred house in a new public plaza and its temporalities. On the first level, both ritual gestures—layering and associated bundling-burying—can be said (1) to prepare the horizontal surface of the earth to be stuccoed and inhabited and (2) to insert into the earth a bundled deposit of specific items. One can interpret these gestures in relation to agriculture—that is, soil preparation, manuring (soil renewing), and sowing—as though the construction of 6E2sub would have been enacted under the cultivation paradigm. In other words, the building of the house, sacred house, or temple would have been thought of as a plant promising fruits, an interpretation that slightly diverges from the one in which buildings are seen as animated beings to be nourished (Harrison-Buck

2004; Vogt 1965). The former interpretation is perhaps more easily understood if one considers the mundane and routinized gestures of infilling a platform and inserting wooden poles when building a simple house made of perishable materials so as to ensure its stability and long-term occupancy (see Pendergast 1988 for the technical importance of fills in Maya architecture). Thus the 6E12sub ritual stratification involves continuity and analogies in gestures and functions with customary construction practices (Brown and Emery 2008; Carlson and Eachus 1977; Monaghan 1996; Vogt 1965). More generally, these place-making rituals that we equate to soil preparation and sowing perhaps also tied the building to a new temporal era, since "sowing, that which is sown" is "a concept that is paired with 'dawning' throughout the text of the *Popol Vuh* as a metaphor for the creation" (Christenson 2003, 51; Mock 1998b).

Ritual layering and piercing burying done before the construction of the exterior and interior floors (resulting in subfloor Strata 577/512 and Cache 579/jade bead) were part of the project of fixing the sacred house, whereas the same gestures done just before infilling its interior space (on floor Strata 574-575/Cache 585) started the operation of its closure/infilling. The latter pertains to a transitional context, since it also initiated the technical foundation of Temple-Pyramid 6E12 to be built on 6E12sub. Both pairs of layers/intrusive deposits are part of the same *chaîne opératoire*, even though the early one can be interpreted as a "dedication" and the later one as a "termination." The perspective of place making through ritual stratigraphy integrates the dedicatory/termination interpretations (see Begel, Chosson, and Becquey, chapter 7, this volume). However, in my case study, the corresponding rituals were embedded in particular historical circumstances (following McAnany and Hodder 2009, 17, "ritual stratigraphy" as part of "social stratigraphy"). This is our second level, that is, the creation of a new public place under the sway of one particular La Joyanca social group—the Guacamaya house (figure 5.1).

Classic Maya caching practices are notably variable in their details on multiple scales, and variation may be explained in terms of particular, local historical sequences. Subfloor Strata 577 and 512 are organic in nature (black earth); on floor Strata 574-575 they are less so, although they contained many charcoal fragments. All three layers contain obvious remains of occupation, with a high density of sherds—some from the same broken recipients (Forné 2006, 315–317), with the addition of a proportion of polychrome sherds in Stratum 512. Strata 577, 512, and 574-575 (all distinct in depth and surface, technically expanded at distinct moments) were each plausibly formed by scouring in situ occupational strata that existed in some residential context away from non-residential 6E12sub—such as domestic middens, hearth ashes, and charcoal—and perhaps from cultivated garden soils or even the remains of feasting events. The material would have been carried into 6E12sub and spread out just below the stuccoed floors. In the case of 6E12sub's historical context as presented above, this material might have originated from the residential compound of the sponsors, the Guacamaya inhabitants (for a case of transported middens in a local historical sequence, see Bazy and Inomata 2017, 90). We were unable to test this idea. It is well-known that the Maya used to incorporate domestic refuse into the fill layers that shaped the house platform (e.g., Arnauld, Dzul Gongora, and Déodat 2010; Pendergast 1988, 1654). Functionally, this practice helped keep exterior spaces clean in cities, but it appears systematic enough even in many unlikely urban contexts to allow us to think that it had some deeper underpinnings. Referring to "ritual rubbish," Joyce and Pollard (2010, 298) propose that "knowledge of their formation and constitution sometimes transformed the currency of middens, such that they became an index of . . . occupational longevity and intergenerational connection—time and group genealogy are worked into the fabric of these structures as much as the materials from which they are composed." The stakes were probably high for mobile farmers with regard to occupational longevity, an achievement that deserved to be communicated to neighbors by means of rubbish accumulations visible in the form of high platforms. The direct association of domestic remains with ancestral persons of the group made them some sort of sacred material to be used in the construction *chaîne opératoire*.

The argument might be explored somewhat further using as an analogy the practice of burying dead inhabitants below the house floor. Although their frequency is unknown, burials in middens have been found at Tikal (Becker 1993, 51–52). Structurally inverse, some burials at Rio Bec have been shown to include a stratification reconstructing forest topsoil (Pereira 2013). More research is needed, yet it seems that evidence exists of an emic, conscious materialization of ancestral inhabitants in middens and associated topsoil. Under 6E12sub, the Stratum 512 ceramic lots are chronologically mixed, with an abnormal quantity of old (Early Classic) types and modes considering our radiocarbon assessment for the same Stratum 512 (table 5.1; Forné 2006, 285). Thus expanding those layers gave the builders of 6E12sub the ritualized opportunity to index a previous occupation, address ancestors, materialize their presence, and thus establish in this locale a physical house as well as a social house, whose members had indeed been living for a long period of time in a distinct locale—the Guacamaya compound.

In this manner, continuity of occupational and generational times was materially expressed and anchored at this place, on the west side of the Main

Plaza where 6E12sub was being built and where in fact there was discontinuity, either spatial discontinuity due to the Main Plaza–Guacamaya compound distance or temporal/social discontinuity in case an earlier structure had existed beneath 6E12sub (lower floors visible on figure 5.6, which we briefly observed in looter holes). Ritual layering created continuity "not necessarily because of continuous occupation, but because of continuities in the transmission of practices and in the memory work of people connected through their performances and practices" (Mills 2009, 39). Autochthonous longevity materialized by an old house was crucial for a social group seeking dynastic stability and legitimacy by "creating an earth-bound genealogy" (McAnany and Hodder 2009, 13)—that is, historical depth and attachment to place.

The termination layer (on floor Strata 574-575) may have had somewhat distinct qualities (less organic earth matrix, a few human bones). It can be positively compared to the widely expanded middens found on patio floors and on partially ruined residences in the Guacamaya compound (Forné 2005).[1] Dated to the Terminal Classic (AD 850–1050), those on-floor middens—which also include human bones—are the remains of termination rituals carried out within the residential compound itself, of which they indexed previous occupations, announced abandonment, and, finally, closed the occupation time (Sion and Arnauld 2015).[2] In Structure 6E12sub, in addition to the same meanings, termination Strata 574-575 prepared the construction of superimposed Structure 6E12 and is thus equivalent to the earlier construction (Strata 512 and 577; compare Newman 2018).

However, Cache 579, which refers to the construction, and Cache 585, which refers to the termination of Structure 6E12sub, differ in their contents. Both pitted deposits contained the same types of small or juvenile animals, but according to the analysis by Emery and Thornton (2008), thirty-three individuals were bundled in Cache 585, whereas only one, probably intrusive (animal?) individual was present in Cache 579, which otherwise had no preserved content; the former pertain only to non-hunted, non-edible bird and water animals of "unusual" species.[3] Those species by themselves perhaps engaged the builders of 6E12 in human and non-human temporalities, animacies, and materialities; and some concept of world miniaturization may also have been involved. But for the sake of my historical argument, I would only emphasize the extraordinary quantity of individuals in Cache 585, interpreted as materializing through multiplicity a desired or anticipated reproductive abundance for the future 6E12 building. This appears consistent with the function of the superimposed Temple-Pyramid 6E12, a much larger and politically more important edifice than 6E12sub for the collective,

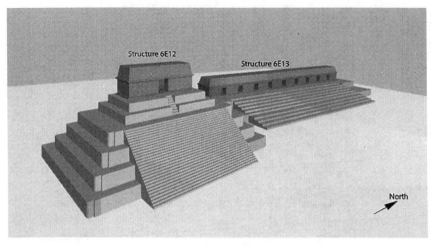

FIGURE 5.7. *Reconstruction of the west side of the Main Plaza, after "entombment" of Structure 6E12sub under Temple-Pyramid 6E12 by AD 750. Drawing by Tristan Saint-Dizier, Projet PNO-La Joyanca.*

communitarian entity. Cache 585 also contained jade, a symbol of fertility and renewal, enhancing the materialization of multiplicity, diversity, and youth through the many buried small animals (for a similar bundled-buried deposit of young animals, although less abundant, see Masson 2004).[4] The promised fruits may have been thought of as future members of the royal house or as the entire political community.

On the Main Plaza, Structure 6E12sub was then carefully filled in without destroying any of its elements, not even its roof *crestería* (figure 5.6). It was actually "entombed" (McAnany and Hodder 2009, 12; figure 5.3). On the 12-m-high pyramid that covered it, the masonry temple was built; stratigraphically contemporaneous, a 52-m-long building of the long hall type (Arnauld 2001) was built abutting the short northern facade of Temple-Pyramid 6E12 to form the west side of the Main Plaza. Both edifices, along with a second pyramid-temple constructed on the east side of the Main Plaza (figure 5.7), formed a political apparatus and landscape of great relevance for the La Joyanca community from AD 720 to perhaps 1050. Having been ritually stratified, the old, now buried sacred house, Structure 6E12sub, ensured the social and cosmic anchoring of the monumental complex, creating the political place in a long-term collective temporality.

CONCLUSION

In this chapter I argue that among the ancient Maya, infilling platforms, either for simple domestic use or for monumental landscaping, required technical and ritual gestures deeply entangled in a series of repeated operations that formed the construction *chaîne opératoire*, with variable stratifications depending on the "historical sequence" (after Hodder 2007) of which it was a part. In the case of La Joyanca Structures 6E12sub and 6E12, the historical sequence involved the creation by a local social group (arguably associated with the Guacamaya compound) of a dynastic place on the public, collective plaza of the local community. Spatial discontinuity with the residential compound of this social group entailed efforts to ensure continuity at the place where the public structures were to be built. Those efforts translated into a ritual stratigraphy that included, among other elements, the making, carrying, and laying of fill strata that originated from distinct occupational contexts and the bundling-burying of an abundance and diversity of young animals. These gestures were constitutive of a long sequence of creation, destruction, and re-creation synchronizing human activities with time dimensions of the world—in that case, generational time of one particular social group with collective times of the community—allowing human groups to settle their residence, establish their (dynastic) longevity, and reproduce themselves: in sum, their "sowing-dawning" according to the agrarian metaphor.

The contribution of the amplified stratigraphic approach (Joyce and Pollard 2010; McAnany and Hodder 2009) is also to stress the culturally peculiar treatment the ancient Maya builders gave to the surface of the earth. First, they maintained clean spaces around their house platforms in urban environments, in strong contrast to Amazonian urban sites where mounds materialize as in situ primary middens (*terra preta*) of domestic occupations (e.g., Browne Ribeiro et al. 2016; Walker 2012; see Joyce and Pollard 2010, 298 on middens). They also repaired the surface damaged by constructive actions (e.g., deep quarry holes under the Main Plaza stuccoed floor close to Structure 6E12), ritually making and expanding layers that by their nature and content engaged ancestors, temporalities, and animacies. "Repairing the earth surface" (see Arnauld and Saint Dizier 2016; Brown and Emery 2008, 329–330; Carlson and Eachus 1977) may not have differed much from preparing soils for cultivation through ritual compensation to the earth in a "settlement" reached with supranatural entities (Vapnarsky and Le Guen 2011). Settling, sedentarizing, memorializing, and using land appear to be deeply intertwined Maya concepts that engaged human and non-human entities through ritual action.

We are still left with the task of furthering the study of relationships between this web of concepts, focused on sedentism as autochthony, and sacred Maya kingship, in which the role of the king as a "tenderer of times" has been recently emphasized by epigrapher David Stuart (2011, 262, 2015). Autochthony and ancestry were pivotal qualities of sacred kingship, yet epigraphic evidence is now mounting in favor of some royal dynasties having been mobile and intrusive in many cities. What were the effects of those particular historical trajectories on Classic Maya societies, and how can we retrieve them archaeologically? Ritual materialization of times and spatial distances may be one important approach.

Acknowledgments. I am indebted to Clarissa Cagnato for revising and improving my English writing.

NOTES

1. When excavated, those middens were considered the remains of a late occupation by squatters (Breuil-Martinez et al. 2003), an interpretation now largely dismissed (e.g., Chase and Chase 2004; Stanton, Brown, and Pagliaro 2008).

2. It is tempting to contrast the inclusion of human bones in those termination ritual layers (see Barrientos et al. 2015) in symmetry with the insertion of burials within the house platform during occupation, as if abandoning the house required that the entire conceptual structure be overturned, with the bones then on the surface.

3. Publication of this analysis is in progress.

4. Except for a large spherical jade bead the looters did not find, present interpretations cannot take into account the exact content of the hypothetical central inner deposit dating to the construction of 6E12sub (see table 5.1, second line).

6

Altars are a key component of public rituals of a political nature carried out by the ancient Maya of the Classic Period. Recorded from the Middle Preclassic in both the highlands and the lowlands, altars, either free-standing or with their associated stelae, express for the archaeologist and probably for the Classic Maya themselves a kind of materialization of public rituals linked to power (mostly royal). The repeated dedication of these monuments in cycles of ten or twenty years over periods of more than six centuries symbolizes and materializes the passage of time. By extension, through these ritualized and cyclical dedications marking important period endings and their portraiture on these long-lived stone monuments, the Maya kings slowly became "lords" of time (Stuart 1996, 167).

Altars were the theater for a series of rituals, probably organized in complex sequences to permit the sacralization of a specific place (place making) or a period of time. It is difficult today for archaeologists to reconstitute the complete sequence of actions, as most of these ephemeral acts (for instance, dancing, chanting, voicing incantations, and sacrificing) did not leave material and identifiable traces in the associated contexts. (For the importance of tone, the rhythm of the voice, and gestures in ritual practices, see Vapnarsky, chapter 4, this volume; see also Le Guen 2011.) Thanks to iconographic and epigraphic studies, these practices, mostly immaterial in nature (e.g., dedication acts, binding of the monuments, sacrifices), can be tracked

The Role of Altars in Maya Public Rituals of the Early Classic Period

Analysis and Contexts of the Associated Deposits

Philippe Nondédéo,
Johann Begel,
Julien Hiquet,
Julie Patrois, Isaac
Barrientos, and M. Luisa
Vázquez de Ágredos
Pascual

https://doi.org/10.5876/9781646422395.c006

in part, while archaeology can recover another range of material elements that constitute the "traces" of some of these actions—complementing in a sense the complex nature of these rituals (Joyce 2015a, 2015b). These physical remains or sometimes material residues whose nature is hard to decipher materialize some practices carried out during the ritual events, allowing us to trace a reduced part of the performance (Johnson 2018b; Joyce and Johnson, chapter 1, this volume). They also suggest the intricate perceptual or multisensorial nature of rituals, through the combination of different matter used as well as of colors and scents. The spatial distribution and organization of all these components, active and agential, sometimes implies a sequential form for these ritual actions, even a certain cyclicity if repeated phenomena, choices, or practices are observed in similar and contemporaneous contexts.

In this chapter, we focus on the material deposits—most of them composed of human remains—found associated with the altars from the site of Naachtun, Guatemala, in order to analyze their relationship first, with the building at the foot of which they are placed and second, with temporalities as the dedication acts form part of a longer sequence of actions that implies the procurement of the artifacts, here the bones, necessary for the ritualization processes. Temporality through the sequence of actions is thus central to tracing, step by step, the order of performances that link altars and deposits. Moreover, the concept of temporality is fundamental in the sense that these rituals seem to correspond, as we shall see, to a tradition specific to the Early Classic Period and are diffused in a restricted area. Two case studies of two similar contexts of deposits linked with stone (or masonry) altars are analyzed, showing a similar and repetitive ritual pattern. These two examples of altars, closely linked with monumental buildings and architectural complexes (which recalls the idea of proximity and axiality: see Hull 2006, 44), illustrate the concept of "structured deposition" (see Arnauld, chapter 5, this volume; Joyce and Pollard 2010): that is, a certain structuring in the deposits placed beneath the altars and a certain sequence of actions in their arrangement, providing some clues about the meaning of these rituals.

MORPHOLOGY AND THE ROLE OF ALTARS

In lowland Maya civilization, altars are morphologically classified in four types. Plain altars can consist of monolithic stone (circular, concave, rectangular, or quadrangular) or masonry (circular) covered by a layer of stucco. Sculpted altars are circular monoliths with carved iconographic motifs or inscriptions, usually on the tops and sides. Some examples can be observed at Tikal Altars 8, 9, and 10 (Jones and Satterthwaite 1982) and Tonina M.149 and M.165 (Graham and Von Euw 1992). The carved motifs and inscriptions are related to political issues and to the sacrifice of captives, as well as to calendrical themes of celebration of a period ending (Stuart 1998). In the Puuc area, carved altars have a truncated conical shape (see the altars of Kabah and Uxmal in Pollock 1980), and in the Petén they are mostly circular or quatrefoil. There are also altars that are true sculptures in the round, as they represent tri-dimensional fantastic heads or skulls, such as Copan Altar CPN8 (Schele and Mathews 1998). At Quirigua, these are called "zoomorphs." They do not depict specific animals but instead fantastical creatures (Maudslay 1889–1902; Stone 1983). Finally, there are composite altars formed by the association of a flat stone (quadrangular or circular) placed horizontally on vertical supports, such as Altar 4 of Piedras Negras supported by four fantastic heads (Maler 1901).

These four types of altars do not seem to present differences at a functional level or in terms of ritual practices. If we judge by the iconographic documen-tation present on polychrome vessels, they almost always appear inside scenes related to the theme of human sacrifice and cardiectomy, or heart extraction (for example, K718, K1377, K928), or more occasionally to decapitation (K5112, K8719).[1] Victims rest directly on the altar, their bodies limp and lifeless, limbs hanging down over the sides of the monument (K8351). They represent the moment of the sacrificial act itself. The images stress this particular moment and do not give information about what precedes the ritual or what happens after it. In these scenes, the shape of the altar does not seem to matter; nei-ther does whether it is decorated. On the other hand, the almost systematic association of altars with stelae, at the foot of which they are placed, prevails in these images. While the prehispanic iconography on vessels emphasizes images of sacrifices on altars, it does not illustrate more everyday actions such as those observed today that consist of depositing food offerings (tamales), flowers, or plants on such ritual supports (Hanks 1990, 2013).

Regarding the role of these altars, some non-negligible differences can be identified in spatial terms and in terms of association with monuments and buildings that could imply distinctions among them. Three types of associa-tions of altars seem to coexist in the same Maya site, each one perhaps with a slightly different role according to its association.

First, the stela-altar pair, or complex, is very widespread in Classic Maya society, and the altar can serve as a receptacle for offerings (Stuart 1996, 149). In other cases, it may represent a theater for the sacrifice of captives in a cult dedicated to the royal king, whose image is portrayed in the accompanying stela. Finally, some were used to make offerings (scattering ritual) related to period endings as part of a *k'altuun* ritual, or "stone-binding ritual" (Stuart 1996, 155). By wrapping or bundling both the stela and the altar (in the same way as the sacred bundles) with sacred paper or clothing, this ritual served to protect the divine essence of the king represented in the stela. As a calendar ritual, it also served to link the stela and altar with time (the "seating" of the monument), as it records the *k'altuun* endings (periods of twenty years to come), and thus to render the image and essence of the king timeless (Houston, Stuart, and Taube 2006, 81–86; Stuart 1996). In the stela-altar complex, the shape of the altar used for the execution of these rituals was not as important.

Second, free-standing altars are located toward the center of a public space such as a plaza or sometimes a courtyard, as in the Puuc area. They show a clear association with a defined and probably sacred public space or with a particular social group rather than with a specific person. Generally plain, this type of monument has not yet been studied by scholars to identify a specific role, although several, following Stuart (1996), consider that they also mark a period ending. Examples are found in Naranjo, Copan, Quirigua, Tikal, and Uxul and in sites of the Puuc area such as Sayil, Xkipché, Oxkintok, and Kabah, where they are very frequent (Baudez 1994; Jones and Satterthwaite 1982; Pollock 1980; Stone 1983).

Finally, there are free-standing altars closely linked to architecture and placed at the foot of pyramidal buildings, platforms, and ritual or funerary complexes. This type of altar, usually plain, at the base of a monumental staircase materializes the central and main axis of a construction, usually the east-west axis but sometimes the north-south axis. Many of the rituals performed there are in relation to the adjacent building, often a building linked to power. Little attention has been given to this type of monument to date, although examples are found in Copan, Altar de Sacrificios, Uaxactun, and Yaxchilan and in sites of the Puuc area such as Labna and Kabah.

In archaeology, the materiality of the rituals performed in relation to altars, or rather the "ritualization" of these monuments, can sometimes be expressed by the presence of deposits placed and buried under the altar. Although this is a rather rare practice, it is common to find beneath the stelae large lithic deposits composed of eccentrics, blades, and flakes of flint and obsidian, as well as greenstone (Coe 1990; Weiss-Krejci 2010). In Tikal, for example, almost all of the systematically excavated altars had an associated deposit, with the exception of Altar 9, Altar 6C-XI, and some masonry altars of residential groups of PP4 type (that is, with a low platform altar in the center of the residential group; Becker 2003, 262–264; Berlin 1951; Laporte and Iglesias Ponce de Léon 2000). In some places, when there are deposits under altars, they are mostly incised flint objects accompanied by vessels, as is the case of La Milpa under a free-standing altar located in the center of Plaza B (Houk and Zaro 2010, 99). Similarly, at Altar de Sacrificios, five deposits (Deposits 3, 5, 6, 7, and 48) were found under altars, all containing, among other materials, eccentrics and flint and obsidian blades (Smith 1972). The presence of so many lithic elements in the deposits associated with stelae and altars, particularly flint and obsidian, is probably due to the fact that these materials are symbolically and epigraphically related to the practice of sacrifice. *Took'*, the word for flint, also means "bloody sacrifice," while obsidian, *ch'ahb*, is related to the instrument of self-sacrifice (Stone and Zender 2011). To reinforce this idea, a stingray spine, the tool *par excellence* for self-sacrifice, is occasionally found in these deposits, as is the case in Deposit 48 of Altar de Sacrificios (Smith 1972, 207–208).

As discussed below, the physical remains and traces left by these dedication rituals are very few compared with the richness and complexity of the sequence of actions performed during these rituals. As carefully detailed by Looper (2009, 23–25), the stone-binding ritual for a period ending was generally a moment of gathering of allied kings and the pretext for dance performances by the kings themselves. He also mentioned that the dance performances were different at every *k'atun* ending according to the events commemorated, which were sometimes military victories (24–26). This example illustrates all of the ephemeral acts performed during these rituals for which we lack traces. But we could also have mentioned music, praying, and censing among the many other actions that left no material evidence for archaeology.

In this chapter, we turn our attention to the stone altars linked to architecture, without association with stelae, and to the material deposits found buried under these monuments. The two case studies come from the Early Classic Period and from the site of Naachtun, and the data gathered resulted from our 2017 investigations. This chapter is an attempt to understand ritual processes over time and through the scope of both materiality and material traces.

CASE STUDY: ALTAR DEPOSITS AT NAACHTUN

Naachtun was a large regional capital of northern Petén, occupied mostly during the Classic Period (150–950/1000 CE). It was the seat of the famous Bat dynasty, K'uhul Suutz' Ajaw, one of the three great dynasties of the region, along with the Kanu'l dynasty of Dzibanche-Calakmul and that of Tikal (Nondédéo, Lacadena, and Cases Martín 2019). The site is composed of three monumental groups of structures, labeled A, B, and C, that occupy around 33 ha and serve as the political-administrative epicenter of the city

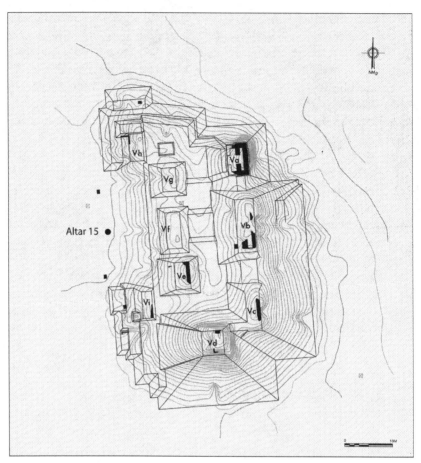

FIGURE 6.1. *Plan of Naachtun's Acropolis V*

with its wide plazas, temples, palaces, funerary acropolis, and political-ritual complexes (including an E-Group assemblage). A widespread residential area of more than 170 ha where we were able to register more than 603 structures distributed in patio groups extends around the epicenter (Hiquet 2020). The development of the site proceeded from the older western sector toward the more recent sectors to the east, thus materializing the political history of the city—formed by several dynastic ruptures, each corresponding to a re-foundation of the city—and of its political center through the construction, always further to the east, of new plazas accompanied by a series of palatial elite compounds for the royal court (Nondédéo 2016; Nondédéo et al. 2021).

The two public and ritual-ceremonial components that interest us here are dated to the Early Classic Period and belong to Group C and Group A. Their functions are very different in nature since the first, Structure V in Group C, corresponds to a royal funerary acropolis where most of Naachtun's rulers from this period were buried. It constitutes a kind of imitation at a lower scale of the model of the North Acropolis of Tikal (Coe 1990; Loten 2003), a city with which Naachtun maintained political, economic, and most likely strong matrimonial ties (Nondédéo, Lacadena, and Garay 2018; Nondédéo et al. 2016). The second case, roughly contemporary or perhaps slightly earlier, comes from Naachtun's E-Group in the northern part of Group A, whose main plaza concentrates most of the political-ritual components such as a ball court and a reservoir where several rituals resulting in deposits were carried out over the long term. E-Group assemblages are one of the oldest types of public complexes built by the Maya, dedicated to agrarian cycles through the observation of the sky and, more generally, to time and the affirmation of reestablished power at the end of each twenty-year period (Aimers and Rice 2006; Andrieu et al. 2017; Freidel et al. 2017). This perhaps explains the concentration of nine stelae and four altars in this political-ritual area, some of them dedicated when the complex was already abandoned.

ACROPOLIS V

The investigation of looters' trenches that penetrated deep into the basal platform of Acropolis V, together with intensive excavations that began in 2017, allowed us to better understand the sequence of construction and the development of this royal funerary complex. Running north-south, the monumental platform measures 65 m × 40 m and from 3.5 m to 6 m high (figure 6.1). It has its main and central axis running east-west materialized by Temples V-b and V-f. It is a succession of funerary platforms and low substructures that were covered by a large final monumental platform on which rest two north-south rows of funerary temples (Temples V-a-c to the east and V-e-g to the west). From the excavations of 2017–2018, we know that Structures V-b and V-c were among the first built, while the other temples of the western row, as well as Structures V-a, V-i, and V-h, were organized around them later. The main facade of the complex faces west by means of three individual staircases flanked by stuccoed masks, which give access to the three central temples (Structures V-e, V-f, and V-g). At the foot of Structure V-f, a limestone monolithic altar was found when looking for the base and center of the access stairway to Structure V-f on the primary axis of the acropolis (Nondédéo, Begel, and Rodas 2018).

This monument, Altar 15, irregular and roughly circular, measures 1.2 m in diameter by 28 cm in thickness (figure 6.2). Excavations carried out at the foot of the altar by Johann Begel and Philippe Nondédéo provided an interesting sequence of structured deposition (Begel and Barrientos 2018). The altar was not set on one of the four stuccoed plaza floors that were identified in all the test pits conducted at the foot of the west and north facades of the acropolis. These four floors encompass the entire sequence of construction and remodeling of the plaza that extends to the west of the complex. They cover much of the Early Classic Period—that is, roughly 400 years. In contrast, below the altar was a single homogeneous and very compact fill, without any existing floor or subdivisions identified up to the natural bedrock, 44 cm below. The altar rested on this compact fill on its west, north, and east sides while on the south side there was a stone support consisting of a well-sculpted sphere with a flat top. These first stratigraphic data indicate that this central sector of the acropolis, at the base of the central staircase where the altar is located, was subject to special treatment—perhaps somewhat late in the history of the funerary complex—that removed all existing floors. Structure V-f, at the foot of which Altar 15 is located, was originally built during the Early Classic (Balam II 300–400/420 CE), as indicated by the fill associated with the base of the staircase (Nondédéo, Begel, and Rodas 2018). The destruction of the earlier plaza floors in this specific area is probably due to the installation of the altar and its associated deposits as part of a first step in the ritual place-making process.

In front of the altar, on its west side, we observed an entire sequence of six deposits located at different depths, from bedrock to the level of the altar. These concentrations of material show different patterns, and almost all are composed of basal flange polychrome vessels, stacked one on top of another or placed lip to lip regardless of whether they have preserved offerings or residue inside. In some cases, however, instead of dishes we found fragments of bowls, jars, or tripod cylindrical vessels. Given the degree of destruction, erosion, and the state of fragmentation of all these vessels due to the compaction of the fill, it was not always possible to identify the potential contents of these ceramics. All are dated from the intermediate phase of the Early Classic Period (Balam II 300–400/420 CE) and are contemporaneous with the occupation of Structure V-f.

Two levels or two stages in the deposition practices were observed. The three lower deposits (39, 34, and 42) were placed directly on bedrock (including Deposit 39, partly excavated into the bedrock) or at a short distance from it. The top three (38, 40, and 41) were located just below the base of the altar,

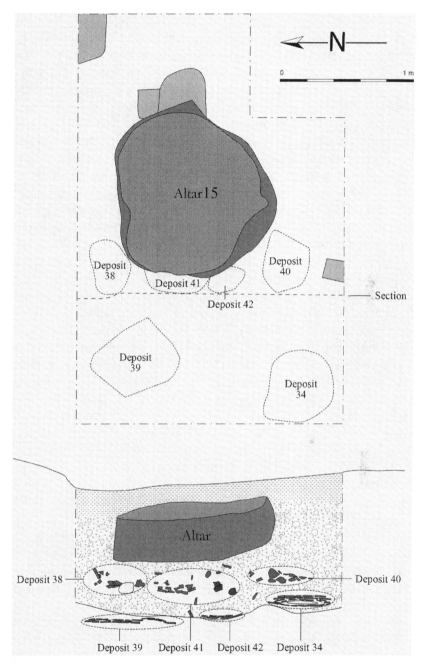

FIGURE 6.2. *Naachtun Altar 15 and associated deposits*

about 20 cm above the others. Among the lower deposits, Deposit 34, southwest of the altar, deserves special mention. It consisted of two plates placed facedown, one on top of the other, on a third placed faceup. The remains of a severely damaged complete skull of an adult individual were located inside the plates arranged lip to lip, while nine additional teeth of another adult (mainly molars) were found outside (Barrientos 2018, 260). Further north, Deposit 39 is composed of two concentrations of artifacts: one to the south with two overlapping vessels, upside down, covering an unidentified organic residue; to the north, two plates arranged lip to lip were associated with two obsidian flakes. The physical-chemical characterization of the organic residues in Deposit 39 suggests that they are a triterpene-type resin, consequently aromatic. The precise identification of this resin is in progress in the laboratories, but undoubtedly its presence in this ritual context is not accidental due to the importance and the sacred character fragrances had for the ancient Maya.[2]

Among the deposits of the upper level, Deposit 38—placed at the foot (northwest) of the altar—consists of two plates, faceup and overlapped, covered by a third. Between the two vessels that were faceup, seven un-erupted teeth (molars and premolars with a canine) belonging to an infant (five to seven years) were collected, apparently without association with other bones (Barrientos 2018, 260). Finally, Deposit 41, the only one in axial position, which extends partially below the altar, is the sole deposit that contained a certain diversity of materials. It probably consisted of an overlapping plate and bowl, both upside down, covering a plate placed faceup. To the south of that first assemblage of artifacts, the remains of an incomplete tripod cylindrical vessel were found. Associated with these containers but with an uncertain original position were an incomplete worked jade plaque—possibly a quatrefoil pendant with an incised curved motif in its center—another jade ornament, a shell ornament, and a fragment of *Spondylus* shell in addition to micro-flakes of flint, obsidian, and greenstone.

While the remains present in these deposits clearly evoke sacrifice through the presence of flint and obsidian, axial Deposit 41, the most symbolically elaborated and the only one with a key central position in relation to the altar, also evokes other themes such as the fertility fostered by rituals through jade (its color and its preciousness evoke water, life, and fertility), while the shells are related to the watery underworld. The quatrefoil design evokes the portal between the terrestrial world and the underworld, in particular the transmission of the benefits of rituals from one world to another, similar to the role of altars (see Guernsey 2010; Stone 1995; Stuart 1987 for the quatrefoil design as a cave and the mouth of the Cauac Monster). It could be a material manifestation of concepts such as centrality and axiality, which in funerary contexts linked with buildings favored the communication between worlds—the axial position acting as a portal, a pathway for the souls (Hull 2006).

The presence of aromatic resins can be explained by the great ritual and symbolic value the Maya assigned to scents and fragrances, as seen in iconography (Vázquez de Ágredos Pascual and Vidal Lorenzo 2017; Vázquez de Ágredos Pascual, Vidal Lorenzo, and Horcajada Campos 2018), especially that of the Classic Period (the Maya gods, for example, appear wrapped in the scent of flowers and other perfumes, mostly from resins). Pine and copal resins recently identified as part of the funerary shrouds of Maya kings and queens are representative of this (Vázquez de Ágredos Pascual 2018; Vázquez de Ágredos Pascual, Tiesler, and Romano Pacheco 2015; Vázquez de Ágredos Pascual, Vidal Lorenzo, and Horcajada Campos 2018). However, it is still difficult for us to explain the presence of skulls and human teeth in such deposits, including un-erupted teeth. Are they from sacrificed victims or carefully selected with soft tissues and dismembered dead? This selection of individuals—sometimes young, sometimes adult—and the mortuary practices associated with this altar illustrate a complex ritual unfortunately without known equivalent in the Maya area. If the individuals were decapitated, we would have a possible evocation of fertility and rebirth, as others have noticed (*inter alia*, Becker 2009, 25), by an allusion to a famous scene in the Popol Vuh where, in the underworld, the decapitated skull of the God Hun Hunahpu manages to fertilize a princess with his saliva and give rise to his sons, the Hero Twins (Chase and Chase 1994, 57; Martin 2006, 163–165). But clearly, in this context there is no evidence in human remains to attest to any decapitation event.

To consider the sequence of ritual actions in relation to this altar, it must be remembered that this area had been subject to extreme manipulation through, first, the removal of all existing floors of the plaza; second, the placement of an initial series of deposits on top of the bedrock; third, the positioning of the upper deposits after a compact fill of 20 cm thick was laid; and fourth, the setting of the altar itself, which partially covers Deposit 41. At this level of analysis, it is still difficult to determine whether the altar was placed before or after the last series of deposits. Axial Deposit 41 is the only one to be partly overlapped by the altar. However, in the absence of pit and floor delimitations, it is impossible to determine if it was placed before the altar was or if it was subsequently intruded in the compact and homogeneous fill. Whatever the sequence, both the altar and the deposits emphasize the central axis of this symbolically and politically important building and show their close relationship with it. Ritualization in this place used specific matter linked to the

Figure 6.3. *Naachtun Deposit 33*

underworld and to concepts such as sacrifice and fertility, while organic matter refers to sensorial effects that, along with the visual effect of the skulls, could have impacted the participants in and observers of this important ritual event.

Another similar deposit, Deposit 33, can help clarify practices observed in relation to Altar 15 (figure 6.3). It is also associated with this same Temple V-f and was found on the northern edge of the same staircase. It was located at the corner between the staircase and an earlier basal platform whose painted orange wall, in the form of a *talud* (later covered by a new version of the basal platform), runs along the west facade. There, under the floor of the earlier basal platform, this corner deposit is composed of a circular pit in which two basal flange polychrome vessels were placed lip to lip (Nondédéo, Begel, and Rodas 2018). Inside, the complete skull of an adult individual was found (Barrientos 2018). The pit was sealed not by a stucco patch but by an 84-cm-thick construction fill of a new stucco floor that covered the final stage of the basal platform. The selected individual, with artificial cranial modification and with dental inlay of jade and pyrite on three of his or her upper incisors, is a person of high social status who may have played a role of guardian of the temple rather than of a sacrificed individual. The bio-anthropological analysis of the first two cervical vertebrae, still in situ, indicates that the skull retained its tissues or ligaments and clearly rules out any intentional death by cranial trauma

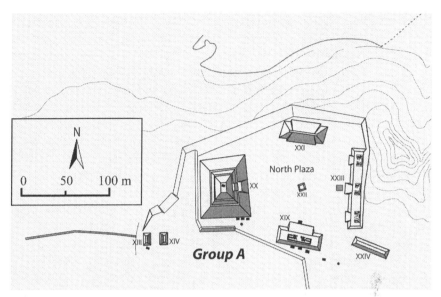

FIGURE 6.4. *Naachtun's E-Group*

resulting from decapitation or intentional dismemberment. No cut marks was observed on the vertebrae, the skull, or the back of the jaw. It is possible, therefore, to interpret this as a postmortem recovery of the skull in an advanced state of decomposition but still with soft tissues and without the need to dismember it. The perfectly preserved dentition (without occlusal wear) allows us to identify this as a young adult. This example of a corner deposit, which perhaps had another symmetrical equivalent on the unexcavated south side of the staircase, is the case that most closely approximates that of the deposits with skulls below Altar 15 of the acropolis. This ritual event with a strong visual impact was intended to sacralize the huge architectural transformation of the west facade of the acropolis. Stratigraphically, it precedes the installation of Altar 15 and its associated deposits and may have inspired the use of skulls in the major rituals of this funerary space.

THE E-GROUP

Another case that is particularly interesting and comparable to the previous one, since it also dates from the Early Classic Period, comes from Structure XXIIIb of Naachtun's E-Group (figure 6.4). This E-Group assemblage consists of a 33-m-high pyramid, Structure XX—which borders a wide plaza to the west—and an elongated supporting platform to the east. More than 83 m long by 20 m wide and 5 m high, this eastern platform, Structure XXIII, is topped by three temples that reach 12 m high from the plaza level: two at its north and south ends and one in the center. Finally, to the north and south, enclosing the plaza, there are two monumental buildings (probably temples because of the narrowness of their rooms); in the center of the public space there is a quadrangular platform altar. These buildings form an E-Group assemblage initiated in the Balam I phase (150–300 CE) of the Early Classic, occupied throughout this period and abandoned toward the beginning of the Late Classic Period. This political and ritual space was reused later, at the end of this period, for the raising of stelae until the last moments of kingship on the site—around 760 CE, as indicated by the latest inscription known from Naachtun, on Stela 10 (Nondédéo et al. 2021).

Structure XXIIIb, which occupies the center of the supporting eastern platform, is also of interest. It is a temple of three successive rooms accessible by a staircase leading to the platform. At the foot of the staircase, excavations carried out by Julien Hiquet (2018, 2020) located a series of constructions and deposits designed to emphasize the central axis of the whole platform. Among these features is a circular masonry altar, Altar 14, perfectly round and finely stuccoed. This plain altar is in a perfect state of conservation, as it was incorporated into the 0.45-m-thick lime-based backfill of a later platform that covered the first steps of the staircase. The altar is slightly displaced toward the north in relation to the very center of the building.

The stratigraphic sequence indicates the presence of two initial low and quadrangular sub-platforms dated from the beginning of the Early Classic (Balam I). They were in the center of what will later be the eastern platform. When constructing the latter topped by the central building, the two previous sub-platforms were covered by the stucco floor of the plaza, which abutted the stairway of the temple. When placing this floor, a ritual deposit (Deposit 45) was installed (completely hidden and sealed by the floor) at the base of the lower step of the staircase. It marks the transverse axis of Temple XXIIIb (figure 6.5). This Deposit 45, interpreted as a dedication deposit for this temple, consists of two flaring monochrome vessels placed lip to lip, containing a reddish pigment and four miniature artifacts: a disk of dark green stone, a tubular jade bead, a spondylus shell bead, and a finely incised anthropomorphic jade figure of the "Charlie Chaplin" type (Johnson 2018a; Lomitola 2012; Moholy-Nagy and Coe 2008). The red pigment is a ferric-based red earth (Fe) rich in manganese (Mn) that is most likely of local origin, since it was also found in Deposits 34 and 39 of the acropolis.

FIGURE 6.5. *Naachtun Deposit 45*

As a stratified deposit, the two containers were covered by a layer of around thirty-five small stones of varying shape—some of them perfectly spherical, others thick discs or squares, and others of more irregular and amorphous shape. The fist-sized stones, embedded in fine sediment, were covered by a limestone disk 30 cm in diameter by 12 cm in thickness that sealed the successive layers. Primarily in light gray limestone, two of the spheres were made of flint and appeared red and yellow. Together with a white and a blackish burned limestone fragments, these four stones, deposited along the north-south and east-west axes, recall the colors of the Maya cosmogram (Houston et al. 2009, 27–28). In this case, the colors do not match the usually accepted cardinal points, except for the east being red. This deposit is reminiscent of another similar context, funerary in nature, from the end of the Late Preclassic–Early Classic Period: Tomb 91B-1 of Las Ruinas del Arenal, Belize, where a cist was dug in the lower part of the staircase of Group A, Structure I. At the individual's head and feet were two pairs of vessels set lip to lip, both north and south of the burial, that express the same idea with deposits that allude to the cosmogram. The north deposit included five "Charlie Chaplin"–type figures made of red, white, black, and yellow materials and placed in a quincunx pattern between the two plates. The central figure was green (Taschek and Ball 1999, 220–225). This representation of the Maya cosmogram is reinforced by a possible interpretation that these figures could represent the Axis Mundi, according to Scherer (2015, 111–112).

FIGURE 6.6. *Naachtun Altar 14 and associated deposits*

With its artifacts, the colors represented by the combination of different matter (earth, flint, limestone, jade, and shell), its composition, and its stratified context, Deposit 45 is probably the most complex and sophisticated and is the earliest of the sequence of three deposits we will analyze. It marks both the main axis of the eastern platform and of the central Temple XXIIIb.

Altar 14 is 1 m away from the lower step of the stairway to Structure XXIIIb (figure 6.6). It measures 90 cm in diameter by 40 cm in thickness. It is accompanied by two intrusive deposits on the plaza floor, each sealed with a stucco patch. The first (Deposit 47), to the south, precedes the placement of the altar since it is partially covered by it. The second (Deposit 48), to the west, has no direct stratigraphic connection with the altar, so it could have been placed either before or after it.

Both deposits included monochrome vessels with basal flanges, whose shape is typical of the Early Classic Period. Deposit 47 (figure 6.7) consists of two plates placed lip to lip and dated from Balam I facet (before AD 300). Inside the vessels, the same pattern as the one observed in the acropolis was repeated—that is, the presence of a human skull as the only remains. Unlike the contexts of the acropolis (Deposit 33 in particular), the skull in Deposit 47 did not have its vertebrae and was already in a skeletal state when it was placed

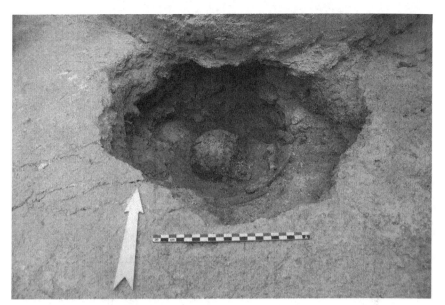

FIGURE 6.7. *Naachtun Deposit 47 with skull in lip-to-lip vessel*

between the vessels (Barrientos 2018). The earth placed with this skull is also a local red earth with iron base but of goethite type (FeOOH).

Deposit 48, to the west (toward the center of the plaza), consists of two pairs of vessels aligned north-south and set lip to lip (figure 6.8). They are assigned to the Balam II facet, slightly later chronologically than Deposit 47. The patch of polished mortar that covered the intrusive pit of Deposit 48 contained a much higher than usual load of charcoal. The practical or ritual significance of such a composition is still to be studied, but this enabled a radiocarbon dating of the deposition. The range 331–432 CE (85%) obtained from this date (1650 ± 30 years BP) is perfectly consistent with the Balam II dating of the two pairs of vessels. Both of them contained human remains: dentition and fragments of bone. In the southern assemblage, scant fragments of cranial bones, a molar tooth, and two jade dental inlays were found; in the northern pair, the bone fragments were deposited in a compact organic mass that included two molars and fragments of cranial bones in a waxy sediment. Both pairs of vessels contained sediments inside that revealed the presence of iron-based red earth; in the southern assemblage this is equivalent to the goethite type in Deposit 47, while in the case of the northern pair it is a ground iron pigment of the ilmenite type ($FeTiO_3$), less common in the Petén but nevertheless very common

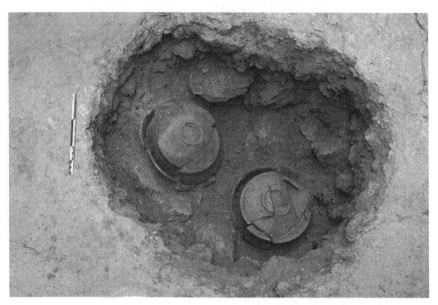

FIGURE 6.8. *Cached vessels set lip to lip in Naachtun Deposit 48*

in the color palette of the ancient Maya. In contrast, a third sample in the same Deposit 48, which comes from the waxy organic mass from the northern assemblage, indicated the presence of very pure hematite (Fe_2O_3).

Later, possibly shortly after the altar was constructed as there was little erosion, this monument and its associated deposits were buried, hidden, and thus protected by thick layers of compact lime mortar forming several levels, the uppermost one covered by a stucco floor that abuts the sixth step of the Temple XXIIIb staircase. Apparently, the upper part of the altar was partially damaged before its burial, as minor deteriorations can be observed on its southeastern and western sides. The fill that covers it was placed during the Balam II phase of the Early Classic, which means a time span shorter than a century after the altar was installed. Interestingly, as noted by Wagner (2006, 63–64), the physical sealing of monuments and buildings generally uses the white color of the *saskab* and lime as part of a protecting and purifying ritual, as this color symbolically purifies what is sealed and protects its essence in a conception similar to closing rituals (*mak*-rituals) (64).

Chronologically, Deposit 45 initiates a sequence of deposition that marks the central axis of the building when laying the plaza floor. This axis was reinforced by the addition of Deposit 47, which marked the first use here of skulls in rituals. Subsequently, this series of ritual events was concluded by the setting of Altar 14 and the double Deposit 48, whose order of deposition could not be established. This conjunction of ritual events was part of the establishment of a newly created sacred area. This space was possibly linked to the observation of the sky, as the central east-west axis, the most important of this complex, is projected far away to the east where isolated buildings recorded intentionally adopted the same alignment (Šprajc 2020).

Finally, in comparison with Acropolis V, the ceramic modes, in particular in Deposit 47, clearly indicate that the deposits buried under Altar 14 are earlier than those of Altar 15. This suggests priority in the E-Group of the practice of skull-in-vessel deposition. The presence of dental inlays in both cases suggests that bones used as offerings were from individuals of high social status.

DISCUSSION

An association between altars and deposits of skulls has not been much reported in the literature (Becker 2009). In contrast, the use of skulls in different archaeological contexts has been abundantly mentioned in reports: it is the case in well-known funeral contexts where an isolated skull can appear as grave goods that accompany the dead, whether it is a deceased adult or child, in individual or collective graves, from the Preclassic or Classic periods, or in domestic or elite contexts. We can mention sites such as Cuello (Robin 1989), Kaminaljuyu (Kidder, Jennings, and Shook 1946, 90), Zaculeu (Woodbury and Trik 1953, 80–81), Nebaj (Smith and Kidder 1951, 27), and Balamku (Michelet et al. 1998, 191–192). Among these funerary contexts, the additional skulls can refer to another (very different) concept and (much more warlike) nature related to trophy heads that can accompany the dead, as in El Tintal (Hansen et al. 2006; see also Berryman 2007; Fitzsimmons 2011, 56–60; López Oliva 2013).

Another example of ritual contexts different in nature in which skulls were used involves termination rituals. These are evident at Colha, Belize, where more than thirty skulls of all ages were arranged in a pit below the staircase of a monumental structure before it was burned (Mock 1998a, 113–114). Several skulls showed traces of decapitation and skinning (Houston and Scherer 2010, 182). Another case, comparable in the number of skulls documented and also in relation to a public building, although with a less clear context (perhaps of dedication), comes from Tikal Temple VI. Inside a kind of *chultun*, sealed and in axial position below the access stairway to the temple, a set of at least fifty-nine Early Classic vessels was placed, some arranged lip to lip. They contained a score of human skulls (some with vertebrae, others without), of which some were pulverized or ground (Loten 2018, 39–44).

Interestingly, skulls may appear in contexts of building dedication, including Tikal's East Plaza (Jones 1996, 63; see also Ruz Lhuillier 1989, 167). They also can be found buried below stone monuments as part of dedication rituals, as in the case of twin pyramid complexes 5B-1, 3D-1, 5C-1, and 4D-1 (Weiss-Krejci 2010, 90) and of Nebaj Stelae D and E (Smith and Kidder 1951, 27), not to mention numerous examples of Classic and Postclassic period secondary deposits that include skulls, among other components. In comparison, contexts in which altars are associated with offerings of skulls, covered by a vessel or placed between two vessels arranged lip to lip, are far less frequent. These skull-in-vessel offerings sometimes occur in association with a building, be it a temple-pyramid or an altar-platform. Some authors who carried out research in Tikal and Uaxactun have noted that the arrangement of a skull between two vessels was more frequent in the Early Classic Period (Coggins 1975, 240; Smith 1950, 93), which fully corresponds to all of the contexts found at Naachtun. The close political relationships that existed between Tikal-Uaxactun and Naachtun throughout the Classic Period and the sharing of these same rituals with skulls could suggest the existence of a regional tradition diffused in Tikal's sphere of influence. This type of deposit is also found in sites such as El Zotz, Yaxha, and Nakum, which formed part of the same sphere for this period (Calderón, Fialko, and Schwendener 2009; Scherer and Houston 2019). We must recognize, however, that in some cases this ritual practice may have extended to the Late Classic Period, as in the case of San José, Belize, where similar deposits were found in a Late Classic "pseudo-E-Group," perhaps with ritual and political meanings different from those of the Early Classic Period (Guderjan 2006, 101).

To illustrate that skull deposits in lip-to-lip vessels represent an Early Classic practice, possibly related to the sphere of Tikal, we can mention the example of the original E-Group of Uaxactun, where under the floors of the three temples of the east platform (Buildings EI–EIII), a series of at least four deposits of skull-in-vessel placed lip-to-lip and sometimes associated with other artifacts was located. The placement of such deposits in E-Group assemblages was a relatively common practice between the Late Preclassic and Early Classic periods. In addition to Uaxactun and Naachtun, similar cases were observed in Cenote, in Burial T1C-3 dated from the Early Classic Period (Chase 1983, 114); in Yaxha, in Deposit 40 in Building 152, with a child's skull; and in Calakmul, in Deposits DR-57 and DR-58 of the Early Classic Period, associated with the plain stelae located at the base of the central temple (IVb) built on the eastern platform of the E-Group (Vázquez Campa 2014, 177). In Nakum, a similar deposit, dated to the transition between the Late Preclassic and Early Classic Periods, has been found on the axis of Ballcourt 2, directly associated with the E-Group (Calderón, Fialko, and Schwendener 2009, 1396). Another interesting case in Nakum but somewhat different in nature comes from Tomb 2 of Structure 15—dated from the Early Classic Period—where a female individual, extended in dorsal decubitus position, had her head placed between two polychrome lip-to-lip vessels decorated with basal flanges, in an identical configuration to that of the deposits we have described (Źrałka, Koszkul, and Hermes 2008, 118–119). This means that this skull-in-vessel practice was not exclusive to ritual deposits and could also be applied to elite funerary contexts.

In earlier deposits from the Late Preclassic Period, the skull can be placed in a single vessel, as in the E-Group of Punta de Chimino, Cache 101 (Bachand 2006, 105), or be found isolated in the fill, exemplified by Burial 17 in the western structure of the E-Group at Chan, Belize (Novotny and Kosakowsky 2009, 77). At Uaxactun and Tayasal, headless bodies were also found buried in E-Groups. Aimers and Rice (2006, 89) relate them to the practice of human sacrifice. However, the link to sacrifice by decapitation is not always explicit. The case of Punta de Chimino is similar to Deposit 43 of Naachtun: the atlas, the axis, and the first cervical vertebrae were present but without showing evidence of violence indicating a decapitation (Bachand 2006, 106). In Uaxactun (Ricketson and Ricketson 1937, 150), the skull found in the south temple (E-III) of the eastern platform was also associated with those same three vertebrae.

Another practice that seems widespread among these deposits is postmortem modification of the skull or manipulations of bones (see Fitzsimmons 2011, 60–63). In Punta de Chimino, the frontal bone of the skull found in Cache 101 was missing (Bachand 2006, 106). At Cenote, the two cranial deposits linked to the E-Group, Burials T1C-3 and T1G-3, lacked the frontal bone, which had been placed on the side of the skull (Chase 1983, 114–115, 209). In Uaxactun, the frontal bone of the skull deposited in the E-III temple was also missing (Ricketson and Ricketson 1937, 150). The front part of this skull "was covered with a friable brown coating" (56). According to Bachand's (2006, 107) interpretation, this could be the remains of a mask, although Ricketson and Ricketson (1937, 150) described it as "a dried periosteum." The presence of black debris on the face of a buried child (Sep. 15) in a two lip-to-lip vessels deposit, Deposit 10, located near Burial 9 of El Zotz, is also explained as remains of masks (Scherer and Houston 2018, 139). As mentioned earlier, the two-lip-to-lip vessels of Naachtun's Deposit 48-north contained fragments and teeth in a compact yet unidentified waxy mass that could indicate in this context a postmortem modification of the skull.

To summarize, it can be said that in Naachtun contexts where cervical vertebrae are preserved, the head had been removed shortly after an individual's death. Decapitation sacrifice cannot be totally ruled out, but data do not particularly support this interpretation. In other Maya sites, the head was in some cases subject to modifications that may have included the partial or total destruction of the skull, the removal of the frontal bones, the disarticulation of the face in relation to the rest of the body (in the case of complete burial of children in vessels), and, perhaps, the placement of a kind of mask.

All this leads us to the thorny issue of sacrifice and beheading in dedication ritual contexts. On the one hand, the analysis of the pigments associated with Naachtun's deposits emphasizes the presence of red color in these contexts, a color generally linked to ritual sacrifice in Maya culture and art. Red or reddish pigments were also thought to confer life on the corpses following the symbolic logic of sympathetic magic, according to which "same begets same." In this sense, the shine and luster of many Mesoamerican red pigments, such as cinnabar and hematite, were probably associated with fire and the solar astral-deity and, consequently, with life, which needs the warmth provided by fire and the sun. Given that a dead body quickly turns cold, it is possible that the red pigments found in Mesoamerica served the purpose of figuratively bringing back the lost body heat—that is, the warmth of blood (Vázquez de Ágredos Pascual 2018).

On the other hand, both in the acropolis and in the E-Group, the osteological analysis of the bones from these contexts indicates a total absence of evidence for decapitation or sacrificial practice instead of a postmortem recovery of the skulls (Barrientos 2018). The only thing that can be said in the case of complete skulls is that some, such as Deposit 33, could have contained soft tissues at the time of their deposition while others (Deposit 47) were already "skeletonized" (2018), a point also observed by Haviland in the skulls of children of Tikal buried under the stelae and subject, according to him, to a long postmortem exposure before burial (cited in Weiss-Krejci 2010, 90).

In an attempt to emically reconstruct the ceremonies and ritual events carried out in E-Group assemblages, based widely on modern ethnographic observations and discussions, May Castillo (2018, 32) suggested that the skulls found deposited in relation to architecture were those of religious leaders and that they were carefully separated from the rest of the body in an event celebrated 260 days after their death. This time span, very significant from a ritual and calendric point of view, is marked by the E-Group. It is sufficient time to allow for the disappearance of most of the soft tissues but not of the most resistant muscles and ligaments, allowing the retrieval of the skull with some cervical vertebrae.

In Maya mythology in general and in the Popol Vuh in particular, the regenerating power of the decapitated skull of the maize god Hun Hunahpu is evoked. Although decapitated, the maize god can continue to give life and keep his fertilizing capacity intact. Death and life are then intimately imbricated. It is possible to wonder if the presence of human skulls (decapitated or not) placed in these deposits could symbolize the divine head of the maize god and therefore fertility through his regenerating power, which is desired for the entire community. In this sense, these deposited skulls can be interpreted as powerful agents of fertility. In addition, they may symbolize the underworld, an aquatic realm materialized by shells and greenstones that can be found in the deposits—an environment conducive to rebirth, as can be seen in iconography (for example, polychrome vessel K5073, where water lilies sprout from the skull). We can also mention the example of the lid K2849, dated from the Early Classic Period, which forms part of a deposit consisting of two large plates set lip to lip (Schele and Miller 1986, 207). The incised motif present on the exterior of the lid depicts the decapitated head of the maize god associated with three bloodletters used for sacrificial acts (obsidian blade, stingray spine, flint knife). Here, the aquatic underworld is represented by the blood of the maize god. The scene thus refers to his sacrifice and links it to rebirth and fertility.

In the iconography of painted vessels, several scenes illustrate the myth of the Popol Vuh (K5615, K1228, K1892). In contrast, the association of decapitation with altars is very uncommon in these representations. When it occurs, as in the case of vessel K8719, the decapitation act is performed on the altar, and the bloody head of the sacrificial victim is exposed as an offering directly placed on top of the stela, without a container or basket to accompany it. Unfortunately, we are not told the fate of this head or of the body later in the scene. In other painted scenes on vessels, the decapitated head is displayed in the hand of the sacrificer, but again, there is no indication of what comes after this. So we cannot establish with certainty a sacrificial link between the altar and the deposits, apart from an obvious spatial connection. In epigraphy, however, a clear relation can be established between the bones—particularly the manipulation of bones—and the dedication rituals of the stelae. The famous Copan Stela H, for instance, mentions in its inscription the "peeling" or "slicing" of the long bones of the deceased king of Copan, Butz' Chan, in front of the monument to be dedicated. As Fitzsimmons (2011, 56) pointed out, this bone manipulation represents the most significant event of this stone-binding ritual, an event that did not result in the deposition of the human remains beneath Stela H.

In the archaeological record, there is a special link between stelae and the deposition of bones (skull, teeth, long bones), since the bones sometimes form part of the artifacts placed in the sub-stela deposits. They thus play a key role in the *k'altuun* ritual (Weiss-Krejci 2011, 22, 27). In the case of the plain stelae of Tikal, which are part of the twin pyramid groups, the skulls (without cervical vertebrae) of children between six and eight years of age were found, among other bones (Weiss-Krejci 2010, 90). Only the individual associated with the famous Stela 16 of Tikal was older (Jones and Satterthwaite 1982, 37), between twelve and twenty years old. This could correspond to the remains of the noble lady Tuun Kaywak, whose long bones and skull are represented on Altar 5 (Weiss-Krejci 2011, 28–31). In this particular case, the deposit of these bones corresponds to an exhumation, a re-entry to the original burial for the extraction of long bones and the skull of a woman deceased eight years before—all this for a probable deposition act of her bones in Tikal (although the text does not specify it), as mentioned and illustrated (Stuart 1998, 407–408). This may have happened at the very foot of Stela 16, which forms a pair with Altar 5, since a deposit containing a skull and bone remains was found during the excavations (Jones and Satterthwaite 1982, 37). This specific case illustrates the increase during the seventh and eighth centuries of manipulations of the dead body for political purposes (Fitzsimmons 2011, 60–63; Weiss-Krejci 2011, 19–21).

Among stela dedication deposits, one can occasionally find complete human remains, as in the case of Stela 26 of Naachtun, found buried inside the Triadic Complex (Structure I)—always in Group C—at a short distance from the acropolis. There, the deposit that accompanied this Early Classic stela consisted of a newborn placed inside two lip-to-lip vessels (Rangel, Alonso, and Reese-Taylor 2013, 46). We do not know in this case if the young child was the object of a sacrifice, but the sacrifice of children was a frequent theme in Maya vase iconography. On vessel K928, a child is sacrificed by cardiectomy on a skull-shaped altar, which reinforces this link between death and sacrifice, as does the presence of a jaguar sitting on the stela, the object of the ritual. In any case, both in Deposit 38 of the Naachtun acropolis and in Deposit 48-north of the E-Group, the remains of children with or without skulls are at issue.

Another case of a stela-burial relationship concerns Stela 1 of El Juilín, a peripheral group located 6.5 km southeast of Naachtun. Stela 1, dating from Cycle 8, was erected there and enclosed inside a two-room building (Andrieu 2016). At the foot of the stela, without any association with an altar, and near its base was found a burial in a cist of a subadult (over ten years old) accompanied by a single vessel. The base of the stela rested against the slabs of the cist roof, indicating not only the close relation between the cist and the stela but also the anteriority of the first in relation to the second (Barrientos 2016, 170–171).

All of these examples—whether in relation to stelae, altars, or buildings—show the close relationship that existed between these ritual deposits (regardless of whether there is sacrifice) and the presence of newborn infants, children, or subadults. This relationship is even closer in the case of Burial 9 of the El Diablo Complex in El Zotz, dated to the Early Classic Period (Scherer and Houston 2018, 136–139). Not only is the buried ruler accompanied by six children placed inside lip-to-lip vessels, but outside the tomb there are two other pairs of lip-to-lip vessels. Each one contains the remains of a single child age, in the first example (Cache 3, Burial 6), between two and four years old and in the second (Burial 15) between four and eight months. The remains of both children, possibly sacrificed, show traces of exposure to fire and appear to have been disarticulated. Both are deposited near an altar. Scherer and Houston (140) relate these sacrifices of children to a pan-Mesoamerican tradition that intensified during the Early Classic Period and was possibly linked to Teotihuacán.

The possible ritual sequence depicted on polychrome vessels—sacrifice and decapitation of the victim on the altar itself, display of the skull on the stela, and burial at the foot of it—does not correspond to the deposits present under Altars 14 and 15 of Naachtun. First, we do not have a stela-altar pair and second, in both cases there is a chronological lag between the burial of several of these deposits and the setting of the altar itself above them. The sequence "sacrifice on the altar; bury the skull at its feet" is not supported by stratigraphy. If the skull of Deposit 34 on the acropolis and Deposit 47 in the E-Group were to be definitively identified as decapitated, these sacrifices could not have been made on top of their respective altars, as the altars were yet to be placed when the skulls were deposited.

Instead, the skull deposits in Naachtun might mainly be related to the buildings' primary axis and not to the altar itself. Examples in other sites show an association between skulls and buildings, marking the central axis of architectural complexes, especially an east-west axis. At Naachtun, in a second stage, this axis is reinforced by setting these altars accompanied by rituals. In this case and in several others, there remains the problem of the origin, or the recruitment, of the individual and of the postmortem treatment of the deposited skeletal remains (re-entry to graves or postmortem dismemberment?), which surely belong to individuals of high social status, as shown by dental inlays. This topic of re-entry is a very pertinent issue at Naachtun, where we identified numerous explicit cases in Late and Terminal Classic residential contexts (Barrientos et al. 2015; Goudiaby and Nondédéo 2020). It is a common practice attested by archaeology and iconography and also mentioned in the inscriptions (see Fitzsimmons 2006, 35–40; Stuart 1998). But, as observed several times (Tiesler Blos and Cucina 2003, 2007; Weiss-Krejci 2010, 90), it is also possible that on some occasions, deposited skulls come from people who died shortly before a ritual. In this sense, one might wonder if such an important death in the community acted as a trigger for a ritual event to come.

CONCLUSION

The purpose of this contribution was to provide a reflection on the sequence of ritual actions as depositional processes and their special link to altars that marked the east-west axial center of monumental architecture. We described the content of those deposits and their possible meaning. We showed that in some cases, the altar was not involved in these ritual events but instead was set *a posteriori* to reinforce an existing link between an axial deposit and a building. These deposits stress the primary axis of the architectural complexes at the foot of which they are located. The review of the literature to investigate similar cases allows us to establish the existence of patterns that can be related to a particular period, namely the Early Classic, with specific architectural configurations: the E-Group assemblages. There seems to be a possible area of diffusion of these ritual practices that encompasses the Tikal political sphere of influence. However, we must admit that isolated cases may be found in other regions and for other periods, indicating perhaps a more widespread practice in Maya society.

The study of these two specific contexts at Naachtun shows a complex set of ritual actions that involved different systems of perception, among them sight activated by the different colors of the artifacts and sediments selected, touch by the diversity of the matter used, and smell by the different scents detected in the residues. All this, along with the skull deposits, contributed to create an impactful ritual event through a complex sequence of actions that runs from the procurement of the skulls through the different phases of depositions to the setting of the altar to the final covering of this monument (in one case). Even if certain gray areas will always remain in the retracing of the ritual process, we trust that in the future, the results of chemical analysis, still in process on the organic materials preserved in these vessels, will elucidate more ritual practices (gestures) related to these skull deposits.

Acknowledgments. The Naachtun Archaeological Project (2010–2022) has been funded by the French Ministry of Europe and Foreign Affairs, the

CNRS, the Foundation Pacunam, the Perenco Company, LabEx DynamiTe, and the Foundation Simome et Cino del Duca. It forms part of Cemca activities in Central America, and its fieldwork was undertaken with permission of the Instituto de Antropología e Historia (IDAEH) de Guatemala. We thank all the members of the Naachtun Project and all the workers from Uaxactun for their contribution and hard work. This research was developed within the RITMO international network (funded by CNRS, France).

NOTES

1. All vessels are identified using Kerr Maya Vase Database numbers and can be consulted at http://research.mayavase.com/kerrmaya.html.

2. The analyses were carried out in the Laboratorio de Análisis y Diagnóstico de Obras de Arte and the Parque Científico of the Universitat de València using optical microscopy, Scanning Electron Microscopy Energy Dispersive X-Ray Analysis (SEM-EDX), Fourier Transform Infrared Spectroscopy (FTIR), and Gas Chromatography–Mass Spectrometry (GC-MS).

7

Materiality and Agentivity of House Building Rituals

An Ethno-Archaeological Approach

Johann Begel,
Marie Chosson, and
Cédric Becquey

In the archaeological record, the existence of Precolumbian rituals associated with structures has been noted in the Maya area since at least the late 1950s, following excavations in Uaxactun and Piedras Negras. Dedication rituals are ceremonies performed immediately before or during the first construction stage of a building. An architectural addition may also imply new offerings. These ceremonial openings have a parallel, the so-called termination or abandonment rituals, characterized by destruction of artifacts or structures.

At the same time, house building rituals were broadly studied by anthropologists for contemporary Maya societies. While the archaeological examples were mostly from ceremonial groups, the ethnographic ones came from residential contexts. Despite the temporal distance and the differences between functions of buildings, this provided archaeologists with some directions in the interpretation of these Precolumbian rituals. Indeed, inspired by the ethnographic investigations of Evon Z. Vogt (1979) and Brian Stross (1998) among the Tzotzils, some archaeological studies suggested that the main purpose of the so-called dedication rituals was to give a soul to the building to bring it to life, an approach we call ensoulment theory (Mock 1998b). In the same large-scale comparative approach, however, it is possible to offer a different axis of interpretation. The review of a corpus of thirty-five different rituals described in the Mesoamerican ethnographic literature (figure 7.1) allows us to question buildings'

https://doi.org/10.5876/9781646422395.c007

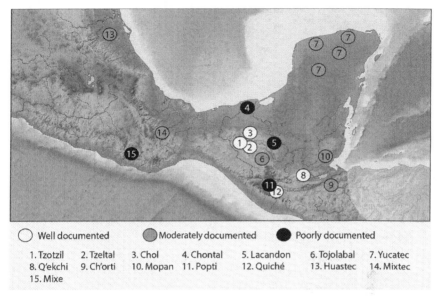

○ Well documented   ◐ Moderately documented   ● Poorly documented

1. Tzotzil	2. Tzeltal	3. Chol	4. Chontal
8. Q'ekchi	9. Ch'orti	10. Mopan	11. Popti
15. Mixe			

5. Lacandon	6. Tojolabal	7. Yucatec
12. Quiché	13. Huastec	14. Mixtec

FIGURE 7.1. *Distribution of ethnographically documented rituals in Mesoamerica*

animation or aliveness. Second, it allows us to examine possible shared features of the material realm in both Precolumbian and contemporary rituals, which might lead to some understanding of the aims of these ceremonies. Finally, while these rituals always mark a break in the type of human occupation, a better understanding of their outcomes and a comparison of their long-term temporalities can open new perspectives that question their benefits and their interpretation as unique foundational events.

WHAT ETHNOLOGY SAYS

The Mesoamerican ethnographic literature provides various descriptions of house building ceremonies, underlining variations in the main purposes attributed to these rituals. One of these outcomes is emphasized by archaeologists in their interpretations: the ensoulment of buildings. This impelled us to research, among all the ethnological material available, references to ritual protocols related to the living nature of buildings. This research revealed that the existence of such practices and beliefs is restricted to the Tzotzil, Tseltal, Yucatec, and Mixtec communities in Mexico and to the K'iche' and Q'eqchi areas in Guatemala (figure 7.2). For Tzotzil people from San Pedro Chenalho,

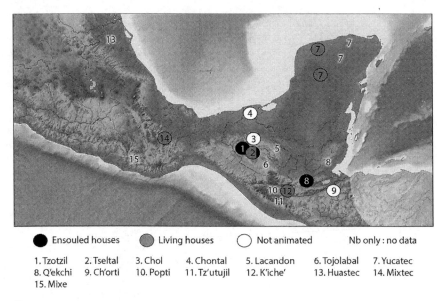

Ensouled houses   Living houses   Not animated   Nb only : no data

1. Tzotzil   2. Tseltal   3. Chol   4. Chontal   5. Lacandon   6. Tojolabal   7. Yucatec
8. Q'ekchi   9. Ch'orti   10. Popti   11. Tz'utujil   12. K'iche'   13. Huastec   14. Mixtec
15. Mixe

FIGURE 7.2. *Distribution of living, ensouled, and non-animated houses*

Calixta Guiteras Holmes (1986 [1961], 144) specifies that "the house has its own *ch'ulel* and it is what eats the people who enter the house without asking the Earth's permission [*La casa tiene su ch'ulel y es esta que se come la gente que entra en la casa sin pedir permiso a la Tierra*]." Maria Esther Hermitte (1970, 58) clarifies the notion of building aliveness among the Tseltal of Pinola, insisting on the process of aging of its components: "The house is alive, the proof is that it gets old, it rots and has worms, and being alive has its *nahual*, a woman, who can turn against the inhabitants. When a new house is inhabited, it needs to be duly fed [*La casa está viva, prueba de ello es que se hace vieja, se pudre y tiene gusanos, y al estar viva tiene su nahual, una mujer, que puede volverse contra sus ocupantes. Cuando se ocupa una casa nueva tiene que ser debidamente alimentada*]." Carlos Rafael Cabarrús (1979, 121) also underlines the necessity among the Q'eqchi of ritual offerings to the living house: "Here it speaks of feeding the walls . . . Every single thing has its *personaje* which has to be fed [*Aquí se habla de alimentar a los muros . . . Todas las cosas tienen su personaje que tiene que ser alimentado*]." The living nature of buildings in these cases is clearly demonstrated and expressed by reference to things that can be considered, such as souls or different forces, variously named according to the different groups: *ch'ulel*, *nahual*, or *personaje*. It appears important at this point to distinguish rituals that aim to satisfy the requirements of living buildings, those that are clearly intended to ensoul the building (figure 7.2), and those that are not related at all to any ensoulment or aliveness notion.

Vogt (1979, 85–90) is the only ethnographer to cite the existence of a ritual protocol specifically dedicated to ensoul the house, in the Tzotzil community of Zinacantan. In other studies that mention the living nature of buildings, this life seems to be linked primarily to the materials used for its construction, the natural landscape where they were extracted, and the masters, or God, of the landscape. Guiteras Holmes (1986 [1961], 30) clarifies: "Prayers are said in order to divert the harmful *tsots* (power), inherent to the new products that have been brought back from the *monte*, which are used in construction [*Se dicen oraciones para desviar el dañino tsots (poder), inherente a los nuevos productos que se han traído del monte y que se emplearon en la construcción*]." Following the same idea, June Nash (1985 [1970], 16) also commented that the house foundation ritual in the Tseltal locality of Amatenango aims, among other goals, at "introducing the spirit of the house inmates to the house spirit," insisting on its materiality: "The idea of the similarity in substance between the house and its inmates originates in the notions about soil (*lum*) and mud (*ahch'al*). An origin myth concerning the creation of man indicates that God created man out of soil and this mythical identification is reiterated in prayers . . . Whatever soil man comes into contact with, in his house, in the backyard or in his travels, may contain some of his soul" (13). Moreover, in this latter case, "the spirits of inhabitants and of the house meet at the center post at the rear wall of the house. The spirit of the house lives in this post . . . The souls of the inmates of the house hover near the center post when they are not in the body" (11–12). The idea of a transfer of what we could call a power, a force, or a soul of natural elements constituting the structure of the house is also attested among the K'iche' at the beginning of the seventeenth century in the testimony of Ximenez, cited by Ruth Leah Bunzel (1959, 39): "When they cut the wood for their houses, they made sacrifices to the God of houses, praying for the house for which they cut the wood to be favored and that they may live within her for many days in joy."

While the ritual described by Vogt is performed to create the domestic unit by conferring a specific soul, in the other groups for which the house is considered to be alive, the ritual protocol is largely intended to mitigate the impact of a changing use of a construction material—for instance, a tree transformed to a post. These rituals require some compensation made of food, or the house could "revolt" against its inhabitants. Hermitte (1970, 58) says, "If the offerings are forgotten, the house begins to feel envy [*Si las ofrendas se olvidan, la casa comienza a tener 'envidia'*]." This is supported by Cabarrús (1979, 121), who writes "and it demands it [compensation] in such a manner that

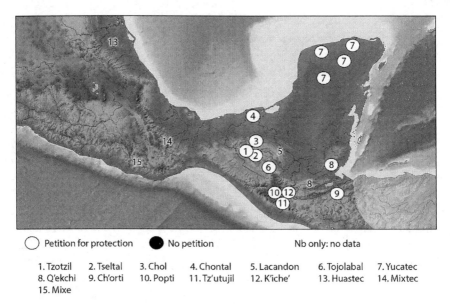

Petition for protection   ● No petition   Nb only: no data

1. Tzotzil	2. Tseltal	3. Chol	4. Chontal	5. Lacandon	6. Tojolabal	7. Yucatec
8. Q'ekchi	9. Ch'orti	10. Popti	11. Tz'utujil	12. K'iche'	13. Huastec	14. Mixtec
15. Mixe						

FIGURE 7.3. *Distribution of protective rituals during house construction*

if it is not complied with, it will take revenge and there will befall bloody misfortunes [*y que lo exige de tal manera que si no se cumple él se vengará y sobrevendrá desgracias sangrientas*]." Insisting on the necessity of the establishment of a harmonious relationship between the two entities, Nash (1985 [1970], 18) also stresses that "the relationship between house spirit and the spirits of the residents is an uneasy one . . . Fear is associated with this capricious spirit." For the human occupants, part of these rituals aims, therefore, to protect them from the dangerous living nature of buildings.

Whether the house could be considered alive, animated, or inert, in almost every study in the corpus, another relationship—with earth-related entities—is ubiquitous. Almost every testimony mentions the necessity to ask earth-related entities' permission to live on a part of their surface and to apologize for the inconvenience (figure 7.3). Mario Ruz (1983, 83) specifies for the Tojolabals that the ritual is performed "with the goal of feeding the 'Holy Mother Earth', at the same time that it asks her forgiveness for having occupied a place that, it can be assumed, belongs only to her and her crops [*Esto se hace con el fin de alimentar a la 'Santa Madre Tierra', al mismo tiempo que se solicita su perdón por haber ocupado un lugar que, se aduce, le pertenece únicamente a ella y a sus cultivos*]." Bunzel (1959, 37–40), mentions two different sequences of the ritual, the first one aiming to warn "the world" about the construction and the other one to thank him/it for having allowed the building to be finished without problems. In at least two cases, there is also an intention to prove the humans' good intentions to the entities related to the earth. Referred to from case to case as a unique entity named Earth or as multitudes of entities, these entities are generally considered masters of the earth. Cabarrús (1979, 118) reports: "It is said that it's [not done] for a bad goal but for the sake of children [*Se dice que no es para mal, sino para el bien de los hijos*]." Bunzel (1959, 37) provides an example (translating as "World" *Mundo*, a term occupying the same place as "Earth" in the previous examples): "Hail World . . . As for me I only wish to provide for my children a place where they may live . . . It is for this, World, that I intrude upon you with my annoyances . . . Pardon me." Like most occupied places, a negotiation with earth-related entities, which requires material compensation, is considered essential to enjoy the usufruct of the land (see also Joyce and Sheptak, chapter 3, this volume).

This request for the occupation of space is always joined to a plea for protection, for the health of occupants and their well-being, often presented to both celestial and chthonian entities. Charles Wisdom (1940, 130), discussing Ch'orti Maya traditions, writes that "the new-house ceremony is performed . . . for the purpose of accepting it into the community and of driving evil spirits out of it." Nash (1985 [1970], 16) also signals that the secondary goal of the ritual is to protect "the house against the intrusion of evil," adding that indeed the upset spirit of the house could make an alliance with these evil spirits and let them come inside. These rituals of protection are not specific to the house but can also apply to other spaces marked by human occupation (such as sugar mills, churches, milpas, *solares*, and even towns). This is widely attested, for example, among the Chols, Chontals, Q'eqchis, Tzotzils, Huastecs, and Yucatecs. This point is particularly well illustrated by *compostura* dedication rituals of the Lenca of Honduras, discussed by Joyce and Sheptak (chapter 3, this volume), which are equivalent for houses, house lots, milpas, and quarries.

While these rituals can be multi-scalar, they can also be multi-layered. While in most of the cases the recipients of these rituals are the chthonian entities such as the earth masters (thirteen of thirty-five rituals reviewed), celestial entities such as God and others whose names at least pertain to Christian tradition can also be invoked (five examples in the thirty-five recorded cases). This segregation is sometimes visible in offerings: those dedicated to celestial entities are displayed at a height, on an altar, while those destined to the chthonian entities are laid on or buried in the floor (Becquey 2017; Cabarrús 1979).

The plea for protection of a building sometimes mentions some kind of "closure" of space, as in Yucatan, where Fabienne de Pierrebourg (1999, 179) observes that the ritual purpose is to forbid evil winds from entering the house. Pedro Pitarch Ramón (1996), discussing the Tseltal of Cancuc, writes about ritual residential protection promoting the sensation of confinement. The ritual words addressed to the entities clearly refer to the circumscription of a definite space, using the pair *makte'* (fence) and *xoral* (corral): "I place myself in a pen, I place myself in a corral." This delimitation of a closed space symbolically realized by the accomplishment of ritual actions in its four corners (discussed below) cannot, however, be considered a definitive closure or an everlasting contract with the masters of spaces.

While de Pierrebourg (1999) underlines the necessity to renew the compact of the ritual named *hetz lu'um*, Pitarch Ramón (1996) states that the house protection ritual must be repeated at least twice a year or if occupants are subjected to numerous nightmares or suffer recurring diseases. A similar situation is encountered among the Chols, where the foundation ritual is supposed to be replayed yearly to sustain the protection asked for the first time. It can also be performed whenever diseases are diagnosed as the result of a lack of protection or due to the malevolence of the master of earth (Becquey 2017). Nash (1985 [1970], 18) also reports that in case of the appearance of diseases, the protection ritual must be started over to "cover the eyes of the devil spirit so it will not enter the house." Guiteras Holmes (1986 [1961], 145) supports the importance of warning *la Tierra* if a new member joins the family, such as a stepdaughter, to give her the same protection. For Cabarrús (1979, 118) and the Q'eqchi', it seems important that all the inhabitants are present during the initial ritual: "It's necessary that everyone be awoken to the extent it's the moment to ask the permission to dwell, that's why they all must be ready [*Ahora es necesario que estén despiertos, puesto que ahore se pide permiso para poder habitar, por eso todos tienen que estar dispuestos*]." Certain sequences of what are considered house building rituals are not only performed during the inauguration but need to be repeated over time during the occupation of the building, raising questions about the temporalities of the ritual process.

Another variation in the corpus shows that the majority of inauguration rituals are performed after completion of the construction of the structure: only seven, including two non-Maya examples, from the thirty-five corpuses are realized before construction. For the most recent examples, with the increasing use of cement floors, which precludes having buried deposits in the house, these rituals are achieved before this construction stage. In cases where the house is considered alive, it seems relevant to underline the existence of two separate sequences or ceremonies, which have explicitly different purposes. For example, for the Tzotzils (Laughlin 1980; Vogt 1998), the Ch'ul *kantela* ceremony aiming to give birth to the house is distinguished from the *Hol Chuk*, dedicated more to the protection of the inhabitants and the indulgence asked of the master of earth for the inconvenience generated by the construction of the structure and its future occupation. In the same way, for the Tseltals of Amatenango, "The first ceremony . . . is for the spirits who reside in the post and the second . . . is to feed 'the spirit of the house earth'" (Nash 1970, 13). The division of the ritual into two distinct sequences also exists in populations for whom the house is considered inert. Among the Chontals, in addition to the protective ritual dedicated to the inhabitants, another is performed for the protection of the house itself (Cedric Bequey, personal observation).

To briefly summarize, the literature concerning modalities of house building rituals and their invoked purposes allows for identification of Mesoamerican convergences. It appears that ritual efforts are commonly focused on negotiations with earth-related entities for the occupation of space and the protection of the house against evil forces, attaching in a small number of groups some ritual protocols related to belief in the living nature of buildings. Humans and non-humans are bound by relations of reciprocity (see Joyce and Sheptak, chapter 3, this volume). Moreover, the descriptions of these rituals offer several lines of thought that might enlighten archaeological interpretation. In the same way, it may be possible to search convergences and even continuities in these rituals, examining more precisely the materiality and agentivity of their offerings.

MATERIALITY AND AGENTIVITY IN HOUSE RITUALS

Ethnography shows that significant commonalities concern the identity of the recipient of such rituals, earthly/tellurian entities, and the propitiatory nature of the ceremony. In the material realm, other shared features can be identified, not only through ethnological data but also through archaeological evidence. This is especially true for buried offerings and the use of a quintipartite device related to the cosmovision. Indeed, the importance of the Mesoamerican cosmogram, materialized in ethnographic cases by ritual performances (e.g., offerings, circuits) in the four corners and in the center, seems to constitute a fundamental element in rituals related to domestic spaces since Precolumbian times.

The Quintipartite Cosmogram

This pattern, known since the Preclassic Period, constitutes a symbol that "fused the horizontal directionality and vertical layering, visually creating a map of how the Maya conceptualized space" (Egan 2011, 97). In the literature

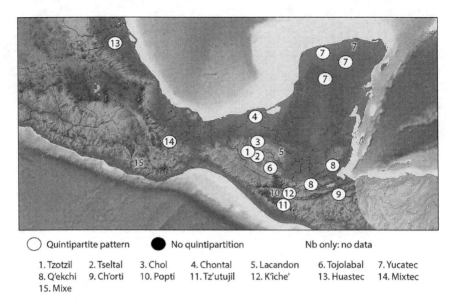

Quintipartite pattern   ● No quintipartition   Nb only: no data

1. Tzotzil   2. Tseltal   3. Chol   4. Chontal   5. Lacandon   6. Tojolabal   7. Yucatec
8. Q'ekchi   9. Ch'orti   10. Popti   11. Tz'utujil   12. K'iche'   13. Huastec   14. Mixtec
15. Mixe

FIGURE 7.4. *Distribution of modern rituals using a quintipartite spatial pattern*

about Precolumbian societies, this kind of cosmogram, broadly shared in Mesoamerica, is commonly interpreted as a cosmic re-creation. This aspect constitutes the basis of the interpretation of many ancient rituals, much architectural organization, and numerous iconographic representations (Mathews and Garber 2004).

Although this cosmological dimension is rarely verbally explicit in ethnological data, we can discern pragmatic employments within the scope of Maya rituals. In some contemporary ceremonies, the circumscription of space follows a flexible quintipartite pattern (figure 7.4). This mainly concerns the localization of four peripherical cardinal points, where ritual actions are realized that can be approximate. For example, a building ritual may involve actions in the four corners of a house, each one associated with a cardinal direction even if this does not conform to the real directions (Becquey, personal data). In other cases, materialized boundaries such as a cross or other territorial marker, supposed to stand in the four cardinal points, are almost never either at the exact cardinal point or on an exact territorial limit (Chosson, personal data).

On the one hand, this flexibility allows for symbolically circumscribing a space thanks to four peripheral markers, related to the four cardinal points (even if in some cases this orientation is more conceptual than absolute). On the other hand, more specifically in relation to the central point, it can also work as a mechanism for "centering the world" (Freidel, Schele, and Parker 1995, 131) and as "a pathway to all three world-levels [underworld, earth, and sky]" (Egan 2011, 84), conferring access to the invisible world and its entities on human beings and thereby creating a liminal space in our material world. Given these different properties, space circumscription, and the nexus with chthonian and celestial worlds, the presence of this symbolic pattern in the context of dedication ritual is not a surprise.

The realization of ritual actions in these five distinct points that form the cosmogram is clearly described in twelve of the modern building inauguration rituals. These spots particularly give rise to ritual circuits or processions, other pivotal and shared practices in most past and present liturgies. In rare studies that describe these circuits in detail for the Chols (Becquey 2017), Tzotzils (Laughlin 1980; Vogt 1998), and Yucatecs (Pierrebourg and Ruz 2014), they always begin at the eastern point before linking the other cardinal points counterclockwise, ending in the center. While the existence of Precolumbian royal processions is well documented by iconography (Morton 2007), if they existed, any specifically related to dedication rituals are totally unknown. One of the only glyphic inscriptions that mentions a list of the four cardinal points, Copan Stela A, does begin with east, followed by west, north, and south, forming a cross-shaped motif. (The text of Stela A at E8-E12 says "*el.k'in, och.k'in, noho'l, xaman, ha'o'b' pasno'm way, makno'm way*," glossed as "in the east, in the west, in the north, in the south, it is they who will open the room, who will close the room.") This kind of oriented cruciform motif is also attested in modern ceremony, in particular when associated with the central point of a space (Becquey 2017, 255). Strikingly, while the ritual associated with Copan Stela A is surely performed on a period ending, the only ritual actions mentioned are an opening and a closure of space.

Other contexts in which we can find a certain relationship between the cosmogram and ritual space enclosure are at Machaquila. At this site, a large number of ritual deposits have been unearthed under a quadrilobate depression in the middle of Plaza A, and some of the stelae around this refer to a space-enclosing ritual, "*umaka'w uway*" (Lacadena García-Gallo 2006). Is this a closure like those we saw previously? Precolumbian rituals related to the quatrefoil symbol are still enigmatic and misunderstood. However, the configuration of architectural groups such as patios (Plaza Plans 3 and 4; Becker 2003, 263), twin pyramid complexes, and triadic groups could refer to mythological notions like quadri-cardinality or the three stones of the domestic fire (the three-stone hearth).

CORNER OFFERINGS

Modern ritual actions and offerings of the peripheral points are mostly associated with building corner posts. Of the fifteen rituals in which this is detailed, twelve imply offerings projected or spread against the posts or poured at their feet. Only six require buried offerings. In addition to artifacts intended to mark the protection of these peripheral points against spirits or malevolent winds such as an adorned cross (4 of 15 cases), holy water (3 of 15), or obsidian flakes or blades (2 of 15), the main goal of these offerings is to feed the entities related to the space delineated by the ritual. This food is mostly composed of sacrificed animals, offered cooked or raw. Often, this is accomplished by spreading some broth (7 of 15 cases) or blood (2 cases for the corners, 4 for the inner walls). In six examples, pieces of meat, cooked or raw, are buried. Beverages often accompany these offerings: alcohol (10 of 15 cases) or *pozol* or *atole* (5 of 15 examples). Some ritual specialists sacrifice cacao (1/15), tortillas (1/15), condiments (salt, pepper, chili, 1/15), or cigars (1/15). Some offerings are soliciting entities while others appeal to their senses, such as candles offered for their visual qualities (8/15) and incense for its fragrance (3/15).

The ethnological pattern composed of corner deposits is not noted by archaeologists. To our knowledge, there is no case of a residential unit where these four positions were occupied by deposits placed during construction. In fact, dedication deposits in domestic contexts are rare (more often, a dedicatory burial is the first settled element). However, most of the time, excavation only reveals the building floor without penetrating the masonry, unless some visible patch indicates a clear occupational deposit or burial. Some examples of corner deposits have been noted, occurring during expansion of existing houses or temples. For instance, in Structure 5N2 of Rio Bec, a jar was deposited in a corner of a new room (Michelet et al. 2010, 172). Other examples are noted at Balamku and Tikal, but all those we have identified consist of a single deposit in one of the corners (Dominique Michelet, personal communication, 2017; Laporte et al. 1992).

Archaeologically, different architectural patterns are documented, such as Becker's (2003) Plaza Plans 2 to 5. Should we search for four-corner deposits in ancient commoners' houses, in the main buildings—supposedly belonging to the patio or lineage chief—or in domestic shrines? In the publications we consulted, none of these examples gave results that corresponded to the ethnological data. By contrast, excavations in Naachtun revealed an intriguing case. Patio 6 of the B group is an elite residence. In Structure 5O-59/65, a series of intrusions was found in the last occupation floor, probably dug just before the abandonment of the building. This could have been an attempt to locate previous deposits or burials before leaving the house for good (Sion and

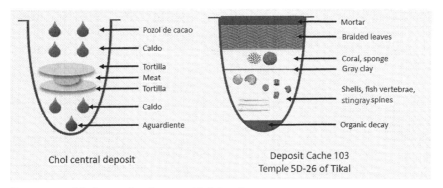

FIGURE 7.5. *Modern and ancient stratified deposits*

Quiñonez 2018). The pertinent point here is that the occupants searched at the exact locations where dedication deposits documented by ethnographers would be found: in the center of the main room and in the corners.

To come back to firmer ground, rarely, some deposits seem to circumscribe a space. At the four corners of Temple II of the Great Plaza of Tikal, for instance, four identical deposits made of a biface and a flint flake were displayed diagonally (Coe 1990). Another case was found in two corners of the palatial Structure 5D-62 of the central acropolis. This very specific arrangement was registered as the "Xik" offertory assemblage (Moholy-Nagy and Coe 2008, 20). In three corners of Copan's Margarita structure, deposits of liquid mercury have been found (Bell 2007, 325–327). These cases are uncommon, but the inner space inside the corners of supporting platforms is rarely excavated, since in general, intrusive explorations of temples are focusing on axial trenches.

Central Deposit

In the present-day rites, the ritual circuit forming the cosmogram is regularly completed by a stratified deposit buried in the center of the house. In the corpus, seventeen central deposits are fully described (figure 7.5). The main element of these deposits is constituted of whole or partial sacrificed animals, mostly poultry (23/35), including turkeys (4/35), hens (14/35), roosters (4/35), and ducks (1/35). In three occurrences, the testimony insists on the importance of black feathers (Tojolabals, Tzotzils, Tzeltals). Other animals can also be sacrificed, sometimes in the same social group, depending on the owner: pigs (2/35), sheep (2/35), and calves or cows (1/35). The animal can be buried intact (6/35, including 1 alive); or only the heart (2/35), the head alone (1/35) or accompanied by the feathers and guts (3/35), only the guts (1 in Yucatan, a solar ritual), or the best pieces (1/35) are buried. Poultry are sometimes hung over the central pit by the feet, then sacrificed (Tzotzils). Their blood can also be poured in the pit (4/35). Generally, the other parts of the animal are cooked to make a broth, which is used to consecrate the corner posts and for the ritual feast.

Other offerings are sometimes components of the central deposit. Thus among some Tzotzils, the chicken is buried alive with flowers, tobacco, incense, and liquor (Hermitte 1970, 58), while other specialists of the same people add twenty pieces of chocolate, thirteen cigarettes, and a bottle of alcohol wrapped in a new cloth (Nash 1985 [1970], 16). For the Chols of La Cascada, *aguardiente*, *caldo*, and *pozol* of cacao surround a ball of meat wrapped between two layers of tortillas (Becquey 2017). This latter pattern is reminiscent of the frequent one used during Precolumbian times when offerings were contained between two vessels set lip to lip. In Yucatan, Robert Wauchope (1938) quotes an informant explaining that the chicken was accompanied by liquor and silver, while in Chan Kom the turkey, consecrated with rum, is not buried.

All this reminds us of the most common form of Precolumbian ritual deposit: an offering placed in an intrusive pit or directly included in newly constructed masonry. In some cases, human remains or remains of sacrificed animals were found—for instance, in Tikal, the skull of a beheaded young man in the cache Esc. PNT-10, a decapitated turtle in Cache 86, two living turtles in the cist Esc. PNT-4, and quetzal wings in problematic Deposit 87 (Coe 1990; Laporte 2002). Frequently, among other artifacts, some deposited offerings are considered to be auto-sacrifice paraphernalia: obsidian lancets, stingray spines and their bone imitations used as bloodletters, and big valves of *Spondylus* to collect the blood drops (Baudez 2012, 143).

While the cosmogram organization has never been fully documented in Classic Period residential areas, some layered deposits may have concentrated the entire symbolism of the quintipartite pattern—the representation of the three levels of the world—in a sole offering (Calligeris 1999; Guderjan et al. 2014, 354, 355). In the ethnographic data, when buried offerings are required, they are always realized in the center of the house, while those of the corners are less common. The latter location can be optional or require other kinds of ritual action, such as aspersion.

In archaeological cases, some deposits had a morphology or a spatial organization that produced a cruciform motif. In Ceibal, during the Middle Preclassic (1000–350 BC), nine occupation deposits revealed jade axes organized in a cruciform pattern or deposited at the center of cross-shaped pits. Burial 153 there also included five possible sacrificial victims following the same pattern. Cache 17, probably a re-foundation of a Terminal Classic pyramid, is also a cruciform deposit, exactly like its distant precursors of the Preclassic Period (Aoyama et al. 2017; Smith and Sabloff 1982, 245). Other quintipartite deposits have been found in El Cival's Structure 12, Tikal's Temple of the Skulls, Nakum's Acropolis, and Copan's 10J-45 complex (Bauer et al. 2005, 199; Laporte 2002, 210; Nakamura 2004, 248; Źrałka et al. 2012, 11). All of these could be devices intending to center the world and figure the axis mundi.

FEAST AND LITURGICAL MATERIALS

Other ritual actions executed during modern house dedications require a large range of objects. Among the most widely shared elements are incense (and probably censers, 19/35), candles (at least 18/35 explicit cases), alcohol (for aspersion, 16/35), flowers (10/35), holy or spring water (8/35), a cross (8/35), and a feast meal (7/35). We suggest from the modern use of these materials that they are unlikely to leave easily identifiable remains archaeologically, so it will be hard to find clues for comparable use in the archaeological data except for substances such as copal. Nevertheless, some hypotheses can be made. For example, the candles consecrated today may have replaced ritual fires noted as used in the past.

Today, the dedication ceremony sometimes ends with a feast (17/35), with dances and music (6/35). This ritual meal and liquor offered to participants could be a continuation of Precolumbian behaviors. Some archaeological finds could refer to feasts or celebrations. A royal feast is portrayed on Panel 3 from Piedras Negras (Houston, Stuart, and Taube 2006, 129). Laura Lucia Gámez Díaz (2013, 103–124) concluded that ritual meals may have been consumed in every layer of society at Yaxha. Some dedication deposits, such as Naachtun's Deposit 22 (Hiquet, González, and Ángel Cano 2014, 97), revealed a large number of empty vessels, which could have been used for serving or cooking.

TO INITIATE, TO PERPETUATE, THEN TO CLOSE: RITUAL TEMPORALITIES

Precolumbian Maya structures are often superimposed over previous construction stages. During these transitions, offerings are generally laid and fires, presumably ritual fires, are sometimes burned before or during the construction. During excavations, deposits are quite frequently identified by archaeologists as dedicatory ones. The most common are concentrations of votive materials, deposited directly in the masonry or in pits intrusive in floors or other architectural elements. This category was established by William R. Coe (1959) at the end of the 1950s. These rites were supposed to dedicate the structure, to open its occupation time, before a so-called termination ritual happened to definitively close the cycle or before a re-dedication ceremony.

Ethnographic studies allow us to question the pertinence of the dedication notion. The repetitive aspect of modern rituals shows few particularities of the initial rite. In some cases, among the Chols, for instance, the repeated ceremony (supposedly once a year) is a simplified form of the initial ritual. Temple 33-1st of Tikal provides one example (among many others). Here, three deposits were placed under successive stairways (Caches 59, 71, 201), and seven ritual fire episodes were practiced at different moments of the construction of the pyramid. This ritual behavior is not specific to foundations since the rituals are repeated during occupation of the house or temple.

On purely stratigraphic grounds, the etic categorization of dedication ritual is archaeologically coherent. But using a material criterion, the difference can be less visible. For Tikal, with a very rich corpus of Precolumbian offerings, Hattula Moholy-Nagy and Coe (2008, 18–21) defined eighteen recurring patterns of offering they called "offertory assemblages." Globally, some offertory assemblages are deposited during events of dedication, as well as during periods of occupation or later reconstructions. Linking depositional and architectural sequences reveals that an identical assemblage is almost never offered in a single structure, either during its construction or after, throughout its occupation. The only exceptions are two very similar "Yikel A" deposits in Temple 22-1st. Thus, at this site, perhaps the best documented, there is no indication of any concept of repetition of an initial ceremony. Variations of a similar assemblage may reflect a very similar petition to the entities, but with a sensibly different message. Some precision in the "vocabulary" could require a little modification of the deposited offering. To conclude, if variations are observed among dedication and occupation deposits inside an offertory assemblage, no clear rule appears.

Numerous glyphic texts of the Precolumbian era, the majority according to David Stuart (1998, 374–376), refer to the completion of new architectural structures (e.g., temples, stairs, benches, stelae, altars) or their dedication rituals. This kind of event is most often referred to by the use of verb forms pointing to the construction stage or the state resulting from this construction, such as *patwaan* or *patlaj* "being constructed, formed" for buildings; *ts'ahpaj/-ts'apa'w* "being planted / having planted" and *wa'waan* "standing" for stelae. These verb forms, even if they belong to the traditional paradigm of *dedication verbs*, do not refer directly to a specific dedication ritual, even if one can be implied.

While the dedication verb *k'al* "to tie" and its derived expression *k'altuun* "stone tying" are well known, characterizing the stela dedication ritual, mentions of ritual actions specifically related to structures are rarer and seem to correspond to three actions. These are *och(i) k'ahk'* "fire entering," the most frequent; *ochnahaj/ochotootaj* "house entering or being inhabited"; and *elnah* "house combustion." Strikingly, these "entering" or "combustion" phrases appear only on marginal occasions combined with an explicit mention of a building's construction, as in the inscriptions of the Cross Group at Palenque (Stuart 1998, 392). Nevertheless, today, the majority of epigraphers consider these expressions references to a monument dedication ritual. A general review shows, however, that a correlation between dedication and entering rituals is not so easy, since "fire-entering" rituals are sometimes associated with funerary actions ("tomb-renewal ceremonies"; 396–369) or occur on birthdays or dates of other events (Schele 1989, 39) and during period-ending rituals.

The expression *och(i) k'ahk'* "fire entering" and its association with building dedication shaped the interpretation of this ritual following Stuart's (1998) fundamental paper on the subject. We can note the ethnographic parallel Stuart made in this same article between *och(i) k'ahk'* and the Tzotzil house ensoulment ritual in Zinacantan, called *Ch'ul kantela* "holy candle" or *och kantela* "candles entering," which favored the diffusion of the ensoulment theory, now prominent (Houston, Stuart, and Taube 2006, 13; Schele and Mathews 1998, 48). But, as we saw, ensoulment rituals are rare ethnographically and only attested in a few modern Tzotzil communities. Interestingly, the literal expression "fire/candles entering" also exists in other Maya languages such as Chol, where *ochel ñichim* (*ñichim* "candle" is a synonym of *k'ahk'* "fire, candle, fever") can be translated as "the action of consecrating/ entering the candles/fire," which designates all kinds of ritual practices involving multiple goals (such as protection, petition for rain, curing rites) but excluding ensoulment.

Uncertainty concerning the true goal or goals of the ancient rituals explains the existence of multiple hypotheses. Among these, we can identify the theory that the goals of these rituals were protection (Plank 2004, 1), consecration (Palka 2014, 92), or to make the house inhabitable (Fitzsimmons 2009, 31) or that they constituted a metaphor for creation, where the rulers "reenact the ordering of the cosmos and compares [*sic*] him to the supernatural beings associated with each of the three stone platforms or thrones" (Looper 2003, 11). Much work remains to be done to pursue these different possibilities.

TERMINATION RITUALS: OFFERINGS OR PRAGMATISM?

If the "dedication" category can be questioned, what about its supposed temporal counterpart, the so-called termination rituals? Archaeologically, they are identified by breakage and scattering of ceramics (including censers), destruction of monuments (stelae, altars), severe burning on floors, charcoal and ash concentrations, and partial demolition of buildings. On the North Acropolis of Tikal, between the end of the Late Classic and the Terminal Classic, pits were dug in every temple to search for ancient deposits, among other termination rituals, on a previously unseen scale. Regarding their materialities, these rituals can be easily and clearly distinguished from dedication or occupation offerings. However, they are still generally considered offerings. These rituals may have been performed to deactivate the magical potential of these objects and temples or to kill them, as well as to close a portal. If we try, here again, to search for modern parallels, the ethnographic literature review did not provide any notion of de-animation or ritual termination of buildings, except for rare and undetailed mentions of post-demolition. Usually, houses are left to rot as if a natural "death" was needed (Hermitte 1970; Figuerola, personal communication, 2017).

The main purpose of modern rituals is to establish and then maintain a contract with an earth-related entity. Without repetition, the deal is void. This explains the lack of modern termination rituals, since the point is to continue the relationship. Following this, observed termination events in archaeological sites may not be so much rituals as display a more pragmatic intention. A new category of deposits was recently identified by Julien Sion (2016, 515) in Naachtun. Named "Guardians deposits," they include specific artifacts such as lithic projectile points and human long bones placed across the access way of structures just before leaving the building, presumably to symbolically preclude anyone's entrance. This closure could have been completed by material and architectural staging, including destruction and fires, to make it visibly inhospitable for squatters, travelers, or passersby.

CONCLUSION

This review of the ethnographic literature, as well as archaeological and epigraphic sources, aimed to clarify present knowledge about house building rituals in the Maya area. In contemporary societies, all the examples of rituals present two objectives often disregarded in possible archaeological interpretation: the necessity to negotiate with the master(s) of earth for the right to occupy a space and the delineation of a protected space against evil spirits, diseases, and calamities. Even if nothing allows us to validate fully or exclude definitely the ensoulment/animation theory for the Classic Period, these observations can allow us, despite the obvious time difference between contemporary and Precolumbian societies, to question the archaeological data and the pertinence of some former hypotheses from a new perspective.

This study allowed us to determine some convergences between ancient and present ritual materialities and agentivities. Beyond these observations, the closer look at the different Precolumbian offertory assemblages related to dedication underlined the importance of distinctions between the types of structure, an aspect we had not been able to verify in the ethnography. While this work was initially focused on understanding the aims of house building rituals, it appears that constant references to their repetition over occupation times could imply new perspectives on the very subject of house dedication. Finally, while the notion of termination rituals seems to be completely absent from ethnographic data, their materiality is completely different from that of offerings. Based on ethnographic and archaeological leads, they may have been a warning to signal that the site was now deserted and inhospitable.

The ritual aims to introduce the building in space, a form of place making (see also Arnauld, chapter 5, this volume). It also makes it possible to initiate the relationship between this space/entity and human beings and to maintain it in time at regular intervals. Rituals are performed to create a safe place, guaranteed by theoretically regular repetitions as these immutable constraints have been imposed by entities since the creation of humanity.

Repetition is usually the consequence of unforeseen human events (e.g., planned renewal, arrival of a new house member, change in building function). These ceremonies make it possible to protect the building itself and its inhabitants for a more or less definite time from the dangers inherent to the occupation, but this temporality is often shortened by various hazards that call for an unexpected repetition of the ritual. Although ideally this relationship with the entities should establish a temporal continuum through preventive ceremonies to anticipate problems, human beings often wait until a crisis occurs to carry out their ritual duty, which then takes on a curative role. These successive ritual temporalities are cyclical at the human scale, whereas at a larger timescale, the long-term relationship with non-humans creates a unified historical framework.

8

Heaps of Prayers

The Materiality of Catholic Prayers, Their Temporal Dimension and Ritual Effectiveness within Nahua Ritual Discourse

ALESSANDRO LUPO

https://doi.org/10.5876/9781646422395.c008

In this chapter I reflect on an aspect of Nahua ritual practices that concerns the "materiality" of something apparently as impalpable and ethereal as words but that nevertheless, from the perspective of the social actors themselves and of their imagined extra-human interlocutors, reveals how verbal utterances are also considered to be endowed with sensory properties and capable of producing "physical" consequences, like many other objects and substances used in ritual actions. It is well-known that for Mexican native cultures—as for countless other peoples of the Americas and other parts of the world—the distinction between matter and spirit, between the dense and tangible and the subtle and intangible, is not ontologically as radical and clear as in the theology and philosophy of Europe and its colonial outposts. Those of us, either anthropologists or historians, who try to understand the thought and actions of our native interlocutors know that for them, reality constitutes a continuum without sharp solutions of continuity, within which there are things and beings that have a thicker and heavier consistence and others that have a thinner and lighter one (López Austin 1994)—so much so that even when they speak of "immaterial" entities as souls, spirits, and extra-human beings, they often refer to substances and entities endowed with a very perceptible material consistence, such as air, wind, clouds, or various kinds of animals (from tiny insects to large mammals).

In the rituals they perform to obtain the intervention and help of their extra-human interlocutors, the

Nahua of the municipality of Cuetzalan combine a complex variety of gestural and verbal acts that from their perspective can have both communicative and pragmatic functions, through the use of substances and objects endowed with multiple perceptible qualities, capable of exerting their effects on a plurality of recipients. Their rituals are therefore configured as performances that produce a wide range of complementary sensory perceptions, which sometimes reveal the differences underlying the perceptive faculties of humans and extra-human entities, highlighting meaningful aspects of the indigenous *sensorium* and the way the effectiveness of ritual action is conceived (see Howes 2003). Above all, to understand the meaning of the vast array of elements used in a ritual act, we must consider that in the extra-human dimension of the beings whose intervention is sought by ritual specialists, what is perceived, acquired, and matters in the ritual exchange it is not the "heavy" and dense matter manipulated by humans but rather the subtle and light essence of things, which animates and vivifies them, surviving their dissolution after death. This is the reason why—especially for the rituals' recipients—some ritual words are equated with other objects and substances by attributing to them properties that normally, in the earthly human dimension, would not be characteristic of something as volatile as words, which to our senses are pure *flatus vocis*, mere sounds, impalpable and ephemeral.

SUPPLICATIONS AND PRAYERS

I do not pretend that the meaning and uses of the materials used in these rituals differ significantly from those studied by the multitude of colleagues who have dealt with this topic in Mesoamerica (Breton and Becquelin-Monod 1989; Bricker 1989 [1974]; Dehouve 2007, 2010, 2013a, 2013b; Edmonson 1970, 1976; Figuerola Pujol 1996a, 1996b, 2011; Gossen 1974, 1976, 1989 [1974]; Hanks 1984, 1990, 1993a, 1993b; Haviland 1992, 2000, 2003; Holland 1978 [1963]; Laughlin 1980, 1983; Monod Becquelin 1986, 1987, 1993, 2000; Pitarch Ramón 1998, 2010 [1996], 2011; Pitrou 2012, 2014a, 2014b, 2016a, 2016b; Reyes García and Christensen 1976; Sandstrom and Gómez Martínez 2004; B. Tedlock 1992 [1982]; D. Tedlock 1983; Vapnarsky 2000, 2008, 2009, 2013a, 2013b, 2014, 2017). Nevertheless, I find it interesting to carefully examine the different verbal genres that accompany these rites, in which some statements reveal a materiality that is not always attributed to words.

In particular, I will rely on the examination of two types of ritual speech genres uttered jointly by the specialists known as *tamatiani* /those who know/ 'wise persons', *tetahtohuiani* /those who speak for someone/ 'spokesmen', *tapalehuiani* /those who help/ 'ritual specialists', or *tapahtiani* /those who cure/ 'healers' (singular *tamatque, tetahtohuihque, tapalehuihque, tapahtihque*) (Lupo 1995b).[1] These are two forms of verbal expression that have a different origin and that indigenous people differentiate conceptually and terminologically.

On the one hand, there are the invocations and supplications (Nahuatl *tatatauhtiliz*, pl. *tatatauhtilime*) with which—almost always using the Nahuatl language—they describe in detail before their interlocutors the identity of the clients, the beneficiaries and possible antagonists, the specific situation and the instances that induce them to perform the rite, the requests addressed to each one of the different addressees, the effects one wishes to obtain from the ritual action, and the term before which these effects are expected to be achieved. On the other hand, there is another type of ritual words that after almost five centuries have become part of Nahua religious tradition: Catholic prayers (*tahtolme* /words/ or *tiotahtolme* /divine words/), mainly uttered in Spanish, which are learned during the catechism or from reading the many prayer booklets circulating in indigenous communities.

Prayers are a verbal form that despite its deep-rooted presence in the religious life of Mesoamerican indigenous peoples has not attracted much attention from anthropologists, perhaps because of its exogenous origin, which characterizes it as something scarcely representative of the autochthonous cultural tradition on which ethnographic research is usually focused. These prayers include the Our Father, the Hail Mary, the Glory Be to the Father, the Hail Holy Queen, the Apostles' Creed, the Act of Contrition, the Requiem, and the Magnificat, as well as the wide variety of litanies, mysteries, and formulas every pious parishioner has the opportunity to hear and learn during their catechetical formation and attending the different church functions provided by the Catholic liturgy, in both the public and private spheres.

Unless Nahua ritual acts are directed to forces and entities other than those that people the extra-human Christian world, such as short spells to ward off the rainbow or invocations to the devil to harm others, all ritual supplication in Nahuatl is accompanied by a variable number of Catholic prayers, which often correspond to the type and quantity fixed for the use of the rosary (figure 8.1). These series—called *tapohual* /count/ or *panti* /line, row, group/—on the one hand reflect the fully orthodox idea that the very act of devotion of the one who recites prayers while in a state of purity and being animated by good intentions can produce effects such as attracting divine benevolence or relieving the pains of penitent souls. But on the other hand, these pre-established series of prayers are also inspired by the very old Amerindian practice of offering to the rituals' recipients a great variety of material objects in the so-called

FIGURE 8.1. *Francisca Tejero using the rosary to pray*

counted bundles, based on the supposition that an important part of the effectiveness of ritual depends on the number, sequence, and arrangement of such objects (compare Dehouve 2001, 2007, 2010, 2011; López Luján 1993, 2009, 2010–2011, 2012, 2015, 2018).

The Nahua are well aware that supplications and prayers are closely complementary but different verbal acts: they not only give them different names—*tatatauhtiliz* for supplications and *tiotahtol* or *oración* for Catholic prayers—but they also manifest full awareness of the distinction between the characteristics and the use of each one: "*Tatatauhtiliz*: lo que pide uno; *tiotahtol*: lo que rezas," "what one asks for," "what you pray" (Miguel Cruz, interview, November 9, 2017).

The first are uttered in Nahuatl, following the models of the indigenous ceremonial discourse (therefore with a frequent use of parallelisms, metaphors, formulas of respect, and archaic terms) and nevertheless with the great flexibility of all oral utterances, which allows them to adapt meticulously to the context of the enunciation and to express the most minute peculiarities of the instances that inspire the ritual (Lupo 1995a, 2013, 135–156). Despite the high formalization that characterizes all ritual discourse, the praying person can concentrate in his or her supplications all the information necessary to ensure that the expected extra-human response produces its effects.

In contrast, Catholic prayers, which have a written source and are subject to the strict control of the clergy, do not allow any margin of variation in their form and content, and whoever prays can only vary their number and order. As Maurice Bloch (1974, 76) observed of the ritual songs of the Merina of Madagascar, "Repetition is the only possibility for emphasis. A frozen statement cannot be expanded, it can only be made again and again and again. Repetition reminds us that we are not dealing with an argument." In other words, recalling the concepts formulated several decades ago by the British philosopher of language John L. Austin (1962) and his Berkeley colleague John R. Searle (1969), we can paraphrase the comment of the aforementioned Nahua ritual specialist, noting that the supplications in Nahuatl are used to express and transmit the "propositional content" of ritual action while the use of Catholic prayers is based on the "illocutionary" and "perlocutionary force" attributed to them: that is, on the one hand, their capacity to produce concrete consequences simply by being pronounced in appropriate conditions that determine their "happiness"; on the other, their ability to persuade extra-human interlocutors to do what they are asked to do, inducing them to intervene on behalf of humans (see Lupo 1995a, 2013, 135–156).

The fact that Catholic prayers are used in rituals in a way analogous to the other substances offered in the "ritual deposits" (*tahpalol* /greeting/ 'offering' or *nezcayot* /what appears, signal/ 'gift, donation') is demonstrated by the phrases used to introduce their utterance during the supplications. These phrases always use verbs related to a material delivery and to the possession and use of concrete goods, such as *mactilia* /to put in hand/ 'to present', *axcatilia* /to give possession of something/, or *entregarohuilia* 'to deliver' (throughout this chapter, in transcription of texts, italics are used to highlight loans from Spanish; bold is used for emphasis):

Nican **nimitzmactiliti** nehin *oraciones*[2]
  Here I am going to present to you these prayers
talticpactzin *de mi alma.*
  Earth[3] of my soul.
  (José Morales, Tacuapan; supplication to cure fright illness,
  November 29, 1988)

Animas benditas,
  Blessed souls,
xic*recibiro*can *santas ofrendas*
  receive the holy offerings
tein tamechaxcatiliah.
  of which we give you possession. [He recites a Glory Be and an
  ejaculation.]
Itech in eyi tapohualme
  In the three counts [the third series of Catholic prayers of the rosary]
oc cepa **namechaxcatiliti** oc ce **namotahtoltzin**
  once more I will give you possession of other Words of yours [prayers]
para namehhuan xic*recibiro*can
  in order that you receive
nehin nemactiliz tein tamechaxcatiliah
  this endowment of which we give you possession
itech nehin tonal,
  in this day,
itech nehin *hora.*
  in this hour.
  (Miguel Cruz, Cihuapilaco; rosary for the dead, November 2, 1988)

Canachi tein nictali nican
  Everything I put here
itech *mesa* yetoc, **namech***entregaro***huilia,**
  [and] it is on the table, I give it to you,
namechmactilia.
  I present it to you.

. . .

Namech*entregaro*huilia ica nehin *oraciones*
I deliver it to you with these prayers
y nehin *ofrenda* nehin *hora* huan nehin tonal.
and this offering [in] this hour and [in] this day.

(Guadalupe Vásquez Bonilla, Tzinacapan, rosary for the dead,
November 2, 1985)

As is evident from the fragments of ritual discourses I just quoted, Catholic prayers are equated with the other objects and substances the specialist has laid on the altar to please, satisfy, and ultimately "nurture" the extra-human entities to whom they are addressed (the Earth, the saints, God, the souls of the dead). It is evident that—depending on the ceremonial occasion—the type, number, and disposition of the offered goods vary considerably. However, both with supplications pronounced for the installation of the *calyolot* /heart of the house/ (Lok 1987) and the hearth (*tixochit*) and in those that precede the sowing of maize, in those to cure illnesses caused by fright (*nemouhtil*) or witchcraft (*amo cuali ehecat*), or in those addressed to the dead on the occasion of All Saints (Lupo 1995a), the altar is always adorned with many flowers, lit candles, and paper or plastic cutouts of various colors; the speaker will also often accompany the salient passages of his invocation by elevating *copal* smoke with a censer (*tecolcaxit*) or sprinkling holy water by means of a flower (Lupo 1995b, 2013, 2018, 2019). The ritual setting, then, manifests the aim to establish a communication/interaction with the extra-human recipients by means of a synesthetic event in which—even if they are imperceptible to those who invoke them—these beings manage to capture the essence of all the goods that are given to them and the gestures that are performed. This is achieved through the clarity of light and the brightness of colors, the fragrance of perfumes, the heat of the flames and freshly cooked dishes, and the sound of words and songs; through the flavor of foods and the delicate rubbing of the rosary on the ground or the violent blows given on the Earth to have it release the patient's shadow (*ecahuil*), which has been stolen after a fright (Lupo 1995b; Signorini and Lupo 1989).

Since in the Nahua conception of the cosmos all beings, including the divine ones to which many invocations and offerings are directed, are believed to take part in the great process of circulation and consumption of energies on which all forms of life depend and are therefore imagined as subject to wear, deficiencies, and appetites similar to those of humans, most ritual acts have—among others—the objective of giving back at least part of the energies human beings receive and consume from them (Lupo 1995b, 2001, 2013). This kind of delivery/restitution of forces is particularly evident with entities such as the Earth-Trinity, which is considered the main source of everything that feeds living beings and therefore is conceived as insatiable, hungry for everything that may fall on its surface (Lupo 1995b, 2011; Signorini and Lupo 1989). The same criterion also inspires invocations addressed to God and to the saints, whose amount of force is evidently not conceived as infinite and inexhaustible but as subject to the gradual deterioration of entropy. Above all, as is easy to guess, a voracious demand to satisfy the lack of worldly goods that death took away from them forever torments the deceased when at the beginning of November they return to visit their homes, richly prepared by the living relatives with all the substances and objects they most enjoyed in their earthly life: food, drinks, cigars, toys, candles, incense, and paper cuttings, among others (Baez Cubero 1996, 2005, 2008; Baez Cubero and Rodríguez Lascano 2008; Chamoux 1997; Good Eshelman 1996; Lok 1991; Lupo 2018, 2019; Nutini 1988; Signorini 2008). The characteristic all these offered goods have in common is to be vehicles of "force," which the Nahua often verbally express in terms of "heat." Due to the fact that extra-human entities have an immaterial, ontologically distinct, or "lighter" and "subtle" nature, they cannot appropriate the material and tangible substance of what is given to them through the organs and senses of proximity, such as touch and taste (whose exertion implies the manipulation and partial destruction of substances); instead, they take their gifts' most impalpable essence, made of clarity (*tanex*), heat (*totoniliz, tecahuaniliz*), smoke (*pocti*), and fragrance (*ahhuiyacayot*), leaving the offerings apparently intact although already emptied of their deepest energetic content.

THE "FORCE" OF PRAYERS

What about the acoustic dimension of ceremonial invocations and prayers? Well, it does not escape the logic that inspires the energetic exchange I just outlined. As observed, Catholic prayers are not used as verbal instruments suited to transmit to the addressees the essential information of ritual, since their propositional content is minimal and extremely rigid, very difficult to adjust to the highly variable demands of the context in which they are uttered; rather, they are recited for the "illocutionary force" attributed to them, which varies according to the identity of the beings they mention and the meaning of their text.

To ask for the disclosure of the cause of an ailment and to be able to make the diagnosis, the therapist Miguel Cruz pronounces a brief invocation to the Sun-Christ, the Virgin, and the angels—reciting just one Our Father, a Hail Holy Queen, and a Glory Be: as the extra-human intervention he invokes is

FIGURE 8.2. *The dancer representing Saint James wielding his sword*

limited to the revelation of something, the number and importance of prayers is rather small (Lupo 1995b, 116–118). On the contrary, to cure a serious illness such as fright, which is attributed to the loss of one of the patient's spiritual components (the *ecahuil* /shadow/) and requires its restitution by the Earth-Trinity that retains it and feeds on it, it is necessary that, in addition to giving the Earth a "replacement" (*iixpatca*) of its prey or a "payment" (*taxtahuil*, which may also consist of a coin), one address a series of prayers to the divine couple that forms the Earth-Trinity and to the main figures of the Catholic "pantheon," such as Saint Michael, Saint Christopher, Saint Raphael, the angel of Mary, the guardian angel, Saint James, Saint Peter, and Saint John (José Morales in Lupo 1995b, 128–136) or Jesus Christ, Our Lady of Sorrows, Saint James (figure 8.2), and Saint Michael (Miguel Cruz in Signorini and Lupo 1989, 204–225).

FIGURE 8.3. *The healer Francisco Landero praying before his home altar*

Here, too, we find the recitation of Our Fathers and Hail Marys, but in the first case the curer utters a single series of seven Our Fathers and seven Hail Marys, while in the second case he dedicates to each of the five recipients one Our Father, seven Hail Marys, and one Glory Be—ending with a final series of one Our Father, one Hail Holy Queen, one Glory Be, one ejaculation, and one Creed. Finally, to heal an act of witchcraft, which supposedly consists of the intrusion into the patient's body of a hostile spirit or "evil air" (*amo cuali ehecat*), it is necessary to seek the help of a higher number of extra-human helpers (Jesus Christ, the Virgins of Guadalupe and of Sorrows, Saint Anthony of Padua, Saint James, Saint Michael, and the angels) and to give them a greater number of Catholic prayers: the therapist dedicates to each of the recipients one Our Father, ten Hail Marys, one Glory Be, and one ejaculation—ending with a final series of one Our Father, one Hail Holy Queen, one Glory Be, one ejaculation, and one Creed (Miguel Cruz 1988, in Signorini and Lupo 1989, 248–273).

To combat witchcraft, other specialists address an even greater number of extra-human helpers, praying up to three Creeds (Guadalupe Vásquez Bonilla, Tzinacapan, personal communication, 1985), since this prayer is considered the most powerful one that can be used: "The Creed is for defense [against witchcraft], it is hot, it is strong. If someone wants to harm you, if he wants to bewitch you, just pray those big prayers and with that they won't do anything to you" (Miguel Cruz 1988 in Signorini and Lupo 1989, 190). The reason why the Creed is attributed a greater amount of heat-force—which explains why during ritual it is prayed a number of times inferior to the other prayers—is that it lists all the main figures and the foundations of the Catholic faith, expressing the firm belief of the one who prays in the truth of what they state (figure 8.3):

> It's hot, it's strong. You can stop any temptation [evil spirit] with the Creed, because it is hotter, it is stronger: it is as if it were Saint James' machete, as if it were the machete of Saint Michael. With that you cut off any temptation: you put your machete crosswise, with that you arrest it. The Creed is strong . . . Well it's hot—they say—stronger, so to say. With that you arrest all bad temptations, all bad vibes. That's why I tell you: you have a weapon . . . That Creed means that I believe [with emphasis] in all things . . . It is belief, it is our belief . . . Belief, believing in the word of the Lord . . . It is strength, because you are with God: you believe before God, you do believe that there is God . . . Faith is hot, it is the most part of everything, of everything you want.[4] (Miguel Cruz, interview, September 9, 2017)

These last words clarify how the Creed's force is derived from both its textual and its semantic extension (it is "big" and mentions many extra-human entities) and even more so from the intentionality of the one who prays; by proclaiming their deep belief in the existence and the power of God, they confer heat-force to what it enunciates, transforming the prayer into an insurmountable barrier: "Those prayers are stronger, it is hotter because it blocks any temptation. Are you willing to put yourself in the fire? Do you? Well, no! So, this is. It's as if it were in the fire" (Miguel Cruz, interview, September 11, 2017).[5] Here is a Nahua variation of the indigenous theory—very widespread in Mesoamerica—that there are types of discourse with a variable charge of "heat." Gary H. Gossen (1974, 1976, 1989 [1974]; see also Haviland 1992, 433; Monod Becquelin 1987, 1993) notes that among the Tzotzil Maya of Chiapas, the higher the degree of formalization of ritual language, the older its origin; the denser, purer, and more charged with force are the words uttered; therefore those forms of language (whose maximum expression is song) are also considered the "hottest": "It is a language so hot that it becomes, as it were, pure essence, like the smoke of tobacco or incense" (Gossen 1989 [1974], 410). Concerning prehispanic Mesoamerica, Mark B. King (1994, 107) interprets as "heat" the fact that in Mixtec pictographic codices, song is represented by the same scrolls that indicate smoke: "I . . . suggest that 'song' and all song-related activities are spiritually heated in nature . . . song [can therefore be conceived] as 'a spiritually heated offering that rises skyward.'"

Although none of my interlocutors has explained the "heat" of Catholic prayers by associating them with their antiquity, we cannot rule out the

FIGURE 8.4. *The healer Miguel Cruz with his rosary before his home altar*

possibility that—like Chamula "ancient words" (Gossen 1989 [1974], 399)—the founding prayers of the Catholic faith such as the Lord's Prayer and the Creed (the first one dictated to the apostles by Jesus's lips) owe their "heat" to the authoritativeness of their origin. What we can surely compare with the "heated heart" of the Chamulas when they utter prayers, ceremonial speeches, and songs is when the Nahua of Cuetzalan devotedly recite the "biggest" Catholic prayers, to which the combination of their dogmatic content and the faith of the speaker confer exceptional strength and warmth. What also seems to fully coincide with the Chamula idea of ritual words is that their high degree of "heat" allows them to cross the ontological gap that separates humans from God, making possible the communication between them and the transmission of energy the rite aims to give back to its source: "Indeed, the 'audible essence' [of ritual language] can be heard at great distances, more so than any of the other forms of 'ancient words'" (Gossen 1976, 55). I think it is superfluous to emphasize the fact that in both contexts—the Maya and the Nahua—sacred words have the same properties as the other substances (e.g., incense, candles, flowers) and that ritual acts seek to activate and make accessible to the extra-human recipients the "essences" they can capture with their "subtle" perceptive faculties, which are typical of incorporeal beings (figure 8.4).

I would like to add another commentary, inspired by what Gossen (1989 [1974], 410–411) says about the Chamula songs: "'Song' may be said the highest form of language addressed to supernaturals . . . 'Song' is . . . an extreme statement of metaphorical heat, for the musical form and the heavily 'stacked' couplet structure together make it possible to repeat them *ad infinitum* until the ritual events they accompany have concluded." Although the Nahua of Cuetzalan do not usually sing their supplications and prayers, it seems to me that Catholic prayers—with their formal fixedness, theological-devotional "heat," and the possibility of being repeated in innumerable series, following the canonical praxis of the rosary—exemplify a type of ritual discourse that shares many traits with the "purest" forms of Tzotzil ceremonial language.

Other faculties attributed by the Nahua to Catholic prayers do not primarily concern the extra-human entities to which they are directed: I mean the indirect effects they may have on the beneficiaries of ritual. In fact, the care in "dosing" prayers is not inspired only by the observance of the canonical liturgical models (which, for example, prescribe the proportion of one Our Father and ten Hail Marys in the rosary) but takes into account the performative consequences their enunciation can determine on the beneficiaries of the supplications. As several scholars have pointed out (Hanks 1984, 1990, 1993a, 1993b; Pitrou 2012, 2014a, 2014b, 2016a, 2016b), it would be a limitation to consider oblational rites as events that only imply a transmission of goods or essences from humans to their extra-human interlocutors, since the very setting of ritual implies the co-presence of a plurality of actors (the ritual specialists, the extra-human recipients, the beneficiaries of ritual action). It is not uncommon that substances and actions that are part of ritual, in addition to reaching their main recipients, may have as a secondary (but carefully considered) consequence an influence on human beings (which may be the ritual actors in person or their beneficiaries, as in healing). This not only concerns substances and goods but sometimes also implies ritual words: among Yucatec Maya healers, William F. Hanks (1984, 1990, 1993a) has observed something similar with respect to the verbal execution of prayers: "In healing rituals, even the speed of verbal articulation and the rhythm of the shaman's corporal gestures vary according to the age and strength of the patient. Strong people can be treated in the 'fast' style . . . while those who are weaker or more vulnerable require a slower and softer type of prayer" (Hanks 1993a, 86–87; see also Hanks 1984, 151).

Among the Nahua, I have not witnessed variations in the style of enunciation of the therapeutic supplications according to the patient's sex, age, or state of health. However, what adapts to his or her varying conditions is the type and number of Catholic prayers, which, as several therapists explained, must respect certain qualitative and quantitative criteria so as not to harm the patient's health: "You must not throw in too many [prayers], otherwise he/she breaks down . . . You cannot increase them too much, because this way what you do doesn't work: it just has to be counted, you must not say too many prayers" (José Morales 1986 in Signorini and Lupo 1989, 190).[6]

The idea underlying these words is that prayers, despite being addressed to the recipients of the supplications within which they are pronounced, also have an effect on the patient's spiritual components, which are somehow co-present in the ritual setting and are affected by this circulation of essences. We must not forget that the main ailments for which ritual therapists are called upon, inducing them to pronounce supplications and prayers, concern the patient's spiritual entities (*ecahuil, yolo*), which in case of fright have left the body and are retained by beings that feed on them and in the case of evil eye or witchcraft are affected by the intrusion of harmful projections or "airs" (Lupo 1995b; Signorini and Lupo 1989, 1992). Therefore, the condition of weakness in which the patient lies requires healers to carefully measure the prayers they are going to address to their extra-human interlocutors, since an excessive dose could harm the patient. If the sick person is gravely ill and requires more intense therapy, then the solution will be to repeat the ritual sessions more frequently, but the number of prayers and other ritual paraphernalia (such as candles) will never be increased indiscriminately: "for *nemouhtil* /fright/ nobody prays more than seven" (Miguel Cruz in Signorini and Lupo 1989, 128):[7]

> Because you put lots of prayers on him and you see his body how it is: [the prayers] are strong and he can get worse. He [the patient] is already like some person [that you] take somewhere: you take a laborer, you grab him and load him—because the wax is wood, the candle is like some wood—you put the load on him, and then you start to put on more. Sure, you loaded him with candles, a piece, you grab and put some more, you put more on him, well, instead of bearing it, instead of carrying it, he falls and cannot stand it. You are doing the same with these prayers: you carry [some] until he endures, and then go and carry more. This way, little by little, it's not all of a pull. (Miguel Cruz 1986 in Signorini and Lupo 1989, 128–129)[8]

This specialist's commentary clarifies in an exemplary way the logic that governs the temporal sequence of ritual practices and the connection between the quantities of offered goods or "essences," their sequential distribution, and the effectiveness of the rite. Just as in supplying food to an organism, one must take into account its metabolic capacities, the same goes for the dispensing of candles, incense, flowers, and prayers—which to achieve the effects expected by the ritual specialist must not exceed the appropriate doses that can be "digested" by the recipients:

I have to pray [some prayers] to all [the saints I invoke in the supplication].
But each one with his rosary. I give you your dish: "This is your dish, food." I
also give his plate to the other one. I also give his plate to the other one. With
measure. You must not go like a fool, running. Everyone with his plate. [A.L.:
But why saying many prayers may hurt the patient?] "Eat and eat!" Before you
already ate a dish and now, I am giving you another one, again and again: I have
already heaped work on you. I'm heaping work on you alone. You're going to
have indigestion later. (Miguel Cruz, interview, September 9, 2017)[9]

It is evident, then, that ritual words reach both the formal recipients to
whom they are addressed (and whom the meticulous descriptions and arguments of the Nahuatl supplications seek to persuade to give their help) and
the human beneficiaries of the rite (more specifically, their spiritual components), which may suffer the effects of an excessive dose of prayers. The
potential harm caused to patients by prayers in excess consists of the risk of
"overloading them," charging them with a disproportioned dose of force issued
in a single moment (remember the analogy of firewood). In parallel, an excess
of prayers is also counterproductive to the extra-human entities to which the
therapist appeals in favor of the patient:

You go to a court, to ask a question to the judge about what you went to
say right now, you went to clarify . . . Tomorrow you go another round for
that same thing. All right. You have to go for the same thing tomorrow. But
tomorrow! Not after a while. He already told you: "Well, I'll see how we solve
it." But after a while [you go] again . . . The judge is going to expel you, he's
going to say: "He's crazy! After [he] came, he just left, he came once again! He
just left; he came once again!" The judge is going to expel you: "Then you do
not really [behave seriously], you're a tattler! Get out!" But no. I already told
you . . . the judge already gave you an appointment for when you have to present yourself: that day you have to go. So, it's the same with prayers: I already
offered you [some]. You already ate, how are you going to eat again right now?
If you have already had lunch, once again they tell you that you are going to
have lunch. "I already ate, I already had breakfast." So why should I harass you?
. . . It's for . . . you [have to] keep waiting, little by little, little by little, until he
obeys us . . . [If] you keep bothering him, he will give you nothing. But if you
leave now, and tomorrow you go once more, then you go again a week later,
thus you are offering little by little . . . The same with God, you have to go in
parts. You have to speak with patience, [like asking] favors . . . Without being
harassing there. Do you [think] that you are the only one to be served? And
the other ones? Are you the only one? There is a shitload of people who are

asking him . . . You have to give him time to think. (Miguel Cruz, interview, September 11, 2017)[10]

The dual analogy chosen by this ritual specialist to clarify the need to present prayers in small doses is not accidental: the imaginary forensic context of the judge who, obsessively urged by the begging one, becomes furious and expels him roughly directly recalls the role of *abogado* (*tetahtohuihque* /one who speaks on behalf of someone/) that is usually attributed to the extra-human address-ees of supplications (such as Catholic saints or the souls of the dead), which are charged to mediate with the supreme divine figures (Christ, the Eternal Father) so they make possible solutions to human problems (recovery of health and social harmony), prosperity of the fields and abundance of crops, fertilizing rains and protection from environmental disasters, and more (see Lupo 1995b, 2013; Signorini and Lupo 1989). But above all, the example of food compul-sively supplied to someone already satiated makes explicit the idea that like the other ritual offerings of incense, candles, and flowers, even the Catholic prayers one actually "delivers" (*mactilia*, *axcatilia*, or *entregarohuilia*) to the recipients of the supplications are considered a kind of food that can satisfy them and, if in excess, produce a sort of "indigestion." This means that conceived as having substance, even these ready-made sets of words are subject to a kind of meta-bolic process, which requires that the extra-human beings are allowed some time for their "digestion" to persuade them of the validity of the human peti-tions and to have them thoughtfully grant what has been requested.

A "RAIN" OF PRAYERS

So far, I have examined the energetic charge (expressed in terms of "heat") Catholic prayers (some more than others) can transmit to the various entities co-present in the ritual setting. However, the supplications the Nahua special-ists direct to various figures of the extra-human world on the occasion of the feast of All Saints, with the aim of appeasing and "refreshing" the souls of the deceased, reveal another facet of the use of Catholic prayers that demonstrates their "otherworldly" materiality. In explaining the meaning of the supplication he was going to say on the eve of the arrival of his dead relatives' souls, when small children are believed to come to visit the living, the old ritual specialist Francisco Antonio Tejero clarified what follows:

Aman yetoqueh *día de vigilia*,
   Today they are on the eve's day,
el día primero de noviembre, sí,

the first of November, yes,
tiquin*rezaro*huiliti in *ánimas benditas difuntitos que* . . .
  we are going to pray to the blessed souls of the Deceased who . . .
tein *viviro*htoqueh ihuan *Dios Padre Eterno*
  who are living with the Eternal Father
ompa *Gloria,*
  there in Heaven,
ánimas angelitos,
  the deceased little angels,
angelitos de Gloria,
  little angels of Heaven,
yetoqueh
  [who] stay
ompa ihuan to *Dios, viviro*htoqueh
  there with our God, they are living
ompa ilhuicac paquiloyan ixochimilpan.
  there in the sky, place of joy [in] His field seeded with flowers.
Nehhua niquin*rezaro*huilia
  I am going to pray
eyi nahui macuil *rosario*
  three, four, five rosaries
de mahmacuil panti
  in series of five
huan *de* chihchicome panti,
  and in series of seven,
para nicmactilia ne ce ne *Dios Padre eterno* huan ne *Jesucristo,*
  so that I give one to the Eternal Father and to Jesus Christ,
para yehhua mah quilhui moyahuili *parejito*
  so that He may tell Him to scatter them evenly
[?? incomprehensible] yetoc ne ilhuicac *para* . . .
  [to whom] is in heaven so that . . .
para nochin quin*tocaroz.*
  so that they may fall to everyone.
Como pues quiere decir: "que los bañe parejo,"
  Well, it means: "may He sprinkle them evenly,"
que los recibe, y las flores
  may they receive them [the prayers], and the flowers
también,
  too,

y los enciensos, los veladoras, todo . . .
   and the incense, the candles, everything . . .

(Francisco Antonio Tejero, interview, November 1, 1997)

The Nahua distinguish the types of dead who are believed to visit the homes of the living: on the first of November the suckling babies arrive, while the adults come on the second, after which the following days are reserved for those who died a violent death (Lok 1991; Signorini 2008). Contrary to those who, having died as adults and having therefore had time to sin, are thought to be spending time in Purgatory expiating their punishment, the infants—in harmony with the teaching of priests—are thought of as little angels who live in Heaven, conceived as a sort of flower garden.

In addition to all the goods arranged on the home altars in view of the arrival of dead relatives—flowers, candles, incense, cut paper ornaments, as well as a wide variety of dishes (fruit, sweet bread, tamales, tortillas, turkey with *mole*, *atole*, coffee, and other beverages; see Lok 1991; Lupo 2018, 2019)—the ritual specialist I observed recites a considerable number of Catholic prayers ("three, four, five rosaries," made mostly of Our Fathers and Hail Marys), which he stacks in series of five and seven (depending on whether the recipients are children or adults). Also, in the offerings placed on the altar of the dead, the children receive a series of five units (e.g., tamales, tortillas, *pan de muertos*, bowls of *atole*, fruit), while the adults are offered a series of seven units (Lok 1991; Lupo 2019). In praying, he follows a personal scheme of his own, which does not reflect the canonical distribution of ten Hail Marys and one Our Father corresponding to the grains of the rosary, but he skips the individual ones and only partially uses (up to five or seven) the series of ten grains for both prayers.

In this way, the ritual specialist consciously undertakes a considerable oratory effort, with the purpose of giving to God and through Him to the dead a great number of prayers, which he explicitly compares to the other substances arranged on the altar and whose abundance is one of the fundamental requisites for the effectiveness of the ritual. The manifest objective of this heterogeneous offering of substances and words is to allow the dead who arrive after a long journey to "rest," recovering their energies through the offerings and "refreshing" themselves. Some similar concepts have been expressed by another ritual specialist, in the supplication he addressed to the deceased adults visiting his house on November 2:

Ica nehon
   So

xicpiyacan *descanso*
  take rest
ica nehin tahtoltzin,
  with these little words,
nehin tapohual
  [with] this count [series]
de oración
  of prayers
tamechaxcatiliah
  of which we give you possession
itech nehin tonal.
  on this day.
Ica nochi nehin
  With all these
panecitos,
  little breads,
tamalitos,
  little *tamales,*
nacatzin,
  little meat,
pahpatatzin,
  little bananas,
xocotzin,
  little oranges,
lo que tein yezqui,
  what will be [whatever is],
cahtzot:
  jícama [*Pachyrhizus erosus*]:
tamechaxcatiliah
  we give you possession [of all this]
itech nehin tonal.
  in this day.
¡Xic*recibiro*can!
  Receive it!

(Miguel Cruz, prayers offered, November 2, 1988)

As we have seen, the Catholic prayers pronounced during the night of the Day of the Dead are explicitly compared with the other substances put on the altar, which the dead are firmly believed to come and take away, thus appeasing their insatiable lack of the earthly goods they left behind when losing their body. As everyone experiences and knows, after the deceased have passed by, the food and other components of the offering do not lose their material consistency; what is lost is their fragrance (*ahhuiyacayot*) because the souls take away the only thing that corresponds to their subtle sensory capacities: the essence. Thus, in the same way food, drinks, fruits, and vegetables provide some nourishment and "rest" to the dead, so do prayers, contributing to "appease" their appetite for earthly things. This action is inspired by the Spanish canonical formula "*que en paz descanse su alma* (may their soul rest in peace)" pronounced in the Requiem that accompanies the supplication and that is metaphorically expressed in Nahuatl with the verb *yolcehui* /to refresh the heart/:

Mah namech**yolcehui** totepixcauh,
　　May our defender [Jesus Christ] cool your heart,
mah namech**yolcehui** ica nehin tahtoltzin.
　　may He refresh your heart with these words [prayers].
Ica xi**yolcehui**can.
　　Refresh your heart with them.
Ica xpiyacan *descanso*
　　With them take rest
namoyolotzin
　　[in] your little heart.

(Miguel Cruz, prayers offered, November 2, 1988)

In Nahuatl, the idea of rest coincides with that of refreshing oneself: someone who works becomes heated and yearns to refresh himself by resting; in fact, the word with which one receives a visit is *ximocehui* /refresh yourself/, even before *xitali* /sit down/. Furthermore, in the words of Miguel Cruz, sin coincides with a condition of overheating: the soul "is heated by sin." The prayers the living say for the deceased who are expiating their sins in Purgatory can attenuate that heat, since they contribute to reducing their punishment.

The exhortative expression (*mah* + verb) addressed to God and the imperative one (*x/xi* + verb) addressed to the souls refer to the condition of lack, sorrow, nostalgia, and concern that are imagined to afflict the dead, causing them an excess of heat. Prayers are believed to have the capacity to sedate and appease that heat, along with the other offerings, through the symbolic action of refreshing the *yolo*, a term that indicates at the same time the heart and the immortal soul, the organ that gives life to the body and the seat of the person's cognitive and volitional faculties (Lupo 2013, 63–90):

Well, with that they rest. With that, the blessed souls take rest, also with prayers: [in the nether world] there is no meat nor is there rum. They want words [prayers], rosaries, holy rosaries, [so that] their souls may rest in peace. Here in the holy Purgatory where they live. They are burning with thoughts, they left the goods, they left other things: here they left their wife, or they left their children. They are wondering if their children misbehave . . . That is why one offers them [prayers]: "My God, let his soul rest in peace, may he not think of bad things. [May he] not always [think of] his goods, nothing. May he cease [thinking about it]. May you receive him to your holy Heaven, where You live with God the Father." (Miguel Cruz, interview, September 14, 2017)[11]

Further evidence of the fact that Catholic prayers in Spanish are tantamount to the other substances donated in the offerings is provided by the evocation of the divine act of distributing them among the deceased. This is an act already present at the beginning of the last quotation, but the supplication directed by Francisco Tejero to God the Father on the occasion of November 1 clarifies it even better:

Mi Dios Padre.
　My God the Father.
Mi Dios Padre eterno Gloria,
　My God eternal Father of Heaven,
Jesucristo de Dios nuestro Señor,
　Jesus Christ of God our Lord,
Gloria santísimo sacramento de altar,
　Holy heavenly sacrament of altars,
altar Gloria.
　altar of Heaven.
Nican ni*reza*roti
　Here I will pray
para los ánimas benditos defuntitos,
　for the blessed souls of the dead little babies,
angelitos angelitas que viven . . .
　little angels that live . . .
tein yetoqueh monahuac ompa *Gloria.*
　that are in your presence there in Heaven.
Yin *hora día,*
　In this hour, [on] this day,
es día primero de noviembre,
　it is the first day of November,

este sábado hora,
    [on] this Saturday [in this] hour,
nican ni*rezar*oti *rosarios oraciones,*
    here I will pray [some] rosaries of prayers,
nimitzmactiliti, nimitzaxcatiliti yin . . .
    I am going to present to you, I am going to give you possession of
    these . . .
yin
    these
mahtacti *rosario*
    ten rosaries
de chihchicome panti.
    [made] of series of five.
Xiqui*recibir*o.
    Receive them.
Cen ahci *puro* nochi
    May they arrive all together
mahtacti *viaje,*
    the ten tours,
mahmacuilpa chihchicome panti *Padrenuestros.*
    five times series of seven Our Fathers.
Xiqui*recibir*o
    Receive them
para mo . . .
    for your . . .
república de Gloria.
    heavenly republic.

. . .

Huan yin *oraciones,*
    And these prayers,
campa [tiyetoc] xicmoyahua
    [there] where [you are], scatter them
huan xiyini
    and sprinkle [spray] them
mo*Gloria*
    [in] your Heaven
para nochin
    for all the

ánimas benditos angelitos,
  blessed souls little angels,
ánimas benditos angelita de Gloria
  blessed souls little angels of Heaven
tein *viviroh*toqueh
  who are living
ompa *cerca* tehhuatzin monahuac.
  there near You, in your presence.
Xiquinquenti
  Cover them [with these prayers]
huan xquinaxcati,
  and make them the owners [of them],
huan xquinnemactili
  and present to them
xochit *cerita,*
  the flowering little candles,
xochit *veladora.*
  the flowering small candles.
No*oraciones* xquinquenti,
  [With] my prayers cover them,
xquinnemactili, xquinaxcatili.
  present them to them, give them possession of them.

(Francisco Antonio Tejero, prayers offered, November 1, 1997)

As can be seen, the speaker does not make any differentiation between the goods placed on the altar and the Catholic prayers he pronounces in large numbers, following the scheme of *"mahmacuilpa viaje cihchicome panti* /10 series of 5 times 7 counts [or rows]/" of Our Fathers and Hail Marys (10 × 5 × 7 = 350 × 2 = 700), so that God may scatter them over the souls of the dead, to whom He donates them together with the other ritual paraphernalia—covering them with prayers as if they formed a protective mantle. The synthetic polysemy that characterizes metaphors clearly expresses the efficacy pursued by the Nahua speaker with his ritual acts: the distribution of such an amount of prayers/gifts among the crowd of purging spirits is assimilated to the rhythmic, slow fall of the drops of rain evoked by the verb *xiyini* /to sprinkle/. Parallel to the widespread identification of the human being with the maize plant, this verb assimilates the actions of the Christian God with those of the pre-colonial agricultural deities (as Pitrou has also observed among the Mixe: Pitrou 2012, 2014a, 2016b), whose main form of intervention in favor of humans consisted of delivering rain.

CONCLUSION

In this chapter I have examined a component widely used in the religious practices of the Mexican natives (whose conversion to Catholicism dates back half a millennium), which, however, has been the subject of little attention from researchers, to the point that very few references to Catholic prayers are found in the ethnographic texts and even fewer that analyze their use in ritual contexts. At least among the Nahua of the Sierra of Puebla, my investigations have shown how prayers constitute an absolutely peculiar typology of verbal utterances the natives use daily, consciously inserting them into the long and detailed invocations and requests in native language that they address to extra-human interlocutors. Nonetheless, the way prayers are used corresponds only partially to the dictates of the church. The fact that they are verbal formulas learned and recited mostly in Spanish, fixed and unchangeable, whose effectiveness the Catholic doctrine itself attributes to recitation in large quantities (through the help of the rosary), has ended up making it so their use does not depend on their propositional content—which is substantially disjointed from the context and unable to communicate with the exactness required by the aims that move the ritual actors (a function performed superbly by the supplications in Nahuatl within which the prayers are inserted). On the contrary, prayers are used above all for the intrinsic variable "force" with which they are believed to be endowed. This use puts them on the same level as the many paraphernalia and substances deployed in the ritual setting, making them "object-prayers"; in some way, they are a sort of inversion with respect to what in a well-known essay Roger Bastide (1998 [1972], 122–123) says about "prayer objects," such as the smoke tacitly offered by the Sioux to their extra-human interlocutors or the sticks the natives of Madagascar plant to the east of their houses after being instigated by the gods: the mere presence of these objects is believed to have the capacity to express "the affective matrix [preexistent to] any discourse . . . the permanence of the appeal addressed by men to the tutelary deities . . . the materialization of prayer . . . the externalized expression of man's feeling of dependence, of his need for adoration or of his act of thanksgiving." According to Bastide, these objects need no verbal accompaniment (or even mental ones) to condense in their mere material presence the affective impulse of the praying person, representing it and transmitting it to the extra-human recipients. Instead, the Catholic prayers the Nahua "deliver" to their interlocutors constitute the imaginary (and nonetheless quite concrete, in the extra-human dimension) materialization of words, made into "objects" that can be donated such as candles, flowers, incense, and food and that cannot exist as such without their actual verbal uttering.

As we have seen, in donating them together with all the other things that are part of the ritual "deposits" or "offerings," the actors use them to transmit to their extra-human recipients (and to some extent also to the human beneficiaries of the ritual, as in the case of people suffering from spiritual illnesses) an amount of "force" that may satisfy their very anthropomorphic need for a supply of energies to ingratiate and induce them to favorably grant to humans what they require. In the administration of Catholic prayers, these are "dosed" carefully according to their variable heat-force, as well as the circumstances, beneficiaries, and recipients of ritual. In this dispensation, the numerical and temporal factors acquire crucial importance. The complex recitation of Catholic prayers is inspired by numerological considerations that, following the distinction proposed by Danièle Dehouve (2007, 2011), are both "qualitative" and "quantitative." The "qualitative" value of the numbers of prayers—which for Dehouve consists of the "conventional symbolism that is attributed [to them]" (2011, 153; see also Dehouve 2007, 96 and following)—can be found, for example, in the fact that on All Saint's Day one must say a series of five Our Fathers and Hail Marys for dead little children and seven for adults (due to the "completeness" this number usually signifies). In spatial terms, this completeness is made evident by the fact that the number seven is the sum of the four cardinal directions and the three levels of the cosmos; within the domestic microcosm, seven is the sum of the corners of the quadrangular box containing the fireplace and the three supports (*tenamazte*) on which the pots and the *comal* are placed. Meanwhile, the Tlapanec studied by Dehouve (2011, 232) associate seven and eight with the living (respectively, women and men) and nine with the dead.

Moreover, during healing rites, specialists usually recite sets of seven prayers to treat a "fright" illness and ten for witchcraft, as the latter is seen as far more serious (see Signorini and Lupo 1989); again, the maximum number allowed for the Creed is three, due to the peculiar "strength" attributed to this prayer, as well as to its explicit Trinitarian connotation. On the other hand, the "quantitative" value of the prayer series is clear in the commitment to recite them—albeit in an orderly form, rationally distributed over time—in very large numbers; especially in the case of rituals dedicated to the dead (in which there are no co-present human beneficiaries, such as the patient in healing rites), the number of prayers offered is directly proportional to the benefits one seeks to obtain (either directly for the addressees or later for humans, thanks to the compensative intervention of the dead). The large number of prayers the speaker is able to offer through the multiplication of the series clearly expresses the ideal abundance of goods, both material and immaterial, the rite aims to propitiate through the idea that the regulated quantification of these powerful "verbal objects" can act by effectively relating the human dimension with cosmic phenomena, which equates to creating a correspondence between microcosm and macrocosm.

As for the temporal factor, it concerns both the ordered dosage of the prayers, which prescribes—just as for food (or pharmaceuticals)—a gradual administration, and the peculiar mode of their delivery, which clearly distinguishes them from the other "objects" donated in the course of ritual activities. In fact, not only are prayers to be recited according to quantities carefully defined in numerical terms, but such quantities must also be adequately spaced over time to let the beneficiaries (who, in addition to the extra-human interlocutors, also include the patient) take advantage of them. The explanations provided by the ritual specialists highlight the clear correspondence of prayers with material substances, which, like any food, require an adequate period of absorption: a too frequent administration would cause the debilitated patient (whose spiritual component is co-present at the ceremony) to fall under their "weight"—as for a load of firewood—and would create a sort of "indigestion" in the extra-human recipient. Moreover, the latter would not be able to examine and weigh carefully (like a judge) the case for which they were consulted, and it would therefore be arduous for them to make the right decision. As Dehouve (2007, 2011) and Pitrou (2014a) rightly point out, the measure and the gradual order in the administration of the goods during ritual are believed to be fundamental for establishing the correct relationship with the extra-human entities and, even more, for determining the modality of the answer one aims to obtain, which also has to be ordered and commensurate with the requests, as well as adequately distributed through the temporal frame.

A second, fundamental temporal aspect of Catholic prayers is the specific way they are provided, which distinguishes them from all other goods offered to ritual's extra-human recipients. Even these goods are, in fact, produced in succession, often with a long process of preparation and presentation. But their material consistence allows them to be mostly presented all together, simultaneously—for example, by placing on the altar flowers next to candles, incense, and food. The effort, dedication, and emotional investment of humans all precede the moment when the offerings are delivered, and they are often considered their main ingredient, the source of the essence the donated goods are deemed to transmit and thus granting their appreciation. Therefore, the recipients can enjoy their components all at once, simultaneously appreciating their quality (e.g., variety, beauty, order) and abundance. In contrast, Catholic prayers must necessarily be recited one by one, in a sequential order that requires a considerable effort on the part of the one who utters them, above all because not everyone is able to sustain their considerable duration. The elderly therapist Francisco Tejero was very proud, at age ninety, to withstand up to six hours praying, and to this he attributed his success as a healer—which allowed him to provide the Eternal Father with a quantity of prayers that would be sufficient for their distribution among all the innumerable cohorts of angels and saints, thus guaranteeing a maximally effective choral extra-human intervention:

> I have worked up to thirty [rosaries]. I did about six hours . . . When I wake up well, I start at three in the morning, I deliver sixteen [rosaries], sixteen [rosaries] I give to God. Then I ask for what I want . . . This amount of rosaries is enough for [those who are] in Heaven, even for the Purgatory. Because . . . Father God needs prayers to maintain the saints of Heaven, and that's what these ones live on, as well as flowers, incense and candles. Yes. That's what God needs . . . But I work hard so that God may have enough for his people, there are many holy miracles [beings] in Heaven, there are many . . . Just prayers, candles and incense. I deliver them in heaven so that the eternal God Jesus Christ may scatter them, so that He may pour them out in Heaven so that . . . so that these [prayers] may serve the angels, the apostles, the holy miracles, all that is in Heaven. It suffices, they say. And their God gives them the blessing so that they may go and see what you ask for. (Francisco Antonio Tejero, interview, October 3, 1997)[12]

The ability to recite interminable sequences of Our Fathers and Hail Marys in orderly series, a truly exhausting verbal effort, clearly produces an emission of force that constitutes the precious essence of the goods being donated, not unlike the way in preparing food for the dead in early November the love, sacrifice, and effort lavished by the living provide what guarantees the offerings' appreciation by the dead. If prayers assure the efficacy of rituals, it is above all because their recitation requires dedication, emotional transport (the profound belief in the existence and benevolence of their extra-human recipients, which confers "heat" to the sacred words), and a long-lasting commitment. In the case of the Nahua, the "heat" of ritual words is not so much attributed to the supplications in Nahuatl, which nonetheless—similar to the ritual songs for the Tzotzil (Gossen 1976, 58–59)—possess a high degree of formalization; rather, it is considered specific to Catholic prayers in Spanish, whose ancient adoption in native ritual practice has led to their use in the same way as the other varieties of substances and objects offered to God, saints, and the entities whose help one invokes. If it is clear that in the earthly world of humans these figures are completely immaterial, in the other dimension to which they all belong—which only the immaterial essence of earthly substances can reach—they are very concretely perceptible, through the very "heat" that summarizes in a polysemic combination the authoritativeness of their origin, the codified strength of their message, and especially the effort and devotion of the praying persons. It is precisely because of the materiality that is attributed to prayers in the extra-human abode of the deities and the dead, where everything is essence and essences have the concreteness of earthly things, that the Nahua can imagine that God generously redistributes and sprinkles them among all His coadjutors, with an action that—similar to the "celestial rain" of Chamula songs (56–57)—can be assimilated into the bestowal of a rhythmic and beneficial, refreshing and regenerating tropical rain.

Acknowledgments. The investigations that allowed for collection of the ethnographic materials on which this chapter is based were developed within the activities of the Italian Ethnological Mission in Mexico, of which I have been a part since 1979 and have directed since 1998. These activities have been supported by the Italian Ministries of Foreign Affairs (MAECI) and of Education, University and Scientific Research (MIUR) and the National Research Council (CNR).

NOTES

1. In translations from Nahuatl into Spanish, I place between transversal bars / . . . / the literal translation and in single quotes '. . .' the free translation. The Nahuatl variant spoken in the municipality of Cuetzalan is characterized, among other aspects, by the substitution of the phoneme /tl/ (present in the variant spoken in the Central Highlands) with the allophone [t]. All translations are by the author.

2. In the transcription of the Nahuatl texts, italics are used to highlight loans from Spanish; bold is used for emphasis.

3. The initial capital letter represents the sense of respect expressed in Nahuatl by the reverential diminutive.

4. Es caliente, es fuerte. Cualisquiera tentación lo paras con el Credo, porque es más caliente, es más fuerte: como si fuera su machete de Santiago, como si fuera su machete del San Miguel. Con ése atajas cualquier tentación: atraviesas tu machete, con ése atajas. El Credo es fuerte . . . Pues es caliente—según—más fuerte, vaya. Con ése atajas todas las malas tentaciones, malas vibras. Por eso te digo: tienes un arma . . . Ese Credo quiere decir que creo [con énfasis] de todas las cosas . . . Es creencia, es nuestra creencia . . . *Taneltocaliz, neltoquilia nitahtol* Señor Creencia, cree en la palabra

del Señor/ . . . Es fuerza, pues tú estás con Dios: crees ante Dios, sí crees que sí hay Dios . . . La fe es caliente, es la mayor parte de todo, de todo lo que tú quieras.

5. "Las oraciones ésas son más fuertes, está más caliente porque ataja a cualisquiera tentación. ¿Apoco tú te vas a meter en la lumbre? ¿A que no? ¡Pues no! Así también esto. Está como si fuera en la lumbre."

6. "No hay que echarle muchas [oraciones], si no se descompone . . . No se le puede aumentar mucho, porque entonces no sirve el trabajo: tiene que ir contado nomás, no hay que pasarle de oraciones."

7. "Para el *nemouhtil* /susto/ nadie reza más que siete."

8. "Porque le metes muchas oraciones y ya ves su cuerpo como está: [las oraciones] son fuertes y se puede apeorar. Éste [el enfermo] viene ya como alguna persona [que tú] llevas de alguna parte: llevas a un mozo, agarras y lo cargas—porque la cera es leña, la vela es como si fuera una leña—le pones la carga, de allí empiezas a ponerle más. Claro, le cargaste la vela, un trozo, agarras y le pones más, le pones más encima, pues en lugar de que lo aguante, que lo traiga, entonces se cae y no aguanta. Así vienes haciendo con estas oraciones: hasta que aguante lo traes, y después vas a traer más. Así poco a poco, no es todo de un jalón."

9. "Tengo que rezar [unas cuantas oraciones] a todos [los santos interpelados en la súplica]. Pero cada quien con su rosario. Yo te doy tu plato: 'Este es tu plato, comida.' Al otro también le doy su plato. Al otro también le doy su plato. Con medida. No vas a ir a lo tonto, a la carrera. Cada quien con su plato. [A.L.: Pero ¿por qué rezar muchas oraciones puede dañar al paciente?] '¡Come y come!.' Antes ya comiste un plato y ya te vuelvo a dar otro plato, te vuelvo a dar otro plato: ya te estoy atareando a ti nomás. Te estoy atareando nomás a ti. Te vas a empachar después."

10. "Vas a un tribunal, a una cuestión con el juez lo que fuiste a decir ahorita, ya fuiste a aclarar . . . Mañana vas otra vuelta a eso mismo. Pues sí. Tienes que ir lo mismo mañana. Pero ¡mañana! No al rato. Ya te dijo: 'Bueno, voy a ver cómo lo resolvemos.' Pero al rato [vas] otra vuelta . . . Te va a correr el juez, va a decir: '¡Está loco! Después de [que] vino, se acaba de ir, ¡otra vuelta vino! Se acaba de ir, ¡otra vuelta vino!.' Te va a correr el juez: 'Entonces tú no de veras, ¡tú eres chismoso! ¡Lárgate!.' Pero no. Ya dije . . . ya te citó el juez que cuando vas a presentarte: ese día tienes que ir. Así también las oraciones: ya te ofrecí. Ya comistes, ¿cómo vas a comer otra vuelta ahorita? Si ya almorzastes, otra vez te dicen que vas a almorzar. 'Ya comí, ya desayuné.' Entonces ¿cómo te voy a atarear? . . . Es por . . . sigues esperando, por etapas, por etapas, por etapas, por etapas, hasta que nos obedezca . . . [Si] lo estás molestando, no te va a dar nada. Pero si te vas ahorita, mañana otra vuelta vas, ocho días te vas, entonces como que más en dejito [poco a poco] le vas ofreciendo . . . Así también con Dios, hay que ir por partes. Vas hablando con paciencia, [pidiendo] favores . . . Sin estar estorbando allí. Nomás tú [piensas] que a ti te atiende, ¿y los

demás? ¿Acaso nomás tú eres? Hay un chingo de gente que está pidiéndole . . . Hay que ir dando tiempo que fue pensando."

11. "Pues, con ése descansan. Con ése *quipiyacan* descanso *in* ánimas benditas *ica no* con oraciones: *amo oncac* carne *nion oncac* aguardiente. *Quinequih tahtoltzin* [rezos], rosario, santo rosario, que en paz descanse[n] sus alma[s]. Aquí en el santo purgatorio donde viven. Están ardiendo de pensamientos, dejaron los bienes, dejaron otras cosas: aquí la señora, o sus hijos dejaron. Están pensando, si se portan mal los hijos . . . Por eso les ofrece uno: 'Dios mio, dale en paz descanso a su alma, que no esté pensando cosas malas. Siempre [en] sus bienes, de nada. Ya que deje. Que lo recibas a tu santa Gloria, donde Tú vives con Dios Padre.'"

12. "Yo he trabajado hasta treinta [rosarios]. Hizo como seis horas . . . Cuando así amanezco bonito, empiezo a las tres de la mañana, entrego dieciseis [rosarios], dieciseis entrego al Dios. Ya pido ya para qué cosa quiero . . . Ese tanto de rosario alcanza para en el cielo, hasta para el Purgatorio. Porque . . . el papá Dios necesitan oraciones para estar manteniendo los santos de Gloria, y con eso se mantiene ése, y [con] flor y incienso y veladora. Sí. Ese necesita el Dios . . . Pero como mi [yo] trabajo mucho para que alcanza para su gente, hay muchos santos milagros de Gloria, hay mucho . . . Puro oraciones y veladoras y incienso. Lo entrega en el cielo y que ya lo aparta el Dios eterno Jesucristo, que lo riegue en el cielo para que . . . para que con ése se sirve con los ángelos, apóstoles, santos milagros, todo lo que hay en el cielo. Alcanza, dice. Y allá el Dios le da la bendición que vayan a ver qué cosa pides tú."

PART THREE
The Materiality of Sound

9

The ephemeral properties of materiality, such as the sound produced from artifacts, are often overlooked in the interpretation of cultural history (Kosyk 2016; Mills 2010; Reznikoff 2006; Waller 2017). This is unfortunate since sound can reflectively engage with humans and non-humans, offering information about people, things, and their environments (Both 2009; Dennett and Kosyk 2013; Kosyk 2016; Till 2014). Sound is unique because it is the product of activity, produced in both unintentional and intentional ways, through everyday practices (Mills 2014). These practices, which correspond to decisions made by a group or groups, maintain and negotiate certain sonic traditions (Spielmann 2002, 195–197). In this chapter, I investigate several ways sound materializes by inferring performative and embodied practices from archaeologically recovered sonorous artifacts (Kosyk 2016, 2019). Building on Lave and Wenger's (1991) communities of practice, I present "communities of engaged performance" as a theoretical framework. It will be used to explore the degree of sonic knowledge transmission, demonstrated through repetition and embodiment of various gestures among sound, an instrumentalist, and an audience in the production and consumption of sonic traditions.

The sonorous instrument collection that will be discussed is associated with an archaeologically known Greater Nicoyan community from the Tempisque period (500 BCE to 300 CE). The collection was recovered by the department of archaeology at the University

Communities of Engaged Performance

Investigating the Materiality of Sound in Precolumbian Greater Nicoya

Katrina Casey Kosyk

https://doi.org/10.5876/9781646422395.c009

195

of Costa Rica from the G-752Rj site near the town of Garza in the Guanacaste province of Costa Rica (Guerrero Miranda 2009, 2011). The collection is currently housed at the Museo Nacional de Costa Rica in San José and consists of 111 ocarinas, 6 tubular flutes, and 3 possible whistles (2009, 2011). A complete catalog of these instruments, with measurements of their features and sound files, is the basis for the analysis presented here (Kosyk 2016). Collectively, these are examples of aerophones, musical instruments from which sound is produced through the vibration of air. These include most wind instruments, of which flutes, whistles, and ocarinas are the most common. The wealth of the aerophone collection recovered from this site presents us with the potential to explore the impact of sound at various scales while maintaining a focus on the interrelationships among sonic events, instrumentalists (players of instruments), and active listeners (an audience). Sonorous instruments, especially ceramic aerophones, which can take various forms and portray culturally specific abstract ideas, offer clues to our understanding of past semiotic practices used by instrumentalists and interpreted by audiences to communicate meaning (Monelle 1992, 3–5). The communication between an instrument and an instrumentalist, expressed as sound, is more than a single identifiable event and is learned through experiential and experimental processes of sound production.

My methodology builds on an existing body of archaeomusicological literature (Both 2009; Davois 1999; Diaz-Andreu and García Benito 2012; Mills 2010; Reznikoff 2006; Waller 2017). As a means of analyzing communities of engaged performance, I investigate variations in the production and consumption of sound. These variations materialize in several ways, such as through the design of the instrument developed during its production and the ways an instrumentalist incorporates repetitive gestures during the playing of an instrument to produce desired tones. This chapter begins with a discussion on the material force of sound where I discuss how sound can engage agentially with various forms of matter. I then introduce communities of engaged performance to better understand the ephemeral properties of knowledge transmission associated with sonic traditions and their visibility in archaeological collections. After this, I discuss identifying various forms of communities of engaged performance in the production and consumption of sonorous instruments from the G-752Rj archaeological site and offer another interpretation for the use of these instruments.

SOUND AS A MATERIAL FORCE

The study of sound has advanced considerably since the nineteenth century, from acoustical studies, understanding the physical properties of sound, to psychoacoustics, understanding the human perception of sound (Harris 1979; Howard and Angus 2006; Mills 2014). Sound is defined as a vibration, an oscillation of matter, that transfers energy from a source through a medium, which possesses inertia and elasticity. As a force that can impact matter, sound has the potential to impede the intentions of humans and manipulate the impacted area, exhibiting properties of its own creation (Bennett 2010). The materiality of sound is in a constant state of becoming as it flows through, vibrates, and collides with various substances, impacting on each other and on other bodies (Ihde 2007). Sound acts as both a physical substance (absorption and diffraction of waves) and a sensual substance (enticing memories and emotions) that is dependent on the complex processes of perception (Downey 2002; Zatorre, Chen, and Penhune 2007). The processes of perception include the cultural background and the way the listener and instrumentalist (the person who plays an instrument) were brought up to experience sound. The listener experiences sound through symbolic and sonic associations that are related to conditioned bodily habits that are socially reinforced in a situated learning environment and acquired through active listening (Downey 2002; Lave and Wenger 1991; Zatorre, Chen, and Penhune 2007). To a listener, there is no distinction between the perception of sound, which is unique for every individual, and the materiality of sound, the forces that create the perception of sound (Zatorre, Chen, and Penhune 2007).

Sound is a process, existing in a constant state of negotiation and becoming. In spaces (especially enclosed spaces), sound waveforms collide with each other and the surrounding environment, producing reverberation, echoes, and resonance (Blesser and Salter 2007; Howard and Moretti 2009). These effects are dependent on the orientation of the matter of the surfaces the sound waves engage. Some matter reflects or absorbs sound better, depending on the dimensions, shape, and properties of the space. Sound is essential for spatial awareness and can influence the character and the effects of the space that is occupied (Blesser and Salter 2007; Mills 2014). These effects of sound have been investigated in archaeological contexts of architectural remains (Cross and Watson 2006; Mills 2014).

Human and non-human bodies receive information through their senses that helps them understand the structure and configuration of their environment (Howes 2003). According to Merleau-Ponty (1962), the structure of a body, which is dependent on age, gender, physical ability, and social identity, has an association with its surroundings that allows it to experience the world in a variety of ways. In most circumstances, the body experiences forms of practical knowledge that allow it to exist within a form of habitus subconsciously aware of the effects the senses have on producing experiences (Howes 2003). The structure of our surrounding and the forms of embodied engagement we have with our environments influence the propagation and the encoding of sound (Mills 2014). For instance, one of the defining aspects of sound is its rhythmic ability. Many non-human sounds have rhythm, known as biorhythm, that is used to structure our timing of the world—such as our heartbeats and breathing rates, which impact the way bodies function, including our ability to talk and walk (King and Ginsborg 2011; Todd 1999; Zatorre, Chen, and Penhune 2007).

In the twenty-first century, sound has become materialized and objectified by various forms of technology—such as musical notation, records, and mp3 files—that allow it to be retrieved instantaneously (Schafer 1985). The objectification of sound has obscured its agential effects on our daily lives. For instance, often unrecognized forms of sound that encompass our surroundings, such as soundscapes and sonic fabrics, are hardly noticed as influential or dependent on the historical and cultural contingencies that make up our worldview. Therefore, the challenge is to develop ways of acknowledging sound as a materialized force in the archaeological record and to better understand how sound contributes to the understanding of various past perspectives and orientations as past bodies experienced their everyday lives.

COMMUNITIES OF ENGAGED PERFORMANCE

The activities that occur in a situated learning environment are encompassed within the central concept of communities of practice. As proposed by Lave and Wenger (1991, 49), communities of practice correspond to the transmission of knowledge among groups of participants, such as those that can be identified within the production of a craft technology (see also Knappett 2011, 99–105; Roddick and Stahl 2016, 2; Stark 2006, 25). The transmission of knowledge is a process that involves the embodied relations among people, places, and things, which take place over time and across generations (Knappett 2011; Minar and Crown 2001; Roddick and Stahl 2016, 3). The concept of communities of practice has the potential in archaeology to surpass the homogenizing character of standard archaeological classifications, such as ceramic-based chronological sequences and cultural affiliations, in favor of a more practice- and process-based approach (Roddick and Stahl 2016). Building on this analytical tool, I propose an accompanying conceptual framework called "communities of engaged performance" to tackle the ephemeral nature of the transmission of knowledge of sound to an audience through performance. To investigate the autonomous forces apparent from sound based on archaeological collections and to assess how sonorous instruments and humans relate to each other, creating agency between them, it is necessary to examine their embodiment of production and consumption.

Communities of engaged performance are oriented around the variable conditions of instrument design, gestures involved in the playing of an instrument, and the resulting sound that is produced. All three of these conditions are dependent on one another and can result in variable group-specific embodied practices. Communities of engaged performance can be used to analyze the differentiation of sound in performances at different scales to examine how traditional ritual practices may be retained, or, alternatively, how new uses of sound for ritual performances can be innovated. The concept denotes group identity based on consistencies within practices rather than by such things as the surface decoration of sonorous ceramic wares. Potential communities of engaged performance can be traced within archaeological material through the transmission of certain sound-related practices and knowledge across generations. The transmission of sound-related knowledge can happen in several ways, all of which incorporate an aspect of the materiality of the force of sound. The following sections discuss the ways we can observe communities of engaged performance in archaeological contexts.

CONTEXT: THE G-752RJ SITE IN GREATER NICOYA

Greater Nicoya is an archaeological region that comprises northwestern Costa Rica and southern Pacific Nicaragua. Within this region, the site G-752Rj, occupied during the Tempisque period (500 BCE to 300 CE), is situated near the town of Garza in the Guanacaste province of Costa Rica (Guerrero Mirando 2009, 2011). The Tempisque period is known for the establishment of settlements, agricultural practices, craft production, and stratified society (Abel-Vidor 1981; Stone 1957; Wingfield 2009; Young-Sánchez 2010). During this period, Greater Nicoya may have been a collective of related chiefdoms (Wingfield 2009, 31–41), a multi-scalar political system incorporating shamans and warriors as leaders who may have had an influential position in society (Day 1994; Day and Tillett 1996; Wingfield 2009, 31–41).

Unfortunately, not much is known about Greater Nicoya's cultural history. There are no identified ethnohistoric records, and what is known is currently being reevaluated (see Dennett and Kosyk 2013; McCafferty and Dennett 2013, 193–195). For instance, recent scholarship has suggested that the Greater Nicoya region may have had an independent ethnogenesis from civilizations to the north and south during the Tempisque period (Dennett 2016; McCafferty and Dennett 2013; McCafferty et al. 2012). Traditionally, scholars have argued that Greater Nicoya's cultural history was dependent on its neighbors from the north and south, supported by an abundant amount of research that connects iconography of Greater Nicoya ceramic wares with symbolic similarities on wares from other parts of Mesoamerica (Day 1984, 1994; McCafferty and Steinbrenner 2005; Stone 1977, 1982a). This macroscale analysis—between regions—has developed a larger picture of culture history dependent on external cultural events. What is lacking in contemporary research within the Greater Nicoya region is a microscale analysis—between individuals, objects, or both—that could tell us how local communities incorporated variations or consistencies within their ceramic ware as internal and external social, political, and economic events impacted society.

The G-752Rj site was excavated as part of a rescue operation by the University of Costa Rica's archaeology department in 2009. The site was being destroyed by developers, who were exposing areas of the site as part of a project to build a resort, and was further damaged by looters (Guerrero Miranda 2009, 2011). The principal investigator, Dr. Juan Vicente Guerrero Miranda, identifies the site as a musicians' cemetery because 111 aerophones were recovered from burial contexts. At least eleven groups of graves, which would have supported multiple individuals, were excavated at the site, only two of which were undamaged by machinery and looters (2009, 2011). The graves were identified by a distinct change of color and texture in the soil and a clustering in the distribution of artifacts, which apart from the aerophones also included tripod vessels with rattle legs, pendants, mace heads, axes, and various other artifacts—most with zoomorphic imagery (2009, 2011). No human remains were excavated due to poor preservation in acid soils. The G-752Rj collection consisted of at least three potential rattles (listed as whistles in the field report) and several varieties of aerophones. The majority of these aerophones are ocarinas, along with three tubular flutes and several whistles.

An ocarina is a multi-hole Helmholtz resonator (sound is produced through the vibration of air) that can take most shapes and forms. Sound vibrations result from the interactions between the fipple assembly that acts as a spring and the chamber of the instrument (figure 9.1). The fipple assembly is tangent with the body of the ocarina and includes a mouthpiece, an airduct, and a fipple mechanism. As air is blown through the mouthpiece, half of the air is directed into the chamber and half is released. The air increases the pressure inside the chamber and forces it out of equilibrium with the air in the surrounding environment. As a result, the air tries to find any means possible

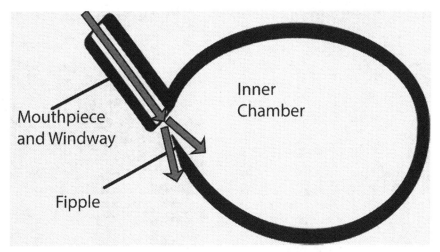

FIGURE 9.1. *Cross-section of an ocarina with the fipple and mouthpiece*

to escape, often through open finger holes and the airduct. The instrument chamber expels so much air that the inner chamber creates a vacuum and pulls in air to compensate. This exchange of expelling and pulling in air is what creates the waves that produce sound.

The frequency and tone of the ocarina are impacted by a variety of factors, such as the inner chamber volume, the size of the finger holes, and the length of the mouthpiece, among others. The sound is also impacted by the chosen material of the instrument. All of the instruments in the G-752Rj collection were ceramic because that is what preserved well. However, ceramic instruments absorb a lot of water from moisture in the breath, which impacts the tone and the length of time the instrumentalist can play the instrument before sound is affected.

The difference between an ocarina and a whistle is the number of tones the instrument can produce. A whistle can only produce one or sometimes two tones. A four-hole ocarina can produce up to sixteen different notes (not including octave differentiation). The ocarinas from the G-752Rj collection were tuned to a non-Western diatonic (consisting of only two whole notes) and hemitonic-pentatonic scales (five-note scales containing half-step intervals).

The aerophones were decorated with zoomorphic imagery, including bird (hawks, ovenbirds, owls, vultures, quails, and wrens), armadillo, turtle, feline, bat, and several unidentifiable mammal representations. Several larger ocarinas had two animal representations, one on either end of the instrument, which

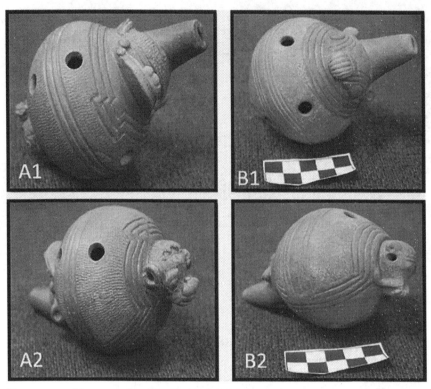

FIGURE 9.2. *Two examples of double-headed globular ocarinas*

include bat and feline, armadillo and vulture, armadillo and feline, as well as bat and bird combinations (figure 9.2). In addition to the zoomorphic iconography, there were anthropomorphized tubular ocarinas that had human-like faces; however, all of these were damaged and were not able to produce a sound. All the zoomorphic ocarinas, except for the turtles, have bodies that were decorated with deep incisions that formed zones resembling an armadillo's carapace (Kosyk 2016, 34–53). The impressions inside the zones were made using rocker stamps, cords, and shells (76). The base of the ocarina supported a hole that may have been used for suspension of the instrument so it could be worn or could have supported a form of organic embellishment (71–73).

There are a limited number of published reports on archaeologically excavated cemeteries in Greater Nicoya, and it is unclear if the number of instruments in this cemetery was an exceptional circumstance or regular practice in the area. Other sonorous instruments of the same ceramic classification

(Marbella zoned incised) exist out of context in museums, such as the Frederick R. Mayer collection at the Denver Art Museum, the Glenbow Museum collection currently housed at the University of Calgary, and Harvard University's Peabody Museum. The stylization and form of these instruments, as well as the measurements of their traits, are comparable across collections. Therefore, it can be assumed that practices using this kind of sonorous instrument were widespread across the Greater Nicoya polity.

Although these artifacts were not associated with every grave cluster in the G-752Rj site, sound instruments, pendants, and mace heads depicting zoomorphic imagery may have been associated with spiritual or ritual practices of the kind identified with shamanic practices. The "shaman" in a broad sense refers to those who are involved with protection, medicine, and spiritual guidance (Stahl 1986, 134–135). Eliade (1964) argues that shamans practice ecstasy through which they can engage in bodily departure and transformation as a means of contacting other realms (Stahl 1986, 135). During ecstasy achieved using hallucinogens, fasting, and musical instruments, the shaman's soul often ascends to other worlds to obtain wisdom or direct evils (Day and Tillett 1996; Stahl 1986, 135). Shamans must master sound to invoke a new way of existing (Reichel-Dolmatoff 1976). The shaman uses sound to reach out to the human and non-human world through song and transformation; depending on the skill of the shaman (as an instrumentalist in some cases), it is possible to take on non-human forms. This may be why the instruments in the G-752Rj collection depicted various animals.

Ethnographically, lower Central American shamanic paraphernalia included a wooden stool, aerophones, wooden staffs, drums, feathers, shells, rattles, and hallucinogens (Day and Tillett 1996). Most of these objects are perishable and would not survive in acidic soils at this site. As mentioned previously, the G-752Rj site assemblage included tripod rattle-leg vessels, possible divination stones, and miniature globular pots that may have held some form of ritual substance (Guerrero Miranda 2011). Based on this, I suggest that the G-752Rj site may have incorporated a variety of individuals with specializations, including shamans (Kosyk 2016).

COMMUNITIES OF ENGAGED PERFORMANCE IN THE PRODUCTION OF SONOROUS INSTRUMENTS

Lave and Wenger (1991) argue that the transmission of knowledge and practice exists in a situated learning environment that incorporates different communities of practice involved in everyday life. A community of practice is formed as individuals come together in a collective learning situation to share knowledge about a skill set (Lave and Wenger 1991; Wenger 1998). Individuals in a collective learning situation, through practice and engagement with the material, embody movements that are copied from a more experienced individual. As a result, these processes are passed down through generations and are constrained by cultural decisions and traditions (Mauss 1979 [1935]). Practices become preserved in a community, and certain practices can distinguish groups from one another (Dobres 2001, 53–54; Gosselain 1998; Minar and Crown 2001). Variation within the practices of the group may be due to negotiation of traditional processes or the introduction of new members who have maintained the practices (and skills) of their originating group (Wenger 1998). This suggests that the relationship between members may change as they move within various communities of practice and that they are not confined to just one group for obtaining knowledge and skills. The transmission of knowledge between individuals and their societal ties leaves traces of identity in technical processes that are observed in ceramic assemblages.

A community of engaged performance recognizes the sharing of knowledge among members of a group but also stresses that there is a degree of information that is shared by engaging with the material used to produce an object. The knowledge process involved in the creation of a sonorous instrument requires a degree of reflexive engagement from the individual and the instrument, which is often communicated through sound. The producer of the instrument is most likely an instrumentalist, given the level of technical knowledge that goes into making a workable ocarina. The embodied practices that are used by the producer of the instrument are observed by members who interpret these gestures in certain ways. More knowledgeable members may understand the use of the techniques by the producer in different ways than would a less skilled member of the group. The goal of producing a sonorous instrument is assumed to ultimately be to produce sound; however, the process to make sound is dependent on the ability of the producer to understand how to communicate with the medium of the instrument. Constructing an instrument that can produce sound is one thing, but the knowledge and skill required for making an instrument that will play desired tones constitutes another level.

As with most ceramics, aspects of the *chaîne opératoire* in sonorous instrument production are destroyed as the instrument is constructed. However, elements that producers have left behind may tell us something of the production process. These include intentional modifications to the inside of the chamber of the instrument body, as well as modifications made to the outside of the

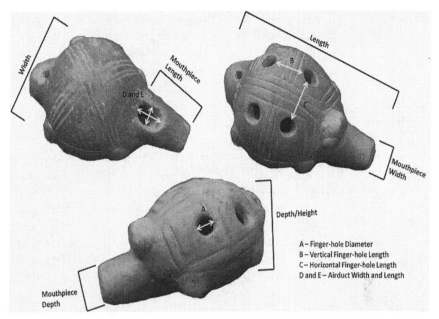

FIGURE 9.3. *Example of various measurements that were taken from the ocarinas*

instrument, to either enhance the appearance or improve sound quality. The traits left behind by the producer were the result of embodied processes and decisions that are maintained in the final product and were communicated by the instrument during the production process to enable sound. I have identified several traits left behind by the producer in the finished sonorous instrument body that would have influenced the tone and style of sound from the G-752Rj collection, which were the result of construction decisions, embodied processes, or both. These traits can influence the pitch, amplitude, volume, and frequency of the instrument that was produced. These traits would determine if the instrument was able to produce sound at all. They include (1) inner chamber volume, (2) inner chamber thickness, (3) structure of the mouthpiece, (4) position of the finger holes in relation to each other, (5) airduct dimensions, and (6) size of the finger holes (figure 9.3).

These traits were among measurements recorded on all complete ocarinas in the collection (66 of the 111 aerophones). The measurements included length, width, and height/depth of the instrument, the thickness of the inner chamber wall (which was measured from the inside of a finger hole using a caliper), the dimensions of the mouthpiece and airduct, and the average dimensions of the finger holes. Unfortunately, most of the tubular ocarinas were damaged and preserved as fragments, so the data in the following section do not include them. The common trait on which all other traits are dependent is the inner chamber volume, which is measured using an ellipsoidal volume equation, accounting for the degree of thickness between the outer and inner chambers. My values will only be approximate and if used in a frequency equation will have marginal error.

Initially, I was going to use animal typology as my common denominator (organizing the ocarinas by their iconography); however, I could not find a correlation between the inner chamber volume and the associated animal. This might be because certain sounds were not required (or desirable) for a specific animal representation. This may suggest that iconography or instrument design was more important than sound in the construction of these instruments.

This theory is supported by timbre modification mechanisms present only on the anthropomorphic tubular ocarinas (9 instruments out of 111 aerophones). The instruments I analyzed had damaged fipples (an essential part of the instrument used to produce sound). This could have been the result of improper cleaning techniques after the instrument was recovered. However, it could have also been intentional and symbolic damaging of the instrument before it was interred in the earth. Smashing or destroying instruments is a typical practice across Precolumbian Latin America as a means of releasing the spirit that resided inside the instrument before final deposition (Santos-Granero 2009, 122–125).

To determine communities of practice, I compared each ocarina trait with inner chamber volume. I used a mean line of regression on each graph to visually demonstrate the level of variability within the G-752Rj collection. If there were multiple communities of engaged performance, then there would be a greater variability of the measurements when compared to the inner chamber volume. For example, the average finger hole diameter of an ocarina is determined by the inner chamber volume. If the finger holes are too large, the instrument will not hold enough air to produce sound. Each of the traits was measured and compared for consistency or variation, which can be attributed to one or more communities of engaged performance in the G-752Rj collection.

The results from the collection of ocarinas demonstrated that most of the traits had tight clustering of measurements, suggesting a small amount of variation in the set (Kosyk 2016). The embodied skills of the producers of the instruments resulted in consistency in the thickness of inner walls (using the pinch and pull technique), finger hole diameter, and positions of finger holes—all of which may support the identification of a community of engaged performance. The finger holes were very consistent, with their diameter ranging between

0.40 cm and 0.90 cm (2016). This suggests that the finger holes may have been constructed with a certain kind of material, such as reed of a certain diameter, to produce holes of a particular size in relation to the size of the inner chamber volume. In addition, finger hole placements in relation to each other (horizontal and vertical placements) were directly related to the size of the inner chamber volume. The positions of the finger holes on each side of the instrument were designed to be closer together, situated on the front side of the instrument. The instrumentalist's hands would have been placed on either side of the ocarina, and the index and middle fingers could have been used to block the finger holes when producing different tones. Typically, the average distance of the horizontal spacing between the finger holes would gradually increase as the size of the inner chamber of the instrument increases, while the vertical spacing would be consistent regardless of this change.

There appears to be greater variation in measurements pertaining to mouthpiece length, ranging between 2.00 cm and 3.50 cm, as well as to airduct diameter. Manipulating the length of the mouthpiece of the ocarina may have been a technique of the producers for achieving desired sounds from the instrument. As the mouthpiece increases in length, the pitch of the instrument also increases to an extent. However, visually and functionally, the ocarina mouthpieces were designed with little to no variation, which would support a community of engaged performance. The variation in airduct measurements may have been a consequence of the manipulation of the length of the mouthpieces. The producer would need to adapt the airduct and fipple system to compensate for the changes in length of the new mouthpieces. The airduct could also be used as a means for manipulating the tone of the ocarina. A larger airduct in relation to inner chamber volume would produce a more earthy and airy tone rather than a strong and clear tone.

The level of consistency in the measurements of the traits suggests a potential that they were employed in standardized practices, supporting the identification of a community of engaged performance. The manipulation of several of the traits that would have impacted the tone of the instruments may demonstrate the level of communication among the ocarina, the sound produced, and the instrument producer.

SONIC GESTURES IN PERFORMANCE

Investigation of the materiality of sound in archaeological collections can extend to how sound, sonorous instruments, and humans relate to each other, creating agency between them. As a means of examining reflective agency, this requires investigating the embodiment of the playing of instruments. Communities of engaged performance are dependent on the relationality among the sound, the sonorous instrument, and the instrumentalist. They are also dependent on the conditions of the receiver of the transmitted information and their skill level when it comes to discerning various gestures relating to sound. The amount of variation in the production of sound may suggest that there are multiple communities of engaged practices. The gestures that go into how the instrument is handled (Kosyk 2019), how sound relays information to listeners, and how that sound is perceived by these individuals may demonstrate variation in the embodiment of sonic practices.

Typically, when playing a sonorous instrument, an instrumentalist is concerned with posture, limb and digit placement, and breathing techniques. These features impact the way the sound is produced. Over time, the skill of the instrumentalist improves through the repetition of these practices, reinforced by the production of a desired sound. Eventually, once an instrumentalist has mastered the instrument, the production of sound becomes an embodied practice and part of the human experience (Shove and Repp 1995; Straw 2012). The focus is no longer on the processes involved in making the sound based on the position of the body and the instrument but on the relations to the external environment and quality of sound. The embodied movements an instrumentalist incorporates in the playing of an instrument potentially include breathing techniques and various bodily postures that shape the way sound is produced. This sound, as well as the postural positioning of the instrumentalist, relays information from the instrument back to the instrumentalist (and any listeners), which may result in the instrumentalist adjusting posture or breathing to account for different auditory, visual, and textural structures.

The sound an instrumentalist makes is called a sonic event (Blesser and Salter 2007, 341) that is perceived by an instrumentalist and anyone else near the sound, called sonic perception. Sonic perceptions and events are elements through which bodies learn to understand spaces. As such, sound becomes a product and producer of various cultural elements over time as reverberation and sonic waves help to shape the space, contributing to group identity through various forms of material agency (Shove and Repp 1995). Sound has the potential to become part of a conceptualized symbolic system through frequencies, tones, timing, rhythm, pitch, and intensity, which are used to better understand the world (Hatten 2008, 1–3). For example, the timing of our walking, our heartbeats, and our breathing are all part of a dynamic system that unconsciously regulates our everyday movements (Gieser 2008, 300–301; Mauss 1979 [1935]; Nijs, Lesaffre, and Leman 2013).

The way an instrumentalist engages with the instrument is a form of knowledge that has been shared through time and generations. This is evident in the consistent design of instruments through time that guides the instrumentalist on how to play the instrument. The transmission of sound-related knowledge can happen in a situated learning environment (such as during performance or practice of the playing of an instrument) where an instrumentalist can both see and hear the production of sound. If a sonic event is heard and the instrumentalist is not seen, then the listener may choose to focus on the dynamics of the sound that is produced, receiving information on the pitch, rhythm, tempo, and quality of the sound. This situated learning environment would rely on the listener's ability and skills to discern certain sounds over others. This kind of learning environment might produce large amounts of variability in sound production, resulting in various communities of engaged performances, since the physical techniques involved in the playing of the instrument would not be observed.

If gestures as well as the sound are observed and heard, then playing techniques may be learned depending on the experience and skill of the observer. For example, an experienced instrumentalist will notice the particulars of another instrumentalist's form when playing an instrument, such as their embouchure position (the way the mouth is applied to the instrument), whereas an individual who has never played an instrument may comprehend the visual and auditory cues of these embodied gestures in another way. Beginner instrumentalists often look at their hands when they play to check the fingering positions. More experienced players could focus instead on the effectiveness and quality of the sound being relayed from their gestures. The instrumentalist's mastery of the embodiment to the instrument, receiving favorable information from sound, can include adjusting their physical postures to improve aspects of the sound quality and adding stylistic playing techniques, creating the persona of their performances (DeNora 2004, 53).

In this sense, I argue for a definition of performance different from the contemporary meaning, as the engagement of the instrumentalist with the instrument and sound in an environment that can be heard by an audience. Performance does not necessarily mean a formal setting to produce sound, although we cannot exclude that possibility (Gritten and King 2011). Rather, whenever an instrumentalist is playing the instrument and sound is produced, it is a form of performance, encompassing all skills levels. In addition, I argue that an audience is made up of those involved in listening to sound. An audience is thus anybody within hearing range of the instrumentalist, whether listening is an intentional act or not. There will always be an audience for the instrumentalist's performance, even if the audience is the instrumentalist. Instrumentalists receive meanings and messages through their own construction of sound and often make necessary corrections to improve or reproduce sounds they have heard before. The process of embodying an instrument takes practice and is dependent on various social conditions of the instrumentalist, such as the player's age and condition (Gritten and King 2011). Within a situated learning environment, an audience may intentionally gather to listen to the instrumentalist, or participation as an audience could be the result of normal daily interaction and activity. There are various forms of listening, depending on the level of engagement between the sonic event (sound) and the person perceiving the sound. Sound is incorporated in the environment of everyday activity, but the extent to which bodies are aware of how sound mediates relations between non-humans and humans is not always clear.

The interaction among the instrument, sound, an instrumentalist, and an audience is a form of situated learning and can be demonstrated by engaging with recovered instruments. Archaeologically, it is not possible to determine emotional responses to sound, but based on the construction of the instrument, it may be possible to examine how the instrument was held and how it produced sound. The various gestures that go into producing sound may provide a way to infer various communities of engaged performance.

COMMUNITIES OF ENGAGED PERFORMANCE IN THE CONSUMPTION OF SONOROUS INSTRUMENTS

Recognizing communities of engaged performance in consumption of the sonorous instruments in the G-752Rj collection can be based on the consistency in the form of the design and production of the ocarinas, discussed previously. The design influences the ways the instrument is held and, ultimately, how it will sound.

The collection supported three different styles of holding the instruments; however, each style had similar attributes with regard to body posture. All instruments required two hands to play, each situated at either side of the instrument body. The finger holes were all positioned at the front of the instrument, forcing the instrumentalist's hands to wrap around the entire instrument, blocking aspects of the zoomorphic iconography when played. The visible section of the instrument when played would have been the head of the instrument situated under the mouthpiece, as well as the decoration that was on the base of the ocarina. When looking directly at the instrumentalist playing the ocarina, the base would have covered various aspects of the instrumentalist's

FIGURE 9.4. *Examples of various sizes of bases of ocarinas*

face, superimposing geomorphic patterns over the mouth and chin region (figure 9.4). The base of the instrument could have been covered with the ring and middle fingers to add additional support if the instrumentalist decided to move with the instrument.

The design of the ocarinas suggests that the fingers would have been positioned relatively close to each other for the smaller instruments and gradually increased in distance as the instrument's inner chamber volume increased. It was not an uncomfortable distance for the larger instruments, but properly playing the larger instruments, such as those with two animal iconographic representations, would have required larger hands (of adults) as well as thicker fingers to cover the entirety of the finger holes to produce good-quality sound. The index fingers of both hands would have been positioned on the finger holes closest to the mouthpiece and either the middle or ring fingers on the two holes furthest away from the mouthpiece. The finger hole positioning was so consistent that all the ocarinas would have been held this way, which supports a possible community of engaged performance. Finger hole positioning is important because it defines the pitch, timbre, and amplitude of the ocarina. Experienced instrumentalists would have kept their finger close to the holes to promote a rapid succession and stability of tones. Smaller to medium-size instruments would have had the capacity to play faster and more high-pitched tunes since the finger holes are closer together and the instrument would not require as much air to sound.

The angling of the mouthpiece of the instrument when it is played impacts the quality of sound as well. Any slight movements of the embouchure or fingers can change the tone of the instrument by several half steps. If instrumentalists were concerned about the consistency of the tone, they probably would have remained still, sitting or standing, when playing the ocarinas. If the variability in sound produced by slight shifts while moving was desired, it indicates a more complex range of possible postures the instrumentalist could have assumed to produce sound. The quality of sound changes so rapidly with ocarinas if they are held in different ways that understanding the expressive gestures an instrumentalist might have incorporated as part of a playing technique is difficult to predict.

Clarke and Davidson (1998, 89) argue that certain body gestures relate to the semiotic associations of the instrumentalist and audience and only occur at specific times in a performance. For instance, body sway, an expressive gesture often resulting from rhythmic embodiment, relies on the instrumentalist's ability to maintain time with a sonic phrase. It is a physical gesture resulting from the embodiment of an instrument and is connected to how an instrumentalist perceives (either subconsciously or consciously) rhythm and movement. Pierce (2003) examines how rhythm and movement impact the balancing and posture necessary to support the instrument to produce solid tones. This kind of movement and balance dependent on an understanding of rhythm is necessary for maintaining gestures and sequences over time (Pierce 2003; Wanderley 1999). Since the archaeological instruments were all various sizes and instrumentalist stylization and rhythm are very subjective, especially without ethnohistorical evidence, it is difficult to say if this would have resulted in variation supporting multiple communities of engaged performance.

Another factor that is influenced by rhythm and the style of holding the instrument is forms of breathing. Breathing techniques can be determined archaeologically based on the size and condition of the instrument. As mentioned, larger instruments require more air to sound than do smaller instruments to establish a strong tone. The intensity of breath impacts the quality and duration of sound. Faster or more intense breaths and slow and less intense breaths may result in off-key tones or the production of "airy" tones. Certain breathing techniques are learned skills that improve through time as the individual becomes more experienced with the instrument. They are also dependent on the instrumentalist's age, gender, and health condition. The longer the initial note on an ocarina is held, the shorter the successive notes would be since the instrumentalist needs time to recover breath. If the instrumentalist runs out of breath, the musical phrase might sound rushed or suffocated and produce a poor quality of sound (Dineen 2011, 142–143). The quality of breath, and therefore sound, is extremely dependent on the materiality of the instrument.

The ocarinas in the collection were ceramic and absorbed moisture from the instrumentalist's breath over time, resulting in a shift of sound quality and tone. In addition, the mouthpiece draws moisture from the instrumental-ist's lips. Based on my experience as a flute player for fifteen years, the larg-est instrument in the collection would have been able to sustain a note for approximately fifteen to twenty seconds without sacrificing the tone of the instrument. The wide variety of ocarinas with different sizes and tones may have supported multiple communities of engaged performance in terms of the capacity for melodic phrasing depending on breathing and finger techniques.

Unfortunately, only 17 of the 111 instruments from the collection were able to produce a scale of five or six notes. The fipples on each of the instruments seemed to have been damaged either in the cleaning process or perhaps ritu-ally when they were interred in the ground. There appeared to be no rela-tionship between the tones produced and the iconography of the instrument. In addition, although most of the instruments that could play produced five or six notes, their tones did not produce a pattern that could be considered consistent with a Western scale. When two or more ocarinas that had similar tonal attributes progressing up a scale were played together, there were micro-tonal distortions that most Western instrumentalists would associate with extreme tuning issues. The fact that many of the instruments in the collection exhibited this trait, the abundance of variation in tonality, makes it difficult to assess if sound supported multiple forms of communities of engaged perfor-mance. Distorted frequencies are common in other museum collections, most likely found in two-tone whistles, and are not unique to this site. It is possible that instrumentalists in the past in Greater Nicoya may have viewed these distortions in symbolic ways, perhaps incorporating them into ritual practices.

As mentioned, the Greater Nicoya region may have supported various kinds of shamanistic practitioners, believed to have been spiritual leaders in com-munities during the Tempisque period (Day and Tillett 1996; Wingfield 2009, 434–435, 445). Shamans achieved ecstasy through various means, including hal-lucinogens and auditory stimulation, through the rhythm of drums and rattles. The microtonal frequencies of two or more ocarinas played simultaneously while playing the same note (as discussed previously) could have had the same effect in inducing trances. Blesser and Salter (2007) describe various ways psychoacoustic qualities of sound in given environmental settings can impact the human body. Extremely low and high frequencies result in harmonic distortions that pro-duce sensations of dizziness, vertigo, nausea, and headaches (2007). These bodily responses to changes in frequencies could have been perceived as essential for conceptions of shamanistic transcendence. Perhaps the zoomorphic decorated instruments from the G-752Rj collection were designed to represent the rela-tionship between human and non-human beings (Sullivan 1988, 434–435).

CONCLUSION

The practice of listening and producing sound in Precolumbian Greater Nicoya demonstrates sonic and physical gestures that may be associated with maintained traditions expressing group identity. I demonstrated several ways to investigate the materialities of sound associated with an archaeologically known Greater Nicoyan community, G-752Rj site in Garza, Guanacaste, from the Tempisque period (500 BCE to 300 CE), which was originally argued to be a musicians' cemetery (Guerrero Miranda 2011). I argue instead that the instruments demonstrate a longstanding tradition that may have been associated with shamanistic practices. The G-752Rj collection consisted of 111 ocarinas, 6 tubular flutes, and 3 possible whistles. The wealth of the aerophone collection recovered from this site presents us with the opportunity to explore the role sound has at various scales as an intermediary among instrumentalists, instruments, and an audience.

The ephemeral properties of materiality, such as sound and gestures associated with playing sonorous instruments, are often overlooked in archaeological analysis. This is unfortunate because sound has the capacity to reflectively engage with humans and non-humans, offering information about the environment and relations between things in space. Sound is the product of daily activity, produced in intended and unintended ways, corresponding to decisions made by groups. Although sometimes not outwardly apparent, these groups can be distinguished by the transmission of knowledge of practices that maintain and negotiate sonic traditions in a situated learning environment. Building on Lave and Wenger's (1991) communities of practice, I proposed "communities of engaged performance" as a framework for exploring the degree of sonic knowledge transmission—demonstrated through performative and embodied practices—among sound, an instrumentalist, and an audience that may be reflected in a group('s) adherence to commonalities in the production and consumption of sonic traditions. The limited variability in instrument construction has restricted sonic and physical gestures in a functional capacity and was likely maintained by a community of engaged performance. Communities of engaged performance have the potential to demonstrate interaction on a sensory level, informing us about desired acoustics of the past.

10

Sensorial practice is the only experience that lets human beings perceive the temporal dimension of the surrounding world. In archaeological contexts, the passing of time leaves material traces, and it is only thanks to the enduring properties of this permanently coeval materiality that time is perceivable for us. But materiality does not act alone in the process of producing culture, and humans are not solely responsible for making sense of the world. Rather, it is an interactive process that gives cultural meaning to the world. Within this process humans and things are perpetually interacting, entangled through time in the same web of creative relationships.

In this chapter I present a particular case study, focused on two Mesoamerican bone rasps (*omichicahuaztli*) currently on display at the Museo delle Civiltà—Museo Preistorico Etnografico "Luigi Pigorini" in Rome, Italy. Both of these sound-related artifacts made of human bone left Mesoamerica centuries ago, to reach a modern European museum case. But although they have crossed different temporalities and regimes of value during the long journey, they have always been materially coeval with whoever experienced them, revealing their property to survive the passing of time in a transcultural dimension. In addition to describing their material aspects in detail, this chapter will also take into account the ways their sound capacities were perceived over time, from the prehispanic context to their present location in a museum glass case. If we

Sensing Time through Materiality

Two Prehispanic Sound-Related Artifacts on Exhibit at the Museo Delle Civiltà, Rome

VALERIA BELLOMIA

https://doi.org/10.5876/9781646422395.c010

consider their main function as musical instruments, reconstructing their cultural biographies can be a good opportunity to discuss archaeological materiality from a multi-sensory perspective. Therefore, this journey through materiality, sounds, and time will lead us to consider Mesoamerican artifacts on display today in a Western museum from a global perspective, where people and things continuously interact in making sense of the surrounding world and in writing a global history.

CULTURAL BACKGROUND

The specimens discussed here are usually referred to as *omichicahuaztli*, which is an indigenous term from the Nahuatl that is composed of the word *omitl* (bone) and *chicahua* (fortify, produce strength). This translates as "bone that gives strength" (Bellomia 2017, 15; Karttunen 1992; Molina 1970 [1571]; Siméon 2007 [1885]). According to Western organology, the *omichicahuaztli* is classified as a scraped idiophone—that is, an instrument that produces sound by the vibration of its own body, without the need for strings, membranes, or columns of air. It is composed of a main sonorous vibrating body with a notched surface and a scraper component, usually classified as a "non-sonorous object" (Sadie 1984, 279, 816).[1] As this chapter will show, the emitted sound is actually affected by the material morphology and characteristics of the object used to scrape the notches, so this is directly involved in the vibration of the body of the instrument. Thus I consider both of the components to be sonorous and from now on prefer to call the second part a "scraper." Sound is produced from the *omichicahuaztli* when the player hits the sonorous object directly or indirectly. During the performance, the scraper moves along the teeth of the notched surface of the sonorous object, direct movement, to be alternately lifted off the teeth and quickly and rhythmically snapped against them—an indirect hit (1984).

In Mesoamerica, such sound-producing devices were manufactured by carving a variable number of transverse incisions, parallel and equally spaced from each other, on a long bone. The hard object used to scrape the notches was usually a shell or a smaller bone, as shown in the prehispanic Mixtec Codex Vindobonensis. Here, on page 24, the deity 9 Wind plays a notched femur by rubbing a scapula on it, on top of a resonance chamber made from a human skull, in the context of ritual consumption of hallucinogenic mushrooms (Anders, Janson, and Pérez Jiménez 1992, 146–149).

The femur was likely chosen as the best raw material to manufacture prehispanic bone rasps based on its robust morphology and resonant natural internal cavity, but we can assume that a symbolic meaning was also involved in this choice. According to the Nahua conception of the human body, a vitalizing energy, *queztcuauhyotl*, resided in long bones—specifically in the femur, making it the most durable and robust bone of the body. This conception probably derived from the physical characteristics of this particular bone: its shaft cavity contains the bone marrow whose texture was compared to human semen by the Nahua (López Austin 1984, 149, 331–333; Mikulska Dabrowska 2008, 219).

Today, hundreds of bone rasps are preserved in various museums in Mexico and the United States, as well as in Europe. Only those that show some figurative decoration have been considered and studied in detail in specific typologies of artifacts from the late nineteenth century onward (Gutiérrez Solana 1983; Lumholtz and Hrdlicka 1898; Seler 1992 [1898], 62–73; Starr 1899; Trejo Mojica 2008, 17–18; von Winning 1959). Only on the basis of the artistic value of the decorative component are they now on display in museums, even in cases where the sound-producing element—that is, the notched surface—is not well preserved. Colonial sources that refer to the Mexicas mention the use of the *omichicahuaztli* exclusively for the commemorative ceremonies of warriors who died on the battlefield (Alvarado Tezozomoc 1943 [1598], ch. 25; Durán 1995 [1581], ch. 18.10). Most of the *omichicahuaztli* we know come from burials, and many are broken as if they had been ritually "killed" before their deposition beside the body of the deceased (McVicker 2005; Pereira 2005). This poor state of preservation makes any organological or acoustic analysis of most specimens difficult. In most of the cases I have observed, the object used to scrape the notches is lacking, which makes any archaeomusicological study even more complicated.

Using a new multifocal approach, I discuss two Mesoamerican bone rasps on display in Rome, with the goal of retracing their cultural biographies (Kopytoff 1986) and of taking into account their material aspects in relation to their peculiar acoustic properties and the way they can be sensorially experienced today in a totally new context: the museum. My theoretical framework has been greatly influenced by the anthropological debate on materiality (Meskell 2005; Miller 2005) and on material culture in archaeology and anthropology (Gosden 2003; Meskell and Preucel 2004; Thomas 1991), which focuses on the infinite ways humans and things are entangled in a dynamic social network (Appadurai 1986; Hodder 2012, 2014). Archaeological artifacts are indicators of past cultural traits to be studied from a "material" point of view. In a museum context, this means recognizing the ability of materiality to dynamically act as a cultural agent, able to convey meanings, stories, knowledge, and creativity (Hendon, Joyce, and Lopiparo 2014). I will try, then, to question materiality to trace the social relations human beings have established with these things through time, inside but also outside Mesoamerica, applying this method to the particular case of a musical instrument today "trapped" in a glass case: the Mesoamerican *omichicahuaztli*.

TWO BONE RASPS, TWO STORIES

Specimen MPE 4209 (figure 10.1) is composed of a left human femur. Anthropometric analysis revealed that it once belonged to a young/adult male individual with a stature of 159 cm (or 5 feet 2 inches). The sound-producing device is composed of nineteen transverse incisions on the anterior face of the femur—four of them perforated at regular intervals—and a shell of a sea snail *Oliva julieta* that was rubbed against the notches of the *omichicahuaztli* to produce sound (Bellomia 2017; Velázquez Castro, Zúñiga Arellano, and Valentín Maldonado 2014). The head and neck of the femur were originally decorated with a mosaic of shell (*Spondylus princeps*) and obsidian, which was glued to the bone with a vegetal resinous material obtained from *Pinaceae* trees (Pecci and Mileto 2017). The mosaic decoration makes this unique among the other known *omichicahuaztli*, though unfortunately the mosaic tesserae are now almost completely lost.

This specimen arrived at the Pigorini Museum as part of an exchange of objects between Luigi Pigorini (1842–1925), an

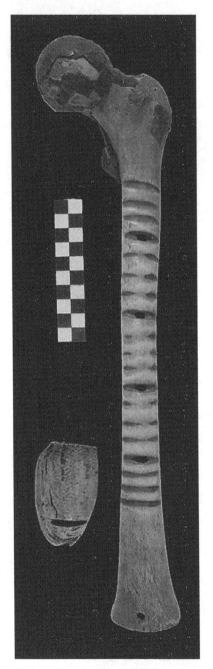

FIGURE 10.1. *Bone rasp MPE 4209*

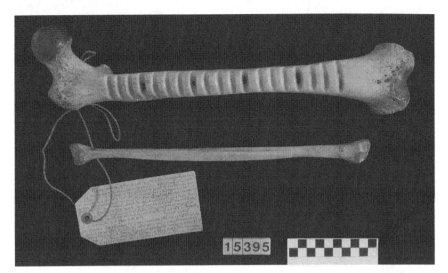

FIGURE 10.2. *Bone rasp MPE 15395/G*

Italian archaeologist and founder of the museum, and the Archaeological Museum of the University of Bologna. It had joined the collection of the Istituto delle Scienze of Bologna through a donation made in 1745 by Pope Benedict XIV (Nobili 1993). Thanks to the recent discovery of an Italian mid-sixteenth-century booklet that contains a list of objects arriving from the American continent, we were able to trace the history of this *omichicahuaztli*. Davide Domenici (2017a) published a detailed description of the booklet and a detailed reconstruction of information about the *omichicahuaztli* MPE 4209 itself (2016) as part of a wider study of Mesoamerican objects that arrived in Italy during the sixteenth century (2017b). The instrument arrived in Europe during the second half of the sixteenth century from the Post-Classic Mixtec kingdom of Tututepec, Oaxaca. The booklet describes the instrument as the "leg of a king," which was originally accompanied by a mosaic-covered human skull, likely its sound box, now lost. Both the *omichicahuaztli* and the human skull are said to have been manufactured from the bones of a "king that was made prisoner in a war by another enemy king" who was eventually sacrificed (2016, 53).

Specimen MPE 15395/G (figure 10.2) is composed of a complete right human femur that once belonged to a young/adult female individual measuring 155 cm tall (or 5 feet 1 inch). It has nineteen transverse incisions on the front face of the bone, four of them perforated at regular intervals (a pattern similar to the other specimen), accompanied by a complete right human fibula used to scrape over the notches to produce sound. This instrument does not have any kind of decoration. It was brought to Paris in 1878 by an anonymous priest, where Enrico Hillyer Giglioli bought it (Bellomia 2017, 222). A label written by Giglioli is still attached to it. There, it is described as coming from a tomb in Quiché, Guatemala.

Giglioli (1845–1909) was an Italian anthropologist, explorer, and collector of exotica. He took part in a circumnavigation of the world for scientific purposes between 1865 and 1868, as assistant to the zoologist Filippo De Filippi. In 1913, Pigorini purchased Giglioli´s entire collection of more than 17,000 objects from all continents.[2] As a result, the notched femur, together with the fibula, was merged into the American collection of the Pigorini Museum (Bellomia 2013, 126–128; Giglioli 1901, 185–186; Nobili 2010).

The main goal of this study was to reconstruct the cultural history of these specimens from their materiality, since that history is inscribed in the material body of objects, which are not only a tangible vehicle to express needs and specific cultural features in positivist terms but also a true social actor that participates actively in the system of relationships that interweave humans and non-humans (Hodder 2012, 88–112, 2014). Through the presentation of some of the results of the interdisciplinary research that involved these two *omichicahuaztli*, I now discuss the manufacture and different uses of these musical instruments during their Mesoamerican and also European social lives, able to cross different epochs and regimes of temporality.

PUTTING HUMAN GESTURES IN SEQUENCE: THE MANUFACTURING PROCESS AND USES THROUGH TIME

Thanks to a detailed taphonomic analysis, I could detect the material aspects of the preparation and manipulation of the human bones as raw material and the process of transformation from body parts to ritual objects, establishing a "before" and an "after" based on the physical relation between the traces of manufacture and use. This *chaîne opératoire* could be detected by the observation of bone surfaces with a stereomicroscope. Such an analysis can reveal the different operations carried out: the disarticulating, cleaning, and manufacturing of the notches; decoration; wear; and finally the attachment of a paper label by the European owners (compare Pereira 2005). Figure 10.3 a hypothetical reconstruction of such an operational sequence for MPE 4209.

The presence of cut marks made by stone tools on the proximal end of MPE 4209 (figure 10.3a)—like those on the distal epiphysis of MPE

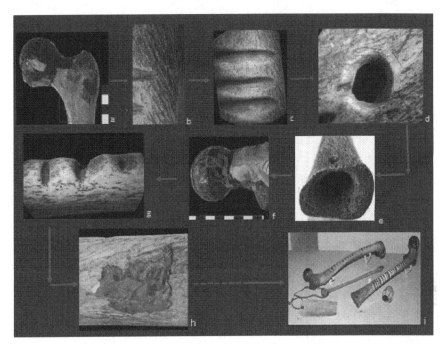

FIGURE 10.3. *Hypothetical* chaîne opératoire *for specimen MPE 4209*

15395/G—confirmed that soft tissue detachment occurred when the corpse of the deceased had not yet begun to decompose, so the degree of humidity was still high in the bone structure, making the bone suitable to be worked (MacGregor 1985, 23–29). The bone became raw material for these musical instruments at a moment relatively close to the deaths of the individuals. These taphonomic data were confirmed by Domenici's discovery of the aforementioned Italian mid-sixteenth-century document, which tells exactly in what circumstances the bone rasp MPE 4209 was manufactured and indicates its origin in the kingdom of Tututepec, Oaxaca. The document mentions that the femur belonging to a "king" made a prisoner in war had been worked immediately after the sacrifice of the victim, according to a common custom among the inhabitants of that region and "*d'altre provintie del mondo novo*" [of other provinces of the New World] (Domenici 2016, 53). The process of manipulation of the body of the sacrificial victim followed the sacrifice, which fully reflects the archaeological records and accounts in colonial sources about the peri-mortem and postmortem treatment of the body of sacrificial victims in different parts of Mesoamerica (López Luján and Olivier 2010; Urcid 2010).

After the disarticulation, the bone surface was then cleaned of the remaining soft tissues (figure 10.3b), and the notches were made (figure 10.3c). Then a circular hole was made on the distal epiphysis (figure 10.3d), and the end of the femur was sectioned to open the inner cavity of the bone (figure 10.3e). The last step of the manufacturing process was the attachment of the mosaic decoration, likely the most delicate operation (figure 10.3f).

Similar to the use-wear marks, the observation of the gradual and oblique erosion of the notches has allowed us to reconstruct the movements the musician made to play the instrument. In the case of the femur MPE 4209, the central notches have a very high percentage of wear of the cortical surface on both their edges, confirming that the notches were rhythmically rubbed in both directions (figure 10.3g). These data also offer very important information about human gestures involved during the performance and their duration. In fact, to date, there are few representations of musicians playing this type of instrument with which we could compare these tracks; one of the clearest ones is found in the aforementioned Codex Vindobonensis, folio 24. The use-wear degree of the 15395/G femur is surprisingly low, although it is clear that in this case it is also oriented in both directions.

After being played for a while in their native context, the femurs then arrived in European possession; it was at that time that a paper label was applied to the rear surface of MPE 4209, likely containing the first description of the specimen as the "leg of a king." Today, the remaining fragment of that label (figure 10.3h) contains the Latin word *"regis"* [king]. After passing from hand to hand in European collections during the following centuries, this bone joined the Pigorini collection. Thirty-five years later, it was joined by its current companion (MPE 15395/G). The latter also had its paper label, made by Giglioli, describing its origin and a sort of transcultural comparison with scraped idiophones of other parts of the world, perfectly in line with cultural evolutionism of nineteenth-century museums (Bellomia 2017, 183; Giglioli 1901, 185). Figure 10.3i shows the current location in the museum exhibition space.

ANCIENT SOUNDS ON DISPLAY: THE
ACOUSTIC EXPERIENCE OF THE PAST

As mentioned, scholars involved in the study of Mesoamerican bone rasps throughout the last century traditionally preferred iconographic or morphological analysis of the single decorated artifact rather than studying its acoustic properties as a sound-producing device. They left aside the function as musical instruments that bone rasps had in their original context, so these objects became the subject of a purely visual contemplation in the exhibition space of Western museums. Only in some recent works has there been an attempt to study the organology of some *omichicahuaztli* (Higelin Ponce De León 2012; Sanchez Santiago and Higelin Ponce De León 2014), although the analysis was based on taphonomic traces and not on directly listening to the sound produced by the instrument. Such musical instruments, now exhibited in Western museums, give us the chance to investigate the different solutions taken to convey information on these specimens, whose presence behind a glass case should not be only visual but also acoustic. Thus an acoustic analysis of the produced sound has become essential for this category of instruments.

Once all the material information described above was obtained, it was possible to return to the initial purpose of analysis, which was to let these sound-related artifacts be experienced by visitors today from a multi-sensory point of view. The main goal of the acoustic analysis was not to reconstruct their original sound performance, which is obviously a chimera, but to let museum visitors have a perception of the extreme sensorial vitality of objects on display, despite the passing of centuries. This can be clearly evident with artifacts that were once experienced with different senses than those that characterize the museum setting, the temple of gaze (Classen and Howes 2006, 207). Taphonomic marks related to the sound-producing activity of both specimens let us detect the ancient performing pattern recorded on the material body of the instruments, giving us the chance to have a confident movement pattern for playing them in a recording session.

The analysis of acoustic properties through the recording of their sound was fundamental to detect the temporal rhythmic pattern materially inscribed in the body of the two bone rasps. This was possible thanks to the exceptional fact that the two instruments are still accompanied by the respective "scraper" objects, which are the olivella shell in the case of the femur 4209 (figure 10.1) and the human fibula in the case of 15395/G (figure 10.2).

The two most important objectives of sound analysis were to quantify how the greater depth of the four perforated notches affects the production of the four corresponding sound impulses and to experimentally verify the presence or absence of any particular rhythmic effect derived from both the depth and position of the perforations at regular intervals. The acoustic analysis of the recorded soundtracks has revealed the presence of a regular rhythmic pattern, which depends in both cases on the placement at regular intervals of the perforated notches. This pattern is visible by observing the spectrograms obtained from the recording of sounds produced by running the scrapers over these two bone rasps, where the peaks of intensity reached by the sound are located in

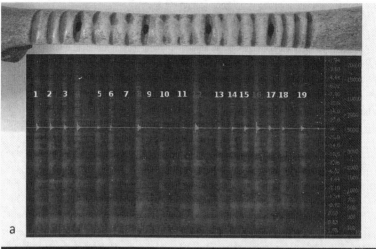

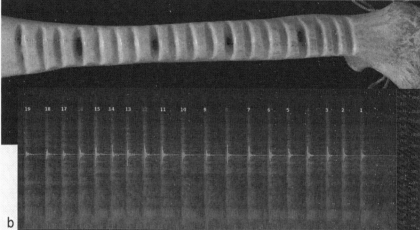

FIGURE 10.4. *Acoustic analysis showing peaks of intensity in a spectrogram from running scrapers over the two bone rasps*

direct correspondence to the four perforated notches (figure 10.4; compare 10.4a with figure 10.1, with its shell scraper, and 10.4b with figure 10.2, showing the bone scraper).

This phenomenon is explained by the greater depth of the perforated notches, connecting directly with the cavity inside the body of the femur. The same bone morphology reveals its peculiar performative ability because it acts as a resonating chamber and thus further amplifies the sound when the scraper is rubbed on the corresponding perforated notch. The intensity of sound differs between the two specimens due to the fact that MPE 4209 is open because it lacks the distal epiphysis, while MPE 15395 is closed, decreasing its resonating chamber.

The difference in shape between the shell used with MPE 4209 and the fibula used with MPE 15395 produced two differently amplified sounds. The empty and open cavity of the shell made it resonate, producing a more complex sound and covering more frequencies than that produced by MPE 15395 with the thin body of the fibula.

Trying to understand the role this sound had in the ceremonies in which the *omichicahuaztli* was played is difficult due to the impossibility of completely reconstructing the musical experience of the past. During past decades, some authors underlined the "hypnotic effect" of the scrapers used in certain indigenous dances (Martí 1968, 65). However, these studies refer to more recent contexts, which are not directly related to the prehispanic ceremonial context in which the bone rasp was played. Many ethnographic examples show the way rhythmic instruments interact with corporal attitudes and determine shared emotive dispositions in collective rituals (Bonfiglioli 2011). Often, they serve as a device able to connect the human temporal dimension with extra-human temporalities (Needham 1967) through their monotonous and repetitive sound.

The use of human bone to manufacture bone rasps to be played during funerals to accompany the *miccacuicatl* has been widely discussed (Bellomia and Fiore 2020; Beyer 1969; Johansson 2014), as has the use of the human body—in particular bones—"as an instrument of lived experience, and as [a] surface of inscription" (Joyce 2005, 140). We can assume that rhythmic musical instruments served to mark the different temporal segments of funerary ritual described by Tezozomoc and Durán, at least among the Mexicas. The repeated movements of the musician producing sound probably helped the vitalizing energy contained in the body of the bone come out and take part in the ritual, as a result of interaction among materiality, human gestures, and performance. This seems to be suggested also by the Nahuatl etymology of the name for the instrument.

The ephemeral nature of acoustic experience makes it even more difficult to offer the same sound to contemporary museum visitors. Although finding a biological basis for the human response to acoustic stimuli has been attempted (Neher 1962), cultural divergences in hearing practices and in individual responses are undeniable, even in a collective dimension where people pertaining to the same cultural background share similar perception categories. Several authors have discussed the risks in attempting a reconstruction of the contexts of an ancient acoustic performance in its entirety (Cox 2015; Rouget and Leiris 1980).

Nevertheless, this acoustic experiment on both of the bone rasps exhibited at the Pigorini Museum also allowed a physical experience of what playing an *omichicahuaztli* means, of the sonic capacities of the matter they are made of—that is, bone and shell—in a dynamic relation with human movements. Although an ancient sound can only be perceived through the cultural distortion of our Western ear, it is possible today to record the sound of archaeological musical instruments and offer it to contemporary museum audiences to give them an idea of what it means to experience the past from an acoustic point of view (Bellomia 2020).

TRANSCULTURAL OR MUSEUM TEMPORALITY: A GLOBAL PERSPECTIVE

As indicated, the "social life" of these artifacts did not end with the conquest. They had to face several changes of identity and meaning through time, within the framework of historical processes of a long duration between America and Europe, until reaching their current museum location. According to Barbara Appelbaum (2007), the cultural life of each museum artifact can be divided into five basic stages: creation, original use, abandonment, collection, and institutional acquisition. Each of these stages always involves "a change of location, change of ownership, and change in use, with accompanying changes in attitudes toward many of its aspects . . . All these changes in the lives of objects are accompanied by changes in values" (124). Panagiotis Poulopoulos (2016), curator at the Deutsches Museum in München, Germany, has applied this biographical model subdivided into stages to musical instruments, taking into account the conditions under which many historical instruments were incorporated into European and American museums during the twentieth century—mainly as acquisitions of private collections by museum institutions.

I propose that Appelbaum's five-stage model can be used effectively to describe the entire life cycle of musical instruments on display, since it emphasizes their transition from sound-producing devices to museum artifacts, in most cases only to be visually experienced in a totally changed performative context. Currently, both of the *omichicahuaztli* discussed here occupy a museum case dedicated to human sacrifice in the Pigorini's exhibition space titled *The Americas*. After having undergone a process of, first, forced decontextualization when traveling to Europe, they are re-contextualized in foreign lands (Thomas 1991), now exhibited in an Italian museum.

Thanks to the layering of meanings and identities through time and space, these two artifacts are a case study of great interest, since they can provide an example of multi-temporality involving both sides of the Atlantic in a broader sense. By entering Italian museum heritage, their material aspects have been preserved for centuries. However, much of the original immaterial performative context is lost. But even so, by their presence, these objects continue to interact with a different humanity in a totally new context: the museum.

Their presence in the Roman museum bears witness to two different historical moments in which the West has confronted the American native world and its materiality. The specimen MNPE 4209 with its "precious" mosaic decoration reached Italy in the first decades of contact with the New World, together with many exotic objects shipped to Europe. With the expansion of knowledge during the Renaissance and Baroque in Europe, Italian aristocrats, scholars, and members of the bourgeoisie started to collect natural and artificial objects from distant lands (Laurencich-Minelli 2015, 219), representing the materiality of another geographically but also temporally distant humanity. In this way, they aspired to possess their own microcosm, a miniaturized model of the whole world, inside their cabinets of curiosities. Within the walls of those private and closed rooms, European intellectuals started to experience the things of the "others." At the same time, the West could exercise a material domain on that newly discovered humanity, physically removing its most representative objects from its context of use. This effectively demonstrated the defeat of native idolatrous practices, in this case materially represented by worked human bones (Domenici 2017a).

Native American artifacts, once they arrived in Europe, were destined to become something different from what they had been until that moment. They entered into another regime of temporality. As socially and culturally salient entities, they changed despite their material stability. The category to which they belonged, the emotion and judgment they prompted, and the narrative they recalled were all historically refigured (Thomas 1991, 125).

The exercise of this coercive power over material objects representing otherness soon translated into a cultural domain of the same others. The symbolic manipulation of the *omichicahuaztli* MNPE 4209 took place over the centuries, transforming it from an emblem of military power and a sound-producing device in native ritual contexts to material proof of native bloody idolatry and of its successful extirpation, passing through the status of "wonder" to be exhibited together with other exotic objects in the Renaissance Wunderkammern. These proto-museums were frequented by European scholars until the seventeenth century, then were opened to visitors as public museums, becoming an expression of modernity.

While MPE 4209 arrived in Italy in the mid-sixteenth century, MPE 15395 is more recent, arriving during the second half of the nineteenth century. While curiosity pushed Western collectors to accumulate exotic objects as a source of value until the eighteenth century, during the following decades the artifacts of non-European cultures had been definitively placed in a historical-temporal "elsewhere" (Fabian 1983). This allochronic operation was necessary to justify the attempt to compare non-European ethnographic artifacts with European prehistoric material culture, an orientation that was spreading in the frame of the evolutionary theoretical model (Biscione 1999; Cardarelli and Pulini 1988; Nobili 1990).

During the mid-nineteenth century, the European appropriation of indigenous material culture by explorers was often justified by the will of the community itself that spontaneously yielded or sold a few selected items. Although this appropriation often lacked any scientific basis, once objects reached the Old World, they were placed at the disposal of a classification system that denied their contemporaneity and used them to develop an allochronic discourse on the others, making them the object of comparative studies with European archaeological remains thousands of years older (Thomas 1991, 141). This is exactly what happened to specimen MPE 15395, which an anonymous priest decided to take to Paris as a prehispanic cultural survival. There it was bought in unclear circumstances by Giglioli and ended up in the Roman Regio Museo Etnografico of Pigorini because it fulfilled the evolutionist scientific need of that time.

It was in the exhibition space of the Pigorini Museum that these two bone rasps met for the first time. Within the walls of an Italian ethnographic museum, they started sharing the same physical location and meaning among objects related to human sacrifice.

FINAL CONSIDERATION

The material presence of these instruments—each time carrying a different evocative charge—has determined their capacity to resist time, which Domenici (2016, 55), referring to Johannes Fabian (1983), calls *enduring coevalness*: the quality of the ancient objects of crossing different temporalities, "being always coeval with different people in different epochs."

Today, the two musical instruments on display at the Pigorini Museum are still "foreigners in a foreign land," but their integration into the American museum collection has preserved their material integrity, keeping them almost intact to the present day. Both artifacts never ceased to be meaningful for those who manipulated them. They crossed different regimes of value through time, and in the transition from native to European temporality they underwent a process of re-definition—each time functional for what the West needed to say about them—up to their current location in the space of a museum. The case that contains them now aims to illustrate to twenty-first-century visitors the material aspects of the practice of human sacrifice in pre-hispanic Mesoamerica.

The analysis of such artefacts could not focus solely on two moments of their life—the manufacturing process and the performance—since certainly their flow within time does not end in these two stages. Rather, it was necessary to create a deep understanding of their multiple transformations through time. If we shift from the concept of biography to that of "itineraries" of things in time, we can consider their social life as "a continual assembling of networks in which materialities that worked as mediators in the past persist in the present and are available for us to incorporate in our accounts" (Joyce 2012b, 120). Then, such rhythmic instruments will appear to be "thick" artefacts, capable of going beyond the mere production of sound in ancient times. As the studies on materiality suggest, the performance of the *omichicahuaztli* resulted from the contact of the human element (the hand that beats the rhythm) with another material element (the bone of the instruments). These two components collaborated in a dynamic interaction. The affordance of materials (following Knappett 2014, 4704; see also Ingold 2019) pushed the hands to make certain movements, literally creating time. Together, they shaped both each other and the context of action and produced meaning. If we extend the hands-bone interaction through time and consider the itinerary of such instruments from hands to hands crossing different epochs, this will show how much more complex and multitemporal the web entangling humans and things actually is. This resulted in an illuminating perspective because it is precisely from this entanglement that the experience of the world is derived.

As Rosemary Joyce (2012b, 2015b, 185–187) suggested, archaeological artefacts are not things recaptured from a past lived experience and revived in our present circumstances; rather, they are traces, signs of history, and they bind different temporalities together. They provide us with abundant material traces of the process of creating social relations. This is true for both the use context and the museum context. Here, the *omichicahuaztli* continue to exercise their agency in producing multiple temporalities in the framework of interaction with curators and visitors, who still shape and "manipulate" them, "giving sense" to their material past. What emerges from this theoretical point of view about the itineraries of things producing changing relationships is that they clearly not only pertain to the past since they are coeval with us, just as they were with their ancient makers and users. Their presence continues to be reinterpreted through time in a never-ending dynamic process, and we as scholars studying them today are part of this process. But this also means they change through time although apparently remaining the same. In other words, they are still moving on their itineraries. Putting together different data with an interdisciplinary focus, I tried to capture the multiplicity of their functions and their multi-layered never-stopping interaction with the human body and thought through time.

Their extreme richness of meanings that cannot be silenced lies precisely in the ability of these objects to cross different temporalities, being permanently coeval. The museum has to put their cultural biographies on display together with the material objects to show the way they changed identity through time, according to what people saw by looking at them at different times but what they also heard by listening to them. The Pigorini Museum curators recently agreed to change the setting of the exhibit space to introduce sound in the future so that future museum visitors will finally be allowed to have a multi-sensory experience of the past. This last consideration is particularly relevant if we think that in its original context the *omichicahuaztli* was a musical instrument, thus made to be listened to and not only to be looked at, in a multi-sensory perspective.

Acknowledgments. I wish to thank Donatella Saviola, curator of the American collection of the Museo delle Civiltà, for giving me full access to the artifacts; my gratitude is also addressed to Luca Bondioli and Alessandra Sperduti Amato of the Bioarchaeology Laboratory of the same museum, who helped me conduct the osteological analysis, and Davide Domenici, who was in charge of the archival research on specimen MPE 4209. Taphonomy was studied with the collaboration of Ivana Fiore, while Adrián Velázquez Castro carried out the shell identification and Alessandra Pecci worked on the chemical identification of the mosaic's resin. I also thank Antonio M. Buonomo, the sound engineer who made possible the acoustic analysis, and last but not least, Alessandro Lupo for supervising the entire research project.

NOTES

1. After MIMO (Musical Instruments Museums Online); *Revision of Hornbostel-Sachs Classification*, 2011, 6; http://network.icom.museum/cimcim/resources/classification-of-musical-instruments/L/1/, viewed August 25, 2018.

2. http://www.pigorini.beniculturali.it/personaggi.html, consulted September 21, 2018.

11

In this chapter, we analyze the role of the *tunk'ul* (a two-tab sound instrument made from a hollow tree trunk) during the festivities of the Pomuch Carnaval, as well as its participation in the ritual and ceremonial song (*k'ay*) titled "Oh, God! [Juanita]" (table 11.1), which was part of a sequence of propitiatory rituals to "pay" (*bo'ol*) spiritual entities for the rains and good harvests during this period. Our chapter explores the materiality of the *tunk'ul*, an instrument of prehispanic origin still in use today in indigenous communities of Mexico, especially among the Maya of Campeche.

Specific rituals are still conducted to manipulate the agency of the *tunk'ul*. The instrument itself is said to have a certain will, but to "activate" it, a ritual specialist has to perform a specific ritual, feeding it with tobacco and rum to enable the reproduction of a specific performance in the hands of practitioners who have learned to play it. This material instrument is linked to (and even defined by) immaterial performative practices that involved processions, songs, and dances—held together as part of cyclical temporality. Each year, a carnival is held in Pomuch to invoke the deities and assure good harvests but also to link the people in a particular place, time, and action—all part of their memory and historical ritual practice, which gives them a sense of being and a special identity directly in relation to the existence and presence of the *tunk'ul*. For these reasons, we analyze the instrument and a specific song that reveals its importance in the carnival and the identity of the

The Importance of the Tunk'ul in the Ritual and Ceremonial Song of the Carnival of Pomuch, Campeche

An Interdisciplinary Study

Francisca Zalaquett Rock,
Olivier Le Guen, Juan
Carrillo González, and
Giovani Balam Caamal

https://doi.org/10.5876/9781646422395.c011

Maya that allows a link between the materiality of the object and the immaterial world that surrounds it.

The musicians Fernando Pool and Miguel Tun still sing the first part of the song we analyze. The second is still being learned; the third is taught by an old man from the community who still remembers it, but the fourth part has not been preserved into the present. There are other songs, also titled "Ay God," that are still performed locally. A version written by Don Pablo Novelo in June 1906 and copied by Tuz Chi (2013b, 4) can be found in the magazine *K'a'ajsaj*. This version has similar aspects although it is of a different nature and is part of a *saka'* or "*atole*" offering in the milpa.

In multiple Spanish-speaking cities, homage is paid to the Dios Momo ("Momo god") during Carnaval. Momo derives from the Greek *mômos*, meaning "mockery, guilt." In Greek mythology, sarcasm, ridicule, jokes, and madness were personified by Momus who was in charge of correcting criticisms of human beings and gods. For this reason, people were allowed to make jokes in public places during these celebrations. Carnivals have their origin in Roman pagan festivals that coincided with the completion of the agricultural work of field preparation. They were conceived as a period of excess, allowed before the abstinence of Lent. During Christianization in Mexico, these celebrations were moved to the dates of Holy Week. Thus the dates of the Carnaval and the performance of the rite and singing in Pomuch vary between the months of January or February, depending on the beginning of Lent.

Since prehispanic times, the *tunk'ul* has been linked to various ritual practices among the Maya and managed to transcend the ravages of the conquest and the censorship of the colonial era. However, today, it is no longer used for such ritual purposes, due mainly to the lack of specialists with the knowledge to carry out the rituals. As Roger Juárez, a native Maya speaker from Ticul, explains, *tunk'ules* and rattles are related to agricultural rites. As the rattle produces noises that sound like rain, it serves to "call the waters" and is used when some songs begin or end.[1] Tuz Chi (2013a, 210–213) adds that the *tunk'ul* is an instrument that calls the thunder, while blowing the conch shell horn "opens the clouds so that the rain falls." The *tunk'ul* is also present in rituals such as the *jéets' méek'*, in which a baby is placed next to the godfather and godmother while blessings are asked for the new member of the family.

It is essential to study the presence and use of the *tunk'ul* during the Pomuch Carnival, since we are still able to access the singing, ritual, and actions of the musicians, which together can give us key clues regarding their interrelation in Maya culture. These data also enable us to provide a more complete analysis to understand the social, linguistic, and sonic variants in *tunk'ul* use.

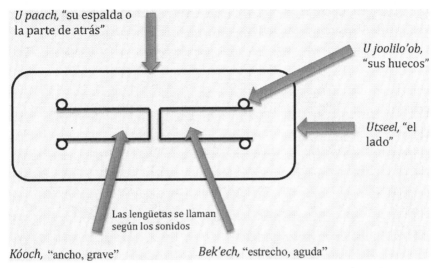

U paach, "su espalda o la parte de atrás"

U joolilo'ob, "sus huecos"

Utseel, "el lado"

Las lengüetas se llaman según los sonidos

Kóoch, "ancho, grave"

Bek'ech, "estrecho, aguda"

FIGURE 11.1. *View of a* tunk'ul *from above, indicating the Maya names for each section*

THE *TUNK'UL* AS AN INSTRUMENT

The *tunk'ul* is made from heart of a tree (*chulúul* in Maya). In the case of Pomuch in Campeche, it comes from a *mora* tree, *Maclura tinctoria*. Musicians from Ticul note that the *tunk'ul* can also be made from other trees such as *zapote, siricote, granadillo*, mountain avocado, and *chakte'*. The tree is cut and left to dry; sometimes a fallen trunk is used. Craftsmen identify the most propitious part of the tree to cut, which will be transformed into the instrument (Carrillo González, Zalaquett, and Sotelo 2014, 113, 116).[2] The portion of the trunk that is used is carefully chosen. It is left to dry for several years before being worked.

A detailed study of the characteristics of the *tunk'ul* and its variations can be found in Carrillo González, Zalaquett, and Sotelo (2014, 112–142). The instrument is composed of an upper section that has two longitudinal and one transversal incisions, which form its wings or tongues, while the back contains an internal fretwork—either rectangular or semicircular—that makes up the resonance chamber (figure 11.1). The techniques used to manufacture this instrument present remarkable continuities that allow us to explain and understand the importance of its structural elements and the range of its tonalities.

In many Maya villages and towns in the Yucatan peninsula, the manufacture of the *tunk'ul* was the responsibility of the person who developed the different *sones*, or musical compositions, played on it (Carrillo González, Zalaquett, and Sotelo 2014, 116–118). However, most of the recent evidence from eastern

Yucatan indicates that "the one who made them was not the one in charge because his work was rewarded with maize. He only had the right to play it if he carried it and took it to where it was going to be played in an event."[3] Data from Kanxoc, Tixhualactun, and San Francisco Tinum in Yucatan and from San Silverio in Quintana Roo indicate that the performer is not necessarily the person who makes the instrument. While the performer is the person responsible for choosing the trunks, the best *j pol(aj) che'*, "wood carver," of the village is responsible for its preparation under the direction of the *tañedor*, or performing musician, so its sound is correct (a process that is also seen among the Maya of the western portion of the peninsula, in Campeche). At the end of his work, the craftsman was rewarded with the payment of an amount referred to as *jun-múut* that was equivalent to 4 kilos of maize (*junmúut xi'im*).

The person in charge of the *tunk'ul* could be given the title of *kuuch paach* or *kuuch tunk'ul*. Literally, both titles reveal the importance of the care of the instrument, as the Maya word *kuuch*, meaning "carry with a *mecapal*," also refers to a "burden" (*cargo* in Spanish) used in a metaphorical sense to allude to the function of caring or being in charge of something. The alternative term, *paach*, emphasizes the position in which the object was carried. Hence *kuuch paach* can be interpreted as "he who carries something on his back," while *kuuch tunk'ul* refers to "the one who carries or cares for the musical instrument" (see also Barrera Vásquez 1980, 343, 615).[4]

Many musicians are said to have a special predisposition or a special gift (*don* in Spanish) to correctly play the *tunk'ul*. Musical instruments can be inherited, along with the necessary knowledge for their manufacture (see Barrera Vásquez 1980, 343, 615).[5] Following from this, it is possible that the knowledge needed to make a *tunk'ul* was inherited along with the instrument itself. A fundamental part of the knowledge required to make and play the instrument, which has to do with the selection of the elements used for its manufacture, is revealed in dreams. On the basis of such dreams, Maya experts know when and where the trunk should be cut, that is, "they know . . . the proper sound" of each tree. Apparently, they can also choose hollow trunks that have a better sound.

ORIGIN AND KEY TERMS ASSOCIATED WITH THE *TUNK'UL*

We find the term *tunk'ul* in sixteenth-century sources, such as the Calepino de Motul (1577), and in the Vocabulary of Vienna (Barrera Vásquez 1980, 845) with the definition "drum" (*atabal* in Spanish). In Yucatec Maya, the word *tunk'ul* is composed of two roots: *tun* "stone" (also *tuunich* in Maya) and *k'ul* "sacred." This means that *tunk'ul* can be translated or understood as "sacred stone." This meaning of "stone" is found in several other Maya languages with the cognate terms to *tun*: in Chorti we have expressions such as *ja'ats' tuun* "the drum beat (lit. of the stone)" as well as several expressions with the same root that refer to the drum (Wisdom 1950, 56). Similarly, we find *tun* or *tunqul* as "drum" in K'iche',[6] *xhtun* in Mam, and *tun* in Kakchiquel (Christenson 2017; Kaufman 2003, 751).

How do we explain the apparent contradiction between the name *tunk'ul* or "sacred stone" and the wooden material used for this instrument? This is addressed in an origin story told by Miguel Tun of Pomuch:

> Lelo' leti'e' jach u ma'alobil le máako'ob je'elo', tumen leti'o'ob yáax fomenta-artej, tumeen le tunk'ulo' ku ya'alale' kaxtbi meeta'anik pero te bin bino'ob te k'áaxo' ka' tu kaxto'ob le tunk'ulo' . . . pero le tunk'ulo' ma' bin de che'i' sinoke de tuunich . . . jaa de tuunich . . . **le beetik ku ya'alal tuun . . . tunk'ul** . . . de tunich ka'a p' u tsikbalko'ob . . . entonses ka bin tu yotaj bin u yéenso'ob bine', ka tu pots'k'abto'ob bine' ka pajchaji' . . . pa'achaj le tunk'ulo' . . . entonses ka' tu tukulto'ob bin le máako' . . . "ba'an ko'on a'al ti' ak taata, ts'o'ok a pa'ik le ba'ala' . . . ba'an ko'on a'al ti' . . . ba'ax ko'on bíis yilej, ba'ax ko'on beetej? ko'ox polik jum'p'éel de che'i'" . . . komo tu yilo'ob bix u formaile', ka' tu beeto'ob bin dee che' . . . tun bisik le tunk'ul orijinal ku ya'alalo' . . . pero ma' beychaji' ma' tu lograrto'obi' . . . tu pajo'ob de tuunich . . . de tuunich le tunk'ulo'.[7]

[They were the wise men because they were the ones who developed it, because it is said that only they encountered the *tunk'ul* in the forest but that the *tunk'ul* wasn't made of wood but of stone, which is why they call it *tunk'ul*, so they say. So, when they tried to bring it down to the ruins and released it, it fell and broke. Then one of the men thought: "What are we going to say to our Father, now that we broke this? What are we going to do? What are we going to bring so that he can see it? What are we going to do? Let's carve one of wood!" As they knew the form, they made one of wood, so they say. They were carrying the original *tunk'ul*, but they did not succeed. They broke the original *tunk'ul*, they broke the one made of stone.] [authors' translation]

We note in this narrative the frequent use of the evidential *bin*, meaning "so they say." This refers to a secondhand source of knowledge. That is, the information was acquired through reported speech, in this case, in all probability through people from the community or relatives. This word implies a trusted source (person or acquaintance), which serves to legitimize this story (see Le Guen 2018). Such a story could be based on an actual event, although it is more likely post facto justification for the name of the instrument. In line with this, a key point made by Miguel Tun is interesting: "that is why it is called stone." Such myths, used to explain the names of animals, artifacts, and animal cries, are fairly common among other Maya groups. In fact, myths like this facilitate the process of memorization and the understanding of cosmology among children.

The root *k'ul* also refers to "an object divided in two," and it is no coincidence that Don Luis Balam, native speaker and *j meen* (ritual specialist) of San Francisco Tinum, explains that *tunk'ul* means "divided stone." Although this interpretation is just a popular etymology, it is interesting that it describes the form of the instrument while at the same time not discarding the homophonous meaning of *k'ul* as "sacred."

In Pomuch, the *tunk'ul* also is given the name *pochob che'* (Tuz Chi 2012, 118; Miguel Tun, personal communication, 2015), which allowed us to understand several aspects that are mentioned in the song and actions that are carried out during the ritual. In some colonial sources, *pocho'* or *pochob* is described as "a forbidden dance, a meeting (*mitotada* in Spanish) of Indians with their tunkules." A dance of prehispanic origin of this same name is performed to this day in Tenosique, Tabasco. Until the second decade of the twentieth century, the *pochob* was danced in unison with singing in Tinum, Campeche (Barrera Vázquez 1980, 660).

Edmonson and Bricker (1985, 49–50) explain that in the Ceremonies of the Katun, the *May* and the *Baktun* were always farces (parodies). Many performances of this kind are named in sixteenth-century dictionaries including *Boox, Hatz'-lam Che, Hech, Pepem, Tzublal, Zabanil,* and *Machlan Kab Okot.* Many were likely prohibited by the church, such as *Maax Okot* (*ma'ax ook'ot*, "the monkey dance"), *Booyal Che* (*bo'oyal che'*, "the shaded tree"), and *Pochob* ("the desire"). The Declaration of Marcos Uc from 1674 mentioned that the *tunk'ul* was used to "light up" nocturnal rainmaking rituals, in which the dances of the *pocho'* and *Ts'ulam* were performed, which served to "revere deities or *pawajtun,* the gods of rains or winds" (see Carrillo González 2012, 130–132).[8] Hernández (1846) relates that the *Kuch,* the *Tich,* and the *Pochob* corresponded to certain "superstitious practices" in use since before the conquest. Two decades later, Brasseur de Bourbourg (1862, 11) stated that "*le Pochob était la danse des amants et des fiancés*" (the Pochob was the dance of lovers and their fiancés) and that "*elle est encore en usage et se danse avec beaucoup de vivacité*" (it is still in use and is danced with great vivacity). However, we do not know if he witnessed it or consulted his sources for this information.

Although these authors claim that the name *pochob* has the meaning of "to desire (erotically)," this could not be confirmed in the consulted vocabularies. In Yucatec Maya, the root *poch* means "gluttonous." It may have a meaning of sexual desire in certain contexts. Used with the suffix *-vb*, an instrumental in Yucatec Maya, it produces the word *poch-ob*, which means "the thing that makes one desire something or someone." This could indeed be the purpose of the song, taken as the instrument of desire.

The *pochob* could also be related to the new year rites in which domestic utensils were broken and during which the "insatiable eaters," patrons of the old year, abandoned their "load" (Acuña 1978, 55). The association between the dance and new year rites could well be related to the introduction and celebration of the carnival by the Spaniards, which, as explained above, originally had to do with agricultural rites of renewal (Pérez Suárez 1994, 249). In Dzitbalché, during Carnaval, some Carnaval groups (*comparsas*) are formed by men of all ages and are called *pochobes*. People explain that they frighten away bad vibrations; they dress like women and scare people as they go dancing from house to house (Quintal et al. 2015, 299). Juan de la Cabada (1899–1986), a writer born in San Francisco, Campeche, alludes to *Pochob* as "a feast of hunger or desire: of the hungry or the desirous. Carnival." One of his characters, called Don Zopilote, is received in the middle of a great celebration, the celebration of the Carnaval and the dance of the *Pochob*, by the inhabitants of *U-cajbaalché* (*ukaaj ba'al-che'*, literally "village of the things of the *monte*, i.e., the animals"), which, as the author points out, we could translate as "*animaletania*," that is, "the capital, city, or town of irrational wooden things or animals."

From all of the above, it can be proposed that the name *pochob che'* given to the *tunk'ul* in Pomuch directly relates to the use of the instrument in rituals performed on the eve of and during Carnaval. There is a relationship between the theme of the song and the ritual, with the "dance of the bride and groom" or that of "desire," which was possibly censored by the priests. In fact, Tomás López Medel, judge and royal representative, ordered in one of his ordinances "that the Indians do not play drum, *toponobuztles*, or *tunkules* at night, and if they were playing it during daylight celebrations, neither during mass or sermon, they shall not use old badges during their dances or songs, apart from what the priest told them" (López de Cogolludo, 1668, book V, chapter XIX, 305).

THE *TUNK'UL* AND SONG DURING THE CEREMONY ON THE EVE OF THE POMUCH CARNAVAL

To understand the role played by the *tunk'ul* in Carnaval and to reconstruct the ceremony related to the song recorded in 1978, formal interviews were conducted with Jorge Pool, the current custodian of an ancient *tunk'ul* in Pomuch, and Fernando Pool and Miguel Tun, musicians who respectively play the *tunk'ul* and the "*filarmónica*" (harmonica), as well as Francisco Ávila, who was a primary schoolteacher in Pomuch.[9] Their testimonies indicate that ritual preparations began when the officiants met in the household of Máximo Poot, the person in charge of keeping the *tunk'ul* and also the sacristan. There, the instrument was unearthed, and people lit tobacco and charcoal to burn copal to conduct the ritual necessary before the *tunk'ul* could be used:

> They held a ceremony, where they took off the cover that it wore, people went singing and dancing to the house where the *tunk'ul* was guarded, and they threw *balché* at it, and they intoxicated it, and here in its little holes [where the wings began to form], they placed some cigars and they lit them so that it could smoke. In fact, it still carries the remains of the cigar here, it never has been removed, they say that this is so that the *tunk'ul* can sing well, to refine his voice with the drink and the cigar.[10]

Both alcoholic drink and tobacco served to modulate the intonation of the instrument. *Balché* was an important cathartic that was produced for and consumed in healing rites, purification ceremonies of farmlands, and *primicias* ceremonies—that is, offerings to reward the supernatural entities for the first crops. This ritual drink was still produced despite prohibition by the Crown, governors, and local mayors. It can be replaced today by other drinks called *x book'*, in the south of Yucatan, and *chak pool*, "head/red cap," in the east, which are "cane liquor."

Fernando Pool explains that once the preparations were finalized, the conch shell trumpet was sounded, indicating the beginning of the ritual. They used two shell trumpets, a large one with a deep sound and a smaller one with a sharper tone. As soon as the first sound was emitted, the person in charge of the song shouted the phrase "*yáawatej paale'ex yuu!*" "Shout it children, *yuu* . . ." in a high voice, and in unison everyone commenced the song (table 11.1).

Meanwhile, the remaining participants excavated the earth and "went on throwing drink, rum, and all were dancing while an old man dressed as a widow along with other men dressed as women with *rebozo* (scarf) and *huipil* (traditional dress)" formed a circle in the place where the *tunk'ul* was guarded below the earth, where it emerged from its annual lethargy. Fernando Pool added that today, "when this instrument comes out, the carnival is about to start within eight or fifteen days, so the people were getting ready from this moment."[11]

The instrument is carried in procession throughout the town, "it is carried using *mecapal*, and it is tied with a rope." While one person carries it on his back, another person plays it: "The holes are left free where the sound comes out, and it is carried upward . . . and the musician plays it with green drumsticks made of palm branches (*guano*), not with normal covered drumsticks, [that's the reason why] when it is carried upright and played this way, it sounds louder."[12]

In the community of Tihosuco (Quintana Roo), the *tunk'ul* is also played during the procession for the celebration of the saint "baby Jesus." Musicians carry the instrument with a *mecapal* (*suum*, or *x tanta'* in Yucatec Maya) while walking from house to house throughout the town. In this case, the instrument hangs on the shoulders with a *mecapal* in front of the person as it is played.

The sound adorns the entire procession while "calling people." Pomuch inhabitants indicate that "if there is a stone, if there is a bench, when the *tunk'ul* arrives at my house . . . there the musicians will sit and sing for us." When the procession finally arrives, the officiants ask for the approval of the *nojoch taata* to play, whether inside or outside the house, all depending on "where the owners of the house give permission."[13]

This ritual marks the beginning of Carnaval, indicating that "the fiesta of the God Momo (the devil) has already started." For this reason, music is played and people dance all around the town. During this festivity the *tunk'ul* continues its journey through the streets, especially because it also accompanies at least a dozen *jaranas* (traditional dances), among them the famous "*cabeza de cochino*" (pig's head).

Later, when the Carnaval is about to come to an end, "the *tunk'ul* has to participate in the *pintadera* day [Martes del Pintadera]." The "town widow" appears in the procession. This is a doll made with old clothes, shoes, scarves, a hat, and some explosives. Its ashes are taken to the church and the cross the next day. Importantly, in the song discussed below, the character Juana is considered the widow of Juan Carnaval. She is the one who carries "Juan Carnaval," followed by the musicians playing the *tunk'ul*. Juan Carnaval is carried because he is supposedly dead, and the widow cries as she goes walking: "Oh, they killed my husband, they killed my husband! How am I going to eat?" Hence, the widow walks from house to house asking for charity.[14]

In the respective households in which the musicians come to play, the women repeat the phrase "I give you money, but only if you dance or play your *tunk'ul*." As the *tunk'ul* begins to play, the widow starts dancing. At the end of the dance, people give "their pennies that are put in a can, and then they go on with their journey throughout town." The donations collected are used for the purchase of the necessary supplies for the celebration of the rites, including the special drinks and food: "Around 4:00 or 5:00 in the afternoon, the widow enters the village meeting room, and once she is in, she does not go out again. Around 12:00 a.m., Juan Carnaval is burned."

On Ash Wednesday the *tunk'ul* is buried again "[because] they say that the fiesta of the god Momo, the devil, is now over. The ritual is carried out again as you heard, the earth is excavated again," and so the *tunk'ul* returns to be deposited in its place. "Before burying it, you burn the cigar and the incense, and you pass it on [to] everyone, and if you were part in taking off the *tunk'ul*, you are carrying *aire* (evil winds that carry illnesses) because, when you take it off the ground it has an *aire*; however, over time we ceased to bury it."[15]

Don Fernando explains that "the ancients" who were in charge of playing the *tunk'ul* were peasants and started dying from accidents in the forest or were run over by cars; for that reason, a special ritual called *k'ex* (literally "change, replacement") was required to offer something in return for the service provided by the *tunk'ul*. Don Fernando also indicated that if they did not light their candles or did not do their ritual properly, they could be harmed and that it was "thanks to God that right now we are all alive. If the *tunk'ul* is not played well, *aires malos* (evil winds) can arise too, but we apply ourselves and that's why nothing happened to us."[16]

Don Fernando Pool notes that the song "begins with 'Oh God!' (*Ay Dios*) because all songs, even if they are evil, have to be directed to God . . . Even if the *tunk'ul* is evil, it remains in God's realm."[17] The fact that the *tunk'ul* originally came from archaeological remains (as claimed by the inhabitants) makes it heavily loaded with *aires malos* considered very dangerous for humans. For the Mayas, the *tunk'ul* is a "sacred" object, that is, an artifact imbued with power and therefore dangerous.

With this background established, in the next section we analyze the ceremonial song in which the *tunk'ul* is mentioned and played. Our purpose is to understand the set of elements that interrelate in this ritual and to propose some interpretations about its content as well as its historical depth.

LINGUISTIC ANALYSIS OF THE SONG

The song was recorded in 1978, performed by Máximo Poot. The song is led by a male, or *aj kuuch* ("leader or person in charge of the ceremony"), a knowledgeable person who acts as an officiant of the song and who was, in this particular case, the sacristan of the church. This latter element is of importance, since the name "sacristan" is mentioned in the song.

"¡*Aay Dios* (Juanita)!" is the first of the four parts that compose the entire song (table 11.1). This song contains a clearly visible rigid structure that delimits its sections. Each unit begins with a phrase that is repeated at the end: *yáawatej paale'ex yuu* . . . "Shout it children, *yuu*. . . ," which incites the participants to repeat each verse sung by the lead singer.

TABLE 11.1. Transcription and translation of the song

#		
#1	*Ayy Dyoos*	Oh God,
	teech Dyoos inyuum	You, God, my father,
	teech Dyoos inko'olele'	you God my mother/Virgin
	tinchéen t'an ka'j k'uchen tujool utaanaj ek taata	I was only talking (singing) when I arrived to the porch of Our Father's house (= the church)
	yéetel inchan paax xan walo' láak'éen	with my little music, would it be too, brothers?
#2	*Ayy Dyoos*	Oh God,
	máaxen tun teech walo' yum	who am I for you then, Lord?!
	inláak'ech	Are you my sibling?
	wáa inko'olelech	Or my woman?
	wáa je' bix ataal ak'áat utoojil inwóol mina'an ujoom áak'a'	How come you to ask me if I am well, there is no hurry in the night,
	xan walo' láak'éen	would it be too, brothers?
#3	*Ayy Dyoos*	Oh God,
	mix tumeen tun inláak'ech walo' Yum	it is not because you are my sister, Lord!
	mix tumeen tun inko'olelech xan walo' Yum	It is not because you are my woman too then, Lord!
	ma' wáa tun tumeen oojela'an yaan teech ugraasya Dyoos xan walo' láak'éen	Isnt' it because it is known that you have the grace of God too then, brothers
#4	*Ayy Dyoos*	Oh God,
	mix achéen oksaj óol teen walo' yum	you did not make me have faith then, Lord!
	wáa ma' tun oojela'an teech utseela'an u'áandas ka yumil ti' Dyoos	If it was not for you known only parts of the prayer Our Father
	yaan teech e x Kruus tak'in walo' láak'éen	you would (not) have the money cross, would it be brothers?
#5	*Ayy Dyoos*	Oh God,
	Kilbalnak	make it crack (like thunder)
	áambalnak	make it tremble
	kuchéen máan e ki'imak óolal te' tujool utáanaj ek taata	the happiness softly passes at the entrance of the house of Our Father
	xan walo' láak'éen	would it be too, brothers?
#6	*Ayy Dyoos*	Oh God,
	wáa yaan tun uk'áanche'ile'	when I have a bench
	wáa yaan tun utuunchile'	when I have a stone (to put the *tunk'ul*)

continued on next page

Table 11.1.—*continued*

	le tun le ki'imak óolal kutaask e mejen áangeleso'	it is then when the happiness is brought by the little angels
	xan walo' láak'éen	would it be too, brothers?
#7	*Ayy Dyoos*	Oh God,
	ka'ap'ée k'iin	two days
	óoxp'ée k'iin	three days
	kuchéen máan upirinsut upool e tooro te' tujool e x nuk táanke'	there goes the turning of the bull's head in front of the big (water) tank
	xan walo' láak'éen	would it be too, brothers?
#8	*Ayy Dyoos*	Oh God,
	ma' tun tuyo'olal Dyoos kinwa'ik teecho' láak' Saakristan Mayorile'	it is was not for the (grace) of God, I am telling you Great Sacristan
	táan wáa tun awu'uyik bix utaal uchun e jaats'o'	Are you hearing how comes the begining of the whipping?
	ba'ale' teeche' tun uchunil	But you'll be the first
	xan walo' láak'éen	would it be too, brothers?
#9	*Ayy Dyoos*	Oh God,
	bin inka'aj tun Kaampech	I am going to Campeche City
	bin inka'aj ko'olele'	I'm leaving woman
	tin chéen t'aan	so I say
	xan walo' láak'éen	would it be too, brothers?
#10	*Ayy Dyoos*	Oh God
	bíin aman tun insiinta	Will you then buy me my ribbon?
	bíin aman inroosaryo	Will you then buy me my rosary?
	ikil abin xan te' Kaampech	While you're going to Campeche
	xan walo' láak'éen	would it be too, brothers?
#11	*Ayy Dyoos*	Oh God
	bix tun siintaile'	What ribbon?
	bix tun roosaryoile'	Which rosary then?
	ken inman teech ti'il inbin xan te' Kaampech	Will I buy you when I'm going to Campeche
	xan walo' láak'éen	would it be too, brothers?
#12	*Ayy Dyoos*	Oh God,
	le tun jach tun awojeel xan tinwéetelo', láak' winkile'	so you know as much as I do, fellow human

continued on next page

TABLE 11.1.—*continued*

	ma' wáa tun teech awilik bix ukuts'ik tuchun ukaala	do you not see how she puts (the rosary) to the base of her neck
	le jach kakbaach jawa'an	this real prostitute on her back
	xan walo' láak'een	would it be too, brothers?
#13	*Ayy Dyoos*	Oh God,
	sobrar(naj) teech x kooralis	you got *x Koralis* in excess
	sobrar(naj) teen e x kastran che'	I got *x Kastranché* in excess
	tin chen t'aan xan walo' láak'een	so I say would it be too, brothers?
#14	*Ayy Dyoos*	Oh God,
	chi'o'ople'e'	tree of *Chioplé*
	x nabanche'e'	tree of *nabanché*
	tin chen t'aan xan walo' láak'een	so I say would it be too, brothers?
#15	*Ayy Dyoos*	Oh God,
	x Jwaana'éen	you Juana
	x Maléen	you x Mal(entia)
	bix ubeel uk'aay inchan troompo tuwu'uyaj teen sáam	how is the song of my little spinning top that you heard earlier
	ka' j máanech te' tujool inbeel	when you passed by my way
	xan walo' láak'een	would it be too, brothers?
#16	*Ayy Dyoos*	Oh God,
	le tun jach tun awojeel xan tinwéetelo', láak' winkile'	so you know as much as I do, fellow human
	ma' wáa tun chéen t'irin	if it does not just move and stretch
	méek'(-ej) inkaal	embrace my neck
	ts'u'uts'(-ej) inchi'	kiss my mouth
	ko'ox te' kaama	let's go to bed
	xan walo' láak'een	would it be too, brothers?
	yáawatil paale'ex yuu::	Its shouting, children! yuu . . .

The song is composed of sixteen stanzas, each delimited by the interjection *Aay Dyoos!* "Oh God!" (from which it received its title). This expression is addressed to God, but it is a lamentation used for rhetorical and dramatic effect. At the end of each verse, the singer ends his song with the expression *xan walo' láak'een*, which we decided to translate quite literally as "Would it be too? my brother(s)." While the meaning in Maya is understandable, there is no simple translation into English. The *xan* particle, "also," points to what was mentioned in this stanza of the song (as well as "and this too") and is some-times absent in certain stanzas. The dubitative particle *wal-* with the distal terminal deictic *-o'* refers to the fact that the content of the stanza reflects a possibility that the audience must validate. This particle is, in fact, very com-mon in ritual discourses (see Vapnarsky 2017, 273–291). The final part of this expression is addressed to the public, here referred to as *laak'*, "brother(s)," and is called with the vocative *-éen* that we find several times in the song, which is also typical of ritual discourses where it is used to address supernatural entities. A possible translation that could convey the meaning of this expression might be "and you brothers, what do you think of that?"

We note other recurring elements that structure the song, such as *tin chéen t'aan*, "so I just say," and *walo' Yum*, "maybe Lord!" (equivalent to the interjec-tion "Oh God!"), which do not add meaning to the content of each stanza but are illocutionary acts that relate the speaker and his interlocutors and serve as a framework within which each stanza develops. The comparison with the version of the 1906 song (Tuz Chi 2013b) is very interesting in this respect because although the content of the song and its nature are very different, the same expressions frame the song.

The text is organized in parallelisms, as in many texts of oral literature of the world (Fox 2014) and, more specifically, of the Maya world (Monod Becquelin and Becquey 2008). A stable element is repeated in the same way (which can be omitted in certain cases), and a second element follows that varies with respect to the stable one. Consider the following example from stanza 3:

mix tumeen tun in**láak'**ech walo' Yum
It's not because you're my sister then, Lord
mix tumeen tun in**ko'olel**ech xan walo' Yum
neither because then you are a woman Lord.

The parts of the parallelism in bold are those that are in parallel and have to be understood with respect to each other in an otherwise stable structure. In this case, the two terms are in opposition: the girl is asked if she is a "sister" or a "woman" (that is, a possible girlfriend). In fact, the same words appear in parallel in the previous stanza (#2) and suggest the same opposition. Parallel-isms can emphasize parts (not limited to words) as opposed, complementary, or *difrasismos*: paired terms that form a metaphorical whole, common in Me-soamerican languages.

The song is undoubtedly a hybrid text, and this is visible on several lev-els. First, we can identify three stories or different narrative lines. The first is related to the fiesta, precisely, the Pomuch Carnaval, in verses 1, 5, 6, 7, 13, 14, and 15. Here we have explicit references to the musicians. The second narrative line deals with the story between a boy and a girl, which has to do with a marriage, in verses 2, 3, 9, 10, 11, 12, and 16. However, these two lines are interrelated, since the song of the lovers takes place in the town of Pomuch and is related to the widow who appears during the Carnaval and the burning of Juan Carnaval. Finally, we have an obvious insertion of two stanzas related to the *Sacristán Mayor* ("great sacristan") in stanzas 4 and 8. These two stanzas deal with a different theme and have a different style: they do not exhibit parallelisms and use a clearly identifiable vocabulary from the so-called *maya reducido*, a Maya modified by the Franciscans along with Yucatec Maya speakers as a tool to evangelize Maya people after the conquest (Hanks 2010).

Considering the content of the text by narrative lines and their interrelation, we find that the first deals with the fiesta, the Carnaval, and the musicians in the town of Pomuch. In the first stanza, a call is made to *yum*, "Lord, God," and *ko'olel*, "Lady, (Catholic) Virgin." Both words are in parallel. This type of opening and calling is very common in ritual texts (Vapnarsky 2008). In the same verse, we have a very clear reference to the church building, described as *tujool utaanaj ek taata*, "the entrance of the house of Our Lord," which in the 1906 version (Tuz Chi 2013b) is mentioned more obviously as *te' tujool u saanto iglesia Po'omuch*, "there at the entrance of the holy church of Pomuch." In stanza 5 the church is mentioned again, now with the roots *kil*, "thunder," and *aam*, "tremble," which are in complementary parallelism with *kilbalnak, áambalnak* "make it crack (like thunder), make it tremble" and possibly refer to the sound of the fiesta and the music as it approaches the church. These two words are based on the same morphological composition and therefore can be considered parallel. The roots *kil*, "lightning, thunder/thunder," and *am*, "tremble," are often used in parallel, referring to "thunder" or "heavy rain," both the sound and the visual event. To the two roots is added the expressive suffix *-bal*, "in movement," along with the anti-passive *-n-* and the subjunctive *-ak*, which allows the construction to be "make it loud, let it tremble."

Stanza 6 mentions the stone and the bench, two indispensable elements for the musicians to play: the stone is used to arrange the *tunk'ul* and the bench allows the musicians to sit (figure 11.2). The song mentions that the music leads to *ki'imak óolal* "joy" and attracts "little angels," which can be various things. While they may be Catholic angels, the contemporary Maya also call the newborn *áanjeles* ("angels"), referring to their character as non-sinners—that is, not yet human. Fernando Pool says, however, that they are indeed *aluxes* (a type of Maya goblin) and alludes to the story of when the *tunk'ul* was discovered by the first *chicleros* who worked near Edzna. This explication is probably idiosyncratic,

FIGURE 11.2. *Don Fernando Pool (left) and Miguel Tun playing the* tunk'ul *and the* filarmónica, *respectively. Note the* guano *palm drumsticks and the sticks at the base of the* tunk'ul, *which allow an opening for sound output.*

a product of a level of interpretation on the part of modern musicians to explain the song. It is likely that this was not the intended meaning in the original song, since the *aluxes* are typically entities of the forest, never associated with the church or the socialized space of the village (Redfield and Villa Rojas 1934, 119).

Verse 7 goes on with the progress of the fiesta for several days, metonymically referred to with the formula "two, three days" (also parallel in Maya). We can also find the expression in parallel in the 1906 text that refers to the same idea of "several days" or "every day" (Tuz Chi 2013b).

During the fiesta, a dance is carried out with bull heads made of paper painted black. In this part, Fernando Pool points out, "they are spinning the head of the bull, they are dancing around it, but the *petate* bull is an entertainment and it is evil. The *petate* bull is carried on Martes del Pintadera and some dress as bullfighters and say *joole*, 'olé!,' some sticks and horn adorn the bull as well as ropes, used to carry it around and to perform the bullfight."[18] The mention of the *x nuk taanke'*, or "big tank," is one of the first indications that directly refers to the ceremonial space of Pomuch. It refers to a water tank from the village around which the bull would have run (according to Fernando Pool).

Stanzas 13 and 14 mention tree names, and while we can link some to the manufacture of the ceremonial drink *balche'* (the *x kooralis*, for example), the meaning of the other plants is less clear. We know, thanks to other sources, that *chi'o'ople'* and *x nabanche'* are ceremonial plants with a strong fragrance that are very much appreciated by supernatural entities (Anderson 2003, 131, 185).[19] In fact, Don Fernando explains that "these plants emit a strong odor and are used as incense burned during ritual."[20]

Finally, the narrative line concerning the fiesta ends with verse 15, which mentions two names of women, Juanita and Mal (or Malentia according to the informants from Pomuch). Both women in the song are asked to judge how the song of the musician's little spinning top is going, a sound that, according to the song, they heard earlier. Informants explained that when they were children, they used to play with spinning tops, which make noise when they rotate, and that this sound is heard when Juan (the protagonist of the song) visits Juanita. This stanza can also be related to the narrative line that alludes to the story of the boy and the girl who, according to the musicians of Pomuch, is indeed Juanita.

The second narrative line deals with the story of Juanita and her boyfriend, which, according to the informants, is developed in additional songs (to which we did not have access). This first song is about how Juanita asks the boy to marry her. A characteristic of this narrative is that it involves a dialogue between the boy and the girl, which we analyze below.

In stanza 2, the boy addresses the girl provocatively, asking if she is either his "sister" or his "wife." The word *laak'* used for sister means "sibling" in Maya and extends to all relatives, that is, people whom one cannot marry. In contrast, the word *ko'olel* "woman" (which here, unlike in other places, does not seem to be related to the meaning of a Catholic Virgin), in a parallelism with opposite meaning, implies that the girl addressed this way is a potential bride. The same is repeated in stanza 3. It is less clear, however, since the girl asked about the boy's "good health" (*toj uyóol* in Maya, literally if "his life energy is straight"). The last phrase of stanza 3 seems to refer to the girl's wealth. This interpretation is based on the fact that the last term, *graasya*, is related to the "grace of God," a very common way to refer to corn in Maya. In the 1906 version of the song, the theme of maize is central and is mentioned several times as "holy grace."

Stanzas 9, 10, and 11 are composed of a dialogue between the boy (who speaks directly to the woman in stanzas 9 and 11) and the girl (who answers in stanza 10). In verse 9, the boy mentions that he will go to Campeche (another mention of a local place), to which the girl responds that he should buy her a ribbon and a rosary, indispensable accessories for the wedding (a feature also mentioned by Fernando Pool). In this stanza, the woman asks the boy to marry her. In his response, the boy, who is obviously not convinced, responds ironically: "What ribbon? Which rosary will I buy you," clearly rejecting the girl's offer.

The parallelisms of stanzas 12 and 16 deal with the theme of the Catholic mass. They start with the same kind of question from the protagonist toward "his fellow men or humans": *le tun jach tun awóojeel xan tinwéetelo', láak' winkile'*, "you know as I do, fellow human." The second part of the construction is given using *ma' wáa tun*, literally "isn't it that then," which is translated differently according to the context of each sentence. In stanza 12, the protagonist asks how it would look if the rosary were put on the *kakbaach*, an offensive word that translates as "prostitute" (Barrera Vásquez 1980, 284), a meaning confirmed by the informants. Here it is not clear who this word refers to: Juanita (the singing girl) or women from Campeche. In stanza 16, the same construction is repeated, but this time it asks *ma' wáa tun chéen t'irin*, "why don't you then keep moving, stretching yourself," and it seems to be addressed directly to the girl of the song.[21] This last stanza seems to celebrate the union of the two betrothed.

In stanza 16, a clear reference to music is made through the use of the lexicalized ideophone *t'irin*, from the root *t'in* "stretch" (from the ideophonic form *t'íijri'in*, which is lexicalized in *t'irin*; see Le Guen 2012). Interestingly, in the song, when *t'irin* is pronounced, the *tunk'ul* starts to embellish the rhythm—giving the sensation of change, a modulation that also denotes the tonal variability (or multiple voices) of the instrument. Based on this evidence, we can infer that the instrument does maintain a close relationship to the elaboration of the messages and the ritual union.

The boy straightforwardly asks the girl to "embrace (his) neck and kiss (his) mouth," gestures very common among the current Maya to show their passion, and also to go "to bed," using a loan from the Spanish. This is particularly interesting since Maya people sleep in hammocks. This puzzling statement raises several possibilities: either we are dealing with the couple having a lot of money (to be able to buy a bed, a rare and expensive object at the time), or they are Ladinos (that is, non-indigenous); even more likely, the Spanish expression is used as a metaphor for sexual union.

Finally, stanzas 4 and 8, the only ones without any parallelism, contain terms of *maya reducido*, which makes us think we are dealing with an older text inserted into the song. In these two stanzas we have another narrative line that is not related to the rest of the song and deals with the *Sacristán Mayor*, a colonial figure. In the two stanzas, the singer directly addresses the sacristan, telling him in verse 4 that he cannot make the singer have faith—using a metaphor from the *maya reducido* developed by the Franciscans, *ok–s–aj óol*, "inculcate the faith," literally, "bring vital energy in" (Hanks 2010, 188–193). The sacristan is accused of knowing only "random parts" (*áandas*, a loan meaning "random, unthinking") of the *Ka Yumil ti' Dios*, the Maya version of the Our Father. This part is clearly a farce that aims to ridicule the sacristan, who is said to barely know the basics of Christian doctrine. Later, the song mentions the *Kruus tak'in*, or "money cross." It is difficult to know exactly what this refers to, but it may be implying that the sacristan was using his ecclesiastical function to get money (a very common accusation throughout the medieval period in Europe and in the Americas as well). The current musicians mention the *Kruus tak'in*, but the term is now integrated into the Carnaval ritual.

In stanza 8, the *Sacristán Mayor* is addressed directly by his title and asked if he is hearing (the sound) of the lash, since he will be the first to feel the rigor of its whip. Could this statement refer to the fact that the Mayas will take revenge on those who abused their position to steal money, or does it suggest that the Spanish will be punishing the inhabitants? It is important to point out that Don Máximo Poot, the singer of the 1978 version, was "the owner of *tunk'ul* and also the sacristan of the church." It is known that despite the fact that the Spanish influx sought to dismantle the apex of the indigenous political organization and priesthood, the intermediate sectors were vital to the organization of the collective survival of the towns. In fact, their intervention can be appreciated over the course of the centuries through the interrelation of their inhabitants with the colonial system. In this context that alludes to cultural transcendence through the capacity of response, we also get a glimpse of the complexity of a social interaction marked by the conflict where, at the same time, the punishments inflicted on the Yucatec Maya for idolatrous practices were whipping, compulsory attendance at mass (on Sundays and other holidays), and compulsory work on church buildings (Quezada 2010, 71).

Due to the complexity and historical depth of this text, it is not surprising that its interpretation is not easy. We point out the different levels of interpretation and above all how our reading of the text from a historical and linguistic point of view can differ from that of the actors themselves, especially the Pomuch musicians. Although as researchers we have at our disposal historical sources and previous works on various types of Maya texts and therefore the possibility to refer back to intertextuality, current Maya speakers have other sources and other aims in their reading of the same text.

We highlight the fact that the Maya who were interviewed did reinterpret the text with elements of their own history, their intuition as native speakers, and their own expectations about the role of this song in the definition of their identity. We conducted interviews with various Pomuch collaborators and asked one who knew the song to sing it *a cappella*. On the basis of these data, we were also able to compare the explanations and interpretations from the two perspectives (academic and local) and analyze how they contrast. Obviously, our purpose is not to determine who is right, since the two perspectives have very different goals and interests, but rather to understand how the Maya today are reinterpreting the text according to their own perspective.

We mentioned that the interpretation of "angels" in the song as *aluxes* is questionable and has no relation to the original meaning. However, this interpretation fits perfectly into the local history of how it is said the *tunk'ul* was found—that is, in the remains of a prehispanic construction in the *monte* (forest), remains considered as guardians created by men but now without owners, preferred places to encounter *aluxes* (Redfield and Villa Rojas 1934).

Thanks to the presence of vocabulary from *maya reducido*, we can confirm that this text is rather old. The presence of several loan words tells us that it was reinterpreted and updated during its transmission over time by the different singers. In fact, the comparison of the *a cappella* song (recorded in 2017) and the interviews conducted with the musicians reveals how certain parts of the song were transmitted in an arbitrary way—that is, without understanding on the part of the speakers—and also reinterpreted. Vapnarsky (2016a) shows a similar phenomenon in analyzing how the Maya of Quintana Roo have perpetuated the transmission of a ritual speech that is totally opaque in its meaning, since it is in Latin, but is actually interpreted as *jach maaya*, "authentic Maya" by the speakers.

Miguel Tun, a Pomuch musician who was in charge of singing and playing the *filarmónica*, in his 2017 version switched several structures, changing older words or constructions in favor of ones more commonly used in everyday speech. For instance, in stanza 10, instead of using the subjunctive prophetic *bíin* (Vapnarsky 2016b), he replaced it with the progressive aspect, more commonly comprehensible to a modern speaker. Similarly, he simplified the structure of the song by changing the person markers in verses 9 to 11 to the first and third person and standardized the song to have only the perspective of the protagonist ("I am going to buy your rosary"; see the analysis of the dialogue above). In addition, we mention above the references to tree names, fairly obscure as they are symbols representing referents probably now lost. It is no surprise to see that they are also difficult for the musicians to explain, and it is no coincidence that Tun omits the entire stanza 14 of the original song, demonstrating how opacity influences (or limits in this case) processes of memorization and transmission of the song.

We cannot fail to mention creative processes. Although the musicians try to be faithful to the original text, they also tend to add more expressiveness, as in the insertion of the root *ki'*, "good," in combination with *chunil*, "beginning" (stanza 8): *ba'ale' teeche' kun uki' chunil le jats' xan walo'*, which we could translate as "but you will be the first to richly start to feel the whip as well," placing emphasis on the mockery of the sacristan.

Further, there are elements and stanzas that are highly ironic and that clearly deviate from traditional Maya speech and customs. We can mention, for instance, the part when the girl requests marriage (stanza 9) or the appeal to the *Sacristán Mayor* (stanza 4). These deviations could be expected due to the nature of the text, produced during Carnaval, a time for the reversal of cultural values (see Da Matta 1991; Turner 1987). This reversal is also visible in other non-linguistic practices, such as the fact that the male musicians who sing this song dress as women.

Finally, in this song the *tunk'ul* has its own voice despite the mixture of influences. The voice of the officiant introduces the rhythm, and beginning with the term *inko'olele'* the *tunk'ul* is incorporated with a rhythmic pattern in measures of 4/4 that is conserved for the length of the *k'ay* ("song"). It is noteworthy that the rhythm of the instrument does not coincide with the beginning or end of the different frames that make up the song. For this reason, it is worth considering the *tunk'ul* as one of the main celebrants, given that it has its own voice, possesses agency, and goes hand in hand with the singer in charge; it also plays along with the chorus. In this sense, it is not just an accompaniment but another voice, and its presence is constant in a similar way throughout the song.

CONCLUSION

The study of the *tunk'ul* with the complexity that encompasses its etymology, history, and manufacture, as well as its participation in ritual and ceremonial singing, brought us new knowledge that requires interdisciplinary work, done through an analysis that reveals the relationships that exist among different layers. Different elements typical of the *tunk'ul* are intertwined with the structure of the ritual and the ceremonial song: its origin story, its name, its caretakers, the musicians and those they visit, its rhythm, the dance, as well as the movement of the participants in the successive directions of the town and their arrival at the Main Plaza. These events are related to a simultaneity of spaces and temporalities. These experiences, related to the song and its ritual actions, in many ways "affect" human beings who codify and reproduce them, assigning them different meanings and values. Such experiences are also dynamic; in spite of the fact that they are collective, each spectator, through his or her particular experience and perception from a specific place, develops a unique and different expectation in each execution.

Through our analysis, we hope to convince readers that study of the complexity of Maya oral transmission and interpretation needs to be deepened. Through the experience of working with Pomuch musicians, we saw how dialogue between researchers and community members should be symmetrical, especially because people want to understand their own tradition more deeply and researchers should provide them with answers. This dynamic enriches and provides new challenges in interpretation. For this reason, we could not advocate more strongly for deeper analysis based on respectful ethnographic work, opening up the possibility of completely clarifying the relationship among materiality, ritual, singing, and orality. In this sense, our study intends to promote more interdisciplinary studies in Maya communities.

Acknowledgments. To Miguel Tun (Chispita), Don Fernando Pool, and Jorge Pool, who have received, sung, and shared all their knowledge. To Lázaro Tuz, who helped us with his comments and corrections in the preliminary version of the chapter. We thank Ángel Agustín Pimentel Díaz and Alejandro Nestor Méndez Rojas for sharing the 1978 recording of the song analyzed herein. This research was carried out thanks to the support of PAPIIT project funds IA400217 "Sonoridad Maya: Diachronic Analysis of Musical Instruments and Elements That Make Up Their Landscape." We also wish to give recognition to the National Council of Science and Technology (CONACYT, Mexico) for the subsidies provided for the development of this work. A preliminary version of this work was presented at the GDRI RITMO conference "Crear, destruir, transformar en Mesoamérica: las modalidades de las acciones rituales y sus dimensiones temporales," October 22–25, 2015, Paris, France.

NOTES

1. Interview with Roger Juárez, Ticul, Yucatan, 2013.
2. Interview with Roger Juárez, Ticul, Yucatan, 2013.
3. Interview with Sara Canché, San Francisco Tinum, Yucatan, January 26, 2016.
4. Interview with Sara Canché, San Francisco Tinum, Yucatan, January 26, 2016.
5. Interview with Sara Canché, Tinum, Yucatan, January 26, 2016.
6. Christenson 2017 (http://www.famsi.org/mayawriting/dictionary/christenson/).
7. Interview with Miguel Tun, Pomuch, Campeche, September 17, 2016.

8. General Archive of the Nation (hereinafter AGN), Inquisition, vol. 629, exp. 4, Declaration of Marcos Uc, Mérida, 1674.

9. We thank Alejandro Néster Méndez and Ángel Agustin Pimental for sharing the 1978 recording of this song, carried out by the Ethnomusicology Unit of the Audiovisual Ethnographic Archive of the National Indigenous Institute. Ángel Agustín Pimental Díaz, Alejandro Néster Méndez Rojas, and J. Jesús Herrera Pimental were in charge of the field research, the musical transcriptions, the content, and the notes from the phonogram. The field recording was made by Rodolfo Sánchez Alvarado. The transcript we present is different from the one they made.

10. Interview with Jorge Pool, Pomuch, Campeche, August 22, 2011.

11. Interview with Fernando Pool, Pomuch, Campeche, September 17, 2016; interview with Francisco Ávila Pérez, Mérida, October 7, 2015.

12. The guano palm (*Sabal* spp., Arecaceae) has been an important vegetal resource for Yucatecans.

13. Interview with Fernando Pool, Pomuch, Campeche, September 17, 2016.

14. Interview with Fernando Pool, Pomuch, Campeche, September 17, 2016.

15. Interview with Fernando Pool, Pomuch, Campeche, September 17, 2016.

16. Interview with Fernando Pool, Pomuch, Campeche, September 17, 2016.

17. Interview with Fernando Pool, Pomuch, Campeche, September 17, 2016.

18. Interview with Fernando Pool, Pomuch, Campeche, September 17, 2016.

19. *Chi'o'ople* (*Eupatorium hemipterapodium*), a vine with large leaves used to treat pain or fever; nabanche'e, *Nursela graveleolens* (Anderson 2003, 131, 185).

20. Interview with Fernando Pool, Pomuch, Campeche, September 17, 2016.

21. Here, we decided to translate it in the second person because of the phrases that follow immediately and that are in second-person imperative:

yáawatil paale'ex yuu::   its shouting, children! yuu::

References

Abel-Vidor, Suzanne. 1981. *Between Continents/Between Seas: Precolumbian Art of Costa Rica.* New York: H. N. Abrams and the Detroit Institute of Arts.

Acuña, René. 1978. *Farsas y Representaciones Escénicas de los Mayas Antiguos.* Mexico City: Universidad Nacional Autónoma de México.

Aimers, James J., and Prudence M. Rice. 2006. "Astronomy, Ritual, and the Interpretation of Maya 'E-Group.'" *Ancient Mesoamerica* 17: 79–96.

Alberti, Benjamin, and Yvonne Marshall. 2009. "Animating Archaeology: Local Theories and Conceptually Open-Ended Methodologies." *Cambridge Archaeological Journal* 19 (3): 344–356.

Alvarado Tezozomoc, Fernando de. 1943 [1598]. *Crónica Mexicana.* Mexico City: Universidad Nacional Autónoma de México.

Anders, Ferdinand, M.E.R.G.N. Jansen, and Gabina Aurora Pérez Jiménez. 1992. *Origen e Historia de los Reyes Mixtecos: Libro explicativo del llamado Códice Vindobonensis.* Mexico City: Fondo de Cultura Económica.

Anderson, Eugene. 2003. *Those Who Bring the Flowers: Maya Ethnobotany in Quintana Roo, Mexico,* with José Cauich Canul, Arora Dzib, Salvador Flores Guido, Gerald Islebe, Felix Medina Tzuc, Sánchez Sánchez, and Partor Valdez Chale. Chetumal, Mexico: El Colegio de la Frontera Sur.

Andrieu, Chloé. 2016. "Operación V.8: Naachtun en su Contexto Regional: Sondeo al Pie de la Estela 1 de El Juilín." In *Proyecto Petén-Norte Naachtun 2015–2018: Informe de la Sexta Temporada de Campo 2015,* ed. Philippe

https://doi.org/10.5876/9781646422395.c012

Nondédéo, Dominique Michelet, Julien Hiquet, and Lilian Garrido, 549–553. Guatemala City: Centro de Estudios Mexicanos y Centroamericanos.

Andrieu, Chloé, Johann Begel, Marie-Charlotte Arnauld, Philippe Nondédéo, Dominique Michelet, Julie Patrois, Naya Cadalen, and Julien Sion. 2017. "Qu'est-ce que Fonder et Refonder Quand le Temps est à la Fois Cyclique et Linéaire? Le cas des Mayas de l'Epoque Classique." In *(Re)fonder: les Modalités du (re)commencement dans le Temps et l'espace*, ed. Phillipe Gervais-Lambony, Frédéric Hurlet, and Isabelle Rivoal, 51–62. Paris: Editions de Boccard.

Aoyama, Kazuo, Takeshi Inomata, Flory Pinzón, and Juan Manuel Palomo. 2017. "Polished Greenstone Celt Caches from Ceibal: The Development of Maya Public Rituals." *Antiquity* 93 (357): 701–717. doi: 10.15184/aqy.2017.44.

Appadurai, Arjun. 1986. *The Social Life of Things: Commodities in Cultural Perspective.* Cambridge: Cambridge University Press.

Appelbaum, Barbara. 2007. *Conservation, Treatment, Methodology.* Oxford: Elsevier.

Ardón Mejía, Mario. 1987. "Religiosidad Popular: el 'Paisanazgo' entre Ojojona y Lepaterique (Honduras)." *Mesoamérica* 13: 125–151.

Ardón Mejía, Mario. 2015. "Panorama del Teatro y de los Bailes Popular-Tradicionales en Honduras." *ISTMICA: Revista de la Facultad de Filosofía* 18: 153–183.

Arnauld, M. Charlotte. 2001. "La 'Casa Grande': Evolución de la Arquitectura del Poder del Clásico al Postclásico." In *Reconstruyendo la Ciudad Maya: el Urbanismo en las Sociedades Antiguas*, ed. Andrés Ciudad Ruiz, María Josefa Iglesias, and Maria C. Martinez, 363–401. Madrid: Sociedad Española de Estudios Mayas.

Arnauld, M. Charlotte. 2004. "La 'Tradition du Petén': Géographie du Sacré à La Joyanca (Petén Nord–Occidental, Guatemala) et à Balamku (sud du Campeche, Mexique)." In *Géographies du Sacré: Dynamiques des Espaces et des Identités Mayas.* Rapport Final, Action Concertee Incitative, Ministere Delegue a la Recherche et aux Nouvelles Technologies Direction de la Recherche. Paris: Université Paris 10. http://www.mae.u-paris10.fr/siteaci/NiveauIII/MMI/peten.html.

Arnauld, M. Charlotte. 2016a. "Entronización y Nuevos Tiempos en Mesoamérica." Paper presented at the RITMO Workshop La Instauración de Nuevas Temporalidades: Rituales de Fundación, Renovación, Nacimiento y Entronización en Mesoamérica, Izamal, Yucatán, July.

Arnauld, M. Charlotte. 2016b. "Rituales de Victoria: Investidura de Reyes Guerreros." Paper presented at the RITMO Workshop El Tiempo en Recomposiciones, Rome, November.

Arnauld, M. Charlotte, Véronique Breuil-Martinez, and Erick Ponciano Alvarado. 2004. *La Joyanca (La Libertad, Guatemala), Antigua Ciudad Maya del Noroeste del Petén.* Guatemala City: Centro de Estudios Mexicanos y Centroamericanos, Asociacion Tikal, and Centro de Investigaciones Regionales de Mesoamérica.

Arnauld, M. Charlotte, Sara Dzul Gongora, and Laure Déodat. 2010. "Evolución de la Ocupación en el Grupo B, Río Bec." In *La Península de Yucatán: Investigaciones Recientes y Cronologías Alternativas*, ed. Ernesto Vargas Pacheco and Antonio Benavides Castillo, 135–154. Campeche: Universidad Autonoma de Campeche.

Arnauld, M. Charlotte, Mélanie Forné, Erick Ponciano, Eva Lemonnier, Mauricio Diaz, Gabriella Luna, Adriana Segura, and Julien Sion. 2013. "Ritos de Transición, Ritos de Crísis: Perspectivas para la Movilidad Poblacional en las Sociedades Mayas Clásicas." In *XXVI Simposio de Investigaciones Arqueológicas en Guatemala, 2012,* ed. Bárbara Arroyo and Luis Alberto Méndez Salinas, 539–552. Guatemala City: Ministerio de Cultura y Deportes, Instituto de Antropología e Historia, and Asociación Tikal.

Arnauld, M. Charlotte, Eva Lemonnier, Mélanie Forné, Laura Gámez, Edy Barrios, and James Fitzsimmons. 2012. "Perspectivas Sobre El Centro–Oeste de Petén desde La Joyanca, Zapote Bobal y Otros Centros Mayas Clásicos, Guatemala." In *XXV Simposio de Investigaciones Arqueológicas en Guatemala,* ed. Barbara Arroyo, Lorena Paiz Aragón, and Hector E. Mejia, 111–125. Guatemala City: Ministerio de Cultura y Deportes, Instituto de Antropología e Historia, and Asociación Tikal.

Arnauld, M. Charlotte, Eva Lemonnier, Mélanie Forné, Erick Ponciano Alvarado, and Julien Sion. 2017. "Early to Late Classic Population Mobility in the Maya Site of La Joyanca and Hinterlands, Northwestern Petén, Guatemala." *Journal of Anthropological Archaeology* 45: 15–37. http://dx.doi.org/10.1016/j.jaa.2016.10.002.

Arnauld, M. Charlotte, and Tristan Saint-Dizier. 2016. "Réparer la Surface de la Terre: Les Restes dans les Rituels de Construction au sein des Villes Mayas Classiques (250–950 apr. J.–C.)." *Techniques and Culture* 65–66: 138–149.

Ashmore, Wendy. 1991. "Site-Planning Principles and Concepts of Directionality among the Ancient Maya." *Latin American Antiquity* 2 (3): 199–226.

Auer, Peter, Elizabeth Couper-Kuhlen, and Frank Müller. 1999. *Language in Time: Rhythm and Tempo of Spoken Interaction.* Oxford: Oxford University Press.

Austin, John L. 1962. *How to Do Things with Words.* Oxford: Clarendon.

Bachand, Bruce R. 2006. "Preclassic Excavations at Punta de Chimino, Petén, Guatemala: Investigating Social Emplacement on an Early Maya Landscape." PhD dissertation, University of Arizona, Tucson.

Baez Cubero, Lourdes. 1996. "*Mo'patla intlakwalle,* el banquete de Todos Santos: Formas de reciprocidad y redistribución entre los nahuas de la Sierra de Puebla." In *Procesos de escenificación y contextos rituales,* ed. Ingrid Geist, 105–120. Mexico City: Universidad Iberoamericana–Plaza y Valdés.

Baez Cubero, Lourdes. 2005. *El juego de las alternancias, la vida y la muerte: Rituales del ciclo vital entre los nahuas de la Sierra de Puebla*. Mexico City: Programa de Desarrollo Cultural de la Huasteca.

Baez Cubero, Lourdes. 2008. "Entre la memoria y el olvido: Representaciones de la muerte entre los nahuas de la Sierra Norte de Puebla." In *Morir para vivir en Mesoamérica*, ed. Lourdes Baez Cubero and Catalina Rodríguez Lascano, 57–84. Veracruz: Consejo Veracruzano de Arte Popular–Instituto Nacional de Antropología e Historia.

Baez Cubero, Lourdes, and Catalina Rodríguez Lascano (eds.). 2008. *Morir para vivir en Mesoamérica*. Veracruz: Consejo Veracruzano de Arte Popular–Instituto Nacional de Antropología e Historia.

Bailey, Geoff. 2007. "Time Perspectives, Palimpsest, and the Archaeology of Time." *Journal of Anthropological Archaeology* 26 (2): 198–223.

Barad, Karen. 2003. "Posthumanist Performativity: Toward an Understanding of How Matter Comes to Matter." *Signs: Journal of Women in Culture and Society* 28 (3): 801–831.

Barad, Karen. 2007. *Meeting the Universe Halfway: Quantum Physics and the Entanglement of Matter and Meaning*. Durham, NC: Duke University Press.

Barnhart, Edwin L. 2007. "Indicators of Urbanism at Palenque." In *Palenque: Recent Investigations at the Classic Maya Center*, ed. Damien B. Marken, 107–119. Lanham, MD: Altamira.

Barrera Vásquez, Alfredo. 1980. *Diccionario Cordemex Maya-Español-Maya*. Mexico City: Ediciones Cordemex.

Barrientos, Isaac. 2016. "Operación II.5: Los Contextos Funerarios y los Procesos de Aglomeración." In *Proyecto Petén–Norte Naachtun 2015–2018: Informe de la Sexta Temporada de Campo 2015*, ed. Philippe Nondédéo, Dominique Michelet, Julien Hiquet, and Lilian Garrido, 161–183. Guatemala City: Centro de Estudios Mexicanos y Centroamericanos.

Barrientos, Isaac. 2018. "Operación IV.4a: Análisis Realizados en los Restos Óseos Humanos." In *Proyecto Petén–Norte Naachtun 2015–2018: Informe de la Octava Temporada de Campo 2017*, ed. Philippe Nondédéo, Dominique Michelet, Johann Begel, and Lilian Garrido, 255–292. Guatemala City: Centro de Estudios Mexicanos y Centroamericanos.

Barrientos, Isaac, Julien Sion, Chloé Andrieu, Daniel Salazar, and Julio Cotom. 2015. "Evidencias de Reingreso a los Espacios Sepulcrales en Grupos Habitacionales del Clásico Tardío-Terminal en Naachtun, Petén, Guatemala." In *XXVIII Simposio de Investigaciones Arqueológicas en Guatemala, 2014*, ed. Bárbara Arroyo, Luis Méndez Salinas, and Lorena Paiz, 465–479. Guatemala City: Ministerio de Cultura y Deportes, Instituto de Antropología e Historia, and Asociación Tikal.

Barth-Weingarten, Dagmar, Elisabeth Reber, and Margret Selting (eds.). 2010. *Prosody in Interaction*. Amsterdam: John Benjamins. doi: 10.1075/sidag.23.

Bastide, Roger. 1998 [1972]. *Il sacro selvaggio e altri scritti*. Milan: Jaca Book.

Baudez, Claude-François. 1994. *Maya Sculpture of Copan: The Iconography*. Norman: University of Oklahoma Press.

Baudez, Claude-François. 2002. *Une Histoire de la Religion des Mayas*. Paris: Albin Michel.

Baudez, Claude-François. 2012. *La Douleur Rédemptrice : l'Autosacrifice Précolombien*. Paris: Riveneuve éditions.

Bauer, Jeremy, Ángel Castillo, Daniel Leonard, Mónica Antillón, Antolín Velásquez, Jennifer M. Johnson, and Joel Zovar. 2004. "El Pasado Preclásico y Monumental de la región de Holmul: Resultados de las temporadas de Campo 2003 y 2004 en Cival Petén." In *XVIII Simposio de Investigaciones Arqueológicas en Guatemala*, ed. Juan Pedro Laporte, 194–205. Guatemala City: Ministerio de Cultura y Deportes, Instituto de Antropología e Historia, and Asociación Tikal.

Bazy, Damien. 2010. "Relation entre Places Publiques et Espaces Privés dans les Basses Terres Mayas Centrales et Méridionales du Préclassique au Classique Terminal (Mexique et Guatemala)." PhD dissertation, Université de Paris 1 Panthéon–Sorbonne, France.

Bazy, Damien, and Takeshi Inomata. 2017. "Multiple Waves of Political Disintegration in the Classic Maya Collapse: New Insights from the Excavation of Group D, Ceibal, Guatemala." *Journal of Field Archaeology* 42 (2): 82–96. doi: 10.1080/00934690.2017.1286928.

Beck, Robin A., Douglas J. Bolender, James A. Brown, and Timothy K. Earle. 2007. "Eventful Archaeology: The Place of Space in Structural Transformation." *Current Anthropology* 48 (6): 833–860.

Becker, Marshall J. 1993. "Earth Offerings among the Classic Period Lowland Maya: Burial and Caches as Ritual Deposits." In *Perspectivas Antropologicas en el Mundo Maya*, ed. Maria Josefa Iglesias Ponce de Leon and Francesc Ligorred Perramon, 45–74. Madrid: Sociedad Española de Estudios Mayas.

Becker, Marshall J. 2003. "Plaza Plans at Tikal: A Research Strategy for Inferring Social Organization and Processes of Culture Change at Lowland Maya Sites." In *Tikal: Dynasties, Foreigners, and Affairs of State: Advancing Maya Archaeology*, ed. Jeremy Sabloff, 253–280. Santa Fe, NM: School of American Research Press.

Becker, Marshall J. 2009. "Skull Rituals and Plaza Plan 4 at Tikal: Lowland Maya Mortuary Patterns." *The Codex* 17 (1–2/2008–2009): 12–41.

Becquey, Cédric. 2017. "Rituel d'inauguration de Maison Chez les Chols: une Étude Ethnolinguistique." Paper presented at the 13th Annual Colloqium of the Maison Archéologie Ethnologie, (Re)Fonder: Modalités du (re)commencement dans le Temps et dans l'espace, Université Paris Ouest Nanterre, June.

Begel, Johann, and Isaac Barrientos. 2018. "Operación V.5: La Estructura V y su Actividad Ritual." In *Proyecto Petén–Norte Naachtun 2015–2018: Informe de la Octava Temporada de Campo 2017*, ed. Philippe Nondédéo, Dominique Michelet, Johann Begel, and Lilian Garrido, 441–456. Guatemala City: Centro de Estudios Mexicanos y Centroamericanos.

Bell, Catherine. 1992. *Ritual Theory, Ritual Practice*. Oxford: Oxford University Press.

Bell, Ellen. 2007. "Early Classic Ritual Deposits within the Copan Acropolis: The Material Foundations of Political Power at a Classic Period Maya Center." PhD dissertation, University of Pennsylvania, Philadelphia.

Bellomia, Valeria. 2013. "Analisi dei due Strumenti Musicali Aztechi in Ossa Umane del Museo Nazionale Preistorico Etnografico Luigi Pigorini." MA thesis, Sapienza Università di Roma.

Bellomia, Valeria. 2017. "Omichicahuaztli dalla Mesoamerica: Studio Comparativo delle Pratiche Museali di Conservazione e Valorizzazione fra Italia e Messico." PhD dissertation, Sapienza Università di Roma.

Bellomia, Valeria. 2020. *Ascoltare un osso umano: L'omichicahuaztli dalla Mesoamerica alla vetrina di un museo*. Avellino, Italy: Il Papavero.

Bellomia, Valeria, and Ivana Fiore. 2020. "The Materiality of Music: Technological and Functional Study of Two Mesoamerican Omichicahuaztli." In *Flower World: Musical Archaeology of the Americas*, volume 6, ed. Matthias Stöckli and Mark Howell, 11–28. Berlin: Ekho Verlag.

Bennett, Jane. 2010. *Vibrant Matter: A Political Ecology of Things*. Durham, NC: Duke University Press.

Benveniste, Émile. 1951. "La Notion de Rythme dans son Expression Linguistique." *Journal de Psychologie Normale et Pathologique* 44 (3): 401–410.

Bergson, Henri. 1999. *Duration and Simultaneity: Bergson and the Einsteinian Universe*. Manchester: Clinamen.

Berlin, Heinrich. 1951. "El Templo de las Inscripciones (VI) de Tikal." *Antropologia e Historia* 3 (1): 3–10.

Berryman, Carrie Anne. 2007. "Captive Sacrifice and Trophy Taking among the Ancient Maya: An Evaluation of the Biarchaeological Evidence and Its Sociopolitical Implications." In *The Taking and Displaying of Human Body Parts as Trophies by Amerindians*, ed. Richard J. Chacon and David H. Dye, 377–379. Boston: Springer.

Beyer, Hermann. 1969. "Un Instrumento Musical de los Antiguos Mexicanos: El Omichicahuaztli." *El México Antiguo* 11: 536–539.

Biscione, Marco. 1999. "I Musei Etnografici come Modelli del Sapere: Il Museo Nazionale Preistorico Etnografico Luigi Pigorini." In *Contesto e Identità: Gli Oggetti Fuori e Dentro i Musei*, ed. Franca di Valerio, 105–111. Bologna: CLUEB.

Blesser, Barry, and Linda-Ruth Salter. 2007. *Spaces Speak, Are You Listening? Experiencing Aural Architecture*. Cambridge: MIT Press.

Bloch, Maurice. 1974. "Symbols, Song, Dance, and Features of Articulation: Is Religion an Extreme Form of Traditional Authority?" *Archives Européennes de Sociologie* 15 (1): 55–81.

Bloch, Maurice. 1989. *Ritual, History Power*. London: Athlone.

Boivin, Nicole. 2000. "Life Rhythms and Floor Sequences: Excavating Time in Rural Rajasthan and Neolithic Catalhoyuk." *World Archaeology* 31 (3): 367–388.

Bonfiglioli, Carlo. 2011. "De la Sipíraka Rarámuri al Omichicahuaztli Mexica: Transformaciones del Concepto de Escalera Cósmica." In *Las vías del noroeste III: genealogías, transversalidades y convergencias*, ed. Carlo Bonfiglioli, 65–102. Mexico City: Universidad Nacional Autónoma de México.

Both, Arnd A. 2009. "Music Archaeology: Some Methodological and Theoretical Considerations." *Yearbook for Traditional Music* 41: 1–11. https://www.jstor.org /stable/25735475.

Brabec de Morí, Bernd, Matthias Lewy, and Miguel A. García (eds.). 2014. *Sudamérica y sus Mundos Audibles: Cosmologías y Prácticas Sonoras de los Pueblos Indígenas*. Berlin: Ibero-Amerikanisches Institut Preuftischer Kulturbesitz.

Bradley, Richard. 1991. "Ritual, Time, and History." *World Archaeology* 23 (2): 209–219.

Bradley, Richard. 2003. "A Life Less Ordinary: The Ritualization of the Domestic Sphere in Later Prehistoric Europe." *Cambridge Archaeological Journal* 13 (1): 5–23.

Brandes, Stanley. 1997. "Sugar, Colonialism, and Death: On the Origins of Mexico's Day of the Dead." *Comparative Studies in Society and History* 39 (2): 270–299.

Brasseur de Bourbourg, Charles. 1862. "Essai sur la Poésie et la Musique, sur la Danse el l'art Dramatique des Anciennes Populations Mexicaines et Guatémaltèques." In *Grammaire de la Langue Quichée, Suivie d'un Vocabulaire et du Drame de Rabinal Achi*, ed. Charles Brasseur de Bourbourg, 5–23. Paris: A. Bertrand.

Breton, Alain, and Aurore Becquelin-Monod. 1989. "'Mais j'ai transmis l'espérance . . .' Etude d'une prière de guérison tzeltal (Maya du Chiapas, Mexique)." *Amérindia* 13 (supplement 1).

Breuil-Martinez, Veronique, Erwin Salvador Loópez, Tristan Saint Dizier, and Laura Gámez (eds.). 2003. *Proyecto Petén Noroccidente–La Joyanca, Informe N°5, cuarta temporada de campo, 2003*. Guatemala City: Centro de Estudios Mexicanos y Centroamericanos.

Bricker, Victoria R. 1989 [1974]. "The Ethnographic Context of Some Traditional Mayan Speech Genres." In *Explorations in the Ethnography of Speaking*, ed. Richard Bauman and Joel Sherzer, 368–388. Cambridge: Cambridge University Press.

Briggs, Charles. 1993. "Personal Sentiments and Polyphonic Voices in Warao Women's Ritual Wailing: Music and Poetics in a Critical and Collective Discourse." *American Anthropologist* 95 (4): 925–957.

Brown, Linda A. 2004. "Dangerous Places and Wild Spaces: Creating Meaning with Materials and Space at Contemporary Maya Shrines on El Duende Mountain." *Journal of Archaeological Method and Theory* 11 (1): 31–58.

Brown, Linda A., and Kitty Emery. 2008. "Negotiations with the Animate Forest: Hunting Shrines in the Guatemala Highlands." *Journal of Archaeological Method and Theory* 15: 300–337.

Brown, Linda A., and William H. Walker. 2008. "Prologue: Archaeology, Animism, and Non-Human Agents." *Journal of Archaeological Method and Theory* 15 (4): 297–299.

Browne Ribeiro, Anna T., Helena P. Lima, Fernando L.T. Marques, Morgan J. Schnmidt, and Kevin C. McDaniel. 2016. "Results from Pilot Archaeological Fieldwork at the Carrazedo Site, Lower Xingu River, Amazonia." *Latin American Antiquity* 27 (3): 318–339.

Bunzel, Ruth Leah. 1959. *Chichicastenango, a Guatemalan Village*. Seattle: University of Washington Press.

Cabarrús, Carlos Rafael. 1979. *La Cosmovisión K'ekchí' en Proceso de Cambio*. San Salvador: UCA Editores.

Calderón, Zoila, Vilma Fialko, and Omar Scwhendener. 2009. "Los Patios de Juego de Pelota de Nakum." In *XXII Simposio de Investigaciones Arqueológicas en Guatemala 2008*, ed. Juan Pedro Laporte, Bárbara Arroyo, and Hector E. Mejia, 1394–1405. Guatemala City: Ministerio de Cultura y Deportes, Instituto de Antropología e Historia, and Asociación Tikal.

Calligeris, Catherine. 1999. "Fonction et Signification des Dépôts de Fondation Mayas, dans les Basses Terres, à la Période Classique." PhD dissertation, Université Paris I Panthéon–Sorbonne, France.

Cardarelli, Andrea, and Ilaria Pulini. 1988. "Il Metodo Comparativo e l'Origine dei Musei Preistorici Etnografici in Europa." *Dialoghi di Archeologia* 4: 71–89.

Carias, Claudia Marcela, Hector Miguel Leyva, Róger Martinez Miralda, Emma Leticia Ordoñez, and Jorge F. Travieso. 2004. *Tradición Oral Indígena de Yamaranguila*, segunda edición. Tegucigalpa, Honduras: Editorial Guaymuras.

Carlson, Ruth, and Francis Eachus. 1977. "The Kekchi Spirit World." In *Cognitive Studies of Southern Mesoamerica*, ed. Helen L. Neuenswander and Dean E. Arnold, 35–65. Dallas: Summer Institute of Linguistics Museum of Anthropology.

Carrillo González, Juan. 2012. "Tunk'ul: Análisis de un Instrumento Musical Maya en Contextos Rituales Durante la Colonia." In *Flower World: Musical Archaeology of the Americas*, volume 1, ed. Matthias Stöckli and Arnd Adje Both, 127–136. Berlin: Ekho Verlag.

Carrillo González, Juan, Francisca Zalaquett, and Laura Sotelo. 2014. "Los Sonidos del Tunkul: Códigos Acústicos Mayas de la Península de Yucatán." In *Entramados Sonoros de Tradición Mesoamericana*, ed. Francisca Zalaquett and Laura Sotelo, 111–149. Mexico City: Centro de Estudios Mayas, Instituto de Investigaciones Filológicas, and Universidad Nacional Autónoma de México.

Chamoux, Marie-Noëlle. 1997. "La cuisine de la Toussaint chez les Aztèques de la Sierra de Puebla (Mexique)." *Babel: Internationale de l'imaginaire* 7 n.s.: 85–99.

Chapman, Anne. 1978. *Los Lencas de Honduras en el Siglo XVI*. Estudios Antropologicos y Historicos 2. Tegucigalpa, Honduras: Instituto Hondureño de Antropología e Historia.

Chapman, Anne. 1985. *Los Hijos del Copal y la Candela [Tomo I]: Tradición Católica de los Lencas de Honduras*. Instituto de Investigaciones Antropológicas, Serie Antropológica 86. Mexico City: Universidad Nacional Autónoma de México.

Chapman, Anne. 1986. *Los Hijos del Copal y la Candela [Tomo II]: Ritos Agrarios y Tradición Oral de Los Lencas de Honduras*. Instituto de Investigaciones Antropológicas, Serie Antropológicas, Serie Antropológica 64. Mexico City: Universidad Nacional Autónoma de México.

Chase, Arlen F. 1983. "A Contextual Consideration of the Tayasal-Paxcaman Zone, El Petén, Guatemala." PhD dissertation, University of Pennsylvania, Philadelphia.

Chase, Arlen F., and Diane Z. Chase. 1994. "Maya Veneration of the Dead at Caracol, Belize." In *Seventh Palenque Round Table 1989*, ed. Merle Greene Robertson, 55–62. San Francisco: Pre-Columbian Art Research Institute.

Chase, Arlen F., and Diane Z. Chase. 2004. "Terminal Classic Status-Linked Ceramics and the Maya Collapse: De Facto Refuse at Caracol, Belize." In *The Terminal Classic in the Maya Lowlands: Collapse, Transition, and Transformation*, ed. Arthur A. Demarest, Prudence M. Rice, and Don S. Rice, 342–366. Boulder: University Press of Colorado.

Chávez Borjas, Manuel. 1992. "Guancasco de Mexicapa, Comunidad Campesina del Occidente de Honduras." *Tramoya: Cuadro del Teatro* 33: 38–45.

Chen, Mel. 2012. *Animacies: Biopolitics, Racial Mattering, and Queer Affect*. Durham, NC: Duke University Press.

Christenson, Allen J. 2003. *Popol Vuh: Sacred Book of the Quiché Maya People*. New York: O Books.

Christenson, Allen. 2017. *K'iche'-English Dictionary*. http://www.famsi.org/maya writing/dictionary/christenson/index.html.

Clarke, Eric, and Jane Davidson. 1998. "The Body in Performance." In *Composition, Performance, Reception: Studies in the Creative Process in Music*, ed. Wyndham Thomas, 74–92. Aldershot: Ashgate.

Classen, Constance, and David Howes. 2006. "The Museum of Sensescape: Western Sensibilities and Indigenous Artifacts." In *Sensible Objects: Colonialism, Museums, and Material Culture*, ed. Elizabeth Edwards, Chris Gosden, and Ruth Phillips, 199–222. Oxford: Berg.

Coe, William R. 1959. *Piedras Negras Archaeology: Artifacts, Caches, and Burials*. Philadelphia: University of Pennsylvania Museum.

Coe, William R. 1990. *Excavations in the Great Plaza, North Terrace, and North Acropolis of Tikal*. Tikal Report 14. Philadelphia: University of Pennsylvania Museum.

Coggins, Clemency. 1975. "Painting and Drawing Styles at Tikal: An Historical and Iconographic Reconstruction." PhD dissertation, Harvard University, Cambridge, MA.

Connolly, William E. 2013. "The 'New Materialism' and the Fragility of Things." *Millenium—Journal of International Studies* 41: 399–412.

Costenla Umaña, Adolfo. 1981. "Comparative Chibchan Phonology." PhD dissertation, University of Pennsylvania, Philadelphia.

Costenla Umaña, Adolfo. 1991. *Las Lenguas del Área Intermedia: Introducción a su Estudio Areal*. San Jose: Editorial de la Universidad de Costa Rica.

Couper-Kuhlen, Elizabeth. 1993. *English Speech Rhythm: Form and Function in Everyday Verbal Interaction*. Amsterdam: John Benjamins. doi: 10.1075/pbns.25.

Couper-Kuhlen, Elizabeth. 2009. "Relatedness and Timing in Talk-in-Interaction." In *Where Prosody Meets Pragmatics*, ed. Dagmar Barth-Weingarten, Nicole Dehé, and Anne Wichmann, 259–278. Bingley, UK: Emerald Group. doi: 10.1163/97890 04253223_012.

Courty, Marie-Agnes, Paul Goldberg, and Richard Macphail. 1989. *Soils and Micromorphology in Archaeology*. Cambridge: Cambridge University Press.

Cox, Travis. 2015. *Pianeta Acustico: Viaggio tra le Meraviglie Sonore del Mondo*. Bari, Italy: Dedalo.

Cross, Ian, and Aaron Watson. 2006. "Acoustics and the Human Experience of Socially Organized Sound." In *Archaeoacoustics*, ed. Christopher Scarre and Graeme Lawson, 107–116. Cambridge: McDonald Institute for Archaeological Research.

Da Matta, Roberto. 1991. *Carnivals, Rogues, and Heroes: An Interpretation of the Brazilian Dilemma*, trans. John Drury. Notre Dame: University of Notre Dame Press.

Davois, Michel. 1999. "Mesures Acoustiques et Témoins Sonores Osseux Paléolithiques." In *Préhistoire d'os: Recueil d'études sur l'industrie osseuse préhistorique offert à Henriette Camps-Fabrer*, ed. Michèle Julien, 165–189. Aix-en-Provence: Université de Provence.

Day, Jane S. 1984. "New Approaches in Stylistic Analysis: The Late Polychrome Period Ceramics from Hacienda Tempisque." PhD dissertation, University of Colorado, Boulder.

Day, Jane S. 1994. "Central Mexican Imagery in Greater Nicoya." In *Mixteca-Puebla: Discoveries and Research in Mesoamerican Art and Archaeology*, ed. Henry B. Nicholson and Eloise Quiñones Keber, 235–248. Culver City, CA: Labyrinthos.

Day, Jane S., and Alice Chiles Tillett. 1996. "The Nicoya Shaman." In *Paths to Central American Prehistory*, ed. Frederick W. Lange, 221–235. Niwot: University Press of Colorado.

Dehouve, Danièle. 2001. "El Fuego Nuevo: interpretación de una 'ofrenda contada' tlapaneca (Guerrero, México)." *Journal de la Société des Américanistes* 87: 89–112.

Dehouve, Danièle. 2007. *La ofrenda sacrificial entre los tlapanecos de Guerrero*. Mexico City: Universidad autónoma de Guerrero, Centro de Estudios Mexicanos y Centroamericanos, Ambassade de France au Mexique, Instituto Nacional de Antropología e Historia, and Plaza y Valdés.

Dehouve, Danièle. 2010. "La polisemia del sacrificio tlapaneco." In *El sacrificio humano en la tradición religiosa mesomaericana*, ed. Leonardo López Luján and Guilhem Olivier, 499–518. Mexico City: Instituto Nacional de Antropología e Historia and Universidad Nacional Autónoma de México.

Dehouve, Danièle. 2011. *L'imaginaire des nombres chez les anciens Mexicains*. Rennes, France: Presses Universitaires de Rennes.

Dehouve, Danièle. 2013a. "El depósito ritual: un ritual figurativo." In *"Convocar a los dioses," ofrendas mesoamericanas: Estudios antropológicos, históricos y comparativos*, ed. Johanna Broda, 605–638. Xalapa, Mexico: Instituto Veracruzano de la Cultura and Consejo Nacional para la Cultura y las Artes.

Dehouve, Danièle. 2013b. "El depósito ritual: una práctica mesoamericana de larga duración." *Confluenze: Rivista di Studi Iberoamericani* 8 (2): 181–206.

de la Cabada, Juan. 1944. *Incidentes Melódicos del Mundo Irracional*. Mexico City: La Estampa Mexicana.

DeLanda, Manuel. 2000. *A Thousand Years of Nonlinear History*. New York: Swerve.

DeLanda, Manuel. 2016. *Assemblage Theory*. Edinburgh: Edinburgh University Press.

DeMarrais, Elizabeth, Luis Jaime Castillo, and Timothy Earle. 1996. "Ideology, Materialization, and Power Strategies." *Current Anthropology* 37 (1): 15–31.

Dennett, Carrie L. 2016. "The Ceramic Economy of Pre-Columbian Pacific Nicaragua (A.D. 1–1250)." PhD dissertation, University of Calgary, Alberta.

Dennett, Carrie L., and Katrina C. Kosyk. 2013. "Winds of Change: Ceramic Musical Instruments from Greater Nicoya." In *Flower World: Musical Archaeology of the Americas*, volume 2, ed. Matthias Stöckli and Arnd Adje Both, 99–119. Berlin: Ekho Verlag.

DeNora, Tia. 2004. "Musical Practice and Social Structure: A Toolkit." In *Empirical Musicology: Aims, Methods, Prospects*, ed. Eric Clarke and Nicholas Cook, 35–57. New York: Oxford University Press.

Diaz-Andreu, Margarita, and Carlos García Benito. 2012. "Acoustics and Levantine Rock Art: Auditory Perceptions in La Valltorta Gorge (Spain)." *Journal of Archaeological Science* 39: 3591–3599.

Dineen, Phillip M. 2011. "Gestural Economies in Conducting." In *New Perspectives on Music and Gesture*, ed. Anthony Gritten and Elaine King, 131–158. Farnham, UK: Ashgate.

Dobres, Marcia-Ann. 2001. "Meaning in the Making: Agency and the Social Embodiment of Technology and Art." In *Anthropological Perspectives on Technology*, ed. Michael B. Schiffer, 47–76. Albuquerque: University of New Mexico Press.

Dolphijn, Rick, and Iris van der Tuin. 2012. *New Materialism: Interviews and Cartographies*. Ann Arbor, MI: Open Humanities Press.

Domenici, Davide. 2016. "The Wandering 'Leg of an Indian King': The Cultural Biography of a Friction Idiophone Now in the Pigorini Museum in Rome, Italy." *Journal de la Société des Américanistes* 102 (1): 43–67.

Domenici, Davide. 2017a. "The Descrittione dell'India Occidentale, a Sixteenth-Century Source on the Italian Reception of Mesoamerican Material Culture." *Ethnohistory* 64 (4): 497–527.

Domenici, Davide. 2017b. *Il Senso Delle Cose: Materialità ed Estetica Nell'arte Mesoamericana*. Bologna: Bononia University Press.

Downey, Greg. 2002. "Listening to Capoeira: Phenomenology, Embodiment, and the Materiality of Music." *Ethnomusicology* 46: 487–509.

Durán, Diego. 1995 [1581]. *Historia de las Indias de Nueva España e islas de Tierra Firme*, ed. Rosa Camelo and José Rubén Romero. Mexico City: Conaculta.

Edmonson, Munro S. 1970. "Metáfora maya en literatura y en arte." In *Verhandlungen des XXXVIII Internationalen Amerikanistenkongresses Stuttgart-München. 12. bis 18: August 1968*, band 2, 37–50. München: Kommisionverlag Klaus Renner.

Edmonson, Munro S. 1976. "Semantic Universals and Particulars in Quiche." In *Meaning in Mayan Languages: Ethnolinguistic Studies*, ed. Munro S. Edmonson, 235–246. The Hague: Mouton.

Edmonson, Munro S., and Victoria Bricker. 1985. "Yucatecan Maya Literature." In *Supplement to the Handbook of Middle American Indians*, volume 3: *Literatures*, ed. Victoria Bricker and Munro S. Edmonson, 44–63. Austin: University of Texas Press.

Egan, Rachel. 2011. "New Perspectives on the Quatrefoil in Classic Maya Iconography: The Center and the Portal." MA thesis, University of Central Florida, Orlando.

Eliade, Mircea. 1964. *Shamanism: Archaic Techniques of Ecstasy*. Princeton, NJ: Princeton University Press.

Emery, Kitty, and Erin Thornton. 2008. *Reporte preliminar de los restos faunísticos recuperados en el sitio de La Joyanca, Peten, Guatemala*. Gainesville: Environmental Archaeology Program, Florida Museum of Natural History.

Fabian, Johannes. 1983. *Time and the Other: How Anthropology Makes Its Object*. New York: Columbia University Press.

Fash, William L., and Leonardo Lopez Luján (eds.). 2009. *The Art of Urbanism: How Mesoamerican Kingdoms Represented Themselves in Architecture and Imagery*. Washington, DC: Dumbarton Oaks.

Feld, Steven, Aaron Fox, Thomas Porcello, and David Samuels. 2004. "Vocal Anthropology: From the Music of Language to the Language of Song?" In *Blackwell Companion to Linguistic Anthropology*, ed. Alessandro Duranti, 321–345. Oxford: Basic Blackwell.

Figuerola Pujol, Helios. 1996a. "L'enfant, les hommes et les dieux: histoire d'une lutte pour la vie: Une prière d'accouchement à Cancuc (Chiapas, Mexique)." *Journal de la Société des Américanistes* 82: 129–158.

Figuerola Pujol, Helios. 1996b. "*Sujtesel*: una oración para buscar el *ch'uhlel* de una persona en la comunidad tzeltal de San Juan Cancuc, en las altas tierras de Chiapas, México." *Amérindia* 21: 173–199.

Figuerola Pujol, Helios. 2010. *Los Dioses, los Hombres y las Palabras*. Mexico City: Universidad Nacional Autónoma de México.

Figuerola Pujol, Helios. 2011. *Les dieux, les paroles et les hommes: Rituels dans une communauté maya du Chiapas*. Paris: Éditions de l'EHESS.

Fischer, Edward F., and Carol Hendrickson. 2003. *Tecpán Guatemala: A Modern Maya Town in Global and Local Context*. Boulder: Westview.

Fitzsimmons, James L. 1998. "Classic Maya Mortuary Anniversaries at Piedras Negras, Guatemala." *Ancient Mesoamerica* 9 (2): 271–278.

Fitzsimmons, James L. 2006. "Classic Maya Tomb Re-entry." In *Jaws of the Underworld: Life, Death, and Rebirth among the Ancient Maya*, ed. Pierre Colas, Geneviève Le Fort, and Bodil Liljefors Persson, 35–40. Markt Schwaben, Germany: Verlag Anton Saurwein.

Fitzsimmons, James. 2009. *Death and the Classic Maya Kings*. Austin: University of Texas Press.

Fitzsimmons, James L. 2011. "Perspectives on Death and Transformation in Ancient Maya Society: Human Remains as a Means to an End." In *Living with the Dead: Mortuary Ritual in Mesoamerica*, ed. James L. Fitzsimmons and Izumi Shimada, 53–77. Tucson: University of Arizona Press.

Forné, Mélanie. 2005. "Etude céramique de la sous-phase chronocéramique Tuspan 2, La Joyanca, Petén, Guatemala." Ms. in possession of M. Charlotte Arnauld.

Forné, Mélanie. 2006. *La Cronología cerámica de La Joyanca, Noroeste del Petén, Guatemala*. BAR International Series 1572. Oxford: Archaeopress.

Fowles, Severin M. 2013. *An Archaeology of Doings: Secularism and the Study of Pueblo Religion*. Santa Fe, NM: School for Advanced Research Press.

Fox, James J. 2014. *Explorations in Semantic Parallelism*. Canberra: Australian National University Press.

Freidel, David A., Arlen F. Chase, Anne S. Dowd, and Jerry Murdock (eds.). 2017. *Maya E Groups: Calendars, Astronomy, and Urbanism in the Early Lowlands*. Gainesville: University of Florida Press.

Freidel, David A., Linda Schele, and Joy Parker. 1993. *Maya Cosmos: 3000 Years on the Shaman's Path*. New York: William Morrow.

Freidel, David A., Linda Schele, and Joy Parker. 1995. Review Feature: "Maya Cosmos: Three Thousand Years on the Shaman's Path." *Cambridge Archaeological Journal* 5 (1): 115–137.

Gámez Díaz, Laura Lucia. 2013. "Cosmology and Society: Household Ritual among the Terminal Classic Maya People of Yaxha (ca. A.D. 850–950), Guatemala." PhD dissertation, University of Pittsburgh, PA.

Gell, Alfred. 1992. *The Anthropology of Time: Cultural Constructions of Temporal Maps and Images*. Ann Arbor: University of Michigan Press.

Gieser, Thorsten. 2008. "Embodiment, Emotion, and Empathy: A Phenomenological Approach to Apprenticeship Learning." *Anthropological Theory* 8: 299–318.

Giglioli, Enrico H. 1901. *Materiali per lo Studio Dell'età Della Pietra, dai Tempi Preistorici all'Epoca Attuale*. Florence: Tipografia di Salvadore Landi.

Gilmore, Zackary I., and Jason M. O'Donoughue. 2015. "Introduction: The Enigma of the Event." In *The Archaeology of Events: Cultural Change and Continuity in the*

Pre-Columbian Southeast, ed. Zackary I. Gilmore and Jason M. O'Donoughue, 1–22. Tuscaloosa: University of Alabama Press.

Goldberg, Paul, Christopher E. Miller, Solveig Schiegl, Bertrand Ligouis, Francesco Berna, Nicholas J. Conard, and Lyn Wadley. 2009. "Bedding, Hearths, and Site Maintenance in the Middle Stone Age of Sibudu Cave, KwaZulu-Natal, South Africa." *Archaeological and Anthropological Sciences* 1 (2): 95–122.

Good Eshelman, Catharine. 1996. "El trabajo de los muertos en la Sierra de Guerrero." *Estudios de Cultura Náhuatl* 26: 275–287.

Gorza, Piero. 2002. *Habitar el Tiempo en San Andrés Larráinzar: Paisajes Indígenas de los Altos de Chiapas*. Turín: Otto Editore.

Gosden, Chris. 2003. *Anthropology and Archaeology: A Changing Relationship*. London: Routledge.

Gosselain, Olivier. 1998. "Social and Technical Identity in a Clay Crystal Ball." In *The Archaeology of Social Boundaries*, ed. Miriam Stark, 78–106. Washington, DC: Smithsonian Institution Press.

Gossen, Gary H. 1974. *Chamulas in the World of the Sun: Time and Space in a Maya Oral Tradition*. Cambridge: Harvard University Press.

Gossen, Gary H. 1976. "Language as Ritual Substance." In *Language in Religious Practice*, ed. William J. Samarin, 40–60. Rowley, MA: Newbury House.

Gossen, Gary H. 1989 [1974]. "To Speak with a Heated Heart: Chamula Canons of Style and Good Performance." In *Explorations in the Ethnography of Speaking*, ed. Richard Bauman and Joel Sherzer, 389–413. Cambridge: Cambridge University Press.

Goudiaby, Hemmamuthé, and Philippe Nondédéo. 2020. "The Funerary and Architectural History of an Ancient Maya Residential Group: Group 5N6, Naachtun, Guatemala." *Journal de la Societé des Américanistes* 106 (1): 19–64.

Graham, Ian, and Eric Von Euw. 1992. *Corpus of Maya Hieroglyphic Inscriptions*, volume 4, part 3: *Uxmal, Xcalumkin*. Cambridge: Peabody Museum of Archaeology and Ethnology, Harvard University.

Gritten, Anthony, and Elaine King. 2011. *New Perspectives on Music and Gesture*. Farnham, UK: Ashgate.

Gubler, Ruth. 2017. *Ritos Agricolas y Ceremonias Curativas en Yucatán*. Mexico City: Universidad Nacional Autónoma de México.

Guderjan, Thomas H. 2006. "E-Groups, Pseudo-E-Groups, and the Development of the Classic Maya Identity in the Eastern Peten." *Ancient Mesoamerica* 17 (1): 97–104.

Guderjan, Thomas H., Steven Bozarth, David Glassman, Robert Lichtenstein, and Norbert Stanchly. 2014. "Mortuary Ritual in the Terminal Preclassic: Evidence from the Maya Site of Blue Creek in Northern Belize." *Research Reports in Beliz-ean Archaeology* 11: 347–359.

Guernsey, Julia. 2010. "A Consideration of the Quatrefoil Motif in Preclassic Meso-america." *RES: Anthropology and Aesthetics* 57–58: 75–96.

Guernsey, Julia, and F. Kent Reilly III (eds.). 2006. *Sacred Bundles: Ritual Acts of Wrapping and Binding in Mesoamerica*. Barnardsville, NC: Boundary End Archae-ology Research Center.

Guerrero, Juan Vicente. 2011. "Entre Instrumentos Musicales, Ritos y Muerte en Garza, Nicoya, Guanacaste (G-752Rj)." *Cuadernos de Antropologia* 21: 1–21.

Guerrero Miranda, Juan Vicente. 2009. "Entre instrumentos Musicales Ritos y Muerte En Garza, Nicoya Guanacaste." Manuscript submitted to the Depart-mento de Antropologia e Historia, Museo Nacional de Costa Rica, San Jose.

Guiteras Holmes, Calixta. 1986 [1961]. *Los Peligros del Alma: Visión del Mundo de un Tzotzil*, trans. Carlos Antonio Castro. Mexico City: Fondo de Cultura Económica.

Gutiérrez Solana, Nelly. 1983. "Sobre un Fémur con Grabados Perteneciente a la Cultura Mexica." *Anales del Instituto de Investigaciones Estéticas* 52: 47–58.

Haber, Alejandro F. 2009. "Animism, Relatedness, Life: Post-Western Perspectives." *Cambridge Archaeological Journal* 19 (3): 418–430.

Hadad, Rémi. 2017. "Ruin Dynamics: Architectural Destruction and the Production of Sedentary Space at the Dawn of the Neolithic Revolution." Paper presented at La Composition du Temps: Prédictions, Événements, Narrations Historiques, annual colloquium of the Maison de l'Archéologie et de l'Ethnologie de Nanterre, Nanterre, June.

Hanks, William F. 1984. "Sanctification, Structure, and Experience in a Yucatec Ritual Event." *Journal of American Folklore* 97 (384): 131–166. doi: 10.2307/540182.

Hanks, William F. 1990. *Referential Practice: Language and Lived Space among the Maya*. Chicago: University of Chicago Press.

Hanks, William F. 1993a. "Copresencia y alteridad en la práctica ritual Maya." In *De palabra y obra en el Nuevo Mundo*, volume 3: *La formación del otro*, ed. Gary H. Gossen, J. Jorge Klor de Alva, Manuel Gutiérrez Estévez, and Miguel León Portilla, 75–117. Madrid: Siglo XXI de España.

Hanks, William F. 1993b. "The Five Gourds of Memory." In *Mémoire de la tradition*, ed. Aurore Becquelin, Antoinette Molinié, and Danièle Dehouve, 319–345. Nan-terre: Société d'Ethnologie.

Hanks, William F. 1996. "Exorcism and the Description of Participant Roles." In *Natural Histories of Discourse*, ed. Michael Silverstein and Greg Urban, 160–200. Chicago: University of Chicago Press.

Hanks, William F. 2000. *Intertexts: Writings on Language, Utterance, and Context.* Lanham, MD: Rowman and Littlefield.

Hanks, William F. 2010. *Converting Words: Maya in the Age of the Cross.* Berkeley: University of California Press.

Hanks, William F. 2013. "Counterparts: Co-presence and Ritual Intersubjectivity." *Language and Communication* 33: 263–277.

Hansen, Richard D., Beatriz Balcárcel, Edgar Suyuc, Héctor E. Mejía, Enrique Hernández, Gendry Valle, Stanley P. Guenter, and Shannon Novak. 2006. "Investigaciones Arqueológicas en el Sitio Tintal, Petén." In *XIX Simposio de Investigaciones Arqueológicas en Guatemala, 2005*, ed. Juan Pedro Laporte, Bárbara Arroyo, and Hector Mejía, 739–751. Guatemala City: Ministerio de Cultura y Deportes, Instituto de Antropología e Historia, Asociación Tikal, and New World Archaeological Foundation.

Harkness, Nicholas. 2014. *Songs of Seoul: An Ethnography of Voice and Voicing in Christian South Korea.* Berkeley: University of California Press.

Harris, Cyril M. 1979. *Handbook of Noise Control.* New York: McGraw-Hill.

Harrison-Buck, Eleanor. 2004. "Nourishing the Animus of Lived Space through Ritual Caching." In *K'axob: Ritual, Work, and Family in an Ancient Maya Village*, ed. Patricia. A. McAnany, 65–85. Los Angeles: Cotsen Institute of Archaeology, University of California.

Harrison-Buck, Eleanor. 2012. "Architecture as Animate Landscape: Circular Shrines in the Ancient Maya Lowlands." *American Anthropologist* 114 (1): 64–80.

Hatten, Robert S. 2008. "A Theory of Musical Gesture and Its Application to Beethoven and Schubert." In *Music and Gesture*, ed. Anthony Gritten and Elaine King, 1–24. Farnham, UK: Ashgate.

Haviland, John B. 1992. "Lenguaje ritual sin ritual." *Estudios de Cultura Maya* 19: 427–442.

Haviland, John B. 2000. "Warding off Witches: Voicing and Dialogue in Zinacantec Prayer." In *Les rituels du dialogue*, ed. Aurore Monod Becquelin and Phillipe Erikson, 367–400. Nanterre: Société d'Ethnologie.

Haviland, John B. 2003. "Dangerous Places in Zinacantec Prayer." In *Espacios mayas: Representaciones, usos, creencias*, ed. Alain Breton, Aurore Monod Becquelin, and Mario Humberto Ruz, 383–428. Mexico City: Universidad Nacional Autónoma de México.

Henderson, John S., and Rosemary A. Joyce. 2001. "Beginnings of Village Life in Eastern Mesoamerica." *Latin American Antiquity* 12 (1): 5–24.

Hendon, Julia A. 2003. "Feasting at Home." In *The Archaeology and Politics of Food and Feasting in Early States and Empires*, ed. Tamara Bray, 203–233. New York: Kluwer Academic/Plenum.

Hendon, Julia A., Rosemary A. Joyce, and Jeanne Lopiparo. 2014. *Material Relations: The Marriage Figurines of Prehispanic Honduras*. Boulder: University Press of Colorado.

Hermitte, Maria Esther. 1970. *Poder Sobre Natural y Control Social*. Mexico City: Instituto Indigenista Interamericano.

Hernández, Juan José. 1846. "Costumbres de las Indias de Yucatán." *Registro Yucateco* 3: 290–298.

Higelin Ponce De León, Ricardo. 2012. "Symbolism and Use of Human Femora by the Zapotecs in Oaxaca, México, during Prehispanic Times." MA thesis, Southern Illinois University, Carbondale.

Hill, Erica. 2008. "Animism and Sacrifice: Reconstructing Moche Religion through Architecture, Iconography, and Archaeological Features." In *Religion, Archaeology, and the Material World*, ed. Lars Fogelin, 38–60. Carbondale: Southern Illinois University, Center for Archaeological Investigations.

Hill, Jonathan D., and Jean-Pierre Chaumeil (eds.). 2011. *Burst of Breath: Indigenous Ritual Wind Instruments in Lowland South America*. Lincoln: University of Nebraska Press.

Hiquet, Julien. 2018. "Operación II.1: Sondeos Estratigráficos en los Grupos A y C." In *Proyecto Petén–Norte Naachtun 2010–2014: Informe de la Octava Temporada de Campo 2017*, ed. Philippe Nondédéo, Dominique Michelet, Johann Begel, and Lilian Garrido, 29–122. Guatemala City: Centro de Estudios Mexicanos y Centroamericanos.

Hiquet, Julien. 2020. "Essor monumental et dynamiques des populations: Le cas de la cité de Naachtun (Guatemala) au Classique ancien (150–550 apr. J.-C.)." PhD dissertation, Université Paris 1 Panthéon-Sorbonne.

Hiquet, Julien, Giovanni González, and Miguel Ángel Cano. 2014. "Operación II.2 bis: Sondeos Estratigráficos en Busca de Ocupaciones del Clásico Temprano en la Periferia Sur de Naachtun." In *Proyecto Petén–Norte Naachtun 2010–2014: Informe de la Quinta Temporada de Campo 2014*, ed. Philippe Nondédéo, Julian Hiquet, Dominique Michelet, Julien Sion, and Lilian Garrido, 57–128. Guatemala City: Centro de Estudios Mexicanos y Centroamericanos.

Hodder, Ian (ed.). 2007. *Religion at the Emergence of Civilization: Çatalhöyük as a Case Study*. Cambridge: Cambridge University Press.

Hodder, Ian. 2012. *Entangled: An Archaeology of the Relationships between Humans and Things*. New York: Wiley and Sons.

Hodder, Ian. 2014. "The Entanglements of Humans and Things: A Long-Term View." *New Literary History* 45: 19–36.

Holland, William R. 1978 [1963]. *Medicina Maya en los Altos de Chiapas*. Mexico City: Instituto Nacional Indigenista.

Houk, Brett, and Gregory Zaro. 2010. "Architectural History and Ritual Planning at La Milpa: A Reconsideration." In *Research Reports in Belizean Archaeology: Papers of the 2009 Belize Archaeology Symposium*, ed. John M. Morris, Sherilyne Jones, Jaime Awe, George Thompson, and Melissa Badillo, 95–102. Belmopan, Belize: Institute of Archaeology, National Institute of Culture and History.

Houston, Stephen D., Claudia Brittenham, Cassandra Messik, Alexandre Tokovinine, and Christina Warinner. 2009. *Veiled Brightness: A History of Ancient Maya Color*. Austin: University of Texas Press.

Houston, Stephen D., Hector Escobedo, Mark Child, Charles Golden, René Muñoz, and Monica Urquizú. 1998. "Monumental Architecture at Piedras Negras, Guatemala: Time, History, and Meaning." *Mayab* 11: 40–56.

Houston, Stephen D., and Andrew K. Scherer. 2010. "La Ofrenda Máxima: El Sacrificio Humano en la Parte Central del Área Maya." In *El Sacrificio Humano en la Tradición Religiosa Mesoamericana*, ed. Leonardo López Luján and Guilhem Olivier, 169–194. Mexico City: Instituto Nacional de Antropología e Historia, Instituto de Investigaciones Históricas, and Universidad Nacional Autónoma de México.

Houston, Stephen, David Stuart, and Karl Taube. 2006. *The Memory of Bones: Body, Being, and Experience among the Classic Maya*. Austin: University of Texas Press.

Howard, Deborah, and Jamie Angus. 2006. *Acoustics and Psychoacoustics*, third edition. Oxford: Focal.

Howard, Deborah, and Laura Moretti. 2009. *Sound and Space in Renaissance Venice: Architecture, Music, Acoustics*. New Haven, CT: Yale University Press.

Howes, David. 2003. *Sensual Relations: Engaging the Senses in Culture and Social Theory*. Ann Arbor: University of Michigan Press.

Hull, Kerry. 2006. "Journey from the Ancient Maya Tomb: Ropes, Roads, and the Point of Departure." In *Jaws of the Underworld: Life, Death, and Rebirth among the Ancient Maya*, ed. Pierre Colas, Geneviève Le Fort, and Bodil Liljefors Persson, 43–52. Markt Schwaben, Germany: Verlag Anton Saurwein.

Humphrey, Caroline, and James Alexander Laidlaw. 1994. *The Archetypal Actions of Ritual: A Theory of Ritual Illustrated by the Jain Rite of Worship*. Oxford: Oxford University Press.

Hymes, Dell. 1977. "Discovering Oral Performance and Measured Verse in American Indian Narrative." *New Literary History* 7: 431–457. doi: 10.2307/468294.

Hymes, Dell. 1981. *"In Vain I Tried to Tell You"*: *Essays in Native American Ethnopoetics.* Philadelphia: University of Philadelphia Press.

Ihde, Don. 2007. *Listening and Voice: Phenomenologies of Sound*, second edition. Albany: State University of New York Press.

Ingold, Tim. 1993. "The Temporality of the Landscape." *World Archaeology* 25 (2): 152–174.

Ingold, Tim. 2010. *Bringing Things to Life: Creative Entanglements in a World of Materials.* NCRM Working Paper Series 05/10. Southampton, UK: ESRC National Centre for Research Methods. http://eprints.ncrm.ac.uk/1306/.

Ingold, Tim. 2011. *Being Alive: Essays on Movement, Knowledge, and Description.* London: Routledge.

Ingold, Tim. 2012. "Towards an Ecology of Materials." *Annual Review of Anthropology* 41: 427–442.

Ingold, Tim. 2019. *Making: Antropologia, Archeologia, Arte, Architettura.* Milan: Cortina.

Inomata, Takeshi. 2017. "Entre Rutinas Cotidianas y Eventos Extraordinarios: las Construcciones de Conceptos Temporales en la Sociedad Maya Prehispánica." *Journal de la Société des Américanistes* online. doi: 10.4000/jsa.15417.

Inomata, Takeshi, Jessica MacLellan, Daniela Triadan, Jessica Munson, Melissa Burham, Kazuo Aoyama, Hiroo Nasu, Flory Pinzón, and Hitoshi Yonenobu. 2015. "Development of Sedentary Communities in the Maya Lowlands: Coexisting Mobile Groups and Public Ceremonies at Ceibal, Guatemala." *Proceedings of the National Academy of Sciences* 112: 4268–4273.

Inomata, Takeshi, and Daniela Triadan. 2015. "Middle Preclassic Caches from Ceibal, Guatemala." *Maya Archaeology* 3: 56–91.

Izquierdo, Ana Luisa, and Guillermo Bernal Romero. 2011. "Los Gobiernos Heterárquicos de las Capitales Mayas del Clásico: El Caso de Palenque." In *El Despliegue del Poder Politico Entre Los Mayas*, ed. Ana Luisa Izquierdo, 151–192. Mexico City: Universidad Nacional Autónoma de México.

Johansson, Patrick. 2014. "Miccacuicatl: Cantos Mortuorios Nahuas Prehispánicos, Textos y 'Con-Textos.'" *Estudio de Cultura Náhuatl* 48: 7–87.

Johnson, Lisa M. 2018a. "Little Helpers, Companions, and Ancestors: Miniature Figures in the Maya Lowland Region during the Late Preclassic and Classic Periods (AD 15–800)." *Latin American Antiquity* 29 (3): 616–622.

Johnson, Lisa M. 2018b. "Tracing the Ritual 'Event' at the Classic Maya City of Palenque, Mexico." PhD dissertation, University of California, Berkeley.

Jones, Andrew. 2004. "Archaeometry and Materiality: Materials-Based Analysis in Theory and Practice." *Archaeometry* 46 (3): 327–338.

Jones, Andrew M., and Nicole Boivin. 2010. "The Malice of Inanimate Objects: Material Agency." In *The Oxford Handbook of Material Culture Studies*, ed. Dan Hicks and Mary C. Beaudry, 333–351. Oxford: Oxford University Press.

Jones, Christopher. 1996. *Tikal Report no. 16: Excavations in the East Plaza of Tikal*. Philadelphia: University of Pennsylvania Museum of Archaeology and Anthropology.

Jones, Christopher, and Linton Satterthwaite. 1982. *The Monuments and Inscriptions of Tikal: The Carved Monuments*. Philadelphia: University of Pennsylvania Museum of Archaeology and Anthropology.

Josserand, J. Kathryn. 1991. "The Narrative Structure of Hieroglyphic Texts at Palenque." In *Sixth Palenque Round Table 1986*, ed. Merle Greene Robertson, 12–31. Norman: University of Oklahoma Press.

Joyce, Rosemary A. 1991. *Cerro Palenque: Power and Identity on the Mesoamerican Periphery*. Austin: University of Texas Press.

Joyce, Rosemary A. 2001. "Burying the Dead at Tlatilco: Social Memory and Social Identities." *Archaeological Papers of the American Anthropological Association* 10 (1): 12–26.

Joyce, Rosemary A. 2004. "Mesoamerica: A Working Model for Archaeology." In *Mesoamerican Archaeology: Theory and Practice*, ed. Julia A. Hendon and Rosemary A. Joyce, 1–42. Malden, MA: Blackwell.

Joyce, Rosemary A. 2005. "Archaeology of the Body." *Annual Review of Anthropology* 34: 139–158.

Joyce, Rosemary A. 2008. "Practice in and as Deposition." In *Memory Work: Archaeologies of Material Practices*, ed. Barbara J. Mills and William H. Walker, 25–39. Santa Fe, NM: School for Advanced Research Press.

Joyce, Rosemary A. 2011. "In the Beginning: The Experience of Residential Burial in Prehispanic Honduras." *Archeological Papers of the American Anthropological Association* 20 (1): 33–43.

Joyce, Rosemary A. 2012a. "From Place to Place: Provenience, Provenance, and Archaeology." In *Provenance: An Alternate History of Art*, ed. Gail Feigenbaum and Inge Reist, 48–60. Los Angeles: Getty Research Institute.

Joyce, Rosemary A. 2012b. "Life with Things: Archaeology and Materiality." In *Archaeology and Anthropology: Past, Present, and Future*, ed. David P. Shankland, 119–132. Oxford: Berg.

Joyce, Rosemary A. 2015a. "Structured Deposition and Commemoration: Classic Period Rituals of Ancestor Veneration in the Ulua Valley, Honduras." Paper presented at the GDRI RITMO Rencontre de Royaumont, Ritual Temporalities: Sequences, Processes, and Action Coordination, Paris, October.

Joyce, Rosemary A. 2015b. "Transforming Archaeology, Transforming Materiality." In *The Materiality of Everyday Life*, ed. Lisa Overholtzer and Cynthia Robin, 181–191. Archaeological Papers of the American Anthropological Association 26. Arlington, VA: American Anthropological Association.

Joyce, Rosemary A. 2017a. *Object Lives and Itineraries: Painted Pottery Traditions of Honduras*. Leiden: Brill.

Joyce, Rosemary A. 2017b. "Religion in a Material World." In *Beyond Integration: Religion and Politics in the Precolumbian Americas*, ed. Sarah Barber and Arthur Joyce, 141–164. New York: Routledge.

Joyce, Rosemary A. 2018. "Becoming Marble." *Scapegoat: Architecture/Landscape/Political Economy* 11: 40–51.

Joyce, Rosemary A. 2021. "Central America: Time for a Paradigm Shift." In *Pre-Columbian Central America, Colombia, and Ecuador: Toward an Integrated Approach*, ed. Colin McEwan and John W. Hoopes, 35–47. Washington, DC: Dumbarton Oaks.

Joyce, Rosemary A., and Susan D. Gillespie (eds.). 2000. *Beyond Kinship: Social and Material Reproduction in House Societies*. Philadelphia: University of Pennsylvania Press.

Joyce, Rosemary A., and Susan D. Gillespie (eds.). 2015. *Things in Motion: Object Itineraries in Anthropological Practice*. SAR, School for Advanced Research Advanced Seminar Series. Santa Fe, NM: School for Advanced Research Press.

Joyce, Rosemary A., and John S. Henderson. 2007. "From Feasting to Cuisine: Implications of Archaeological Research in an Early Honduran Village." *American Anthropologist* 109 (4): 642–653.

Joyce, Rosemary A., and Joshua Pollard. 2010. "Archaeological Assemblages and Practices of Deposition." In *The Oxford Handbook of Material Culture Studies*, ed. Dan Hicks and Mary Beaudry, 289–304. Oxford: Oxford University Press.

Karttunen, Frances. 1992. *An Analytical Dictionary of Nahuatl*. Norman: University of Oklahoma Press.

Kaufman, Terrence. 2003. *A Preliminary Maya Etymological Dictionary*. http://www.famsi.org/reports/01051/pmed.pdf.

Kidder, Alfred, Justin Jennings, and Edwin Shook. 1946. *Excavations at Kaminaljuyu, Guatemala*. Washington, DC: Carnegie Institution of Washington.

King, Elaine, and Jane Ginsborg. 2011. "Gestures and Glances: Interactions in Ensemble Rehearsal." In *New Perspectives on Music and Gesture*, ed. Anthony Gritten and Elaine King, 177–202. Farnham, UK: Ashgate.

King, Mark B. 1994. "Hearing the Echoes of Verbal Art in Mixtec Writing." In *Writing without Words: Alternative Literacies in Mesoamerica and the Andes*, ed.

Elizabeth H. Boone and Walter D. Mignolo, 102–136. Durham, NC: Duke University Press.

Knappett, Carl. 2011. "Networks of Objects, Meshworks of Things." In *Redrawing Anthropology: Materials, Movements, Lines*, ed. Tim Ingold, 45–63. Ashgate, UK: Anthropological Studies of Creativity and Perception.

Knappett, Carl. 2014. "Materiality in Archaeological Theory." In *Encyclopaedia of Global Archaeology*, ed. Claire Smith, 4700–4708. New York: Springer.

Kohn, Eduardo. 2013. *How Forests Think: Toward an Anthropology Beyond the Human.* Berkeley: University of California Press.

Kopytoff, Igor. 1986. "The Cultural Biography of Things: Commoditization as Process." In *The Social Life of Things*, ed. Arjun Appadurai, 64–91. Cambridge: Cambridge University Press.

Kosyk, Katrina C. 2016. "Notes from the Past: Examining Intra-Site Micro-Scale Communities of Practice within Greater Nicoya Aerophones from the Tempisque Period (500 B.C.–A.D. 300)." MA thesis, University of Victoria, Canada.

Kosyk, Katrina C. 2019. "Interfaces Gestuelles: Reconnaître les Pratiques Sonores dans une Collection Archéologique du Grand Nicoya." *Anthropologie et Sociétés* 43 (1): 117–139.

Kubiëna, Walter L. 1938. *Micropedology.* Ames, IA: Collegiate Press.

Kubiëna, Walter L. 1970. *Micromorphological Features of Soil Geography.* New Brunswick, NJ: Rutgers University Press.

Kus, Susan. 1992. "Toward an Archaeology of Body and Soul." In *Representations in Archaeology*, ed. Christopher Peebles and Jean-Claude Gardin, 168–177. Bloomington: Indiana University Press.

Lacadena, Alfonso. 2006. "Excavaciones en Machaquilá, Temporada 2005: El Recinto Cuadrilobulado de la Plaza A." In *Exploraciones arqueológicas en el sureste y centro-oeste de Petén*, ed. Juan Pedro Laporte and Hector Mejia, 74–123. Guatemala City: Atlas Arqueológico de Guatemala and Área de Arqueología de la Universidad de San Carlos.

Laporte, Juan Pedro. 2002. "Exploración y Restauración en el Templo de Las Calaveras, Mundo Perdido, Tikal (estructura 5D-87)." In *XV Simposio de Investigaciones Arqueológicas en Guatemala, 2001*, ed. Juan Pedro Laporte, Hector L. Escobedo, and Bárbara Arroyo, 207–227. Guatemala City: Ministerio de Cultura y Deportes.

Laporte, Juan Pedro, Bernard Hermes, Lilian de Zea, and Maria Josefa Iglesias. 1992. "Nuevos Entierros y Escondites de Tikal, Subfases Manik 3a y 3b." *Ceramica de Cultura Maya* 16: 30–101.

Laporte, Juan Pedro, and Maria Josefa Iglesias Ponce de León. 2000. "Más Allá de Mundo Perdido: Investigación en Grupos Residenciales de Tikal." *Mayab* 12: 32–57.

Lara Pinto, Gloria. 2011. "Dicotomía de una Ciudad: Las Raíces Indígenas de Tegucigalpa y Comayagüela." *Paradigma: Revista de Investigación Educativa* 20 (30): 179–203.

Laughlin, Robert M. 1980. *Of Shoes and Ships and Sealing Wax: Sundries from Zinacantán.* Washington, DC: Smithsonian Institution Press.

Laughlin, Robert M. 1983. "Plegarias de los agricultores zinacantecos de Chiapas." *Mesoamérica* 5: 128–167.

Laurencich-Minelli, Laura. 2015. "Flight of Feathers in Italian Collections from the Sixteenth and Seventeenth Centuries." In *Images Take Flight: Feather Art in Mexico and Europe 1400–1600*, ed. Alessandra. Russo, Gerhard Wolf, and Diana Fane, 218–227. Munich: Hirmer Verlag.

Lave, Jean, and Etienne Wenger. 1991. *Situated Learning: Legitimate Peripheral Participation.* Cambridge: Cambridge University Press.

Le Guen, Olivier. 2011. "Speech and Gesture in Spatial Language and Cognition among the Yucatec Mayas." *Cognitive Science: A Multidisciplinary Journal* 35 (5): 905–938.

Le Guen, Olivier. 2012. "Ideophones in Yucatec Maya." In *Proceedings of the Conference on Indigenous Languages of Latin America–V.* Austin, TX, October 2011. https://ailla.utexas.org/node/97.

Le Guen, Olivier. 2018. "Managing Epistemicity among the Yucatec Mayas (Mexico)." In *Metacognitive Diversity: An Interdisciplinary Approach*, ed. Joëlle Proust and Martin Fortier, 193–222. Oxford: Oxford University Press.

Lemonnier, Eva. 2009. *La Structure de l'habitat du Site Maya Classique de La Joyanca dans son Environnement local (Petén, Guatemala).* Paris Monographs in American Archaeology 23. BAR International Series 2016. Oxford: Archaeopress.

Liendo Stuardo, Rodrigo. 2016. *El Grupo IV de Palenque, un Espacio Residencial de Élite en la Antigua Ciudad de Lakamha': Informe Parcial de Actividades, Temporada 2016.* Mexico City: Universidad Nacional Autonoma de México.

Lok, Rossana. 1987. "The House as a Microcosm: Some Cosmic Representations in a Mexican Indian Village." In *The Leiden Tradition in Structural Anthropology: Essays in Honour of P. E. de Josselin de Jong*, ed. Rob de Ridder and Jan A.J. Karremans, 211–233. Leiden: E. J. Brill.

Lok, Rossana. 1991. *Gifts to the Dead and the Living: Forms of Exchange in San Miguel Tzinacapan, Sierra Norte de Puebla, Mexico.* Leiden: Centre of Non Western Studies, Leiden University.

Lomitola, Lisa. 2012. "A Contextual Analysis of the 'Charlie Chaplin' Figures of the Maya Lowland." MA thesis, University of Central Florida, Orlando.

Looper, Matthew G. 2003. *Lightning Warrior: Maya Art and Kingship at Quirigua.* Austin: University of Texas Press.

Looper, Matthew G. 2009. *To Be Like Gods: Dance in Ancient Maya Civilization.* Austin: University of Texas Press.

López Austin, Alfredo. 1984. *Cuerpo Humano e Ideología: Las Concepciones de los Antiguos Nahuas.* Mexico City: Universidad Nacional Autónoma de México.

López Austin, Alfredo. 1994. *Tamoanchan y Tlalocan.* Mexico City: Fondo de Cultura Económica.

López Bravo, Roberto. 2004. "State and Domestic Cult in Palenque Censor Stands." In *Courtly Art of the Ancient Maya,* ed. Mary Ellen Miller and Simon Martin, 256–258. New York: Thames and Hudson.

López De Cogolludo, Diego. 1668. *Historia de Yucathan.* Madrid: Editorial Juan García Infanzón.

López Luján, Leonardo. 1993. *Las ofrendas del Templo Mayor de Tenochtitlan.* Mexico City: Instituto Nacional de Antropología e Historia.

López Luján, Leonardo. 2009. "Aguas petrificadas: Las ofrendas a Tláloc enterradas en el Templo Mayor de Tenochtitlan." *Arqueología mexicana* 96: 52–57.

López Luján, Leonardo. 2010–2011. "Les dépôts rituels et les cérémonies de reconstitution de l'univers à Teotihuacan, Mexique." *Annuaire EPHE, Sciences religieuses* 119: 49–63.

López Luján, Leonardo. 2012. "Un portal al inframundo: Ofrendas de animales sepultadas al pie del Templo Mayor de Tenochtitlan." *Estudios de Cultura Náhuatl* 44: 9–40.

López Luján, Leonardo. 2015. "Los depósitos rituales y las ceremonias de reconstitución del universo en Teotihuacan." In *Los rumbos del pensamiento: Homenaje a Yólotl González Torres,* ed. Félix Báez-Jorge and Isabel Lagarriga Attias, 75–98. Mexico City: Instituto Nacional de Antropología e Historia.

López Luján, Leonardo (ed.). 2018. *Estrellas de mar y cocodrilos en las ofrendas del Templo Mayor.* A temporary exhibition in the Zona Arqueológica del Templo Mayor, coordinated by Erika Robles Cortés and Belem Zúñiga-Arellano. Mexico City: Instituto Nacional de Antropología e Historia.

López Luján, Leonardo, and Guilhem Olivier. 2010. *El Sacrificio Humano en la Tradición Religiosa Mesoamericana.* Mexico City: Instituto Nacional de Antropología e Historia and Instituto de Investigaciones Históricas, Universidad Nacional Autónoma de México.

López Oliva, Macarena Soledad. 2013. "El Ritual de la Decapitación y el Culto a las Cabezas Trofeo en el Mundo Maya." MA thesis, Universidad Nacional Autónoma de México, Mexico City.

Lopiparo, Jeanne. 2006. "Crafting Children: Materiality, Social Memory, and the Reproduction of Terminal Classic House Societies in the Ulúa Valley, Honduras." In *The Social Experience of Childhood in Ancient Mesoamerica*, ed. Traci Ardren and Scott Hutson, 133–168. Boulder: University Press of Colorado.

Loten, Stanley H. 2003. "The North Acropolis: Monumentality, Function, and Architectural Development." In *Tikal: Dynasties, Foreigners, and Affairs of State*, ed. Jeremy A. Sabloff, 227–252. Santa Fe, NM: School of American Research Press.

Loten, Stanley H. 2018. *Miscellaneous Investigations in Central Tikal—Great Temples III, IV, V, and VI.* Philadelphia: University of Pennsylvania Museum of Archaeology and Anthropology.

Love, Bruce. 2012. *Maya Shamanism Today: Connecting with the Cosmos in Rural Yucatan.* San Francisco: Precolumbia Mesoweb Press.

Lumholtz, Carl, and Aleš Hrdlicka. 1898. "Marked Human Bones from a Prehistoric Tarasco Indian Burial Place in the State of Michoacan, Mexico." *Bulletin of the American Museum of Natural History* 10: 61–79.

Lupo, Alessandro. 1995a. "La oración, estructura, forma y uso: Entre tradición escrita y oral." In *Antropología y Literatura*, ed. Carmelo Lisón Tolosana, 49–66. Zaragoza: Gobierno de Aragón, Dep. de Educación y Cultura.

Lupo, Alessandro. 1995b. *La Tierra nos escucha: La cosmología de los nahuas de la Sierra a través de las súplicas rituales.* Mexico City: Instituto Nacional Indigenista, Consejo Nacional Para la Cultura y las Artes.

Lupo, Alessandro. 2001. "La cosmovisión de los nahuas de la Sierra de Puebla." In *Cosmovisión, ritual e identidad de los pueblos indígenas de México*, ed. Johanna Broda and Félix Báez-Jorge, 335–389. Mexico City: Fondo de Cultura Económica.

Lupo, Alessandro. 2013. *El maíz en la cruz: Prácticas y dinámicas religiosas en el México indígena.* Xalapa: Instituto Veracruzano de la Cultura, Consejo Nacional para la Cultura y las Artes.

Lupo, Alessandro. 2018. "Essences, flux et réceptacles: réflexions ethnologiques sur le sacrifice humain et le cannibalisme aztèque." Paper presented at the seminar Mises à mort ritualisées en Amériques indigènes of the Laboratoire d'ethnologie et de sociologie comparative, Université de Paris X, Paris, May.

Lupo, Alessandro. 2019. "Comer (con) los difuntos: las ofrendas comestibles de Todos los Santos y las lógicas de la comensalía entre vivos y muertos en la Sierra de Puebla." *Estudios de Cultura Náhuatl* 58: 223–264.

MacGregor, Arthur. 1985. *Bone, Antler, Ivory, and Horn: Technology of Skeletal Materials since the Roman Period*. London: Routledge.

Macphail, Richard I., Marie-Agnés Courty, and Paul Goldberg. 1990. "Soil Micromorphology in Archaeology." *Endeavor* 14 (4): 163–171.

Macphail, Richard I., and Paul Goldberg. 2018. "Archaeological Materials." In *Interpretation of Micromorphological Features of Soils and Regoliths*, ed. Georges Stoops, Vera Marcelino, and Florias Mees, 779–819. Amsterdam: Elsevier.

Maler, Teobert. 1901. *Researches in the Central Portion of the Usumacinta Valley*. Cambridge: Peabody Museum of American Archaeology and Ethnography, Harvard University.

Martì, Samuel. 1968. *Instrumentos Musicales Precortesianos*. Mexico City: Instituto Nacional de Antropología e Historia.

Martin, Simon. 2006. "Cacao in Ancient Maya Religion: First Fruit from the Maize Tree and Other Tales from the Underworld." In *Chocolate in Mesoamerica: A Cultural History of Cacao*, ed. Cameron L. McNeil, 154–183. Gainesville: University Press of Florida.

Masson, Marilyn. 2004. "Contributions of Fishing and Hunting to Subsistence and Symbolic Expression." In *K'axob: Ritual, Work, and Family in an Ancient Maya Village*, ed. Patricia A. McAnany, 382–397. Los Angeles: Cotsen Institute of Archaeology, University of California.

Mathews, Jennifer P., and James F. Garber. 2004. "Models of Cosmic Order: Physical Expression of Sacred Space among the Ancient Maya." *Ancient Mesoamerica* 15: 49–59.

Matthews, Wendy, Charley Al French, Thomas Lawrence, David F. Cutler, and Martin K. Jones. 1997. "Microstratigraphic Traces of Site Formation Processes and Human Activities." *World Archaeology* 29 (2): 281–308.

Maudslay, Alfred P. 1889–1902. *Archaeology: Biologia Centrali-Americana*. London: R. H. Porter and Dulau.

Mauss, Marcel. 1979 [1935]. "The Notion of Body Techniques." In *Sociology and Psychology: Essays*, 97–123. London: Routledge and Kegan Paul.

May Castillo, Manuel. 2018. "Time and the E-Group: A Hermeneutical Reflection on Maya Ceremonial Centers." *Indiana* 35 (1): 9–38.

McAnany, Patricia A., and Ian Hodder. 2009. "Thinking about Stratigraphic Sequence in Social Terms." *Archaeological Dialogues* 16 (1): 1–22. doi: 10.1017/S1380200948.

McCafferty, Geoffrey, Fabio E. Amador, Silvia S. Gonzàlez, and Carrie Dennett. 2012. "Archaeology on Mesoamerica's Southern Frontier." In *Oxford Handbook of Mesoamerican Archaeology*, ed. Deborah L. Nichols and Christopher A. Pool, 83–105. Oxford: Oxford University Press.

McCafferty, Geoffrey, and Carrie L. Dennett. 2013. "Ethnogenesis and Hybridity in Proto-Historic Period Nicaragua." *Archaeological Review from Cambridge* 28 (1): 191–212.

McCafferty, Geoffrey, and Larry L. Steinbrenner. 2005. "The Meaning of the Mixteca-Puebla Style: A Perspective from Nicaragua." In *Art for Archaeology's Sake: Material Culture and Style across the Disciplines*, ed. Andrea Waters-Rist, Christine Cluney, Calla McNamee, and Larry Steinbrenner, 282–292. Calgary: University of Calgary Archaeological Association.

McVicker, Donald. 2005. "Notched Human Bones from Mesoamerica." *Mesoamerican Voices* 2: 1–31.

Meluzin, Sylvia. 1997. "Ritual Use of Bromeliads in the Maize-Planting Ceremony of the Lenca of Honduras: Part 1." *Journal of the Bromeliad Society* 47: 252–260.

Merleau-Ponty, Maurice. 1962. *Phenomenology of Perception*, trans. Colin Smith. London: Routledge.

Meskell, Lynn (ed.). 2005. *Archaeologies of Materiality*. Oxford: Blackwell.

Meskell, Lynn, and Robert W. Preucel (eds.). 2004. *A Companion to Social Archaeology*. Oxford: Blackwell.

Michelet, Dominique, M.-Charlotte Arnauld, Philippe Nondédéo, Grégory Pereira, Fabienne de Pierrebourg, and Eric Taladoire. 1998. "La Saison de Fouille de 1998 à Balamku (Campeche, Mexique): des Avancées Aubstantielles." *Journal de la Société des Américanistes* 84 (1): 183–199.

Michelet, Dominique, Philippe Nondédéo, Grégory Pereira, Julie Patrois, Marie Charlotte Arnauld, and Alfonso Lacadena. 2010. "Rituales en una Sociedad 'sin' Reyes: el caso de Río Bec y del Edificio A (5N2) en Particular." In *El ritual en el Mundo Maya: de lo Privado a lo Público*, ed. Andrés Ciudad Ruiz, M. Josefa Iglesias Ponce de León, and Miguel Sorroche Cuerva, 153–180. Madrid: Sociedad Española de Estudios Mayas.

Mikulska Dabrowska, Katarzyna. 2008. *El Lenguaje Enmascarado: Un Acercamiento a las Representaciones de Deidades Nahuas*. Mexico City: Instituto de Investigaciones Antropologicas, Universidad Nacional Autónoma de México.

Miller, Daniel (ed.). 2005. *Materiality*. Durham, NC: Duke University Press.

Mills, Barbara J. 2009. "From the Ground Up: Depositional History, Memory, and Materiality." *Archaeological Dialogues* 16 (1): 38–40.

Mills, Steve. 2010. "The Contribution of Sound to Archaeology." *Buletinul Muzeului Județean Teleorman* 2: 179–195. http://muzeulteleorman.ro/files/010_Mills_BMJT2.pdf.

Mills, Steve. 2014. *Auditory Archaeology: Understanding Sound and Hearing in the Past.* Walnut Creek, CA: Left Coast Press.

Minar, C. Jill, and Patricia Crown. 2001. "Learning and Craft Production: An Introduction." *Journal of Anthropological Research* 57 (4): 369–380.

Mock, Shirley Boteler. 1998a. "The Defaced and the Forgotten: Decapitation and Flaying/Mutilation as a Termination Event at Colha, Belize." In *The Sowing and the Dawning: Termination, Dedication, and Transformation in the Archaeological and Ethnographic Record of Mesoamerica*, ed. Shirley Boteler Mock, 112–123. Albuquerque: University of New Mexico Press.

Mock, Shirley Boteler (ed.). 1998b. *The Sowing and the Dawning: Termination, Dedication, and Transformation in the Archaeological Record of Mesoamerica.* Albuquerque: University of New Mexico Press.

Moholy-Nagy, Hattula, and William Coe. 2008. *Tikal Report no. 27a: The Artifacts of Tikal: Ornamental and Ceremonial Artifacts and Unworked Material.* Philadelphia: University of Pennsylvania Museum of Archaeology and Anthropology.

Molina, Alonso de. 1970 [1571]. *Vocabulario en Lengua Castellana y Mexicana y Mexicana y Castellana.* Mexico City: Editorial Porrua.

Monaghan, John. 1996. "Fiesta Finance in Mesoamerica and the Origins of a Gift Exchange System." *Journal of the Royal Anthropological Institute* 2: 499–516.

Monelle, Raymond. 1992. *Linguistics and Semiotics in Music.* Chur, Switzerland: Harwood Academic.

Monod Becquelin, Aurore. 1986. "Le sang et le corps, ou le blanc et le noir? Contribution à l'étude du parallélisme dans la tradition orale des Maya." *Journal de la Société des Américanistes* 72: 7–31.

Monod Becquelin, Aurore. 1987. "Le tour du monde en quelques couplets: le parallélisme dans la tradition orale maya." In *Kalevala et traditions orales du monde*, ed. M. M. Jocelyne Fernandez-Vest, 467–488. Paris: Editions du Centre National de la Recherche Scientifique.

Monod Becquelin, Aurore. 1993. "Monologues polyphoniques: les discours rituels maya." In *Pour une anthropologie des voix*, ed. Nicole Revel and Diana Rey-Hulman, 295–327. Paris: L'Harmattan, Institut national des langues et civilisations orientales.

Monod Becquelin, Aurore. 2000. "Polyphonie Thérapeutique: une Confrontation pour la Guérison en Tzeltal." In *Les Rituels du Dialogue*, ed. Aurore Monod Becquelin and Phillipe Erikson, 511–554. Nanterre: Société d'Ethnologie.

Monod Bequelin, Aurore, and Cédric Becquey. 2008. "De las Unidades Paralelísticas en las Tradiciones Orales Mayas." *Estudios de Cultura Maya* 32: 111–153.

Monod Bequelin, Aurore, and Alain Breton. 2002. *La Guerre Rouge ou une Politique Maya du Sacré: Un Carnaval Tzeltal au Chiapas, Mexique*. Paris: Centre National de la Recherche Scientifique Editions. doi: 10.19130/iifl.tlalocan.2008.195.

Monod Becquelin, Aurore, Valentina Vapnarsky, Cédric Becquey, and Alain Breton. 2010. "Decir y Contar la Diversidad: Paralelismo, Variantes y Variaciones en las Tradiciones Mayas." In *Figuras Mayas de la Diversidad*, ed. Aurore Monod Becquelin, Alain Breton, and Mario H. Ruz, 101–155. Mérida: Centro Peninsular en Humanidades y en Ciencias Sociales, Universidad Nacional Autónoma de México.

Morehart, Christopher T. 2017. "Ritual Time: The Struggle to Pinpoint the Temporality of Ritual Practice Using Archaeobotanical Data." In *Social Perspectives on Ancient Lives from Paleoethnobotanical Data*, ed. Matthew P. Sayre and Maria Bruno, 145–158. New York: Springer.

Morton, Shawn. 2007. "Procession Ritual at Naachtun, Guatemala during the Late Classic Period." MA thesis, University of Calgary, Alberta.

Murray, Tim (ed.). 1999. *Time and Archaeology*. London: Routledge.

Nakamura, Seiichi. 2004. "Culto Funerario de Copan en el Siglo VI: un Estudio de Caso en el Conjunto 10J-45." In *Culto Funerario en la Sociedad Maya: Memoria de la Cuarta Mesa Redonda de Palenque*, ed. Rafael Cobos, 245–254. Mexico City: Instituto Nacional de Antropología e Historia.

Nash, June. 1985 [1970]. *In the Eyes of the Ancestors: Belief and Behavior in a Maya Community*. Prospect Heights, IL: Waveland.

Needham, Rodney. 1967. "Percussion and Transition." *Man* n.s. 2 (4): 606–614.

Neher, Andrew. 1962. "A Physiological Explanation of Unusual Behavior in Ceremonies Involving Drums." *Human Biology* 34 (2): 151–160.

Newman, Sarah E. 2018. "Rubbish, Reuse, and Ritual at the Ancient Maya Site of El Zotz, Guatemala." *Journal of Archaeological Method and Theory* 10: 1–38.

Newson, Linda A. 1986. *The Cost of Conquest: Indian Decline in Honduras under Spanish Rule*. Boulder: Westview.

Nicosia, Cristiano, and Georges Stoops (eds.). 2017. *Archaeological Soil and Sediment Micromorphology*. Hoboken, NJ: Wiley-Blackwell.

Nijs, Luc, Micheline Lesaffre, and Marc Leman. 2013. "The Musical Instrument as a Natural Extension of the Musician." In *Proceedings of the 5th Conference of Interdisciplinary Musicology*, ed. Michèle Castellango and Hugues Genevois, 467–484. Delatour, France: LAM-Institut Jean Le Rond d'Alembert.

Nobili, Carlo. 1990. "Per una Storia Degli Studi di Antropologia Museale: il Museo 'Luigi Pigorini' di Roma." *Lares* 56 (3): 321–329.

Nobili, Carlo (ed.). 1993. *Prima America: Gli Oggetti Americani Nelle "Camere delle Meraviglie."* Rome: Museo Nazionale Preistorico Etnografico L. Pigorini.

Nobili, Carlo. 2010. "Luigi Pigorini, Collezionisti e Criteri di Raccolta Etnografica." *Forma Urbis* 5: 14–15.

Nondédéo, Philippe. 2016. "Naachtun: Organisation, Essor et Histoire d'une Capitale Régionale Maya." *Compte Rendus de l'Académie des Inscriptions and Belles-Lettres* 2016 (3): 1211–1228.

Nondédéo, Philippe, Johann Begel, and Ricardo Rodas. 2018. "Operación V.2: la Estructura V y la Cuestión Funeraria." In *Proyecto Petén–Norte Naachtun 2015–2018: Informe De La Octava Temporada De Campo 2017*, ed. Philippe Nondédéo, Dominique Michelet, Johann Begel, and Lilian Garrido, 377–440. Guatemala City: Centro de Estudios Mexicanos y Centroamericanos.

Nondédéo, Philippe, Alfonso Lacadena, and Juan Ignacio Cases Martín. 2019. "Teotihuacanos y mayas en la 'entrada' de 11 Eb'(378 dC): nuevos datos de Naachtun, Petén, Guatemala." *Revista Española de Antropología Americana* 49: 53–75.

Nondédéo, Philippe, Alfonso Lacadena, and Alejandro Garay. 2018. "Apuntes Epigráficos: la Temporada 2015 del Proyecto Naachtun." In *Tiempo Detenido, Tiempo Suficiente: Ensayos y Narraciones Mesoamericanistas en Homenaje a Alfonso Lacadena García-Gallo*, ed. Harri Kettunen, Verónica Amellali Vázquez López, Felix Kupprat, Cristina Vidal Lorenzo, Gaspar Muñóz Cosme, and María Josefa Iglesias Ponce de León, 329–350. Couvin, Belgium: Wayeb Publication Series.

Nondédéo, Philippe, Alejandro Patiño, Alfonso Lacadena, Ignacio Cases, Julien Hiquet, Dominique Michelet, Chloé Andrieu, and Lilian Garrido. 2016. "El Papel de Teotihuacán en la Formación de una Capital Regional Maya: el Caso de Naachtun, Peten." In *XXIX Simposio de Investigaciones Arqueológicas en Guatemala, 20–24 de julio de 2015*, ed. Bárbara Arroyo, Luis Alberto Mendez, and Gloria Ajú, 91–101. Guatemala City: Ministerio de Cultura y Deportes, Instituto de Antropología e Historia, and Asociación Tikal.

Nondédéo, Philippe, Julien Sion, Alfonso Lacadena, Ignacio Cases, and Julien Hiquet. 2021. "From Nobles to Kings: The Political and Historical Context of Naachtun at the End of the Classic Period." In *Maya Kingship: Rupture or Transformation from Classic to Postclassic Times*, ed. Tsubasa Okoshi, Arlen Chase, Philippe Nondédéo, and M.-Charlotte Arnauld, 86–105. Gainesville: University Press of Florida.

Novotny, Anna C., and Laura J. Kosakowsky. 2009. "Burials and Caches from the Chan Site E-Group: A Bioarchaeological Perspective on Ritual and Social Complexity at an Ancient Maya Farming Community." *Research Reports in Belizean Archaeology* 6: 73–81.

Nutini, Hugo G. 1988. *Todos Santos in Rural Tlaxcala: A Syncretic, Expressive, and Symbolic Analysis of the Cult of the Dead*. Princeton, NJ: Princeton University Press.

Olsen, Bjørnar. 2003. "Material Culture after Text: Re-membering Things." *Norwegian Archaeological Review* 36 (2): 87–104.

Orellana Peña, Jorge Humberto, and Leivi Aravey Orellana. 2015. "Costumbres, Creencias y Tradiciones como Expresiones de Identidad Cultural en la Región Occidental de Honduras." *Revista Ciencia y Tecnología* 15: 94–110.

Ortíz Ceballos, Ponciano, and María Del Carmen Rodríguez. 1999. "Olmec Ritual Behavior at El Manatí: A Sacred Space." In *Social Patterns in Pre-Classic Meso-america*, ed. David C. Grove and Rosemary A. Joyce, 225–254. Washington, DC: Dumbarton Oaks.

Palka, Joel. 2005. *Unconquered Lacandon Maya: Ethnohistory and Archaeology of Indigenous Culture Change*. Gainesville: University Press of Florida.

Palka, Joel. 2014. *Maya Pilgrimage to Ritual Landscapes: Insights from Archaeology, History, and Ethnography*. Albuquerque: University of New Mexico Press.

Pecci, Alessandra, and Simona Mileto. 2017. "Preliminary Report of the Analysis of Two Resinous Samples from the Omichicahuaztli of the Pigorini Museum." Unpublished Project Report, Universitat de Barcelona.

Pendergast, David M. 1988. "Engineering Problems in Ancient Maya Architecture: Past, Present, and Future." In *Engineering Geology of Ancient Works, Monuments, and Historical Sites*, ed. Paul G. Marinos and George C. Koukis, 1653–1660. Rotterdam: Balkema.

Pereira, Grégory. 2005. "The Utilization of Grooved Human Bones: A Reanalysis of Artificially Modified Human Bones Excavated by Carl Lumholtz at Zacapu, Michoacán, Mexico." *Latin American Antiquity* 16 (3): 293–312.

Pereira, Grégory. 2013. "Ash, Dirt, and Rock: Burial Practices at Río Bec." *Ancient Mesoamerica* 24 (2): 449–468.

Pérez Suárez, Tomás. 1994. "El Pochó: una Danza Indígena Bailada por Ladinos en Tenosique, Tabasco." In *Antropología, Historia e Imaginativa: En Homenaje a Eduardo Martínez Espinosa*, ed. Carlos Navarrete and Carlos Álvarez, 237–271. Ocozocoautla, Mexico: Instituto Chiapaneco de Cultura.

Pierce, Alexandra. 2003. "Letting Gesture Through: The Practice of Reverberation." Paper presented at the First International Conference on Music and Gesture, University of East Anglia, Norwich, UK, August.

Pierrebourg, Fabienne de. 1999. *L'espace Domestique Maya: Une Approche Ethnoarchéologique au Yucatan (Mexique)*. Paris Monographs in American Archaeology 3. BAR International Series 764. Oxford: Archaeopress.

Pierrebourg, Fabienne de, and Mario Humberto Ruz (eds.). 2014. *Nah Otoch: Concepción, Factura y Atributos de la Morada Maya*. Mexico City: Universidad Nacional Autónoma de México and Instituto de Investigaciones Filológicas, Mérida, Yucatán.

Pitarch Ramón, Pedro. 1996. *Ch'ulel: Una Etnografía de las Almas Tzeltales*. Mexico City: Fondo de Cultura Económica.

Pitarch Ramón, Pedro. 1998. "En mitad del cielo: Una oración chamánica tzeltal dirigida a defender un nahual-rayo." *Revista Española de Antropología Americana* 28: 215–241.

Pitarch Ramón, Pedro. 2010 [1996]. *The Jaguar and the Priest: An Ethnography of Tzeltal Souls.* Austin: University of Texas Press.

Pitarch Ramón, Pedro. 2011. "The Two Maya Bodies: An Elementary Model of Tzeltal Personhood." *Ethnos* 77 (1): 93–114.

Pitrou, Perig. 2012. "Figuration des processus vitaux et co-activité dans la Sierra Mixe de Oaxaca (Mexique)." *L'Homme* 202 (2): 77–112.

Pitrou, Perig. 2014a. "Le comptage rituel en Mésoamérique comme dispositif de mise en relation." *ethnographiques.org* 29 [n. mon "Ethnologie et mathématiques"]. http://www.ethnographiques.org/2014/Pitrou.

Pitrou, Perig. 2014b. "Nourrir les morts ou 'celui qui fait vivre', les différents régimes de commensalité rituelle chez les Mixe (Oaxaca, Mexique)." *Journal de la Société des Américanistes* 100 (2): 45–71.

Pitrou, Perig. 2016a. *Le chemin et le champ: Parcours rituel et sacrifice chez les Mixe de Oaxaca (Mexique).* Nanterre: Sociéte d'ethnologie.

Pitrou, Perig. 2016b. "Co-activity in Mesoamerica and in the Andes." *Journal of Anthropological Research* 72 (4): 465–482.

Plank, Shannon. 2004. *Maya Dwellings in Hieroglyphs and Archaeology: An Integrative Approach to Ancient Architecture and Spatial Cognition.* BAR International Series 1324. Oxford: Archaeopress.

Pohl, Mary E.D., and John M.D. Pohl. 1994. "Cycles of Conflict: Political Factionalism in the Maya Lowlands." In *Factional Competition and Political Development in the New World*, ed. Elizabeth M. Brumfiel and John W. Fox, 138–157. Cambridge: Cambridge University Press.

Pollock, Harry E.D. 1980. *The Puuc: The Architectural Survey of the Hill Country of Yucatan and Northern Campeche, Mexico.* Cambridge: Peabody Museum of Archaeology and Ethnology, Harvard University.

Poulopoulos, Panagiotis. 2016. *New Voices in Old Bodies: A Study of "Recycled" Musical Instruments with a Focus on the Hahn Collection in the Deutsches Museum.* Münster, Germany: MV Wissenschaft.

Quezada, Sergio. 2010. *Breve Historia de Yucatán.* Mexico City: El Colegio de México, Fondo de Cultura Economica.

Quintal, Ella, Martha Medina, Alejandro Cabrera, María J. Cen, and Ileana Ruíz. 2015. "Ceibas, chi'ikes y 'osos': Fiestas Patronales y Carnavales entre los Mayas de la Península de Yucatán." In *Develando la Tradición: Procesos Rituales en las Comunidades Indígenas de México*, volume I, ed. Lourdes Báez, 297–357. Mexico City: Instituto Nacional de Antropología e Historia.

Rands, Barbara C., and Robert L. Rands. 1961. "Excavations in a Cemetery at Palenque." *Estudios de Cultura Maya* 1: 87–106.

Rangel, Martin, Alejandra Alonso, and Kathryn Reese-Taylor. 2013. "Excavación y Documentación de la Estela 26, Estructura I-d, Grupo C." In *Proyecto Arqueológico Naachtun 2004–2009, Informe no. 2: Segunda Temporada de Campo en el Sitio Arqueológico Naachtun,* ed. Martin Rangle and Kathryn Reese-Taylor, 37–56. Guatemala City: Proyecto Arqueologico Naachtun.

Rápalo Flores, Oscar. 2008. "El Guancasco entre Mexicapa y Gracias: una Interpretación desde la Antropología de la Religión." *Yaxkin* 24 (1): 172–183.

Redfield, Robert, and Alfonso Villa Rojas. 1934. *Chan Kom: A Maya Village.* Washington, DC: Carnegie Institution of Washington.

Reichel-Dolmatoff, Gerardo. 1976. "Training for the Priesthood among the Kogi of Colombia." In *Enculturation in Latin America: An Anthology,* ed. Johannes Wilbert, 265–288. Los Angeles: UCLA Latin American Center Publications.

Revel, Nicole, and Diana Rey-Hulman. 1993. *Pour une Anthropologie des Voix.* Paris: L'Harmattan.

Reyes García, Luís, and Dieter Christensen. 1976. *Der Ring aus Tlalocan: Mythen und Gebete, Lieder und Erzählungen der heutigen Nahua in Veracruz und Puebla, Mexiko.* Berlin: Gebr. Mann Verlag.

Reznikoff, Iégor. 2006. "The Evidence of the Use of Sound Resonance from Palaeolithic to Medieval Times." In *Archaeoacoustics: Acoustics, Space, and Intentionality: Identifying Intentionality in the Ancient Use of Acoustic Spaces and Structures,* ed. Chris Scarre and Graeme Lawson, 77–84. Cambridge: McDonald Institute for Archaeological Research.

Richards, Colin, and Julian Thomas. 1984. "Ritual Activity and Structured Deposition in Later Neolithic Wessex." In *Neolithic Studies: A Review of Some Current Research,* ed. Richard Bradley and Julie Gardiner, 189–218. Oxford: British Archaeological Reports.

Ricketson, Oliver G., and Edith B. Ricketson. 1937. *Uaxactun, Guatemala: Group E 1926–1931.* Washington, DC: Carnegie Institution of Washington.

Riquelme, Francisco, Jesús Alvarado-Ortega, Martha Cuevas-García, José Luis Ruvalcaba-Sil, and Carlos Linares-López. 2012. "Calcareous Fossil Inclusions and Rock Source of Maya Lime Plaster from the Temple of the Inscriptions, Palenque, Mexico." *Journal of Archaeological Science* 39 (3): 624–639.

Robin, Cynthia. 1989. *Preclassic Maya Burials at Cuello, Belize.* BAR International Series 480. Oxford: British Archaeological Reports.

Roddick, Andrew P., and Ann B. Stahl. 2016. "Introduction: Knowledge in Motion." In *Knowledge in Motion: Constellations of Learning across Time and Place,* ed. Andrew P. Roddick and Ann B. Stahl, 1–35. Tucson: University of Arizona Press.

Rouget, Gilbert, and Michel Leiris. 1980. *La Musique et la Trance: Esquisse d'une Théorie Générale des Relations de la Musique et de la Possession*. Paris: Gallimard.

Ruz, Mario (ed.). 1983. *Los Legítimos Hombres: Aproximación Antropológica al Grupo Tojolabal*. Mexico City: Centro de Estudios Mayas, Universidad Nacional Autónoma de México.

Ruz Lhuillier, Alberto. 1952. "Exploraciones Arqueológicas en Palenque: 1950–1951." *Anales del Instituto Nacional de Antropología e Historia* 5 (33): 25–66.

Ruz Lhuillier, Alberto. 1989. *Costumbres Funerarias de los Antiguos Mayas*, 2nd ed. Mexico City: Fondo de Cultura Economica.

Sadie, Stanley (ed.). 1984. *The New Grove Dictionary of Musical Instruments*. London: Macmillan.

Sagrario Torres, Claudia, and Raquel Lobo Morales. 2015. "Son las Cosas Pequeñas las que Cuentan: El uso del Diminutive en la Tradición Oral Lenca." *Revista Ciencia y Tecnología* 3: 72–93.

Sahagún, Bernardino de. 1982. *Florentine Codex: General History of the Things of New Spain*, trans. Arthur J.O. Anderson and Charles E. Dibble. Salt Lake City: University of Utah Press.

Sahlins, Marshall. 1985. *Islands of History*. Chicago: University of Chicago Press.

Sánchez Santiago, Gonzalo, and Ricardo Higelin Ponce De León. 2014. "El Quego Xilla en la Antigua Oaxaca: Una Aproximación a los Idiófonos de Ludimiento." In *Flower World: Musical Archaeology of the Americas*, volume 3, ed. Matthias Stöckli and Mark Howell, 101–121. Berlin: Ekho Verlag.

Sandstrom, Alan R., and Arturo Gómez Martínez. 2004. "Petición a Chicomexóchitl: Un canto al espíritu del maíz por la chamana nahua Silveria Hernández Hernández." In *La Huasteca, un recorrido por su diversidad*, ed. Jesús Ruvalcaba Mercado, Juan Manuel Pérez Zevallos, and Octavio Herrera, 343–365. Mexico City: Centro de Investigaciones y Estudios Superiores en Antropología Social, El Colegio de San Luis, and El Colegio de Tamaulipas.

Santos-Granero, Fernando. 2009. *The Occult Life of Things: Native Amazonian Theories of Materiality and Personhood*. Tucson: University of Arizona Press.

Schafer, R. Murray. 1985. "Acoustic Space." In *Dwelling, Place, and Environment: Towards a Phenomenology of Person and World*, ed. David Seamon and Robert Mugerauer, 87–98. Dordrecht: Martinus Nijhoff.

Schele, Linda. 1989. *Notebook for the 13th Maya Hieroglyphic Workshop at Texas: The Dynastic History of Copan*. Austin: University of Texas.

Schele, Linda. 1991. "The Demotion of Chack-Zutz': Lineage Compounds and Subsidiary Lords at Palenque." In *Sixth Palenque Round Table, 1986*, ed. Merle Greene Robertson, 6–11. Norman: University of Oklahoma Press.

Schele, Linda, and Peter Mathews. 1998. *The Code of Kings: The Language of Seven Sacred Maya Temples and Tombs*. New York: Simon and Schuster.

Schele, Linda, and Mary Ellen Miller. 1986. *The Blood of Kings: Dynasty and Ritual in Maya Art*. Fort Worth: Kimbell Art Museum.

Scherer, Andrew K. 2015. *Mortuary Landscapes of the Classic Maya*. Austin: University of Texas Press.

Scherer, Andrew K., and Stephen D. Houston. 2018. "Blood, Fire, Death: Covenants and Crises among the Classic Maya." In *Smoke, Flames, and the Human Body in Mesoamerican Ritual Practice*, ed. Vera Tiesler and Andrew K. Scherer, 109–150. Washington, DC: Dumbarton Oaks.

Searle, John R. 1969. *Speech Acts: An Essay in the Philosophy of Language*. Cambridge: Cambridge University Press.

Sedov, Sergey, Elizabeth Solleiro-Rebolledo, Scott L. Fedick, Teresa Pi-Puig, Ernestina Vallejo-Gómez, and María de Lourdes Flores-Delgadillo. 2008. "Micromorphology of a Soil Catena in Yucatán: Pedogenesis and Geomorphological Processes in a Tropical Karst Landscape." In *New Trends in Soil Micromorphology*, ed. Selim Kapur, Ahmet Mermut, and Georges Stoops, 19–37. Berlin: Springer.

Seler, Edward. 1992 [1898]. "Ancient Mexican Bone Rattles." In *Collected Works in Mesoamérican Linguistics and Archaeology*, volume 3, trans. J. Eric S. Thompson and Francis B. Richardson, ed. Frank E. Comparato, 62–73. Culver City, CA: Labyrinthos.

Sewell, William H. 2005. *The Logics of History: Social Theory and Social Transformation*. Chicago: University of Chicago Press.

Sheptak, Russell N. 2004. "Noticias de un cacique indígena de la época colonial: Una contribución a la historia colonias de Honduras." Paper presented at the VII Congreso Centroamericano de Historia, Tegucigalpa, Honduras, July.

Sheptak, Russell N. 2007. "Los Toqueguas de la Costa Norte de Honduras en la Época Colonial." *Yaxkin* 13 (2): 140–157.

Sheptak, Russell N. 2013. "Colonial Masca in Motion: Tactics of Persistence of a Honduran Indigenous Community." PhD dissertation, Leiden University, The Netherlands.

Sheptak, Russell N. 2019. "Moving Masca: Persistent Indigenous Communities in Spanish Colonial Honduras." In *Indigenous Persistence in the Colonized Americas*, ed. Heather Law Pezzarossi and Russell N. Sheptak, 19–38. Albuquerque: University of New Mexico Press.

Sheptak, Russell N., Rosemary A. Joyce, and Kira Blaisdell-Sloan. 2011. "Pragmatic Choices, Colonial Lives: Resistance, Ambivalence, and Appropriation in Northern

Honduras." In *Enduring Conquests*, ed. Matthew Liebmann and Melissa Murphy, 149–172. Santa Fe, NM: School for Advanced Research Press.

Sherzer, Joel, and Greg Urban. 1986. *Native South American Discourse*. Berlin: Mouton de Gruyter.

Shillito, Lisa-Marie, and Philippa Ryan. 2013. "Surfaces and Streets: Phytoliths, Micromorphology, and Changing Use of Space at Neolithic Çatalhoyuk (Turkey)." *Antiquity* 87: 684–700.

Shove, Patrick I., and Bruno Repp. 1995. "Musical Motion and Performance: Theoretical and Empirical Perspectives." In *The Practice of Performance: Studies in Musical Interpretation*, ed. John Rink, 55–83. Cambridge: Cambridge University Press.

Signorini, Italo. 2008. "El regreso de los difuntos en el mundo indígena mesoamericano contemporáneo." In *Morir para vivir en Mesoamérica*, ed. Lourdes Baez Cubero and Catalina Rodríguez Lascano, 249–258. Veracruz: Consejo Veracruzano de Arte Popular, Instituto Nacional de Antropología e Historia.

Signorini, Italo, and Alessandro Lupo. 1989. *Los tres ejes de la vida: Almas, cuerpo, enfermedad entre los nahuas de la Sierra*. Xalapa, Mexico: Universidad Veracruzana.

Signorini, Italo, and Alessandro Lupo. 1992. "The Ambiguity of Evil among the Nahua of the Sierra (Mexico)." *Etnofoor* 5 (1–2): 81–94.

Siméon, Rémi. 2007 [1885]. *Diccionario de la Lengua Náhuatl o Mexicana*. Mexico City: Siglo XXI.

Sion, Julien. 2016. "La Caractérisation Socio-Économique des Élite Mayas au Classique Terminal (AD 800–950/1000): le Groupe B-Sud de Naachtun (Guatemala)." PhD dissertation, Université Paris I Panthéon–Sorbonne, France.

Sion, Julien, and M. Charlotte Arnauld. 2015. "Abandonando la Casa: Última Actividad Sobre Pisos." Paper presented at the GDRI RITMO Rencontre de Royaumont, Ritual Temporalities: Sequences, Processes, and Action Coordination, Paris, October.

Sion, Julien, and Jacqueline Quiñonez. 2018. "Excavaciones en el Complejo Oeste del Grupo B, Patio 6." In *Proyecto Petén–Norte Naachtun 2015–2018: Informe De La Octava Temporada De Campo 2017*, ed. Philippe Nondédéo, Dominique Michelet, Johann Begel, and Lilian Garrido, 169–212. Guatemala City: Centro de Estudios Mexicanos y Centroamericanos.

Smith, Ledyard A. 1950. *Uaxactun, Guatemala: Excavations of 1931–1937*. Washington, DC: Carnegie Institution of Washington.

Smith, Ledyard A. 1972. *Excavations at Altar de Sacrificios: Architecture, Settlement, Burials, and Caches*. Cambridge: Peabody Museum of Archaeology and Ethnology, Harvard University.

Smith, Ledyard A., and Alfred Kidder. 1951. *Excavations at Nebaj, Guatemala*. Washington, DC: Carnegie Institution of Washington.

Smith, Ledyard A., and Jeremy Sabloff. 1982. *Excavations at Seibal, Department of Peten Guatemala*. Cambridge: Peabody Museum of Archaeology and Ethnology, Harvard University.

Solís-Castillo, Berenice, Alexandra Golyeva, Sergey Sedov, Elizabeth Solleiro-Rebolledo, and Sara López-Rivera. 2015. "Phytoliths, Stable Carbon Isotopes, and Micromorphology of a Buried Alluvial Soil in Southern Mexico: A Polychronous Record of Environmental Change during Middle Holocene." *Quaternary International* 365: 150–158.

Spielmann, Katherine A. 2002. "Feasting, Craft Specialization, and the Ritual Mode of Production in Small-Scale Societies." *American Anthropologist* 104 (1): 195–207. https://www.jstor.org/stable/683770.

Šprajc, Ivan. 2020. "Alineamientos astronómicos en la arquitectura de Naachtun." In *Proyecto Petén-Norte Naachtun 2019–2022: Informe De La Decima Temporada De Campo 2019*, ed. Philippe Nondédéo, Johann Begel, and Lilian Garrido, 11–28. Guatemala City: Centro de Estudios Mexicanos y Centroamericanos.

Stahl, Peter W. 1986. "Hallucinatory Imagery and the Origin of Early South American Figurine Art." *World Archaeology* 18 (1): 134–150.

Stanton, Travis W., M. Kathryn Brown, and Jonathan B. Pagliaro. 2008. "Garbage of the Gods? Squatters, Refuse, Disposal, and Termination Rituals among the Ancient Maya." *Latin American Antiquity* 19 (3): 227–247.

Stark, Miriam T. 2006. "Glaze Ware Technology, the Social Lives of Pots, and Communities of Practice in the Late Prehistoric Southwest." In *The Social Life of Pots: Glaze Wares and Cultural Dynamics in the Southwest, AD 1250–1680*, ed. Judith A. Habicht-Mauche, Suzanne L. Eckert, and Deborah L. Huntley, 17–33. Tucson: University of Arizona Press.

Starr, Frederick. 1899. "Notched Bones from Mexico." *Proceedings of the Davenport Academy of Sciences* 7: 101–107.

Stone, Andrea. 1983. "The Zoomorphs of Quirigua." PhD dissertation, University of Texas, Austin.

Stone, Andrea. 1995. *Images from the Underworld: Naj Tunich and the Tradition of Maya Cave Painting*. Austin: University of Texas Press.

Stone, Andrea, and Marc Zender. 2011. *Reading Maya Art: A Hieroglyphic Guide to Ancient Maya Painting and Sculpture*. London: Thames and Hudson.

Stone, Doris Z. 1948. "The Northern Highland Tribes: The Lenca." In *Handbook of South American Indians*, volume 4: *The Circum-Caribbean Tribes*, ed. Julian H. Steward, 205–217. Washington, DC: Smithsonian Institution.

Stone, Doris Z. 1954. "El Guancasco de Intibucá y Yamaranguila." *Revista del Archivo y Biblioteca Nacional de Honduras* 33: 270–275.

Stone, Doris Z. 1957. *The Archaeology of Central and Southern Honduras*. Cambridge: Peabody Museum, Harvard University.

Stone, Doris Z. 1977. *Precolumbian Man in Costa Rica*. Cambridge: Peabody Museum Press.

Stone, Doris Z (ed.). 1982. *Aspects of Mixteca-Puebla Style and Mixtec and Central Mexican Culture in Southern Mesoamerica*. New Orleans: Middle American Research Institute, Tulane University.

Straw, Will. 2012. "Music and Material Culture." In *The Cultural Study of Music: A Critical Introduction*, ed. Martin Clayton, Trevor Herbert, and Richard Middleton, 227–236. London: Routledge.

Stross, Brian. 1998. "Seven Ingredients in Mesoamerican Ensoulment: Dedication and Termination in Tenejapa." In *The Sowing and the Dawning: Termination, Dedication, and Transformation in the Archaeological and Ethnographic Record of Mesoamerica*, ed. Shirley Boteler Mock, 31–39. Albuquerque: University of New Mexico Press.

Stuart, David. 1987. "Ten Phonetic Syllables." Research Reports on Ancient Maya Writing 14. Washington, DC: Center for Maya Research.

Stuart, David. 1996. "Kings of Stone: A Consideration of Stelae in Ancient Maya Ritual and Representation." *RES: Anthropology and Aesthetics* 29–30: 148–171.

Stuart, David. 1998. "'The Fire Enters His House': Architecture and Ritual in Classic Maya Texts." In *Function and Meaning in Classic Maya Architecture*, ed. Stephen Houston, 373–425. Washington, DC: Dumbarton Oaks.

Stuart, David. 2010. "Shining Stones: Observations on the Ritual Meaning of Early Maya Stelae." In *The Place of Stone Monuments: Context, Use, and Meaning in Mesoamerica's Preclassic Transition*, ed. Julia Guernsey, John E. Clark, and Barbara Arroyo, 283–298. Washington, DC: Dumbarton Oaks.

Stuart, David. 2011. *The Order of Days*. New York: Three Rivers.

Stuart, David. 2015. "Meaning in Ancient Maya Rituals of Temporal and Cosmic Renewal." Paper presented at the GDRI RITMO Rencontre de Royaumont, Ritual temporalities: sequences, processes, and action coordination, Paris, October.

Stuart, David, and George Stuart. 2008. *Palenque: Eternal City of the Maya*. London: Thames and Hudson.

Sullivan, Lawrence E. 1988. *Icanchu's Drum: An Orientation to Meaning in South American Religions*. New York: Macmillan.

Swenson, Edward. 2015. "The Archaeology of Ritual." *Annual Review of Anthropology* 44: 329–345.

Taschek, Jennifer T., and Joseph W. Ball. 1999. "Las Ruinas de Arenal: Preliminary Report on a Subregional Major Center in the Western Belize Valley (1991–1992 Excavations)." *Ancient Mesoamerica* 10 (2): 215–235.

Taube, Karl A. 1998. "The Jade Hearth: Centrality, Rulership, and the Classic Maya Temple." In *Function and Meaning in Classic Maya Architecture*, ed. Stephen D. Houston, 427–478. Washington, DC: Dumbarton Oaks.

Taube, Karl A. 2004. "Flower Mountain: Concepts of Life, Beauty, and Paradise among the Classic Maya." *RES: Anthropology and Aesthetics* 45: 69–98.

Taylor, Anne-Christine. 2017. "L'art d'infléchir les âmes." *Terrain* 68: 46–67. doi: 10.4000/terrain.16291.

Tedlock, Barbara. 1992 [1982]. *Time and the Highland Maya*. Albuquerque: University of New Mexico Press.

Tedlock, Dennis. 1971. "On the Translation of Style in Oral Narrative." *Journal of American Folklore* 84: 114–133. doi: 10.2307/539739.

Tedlock, Dennis. 1983. *The Spoken Word and the Work of Interpretation*. Philadelphia: University of Pennsylvania Press.

Thomas, Nicholas. 1991. *Entangled Objects: Exchange, Material Culture, and Colonialism in the Pacific*. Cambridge: Harvard University Press.

Tiesler Blos, Vera, and Andrea Cucina. 2003. "Sacrificio, Tratamiento y Ofrenda del Cuerpo Humano entre los Mayas del Clásico: una Mirada Bioarqueológica." In *Antropología de la Eternidad: La Muerte en la Cultura Maya*, ed. Andres Ciudad Ruíz, Mario H. Ruz, and Maria Josefa Iglesias, 337–354. Madrid: Sociedad Española de Estudios Mayas.

Tiesler Blos, Vera, and Andrea Cucina. 2007. *New Perspectives on Human Sacrifice and Ritual Body Treatments in Ancient Maya Society*. New York: Springer.

Tiesler, Vera, and Andrew K. Scherer (eds.). 2018. *Smoke, Flames, and the Human Body in Mesoamerican Ritual Practice*. Cambridge: Harvard University Press.

Till, Rupert. 2014. "Sound Archaeology: Terminology, Palaeolithic Cave Art, and the Soundscape." *World Archaeology* 46 (3): 292–304.

Todd, Neil P.M. 1999. "Motion in Music: A Neurobiological Perspective." *Music Perception* 17 (1): 115–126. http://mp.ucpress.edu/content/17/1/115.

Trejo Mojica, Juana A. 2008. "Los Restos Óseos Humanos Como Objetos Ideológicos del Periodo Clásico Maya." *Dimensión Antropológica* 42: 7–32.

Trigger, Bruce. 1996. "Comments on Special Section: Agency, Ideology, and Power in Archaeological Theory." *Current Anthropology* 37 (1): 63–64.

Tucker, Catherine M. 2008. *Changing Forests: Collective Action, Common Property, and Coffee in Honduras*. New York: Springer.

Tulving, Endel. 1993. "What Is Episodic Memory?" *Current Directions in Psychological Science* 2 (3): 67–70.

Turner, Paul R. 1971. *The Highland Chontal*. New York: Holt, Rinehart and Winston.

Turner, Victor. 1987. *The Anthropology of Performance*. New York: PAJ Publications.

Tuz Chi, Lázaro Hilario. 2012. *Jaalal T'aan: Bobatilt'aan yéetel jaajil tu tuukul maaya kaaj*. Valladolid, Mexico: Universidad de Oriente.

Tuz Chi, Lázaro Hilario. 2013a. *Aj balam yuumtsilo'ob, cosmovisión e identidad en los rituales agrícolas de los mayas peninsulares*. Mérida: Secretaría de Educación del Gobierno del Estado de Yucatán.

Tuz Chi, Lázaro Hilario. 2013b. "Manuscrito de don Pablo Novelo, junio 1906, origen Pomuch, Campeche." *K'a'ajsaj* 1 (2): 4.

Urcid, Javier. 2010. "El Sacrificio Humano en el Suroeste de Mesoamérica." In *El Sacrificio Humano en la Tradición Religiosa Mesoamericana*, ed. Leonardo López Luján and Guilhem Olivier, 115–168. Mexico City: Instituto Nacional de Antropología e Historia and Instituto de Investigaciones Históricas, Universidad Nacional Autónoma de México.

Valdés, Juan Antonio. 2001. "Palaces and Thrones Tied to the Destiny of the Royal Courts in the Maya Lowlands." In *Royal Courts of the Ancient Maya*, volume 2: *Data and Case Studies*, ed. Takeshi Inomata and Stephen D. Houston, 139–164. Boulder: Westview.

Van Oyen, Astrid. 2018. "Material Agency." In *The Encyclopedia of Archaeological Sciences*, ed. Sandra L. López Varela. Malden, MA: Wylie and Sons. Published online November 26, 2018. https://doi.org/10.1002/9781119188230.saseas0363.

Vapnarsky, Valentina. 2000. "De dialogues en prières, la procession des mots." In *Les rituels du dialogue: Promenades ethnolinguistiques en terres amérindiennes*, ed. Aurore Monod Becquelin and Philippe Erikson, 431–479. Nanterre: Société d'ethnologie.

Vapnarsky, Valentina. 2008. "Paralelismo, ciclicidad y creatividad en el arte verbal maya yucateco." *Estudios de Cultura Maya* 32: 151–196. doi: 10.19130/iifl.ecm.2008.32.71.

Vapnarsky, Valentina. 2009. "Predicción y performatividad en la memoria histórica maya yucateca." In *Text and Context: Yucatec Maya Literature in a Diachronic Perspective*, ed. Antje Gunsenheimer, Tsubasa Okoshi Harada, and John F. Chuchiak, 257–288. Aachen, Germany: Shaker Verlag.

Vapnarsky, Valentina. 2013a. "Mandatos y solicitudes: el arte cotidiano del pedir en maya yucateco." In *Maya Daily Lives*, ed. André Breton and Philippe Nondédéo, 169–183. Markt Schwaben, Germany: Verlag Anton Saurwein.

Vapnarsky, Valentina. 2013b. "Le passif peut-il éclairer les esprits? Agentivités, interactions et esprits-maîtres chez les Mayas." *Ateliers d'Anthropologie* 39 (2). http://ateliers.revues.org/9449. doi: 10.4000/ateliers.9449.

Vapnarsky, Valentina. 2014. "Briser les vents et échanger les coeurs: art et performance dans les discours rituels mayas contemporains." In *Mayas: Révélations d'un temps sans fin*, ed. Dominique Michelet, 123–129. Paris: Réunion des musées nationaux.

Vapnarsky, Valentina. 2016a. "Del latin al jach maaya: captación de lenguas y apropiaciones del poder entre los mayas cruso'ob." Paper presented at the X Congreso Internacional de Mayistas, Izamal, Mexico, June.

Vapnarsky, Valentina. 2016b. "No Escape from the Future: Temporal Frames and Prediction in Yucatec Maya." In *Aspectuality and Temporality: Descriptive and Theoretical Issues*, ed. Zlatka Guentchéva, 643–678. Amsterdam: John Benjamins.

Vapnarsky, Valentina. 2017. "Les Sens du Temps: Temporalités et temporalisations des paroles, expériences et mémoires mayas / Senses of Time: Exploring Temporality in Mayan Discourses, Experiences, and Remembrances." Manuscript submitted for the Habilitation à Diriger des Recherches. Paris: L'École des Hautes Études en Sciences Sociales.

Vapnarsky, Valentina, Claude Barras, and Cédric Becquey. 2018. "*Ujuum payalchi'* el Sonido de los Rezos: Nuevas Perspectivas para el Estudio de los Discursos Rituales Mayas, sus Cualidades Vocales y Variaciones." *Cuadernos de Lingüística de El Colegio de México* 5 (1): 470–505. https://cuadernoslinguistica.colmex.mx/index.php/cl/issue/view/7.

Vapnarsky, Valentina, Claude Barras, Cédric Becquey, David Doukhan, Martine Adda-Decker, and Lori Lamel. 2015. "Analyzing Rhythm in Ritual Discourse in Yucatec Maya Using Automatic Speech Alignment." In *INTERSPEECH 2015: Proceedings of the 16th International Speech Communication Association Annual Conference*, 344–348. Red Hook, NY: Curran Associates.

Vapnarsky, Valentina, and Olivier Le Guen. 2011. "The Guardians of Space and History: Understanding Ecological and Historical Relationships of the Contemporary Yucatec Maya to Their Landscape." In *Ecology, Power, and Religion in Maya Landscapes*, ed. Christian Isendahl and Bodil Liljefors Persson, 191–208. Markt Schwaben, Germany: Verlag Anton Saurwein.

Vazquez Campa, Violeta. 2014. "Depósitos Rituales Arqueológicos del Periodo Clásico en Campeche." *Estudios de Cultura Maya* 44: 167–202.

Vázquez de Ágredos Pascual, Ma. Luisa. 2018. "Painting the Skin in Ancient Mesoamerica." In *Painting the Skin: Pigments on Bodies and Codices in Pre-Columbian Mesoamerica*, ed. Élodie Dupey García and Ma. Luisa Vázquez de Ágredos Pascual, 11–23. Tucson and Mexico City: University of Arizona Press and Universidad Nacional Autónoma de México.

Vázquez de Ágredos Pascual, Ma. Luisa, Vera Tiesler, and Arturo Romano Pacheco. 2015. "Perfumando al Difunto: Fragancias y Tratamientos Póstumos entre la Antigua Aristocracia Maya." *Arqueología Mexicana* 23 (135): 30–35.

Vázquez de Ágredos Pascual, Ma. Luisa, and Cristina Vidal Lorenzo. 2017. "Fragrances and Body Paint in the Courtly Life of the Maya." In *Pre-Hispanic Mesoamerican Traditions for Constructing Power and Place*, ed. Meredith Paxton and Leticia Staines Cicero, 155–169. Albuquerque: University of New Mexico Press.

Vázquez de Ágredos Pascual, Ma. Luisa, Cristina Vidal Lorenzo and Patricia Horcajada Campos. 2018. "Face Painting among the Classic Maya Elite: An Iconographic Study." In *Social Skins of the Head: Body Beliefs and Ritual in Ancient Mesoamerica and the Andes*, ed. Vera Tiesler and María Cecilia Lozada, 93–107. Albuquerque: University of New Mexico Press.

Vázquez de Ágredos Pascual, Ma. Luisa, Cristina Vidal Lorenzo, Patricia Horcajada Campos, and Vera Tiesler. 2018. "Body Color and Aromatics in Maya Funerary Rites." In *Painting the Skin: Pigments on Bodies and Codices in Pre-Columbian Mesoamerica*, ed. Élodie Dupey García and Ma. Luisa Vázquez de Ágredos Pascual, 56–74. Tucson and Mexico City: University of Arizona Press and Universidad Nacional Autónoma de México.

Velázquez Castro, Adrián, Belem Zúñiga Arellano, and Norma Valentín Maldonado. 2014. "Identificación de las Piezas de Concha del Omichicauaztli del Museo Nazionale Preistorico Etnografico Luigi Pigorini de Roma." Unpublished research report, Museo del Templo Mayor, Mexico City.

Villa Rojas, Alfonso. 1945. *The Maya of East Central Quintana Roo*. Washington, DC: Carnegie Institution of Washington.

Vogt, Evon Z. 1965. *Tortillas for the Gods: A Symbolic Analysis of Zinacanteco Rituals*. Norman: University of Oklahoma Press.

Vogt, Evon Z. (ed.). 1969. *Handbook of Middle American Indians: Ethnology*. Austin: University of Texas Press.

Vogt, Evon Z. 1979. *Ofrendas para los Dioses: Análisis Simbólico de Rituals Zinacantecos*. Mexico City: Fondo de Cultura Económica.

Vogt, Evon Z. 1998. "Zinacanteco Dedication and Termination Rituals." In *The Sowing and the Dawning: Termination, Dedications, and Transformation in the Archaeological and Ethnographic Record of Mesoamerica*, ed. Shirley Boteler Mock, 21–30. Albuquerque: University of New Mexico Press.

von Winning, Hasso. 1959. "A Decorated Bone Rattle from Culhuacan, Mexico." *American Antiquity* 25 (1): 86–93.

Wagner, Elisabeth. 2006. "White Earth Bundles: The Symbolic Sealing and Burial of Buildings among the Ancient Maya." In *Jaws of the Underworld: Life, Death, and Rebirth among the Ancient Maya*, ed. Pierre Colas, Geneviève Le Fort, and Bodil Liljefors Persson, 55–69. Markt Schwaben, Germany: Verlag Anton Saurwein.

Walker, John H. 2012. "Recent Landscape Archaeology in South America." *Journal of Archaeological Research* 20: 309–355. doi: 10.1007/s10814-012-9057-6.

Walker, William H. 2008. "Practice and Nonhuman Social Actors: The Afterlife Histories of Witches and Dogs in the American Southwest." In *Memory Work: Archaeologies of Material Practices*, ed. Barbara J. Mills and William H. Walker, 137–157. Santa Fe, NM: School for Advanced Research Press.

Walker, William H., and Lisa J. Lucero. 2000. "The Depositional Histories of Ritual and Power." In *Agency in Archaeology*, ed. Mary Dobres and John Robb, 130–147. London: Routledge.

Waller, Steven. 2017. "A Theoretical Framework for Archaeoacoustics and Case Studies." *Journal of the Acoustical Society of America* 141: 4000. https://doi.org/10.1121/1.4989171.

Wanderley, Marcelo M. 1999. "Non-Obvious Performer Gestures in Instrumental Music." In *Gesture-Based Communication in Human-Computer Interaction*, ed. Annelies Braffort, Rachid Gherbi, Sylvie Gibet, James Richardson, and Daniel Teil, 37–48. International Gesture Workshop. Berlin: Springer.

Watts, Christopher (ed.). 2013. *Relational Archaeologies: Humans, Animals, Things*. London: Routledge.

Wauchope, Robert. 1938. *Modern Maya Houses*. Washington, DC: Carnegie Institution of Washington.

Weiss-Krejci, Estella. 2010. "Depósitos Rituales en los Complejos de Pirámides Gemelas de Tikal." In *El Ritual en el Mundo Maya: de lo Privado a lo Público*, ed. Andrés Ciudad Ruíz, María Josefa Iglesias Ponce de León, and Miguel Andel Sorroche Cuerva, 83–105. Madrid: Sociedad Española de Estudios Mayas, Grupo de Investigación, Andalucía América: Patrimonio Cultural y Relaciones Artísticas (PAI: HUM-806) Centro Peninsular en Humanidades y Ciencias Sociales, Universidad Nacional Autónoma de México.

Weiss-Krejci, Estella. 2011. "The Role of Dead Bodies in Late Classic Maya Politics: Cross-Cultural Reflections on the Meaning of Tikal Altar 5." In *Living with the Dead: Mortuary Ritual in Mesoamerica*, ed. James L. Fitzsimmons and Izumi Shimada, 17–52. Tucson: University of Arizona Press.

Wells, E. Christian. 2007. "Faenas, Ferias, and Fiestas: Ritual Finance in Ancient and Modern Honduras." In *Mesoamerican Ritual Economy: Archaeological and Ethnological Perspectives*, ed. Karla Davis-Salazar and E. Christian Wells, 29–65. Boulder: University Press of Colorado.

Wells, E. Christian, and Karla Davis-Salazar. 2008. "Environmental Worldview and Ritual Economy among the Honduran Lenca." *Research in Economic Anthropology* 27: 189–217.

Wenger, Etienne. 1998. *Communities of Practice: Learning, Meaning, and Identity.* Cambridge: Cambridge University Press.

Wichmann, Anne, Nicole Dehé, and Dagmar Barth-Weingarten. 2009. "Where Prosody Meets Pragmatics: Research at the Interface." In *Where Prosody Meets Pragmatics*, ed. Dagmar Barth-Weingarten, Nicole Dehé, and Anne Wichmann, 1–20. Bingley, UK: Emerald Group Publishing Ltd. doi: 10.1163/9789004253223_002.

Wilkinson, Darryl. 2017. "Is There Such a Thing as Animism?" *Journal of the American Academy of Religion* 85: 289–311.

Wingfield, Laura. 2009. "Envisioning Greater Nicoya: Ceramic Figural Art of Costa Rica and Nicaragua c. 800 BCE–1522 CE." PhD dissertation, Emory University, Atlanta, GA.

Wisdom, Charles. 1940. *The Chorti Indians of Guatemala.* Chicago: University of Chicago Press.

Wisdom, Charles. 1950. *Chorti Dictionary.* Extract from a collection of unpublished manuscripts on the Chorti, transcribed and transliterated by Brian Stross. Austin: University of Texas Press.

Woodbury, Richard, and Aubrey Trik. 1953. *The Ruins of Zaculeu, Guatemala.* Richmond, VA: United Fruit Company.

Young-Sánchez, Margaret. 2010. *Nature and Spirit: Ancient Costa Rican Treasures in the Mayer Collection at the Denver Art Museum.* Denver: Denver Art Museum.

Zatorre, Robert J., Joyce L. Chen, and Virginia B. Penhune. 2007. "When the Brain Plays Music: Auditory-Motor Interactions in Music Perception and Production." *Nature Reviews Neuroscience* 8: 547–558. https://www.nature.com/articles/nrn2152.

Zedeño, Maria. 2008. "Bundled Worlds: The Roles and Interactions of Complex Objects from the North American Plains." *Journal of Archaeological Method and Theory* 15 (4): 362–378.

Źrałka, Jaroslaw, Wieslaw Koszkul, and Bernard Hermes. 2008. "Investigaciones en Nakum, Peten, Guatemala: Resultados de las Excavaciones Realizadas por el Proyecto Arqueológico Nakum en los Años 2006 y 2007." In *Polish Contributions in New World Archaeology*, ed. Janusz Kozlowski and Jaroslaw Źrałka, 73–128. Cracow: Polish Academy of Arts and Sciences, Jagiellonian University.

Źrałka, Jarosław, Wieslaw Koszkul, Bernard Hermes, and Simon Martin. 2012. "Excavations of Nakum Structure 15B: Discovery of Royal Burials and Accompanying Offerings." *PARI Journal* 12 (3): 1–20.

Cabada, Juan de la, 237
Cabarrús, Carlos Rafael, 146, 147, 149, 150
Calakmul, 121, 136
Campeche, 231–252
Cancuc, 150
Carias, Claudia Marcela, 53
Carnaval, 231–232, 237–240, 244–245, 249, 251
Ceibal, 156
Cerro Palenque, 67–69
chaîne opératoire, 9, 20, 110–112, 115, 204–205, 220–222
Chamula, 173, 189
Chan, 137
Chan Kom, 156
chanting, 40, 93, 117; materiality of, 12, 14; as ritual action, 3, 72–73
Chapman, Anne, 52–57, 60, 61, 63
Chávez Borjas, Manuel, 52, 61
Chinda, 61
Chol, 149, 150, 153, 156, 158, 159
Chontal, 149, 151
Chorti, 50, 149, 235
Chosson, Marie, 7–8, 16–17
Clarke, Eric, 212
co-activity, 5, 11
Codex Vindobonensis, 216, 222
Coe, William, 158
coevalness, 215, 228, 230. *See also* temporality
cofradia, 61–63
Colha, 135
community of practice, 9, 195, 198; defined, 203–204
community of engaged performance, 198–199, 204, 206–207, 210–213, 214
compostura, 14, 54–56, 149; archaeological analogues of, 64–69; colonial analogues of, 57–60; described, 51; ethnographic descriptions of, 51–55
Connolly, William, 40
convite. *See* guancasco
Copan, 119, 120, 139, 153, 155, 157
Costa Rica, 5, 9, 18–19, 195–214
Costenla Umaña, Adolfo, 50
Cuello, 135
Cuetzalan, 162, 173, 174
Currusté, 66–67
cycles, 13, 15, 52, 55, 70, 99; agricultural, 55–56, 75, 97, 123; calendrical, 70, 101, 117, 140, 231; in construction, 110–111, 115; in human life,

33–36, 41, 226; linguistic, 74, 76, 81, 84; ritual, 58, 61, 69, 158; seasonal, 38–39

dance, 70, 157, 231, 251; colonial, 236–237; contemporary, 51, 54, 61, 236, 239, 246; prehispanic, 121, 225
Davidson, Jane, 212
Davis-Salazar, Karla, 64
dedication, 16–17, 138, 153; of buildings, 34, 111, 121, 135–136, 157; deposits, 130, 154–155; of monuments, 117–118, 139–140; questioned, 158, 160; rituals, defined, 144; of ritual offerings, 75–76, 83–84; words for, 159
Dehouve, Daniéle, 186, 187
DeLanda, Manuel, 17, 21, 28
deposition, structured, 15, 27, 98–100, 110, 118, 124
Despoloncal, 62
Domenici, Davide, 219, 221, 228
Dzibanche, 121
Dzitbalché, 237

Edmonson, Munro, 236
Edzna, 245
El Cival, 157
El Juilín, 140
El Salvador, 51, 62, 63
El Tintal, 135
El Zotz, 136, 137, 141
Eliade, Mircea, 203
Emery, Kitty, 113
event, 4, 7, 14–16, 21, 27; defined, 13, 28–30; methodological considerations, 31–32; ritual-as-event, 67; sonic, 196, 208–210; synesthetic, 168

Fabian, Johannes, 228
filarmónica, 238, 250
fire, 138, 141, 153, 160, 186–187; as animating substance, 33; archaeological evidence for, 38–44, 65–66; rituals of, 34, 75, 157–159; sensory effect, 40, 172; *see also* heat
Fitzsimmons, James, 34, 139
Fowles, Severin, 28
fragrance. *See* scent

Gámez Díaz, Laura, 157
Garza (Costa Rica), 196, 199, 214
Gell, Alfred, 29, 40

gesture, 14, 50, 70, 248; accompanying music, 195–196, 198, 204, 207–210, 212, 222, 225; accompanying narration, 91; ritual 67–69, 76, 83, 110–111, 168, 174

Giglioli, Enrico Hillyer, 220, 222, 228

Gilmore, Zackary, 30

Gossen, Gary, 172, 173

Gualala, 54, 61

guancasco, 14, 50, 54; archaeological analogues of, 64–69; colonial analogues of, 60–63; described, 51–52; of La Campa, 53–54; of Yamaranguila, 53

Guerrero Miranda, Juan Vicente, 200

Guiteras Holmes, Calixta, 146, 147, 150

Hanks, William, 73, 91, 174

Haviland, William, 138

heat, 138, 168; as vital force, 169, 171–174, 177, 181, 186, 188–189

Hermitte, Maria Esther, 146, 147

Hernández, Juan José, 236

Hiquet, Julien, 130

Hodder, Ian, 26, 97, 103

Honduras, 5, 7–8, 14, 49–69, 149

Huastec, 149

Ilama, 54, 61

Ingold, Tim, 29

Inomata, Takeshi, 101

Intibuca, 53, 54, 56, 66

intra-action, 12, 16, 18, 21–22

itineraries, of things, 19–20, 229–230

Jetegua, 58–59

Johnson, Lisa, 7, 11, 13–14, 17, 67

Joyce, Rosemary, 7–8, 11, 14, 17, 20, 26, 98, 112, 149, 229

Juárez, Roger, 232

K'iche', 145, 147, 235

Kabah, 119, 120

Kakchiquel, 235

Kaminaljuyu, 135

Kanxoc, 234

King, Mark, 172

knowledge, 16, 19, 101, 112, 196, 232–234; embodied, 197–198; esoteric, 72, 89; exclusionary, 105; sonic, 195, 198–199, 209, 214; transmission of, 203–204, 214

Kopytoff, Igor, 19

Kosyk, Katrina, 8–9, 18–20

Kus, Susan, 40

La Campa, 53, 55–56, 66, 68

La Joyanca, 6, 8, 16, 20, 98; description, 102–107; Guacamaya Group at, 111–113, 115

La Milpa, 121

Labna, 120

Las Ruinas de Arenal, 131

Lave, Jean, 195, 198, 203, 214

Lenca, 7–8, 14, 17, 20, 149; archaeology of, 64–69; colonial history, 57–63; ontology, 49–50; ritual, 50–56

Leyva, Hector Miguel, 53

Liendo Stuardo, Rodrigo, 44

Lobo Morales, Raquel, 52

López Medel, Tomás, 237

Lopiparo, Jeanne, 64, 66–67

Lupo, Alessandro, 9–10, 16, 17–19

Machaquila, 153

Mam, 235

Mantecales, 65–66, 67

Martinez Miralda, Róger, 53

materiality, as active, 5, 7, 11–12; defined, 12; and ritualization, 11–12. *See also* new materialism

May Castillo, Manuel, 138

Maya 6–8, 13–17, 20, 27–29, 32, 59; agricultural rituals, 75–82; altars, 118–121; architecture, 38, 102–114, 129–135; building rituals, 144–157; burial practices, 39–45; cleansing ceremony, 82–88; earth rituals, 52–53, 160–161; historical inscriptions, 36–37, 46, 158–159; kingship, 116, 117; language, 50; ontology, 32–35; place-making, 97–102, 115, 121–129; music, 231–251; ritual speech, 71–74, 88–93, 172, 173, 174; sacrifice, 138–140

McAnany, Patricia, 26, 103

memory, 26, 40–42, 99–101, 105, 231; episodic, 29; semantic, 29; work, 30, 113

Merleau-Ponty, Maurice, 197

methodology, 5–10, 31–32, 205–207; archaeomusicological, 196; linguistic, 78–80; microresidue, 26, 31, 46, 48

Mexica, 217, 225

Mexico, 3, 4, 5, 7, 8, 9; archaeobotanical remains in, 34; Christianization in, 232;

museums in, 217; musical instruments of, 18; ritual practices in, 21

micromorphology, 30–32, 42, 46, 48. *See also* microstratigraphy; residues, microscopic

microstratigraphy, 13, 26–27, 30–32, 35–46

Mills, Barbara, 103

Mixtec, 145, 219; music, 216; song, 172

Moholy-Nagy, Hattula, 158

Monod Becquelin, Aurora, 73, 172

museum context, 19–20, 217–220, 222–230

music, 7–9, 34, 40, 63, 121, 245–251; materiality of, 12, 18–20, 198; performance, 212, 222, 225, 232–234, 237–239; in ritual, 51, 54, 70, 157, 174

musical instruments, 8–9, 18–20; aerophones, 196, 200–201, 203; bells, 63; drum, 51, 54, 203, 213, 231, 233–236; harmonica, 238, 250; idiophone, 216, 222; ocarina, 195–214; rasp, 215–230

Naachtun, 6, 8, 20; altars at, 16, 17, 118, 121–123, 141; dedication deposits at, 154, 157; E-Group at, 129–135; funerary acropolis at, 123–129; guardian deposits at, 160; ritual use of skulls at, 135–138, 141; stelae at, 140

Nahua (people), 9–10, 17–18, 19, 162–191

Nahuatl (language), 9, 164–166, 176, 181, 185, 188; etymologies, 216, 225; as prestige language, 59

Nakum, 136, 137, 157

Naranjo, 120

Nash, June, 147–150

Nebaj, 135, 136

new materialism, 28. *See also* agential realism; animacy; assemblage: theory; co-activity; event; intra-action; ontology

Newson, Linda, 59

Nicaragua, 51, 199

Nicoya, 9, 195, 203, 213, 214; archaeology of, 199–200; cemeteries in, 202. *See also* Costa Rica; Nicaragua

Nondédéo, Phillippe, 6–7, 16, 17, 124

Novelo, Pablo, 232

O'Donoughue, Jason, 30

omichicahuaztli, 216. *See also* musical instruments: rasp

ontology, 11, 13, 89, 162; Lenca, 50, 60, 69; Maya, 33, 89; Nahua, 169, 173; relational, 33

Ordoñez, Emma Leticia, 53

Orellana, Leivi, 53

Orellana Peña, Jorge, 53

Oxkintok, 120

paisanazgo. *See* guancasco

Palenque, 6, 8, 13, 17, 20, 25–48; feasting at, 40–42, 44; historical inscriptions at, 32, 36–37, 44, 46, 159; mortuary event at, 29–30, 34–39; use of micromorphology at, 31–32, 42–43, 45

Petén, 102, 119, 121, 133

Petoa, 62–63

Piedras Negras, 43, 46, 119, 144, 157

Pierce, Alexandra, 212

Pierrebourg, Fabienne de, 149, 150

Pigorini, Luigi, 218, 220

Pinola, 146

Pitarch Ramón, Pedro, 150

Pitrou, Perig, 5, 187

place-making, 15–16, 97–102, 111, 117, 124, 161

Pollard, Joshua, 98, 112

Pomuch, 231–252

Pool, Fernando, 232, 237, 238, 240, 245–248

Pool, Jorge, 237

Poot, Máximo, 238, 240, 249

Pope Benedict XIV, 219

Popol Vuh, The, 111, 127, 139

Porter, James, 101

Posta, 61, 69

Poulopoulos, Panagiotis, 226

prayers, 9–10, 14–15, 17–18, 84, 88–91; in Lenca ritual, 56; in Maya ritual, 73–76, 79–82, 147; in Nahua ritual, 162–191

Punta di Chimino, 137

Q'eqchi, 145, 146, 149, 150

Quiché (site), 220

Quintana Roo, 70, 234, 239, 250

Quirigua, 119, 120

Rápalo Flores, Oscar, 52

religion, 11, 52, 57, 97; Roman Catholic, 9–10, 60–62, 74, 162–188, 245–248; syncretic, 49, 53, 56. *See also* ritualization; ritual time

residues, microscopic, 6, 13, 17, 32, 118, 126. *See also* microstratigraphy

rhythm, 19–20, 208–209, 212–213, 223, 248, 251; bodily, 82–88, 174, 198; daily, 31; defined, 71–75; of speech, 75–82

M. Charlotte Arnauld, directrice de recherche émérite, ArchAm Lab (Archéologie des Amériques), Centre National de la Recherche Scientifique and Université de Paris 1 Panthéon–Sorbonne

Giovani Balam Caamal, participant, Universos Sonoros Mayas, Universidad Nacional Autónoma de México.

Isaac Barrientos, masters candidate, Éstudios Meso-americanos, Universidad Nacional Autónoma de México, and investigator, Centro de Estudios Mexicanos y Centroamericanos

Cédric Becquey, research associate, Centro de Estudios Mayas, Instituto de Investigaciones Filológicas, Universidad Autónoma Nacional de México

Johann Begel, post-doctoral researcher, ArchAm Lab (Archéologie des Amériques), Centre National de la Recherche Scientifique and Université de Paris 1 Panthéon–Sorbonne

Valeria Bellomia, post-doctoral lecturer, Sapienza Università di Roma

Juan Carrillo González, participant, Universos Sonoros Mayas, Universidad Nacional Autónoma de México

Marie Chosson, assistant professor, Institut National del Langues et Civilisations Orientales (INALCO) and Centre d'études en sciences sociales sur les mondes africains, américains et asiatiques (CESSMA)

Julien Hiquet, post-doctoral researcher, ArchAm Lab (Archéologie des Amériques), Centre National de la Recherche Scientifique and Université de Paris 1 Panthéon–Sorbonne

Lisa M. Johnson, assistant professor-in-residence, University of Nevada, Las Vegas

Rosemary A. Joyce, professor of anthropology, University of California, Berkeley

Katrina Casey Kosyk, doctoral candidate, McGill University

Olivier Le Guen, professor and researcher, Centro de Investigaciones y Estudios Superiores en Antropología Social, Mexico City

Alessandro Lupo, professor, Sapienza Universitá di Roma

Philippe Nondédéo, Mayanist archaeologist and researcher at the ArchAm Lab (Archéologie des Amériques), Centre National de la Recherche Scientifique and Université de Paris 1 Panthéon–Sorbonne

Julie Patrois, Mayanist researcher in iconography, l'Ecole du Louvre and ArchAm Lab (Archéologie des Amériques), Centre National de la Recherche Scientifique and Université de Paris 1 Panthéon–Sorbonne

Russell N. Sheptak, research associate, University of California, Berkeley

Valentina Vapnarsky, director of research, Laboratoire d'Ethnologie et de Sociologie Comparative, Centre National de la Recherche Scientifique and Université Paris Nanterre

M. Luisa Vázquez de Ágredos Pascual, profesora titular en la Facultat de Geografia i Història, Universitat de València, Spain

Francisca Zalaquett Rock, professor and researcher, Centro de Estudios Mayas, Instituto de Investigaciones Filológicas, Universidad Nacional Autónoma de México